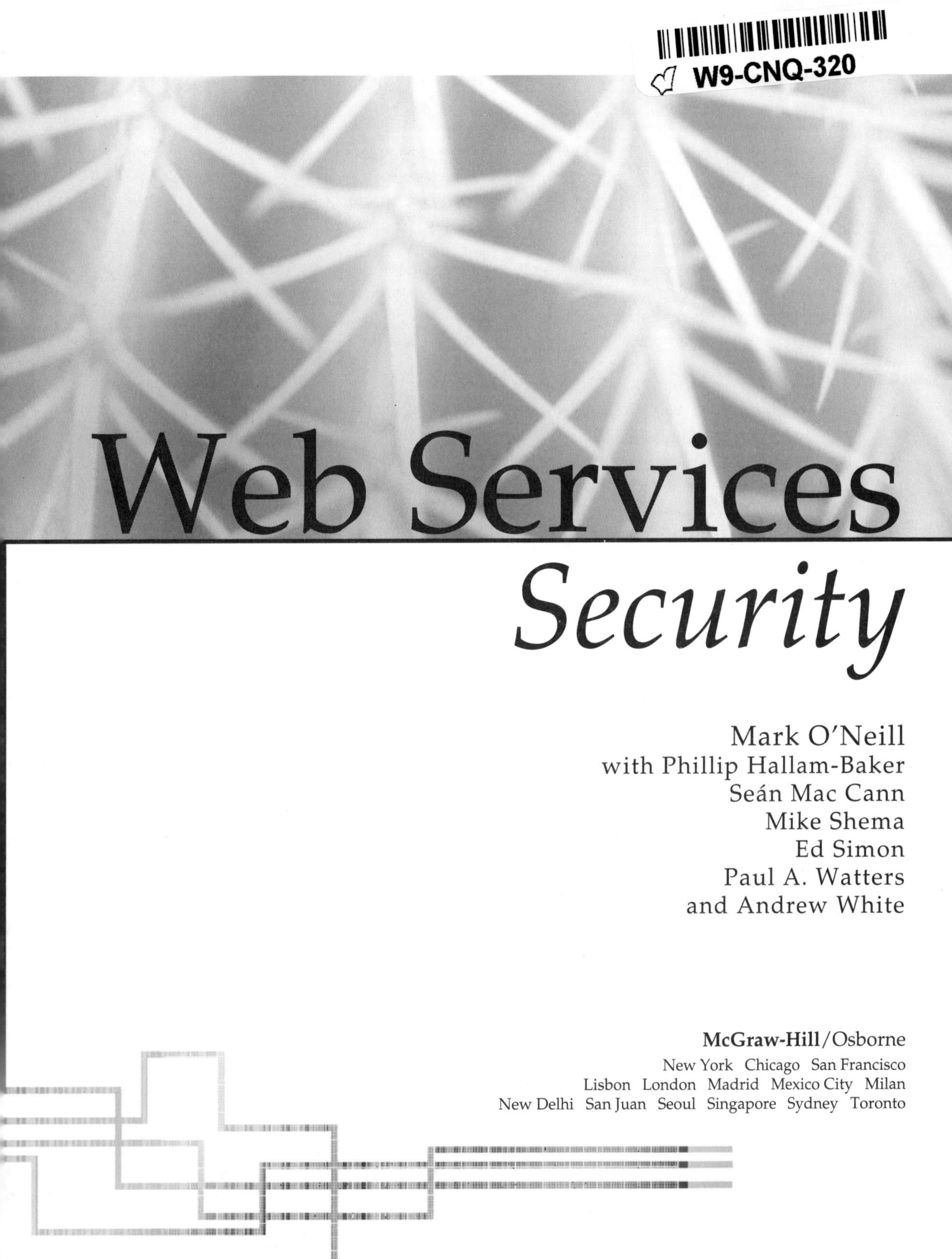

Web Services Security

Mark O'Neill
with Phillip Hallam-Baker
Seán Mac Cann
Mike Shema
Ed Simon
Paul A. Watters
and Andrew White

McGraw-Hill/Osborne
New York Chicago San Francisco
Lisbon London Madrid Mexico City Milan
New Delhi San Juan Seoul Singapore Sydney Toronto

The McGraw·Hill Companies

McGraw-Hill/Osborne
2600 Tenth Street
Berkeley, California 94710
U.S.A.

To arrange bulk purchase discounts for sales promotions, premiums, or fund-raisers, please contact McGraw-Hill/Osborne at the above address. For information on translations or book distributors outside the U.S.A., please see the International Contact Information page immediately following the index of this book.

Web Services Security

34567890 CUS CUS 01987654

ISBN 0-07-222471-1

Publisher
Brandon A. Nordin
Vice President & Associate Publisher
Scott Rogers
Editorial Director
Tracy Dunkelberger
Project Editors
Elizabeth Seymour, LeeAnn Pickrell
Acquisitions Coordinator
Martin Przybyla
Technical Editor
Ed Simon
Copy Editor
Dennis Weaver

Proofreader
Mike McGee
Indexer
Robert J. Richardson
Computer Designers
George T. Charbak, Melinda Lytle
Illustrators
Melinda Lytle, Michael Mueller, Lyssa Wald
Series Design
Peter Hancik, Lyssa Wald
Cover Series Design
Jeff Weeks

This book was composed with Corel VENTURA™ Publisher.

To Kristen and Ben.
—Mark O'Neill

For Karen.
—Phillip Hallam-Baker

To Orla, Seán Óg, and Neil.
—Seán Mac Cann

To my family, for all your support throughout the years.
—Ed Simon

My chapters are dedicated to my new daughter Nellie.
—Paul Watters

I'd like to dedicate my contribution to this book to my parents, who gave me my past, and to Anne, Robbie and Becky, who are creating my present.
—Andrew White

ABOUT THE AUTHORS

Mark O'Neill

As Chief Technical Officer at Vordel, Mark O'Neill oversees the development of Vordel's technical strategy and product development in the areas of XML and security. Mr. O'Neill is also an advisor to the XML.org industry newsletter. He regularly presents at industry conferences on the security issues affecting Web Services and writes in publications including *Web Services Journal, XML Journal, EAI Journal, ComputerWeekly,* and the *Identrus eTrend Quarterly.*

Prior to Vordel, Mr. O'Neill designed and implemented EDI-over-Internet solutions for Ireland's largest EDI Value-Added Network. He then formed a software development company, developing security solutions for clients including Sony Europe, Intel, Royal & SunAlliance, AXA Group, the Irish Government, and Critical Path. Mr. O'Neill holds a double major in Mathematics and Psychology from Trinity College Dublin and studied neural network modelling at Oxford University.

Phillip Hallam-Baker

Dr. Phillip Hallam-Baker BSc, DPhil, FBCS, C.Eng is a leading contributor to numerous XML and Web Services security standards including XKMS (Editor), SAML (co-Editor), WS-Security (co-Editor), XML Signature, and XML Encryption. In addition to speaking at numerous conferences, he was the co-chair of the recent ACM Workshop on XML Security.

Before joining VeriSign, Dr. Hallam-Baker held research posts at the MIT Laboratory for Computer Science and Artificial Intelligence Laboratory, CERN, and DESY where he contributed to the design of HTTP and the World Wide Web. Dr. Hallam-Baker holds degrees from Oxford University and Southampton University and is a Fellow of the British Computer Society.

Seán Mac Cann

Seán Mac Cann is a commercial lawyer from Co. Tyrone, Ireland. He has worked in private practice as a commercial litigator with the London City law firm, DJ Freeman, and as a commercial lawyer with the Dublin commercial firm Gerrard, Scallan & O'Brien. He has worked in the public sector for the Irish telecommunications regulator, ComReg, as its Internet lawyer. He has also worked in industry for a wide variety of public and private companies, such as Shell (energy) and Burberry Limited (fashion). He helped to set up Vordel Limited. Currently, he works mostly with technology start-ups. He maintains a free tech-legal weblog at http://www.maccann.com.

Mike Shema

Mike Shema is a security consultant and trainer for Foundstone. He has performed dozens of security reviews for clients in the financial, telecommunications, software, and e-commerce industries. His familiarity with computer technology ranges from firewalls, to Windows platforms, to several Unix platforms. In addition to network security, Mr. Shema has worked on Web application security assessments and computer forensics investigations. He used his experience with computer security to co-author two titles from McGraw Hill/Osborne: *The Anti-Hacker Toolkit* and *Hacking Exposed: Web Applications*.

Mr. Shema has also worked at a product development company where he configured and deployed high-capacity Apache Web and Oracle database servers used in e-commerce applications. Previous to that, he worked at Booz, Allen & Hamilton where he conducted information assurance reviews for government and military clients. Mr. Shema holds a B.S. in Electrical Engineering and a B.S. in French from Penn State University.

Ed Simon (Contributing Author and Technical Editor)

Ed Simon has been an ardent advocate and implementer of XML since 1997 and is co-author of both the XML Signature and XML Encryption specifications. Today, he provides consulting and training services in the area of XML, Web Services, and security through his company XMLsec (www.xmlsec.com).

Prior to starting XMLsec, Mr. Simon served as Entrust's XML Security Architect, explored new online information technologies at IBM, and developed biomedical research software at the University of Calgary's Faculty of Medicine. Mr. Simon holds a Master of Engineering degree from the University of Alberta.

Paul A. Watters

Paul A. Watters received his Ph.D. in computer science from Macquarie University. He also has degrees from the University of Cambridge, the University of Tasmania, and the University of Newcastle. He has worked in both commercial and R&D organizations, designing systems and software on the Solaris platform. His commercial interests are focused on Java, Web Services, and e-commerce systems in the enterprise. His research areas include virtual enterprises, secure distributed storage, and complex systems. He has previously written *Solaris 9: The Complete Reference* and *Solaris 9 Administration: A Beginner's Guide,* both published by McGraw Hill/Osborne.

Andrew White

Andrew White is Chief Security Architect at Vordel. He has been working in software development for twenty years, and in that time has been involved in a broad range of application areas, including financial services, CRM, and intruder/fire detection systems. For the past ten years, he's been working in the information security field. Specific security related projects he's been involved with in previous employments include HushMail, the award winning secure Web-based e-mail solution, and a number of high-value financial systems for European financial institutions.

Married with two children, Mr. White's hobbies include walking Wicklow hills and tending to the growing inventory of his personal antique computer museum, the latter causing much discord with his wife.

CONTENTS

FOREWORD

Many people have asked whether Web Services is an evolutionary or revolutionary technology. From my perspective, it is both. One of the core specifications used in creating Web Services is SOAP. The authors of *Web Services Security* describe both RPC-based (Remote Procedure Call) SOAP and Document-based (messaging) SOAP. Both of these techniques have been in use in the Information Technology industry for at least 25 years.

So SOAP-based Web Services can be considered an evolutionary technology. There is nothing new about programmers writing applications where one software module does a RPC request to another module, either within the same system, over a Local Area Network (LAN), or even over a Wide Area Network (WAN). What enabled companies to deploy distributed data-exchange applications over the past 25 years was their ability to reply on a seamless security structure as long as they implemented their distributed applications using the same hardware and software architecture (e.g., IBM's SNA or DEC's DECnet). In a similar manner companies have been exchanging document-based messages in application-to-application environments over WANs for more than 25 years. This has been done using Electronic Data Interchange (EDI) standards. While EDI did free the sending and receiving party from having to use the same hardware/software architecture, they usually had to subscribe to the same Value Added Network (VAN) service provider, who provided the end-to-end security necessary to be sure that these transactional "documents" arrived securely. These VAN operators provided the "reliable messaging" infrastructure that enabled electronic commerce to take hold—at least between large enterprises.

The revolutionary nature of the Web Services technology is that companies can now create and deploy distributed applications without regard to the hardware platform, operating system, programming language, or network topology of either party wishing to communicate with the chosen Web Service application. What's missing in the current core set of Web Services specifications is a unifying set of security standards. The IT industry professionals have spent over 25 years developing methods for enabling secure communication of applications in a WAN distributed environment. Quite naturally, companies expect that their use of Web Services to deploy application over the Internet will also have to provide a strong foundation for security.

Web Services Security does an excellent job of explaining the need for security in the emerging Web Services environment and clearly describes the various security standards that are being developed to meet the needs for deployment of "secure" Web Services. Many of the security standards that are needed for deployment of Web Services are being developed within the open environment provided by not-for-profit, global organizations such as the World Wide Web Consortium (W3C) and OASIS (Organization for the Advancement of Structured Information Standards).

The author points out, "At this stage, it should be obvious that the prospect of software from different companies communicating together, while powerful, is fraught with security concerns. In fact, without a convincing security model, the Web Services framework we've outlined would be next to useless."

The authors provide clear analogies to help the reader understand the concepts needed to understand Web Services Security, like the type of security needed for information that is in transit—"However, when it is in transit, a more appropriate analogy may be that of an armed escort who accompanies the information to make certain that it arrives intact at its destination. The escort ensures not only that the data is protected, but that it travels intact from the sender to the recipient. This ensures that not only the data is secure, but the *process* is secure also."

The understanding of Web Services Security can not be achieved by looking at the latest security standards for Web Services. So here the reader is provided with a rich set of examples to demonstrate the inter-relationships between the new Web Services Security techniques and the foundational security standards that have existed for a number of years such as Public Key Infrastructure (PKI), Digital Certificates, and Digital Signatures.

An important aspect of this book is the timeliness of the topic. It is very difficult for a book, which is a snapshot of information at a particular point in time, to be written about technology standards that are still under development. This author provides such sound and practical knowledge for these emerging standards, that the information will remain relevant as these standards for Web Services Security emerge from the standards development organizations and begin the process of achieving wide-spread adoption. It is only through the actual efforts of the author participating in the security standards process that he is able to bring to the reader a firm grasp of the fundamental aspects of these standards that is unlikely to change dramatically in the next few years. As new advances are made in the security arena, this book will serve for many years as an important foundational work describing these security standards for Web Services, upon which other standards will likely be based.

An added bonus for readers of this book is the work presented in Part IV. Here the author provides an effective view of how security principles in general and Web Services Security in particular can be used with other major standards that are considered an important part of enterprise Web Services. These include Liberty Alliance, UDDI, and ebXML. Here they provide an excellent explanation of the security principles and security standards described in detail in the earlier chapters and either incorporated within these other standards, or how the implementation of these standards can be accomplished in conjunction with the Web Services Security specifications. For example, they begin their description of security with respect to ebXML thusly: "The good news from a security aspect is that ebXML was conceived and designed from the ground up with security in mind, in contrast to other protocols or standards where security was never considered at all at the design stage."

Another added bonus is the author's practical view towards the topic of security summed up in these questions, "We need to ask ourselves: 'If security is the answer, then exactly what is the question?' The question is unequivocal: What sort of security is needed to ensure that you can contract [do business] online?"

I highly recommend this book on Web Services Security that covers the broad background necessary for this topic, delves into sufficient detail to provide an education just short of reading the specifications themselves, and then rounds it out by providing practical examples of the environment wherein these specifications and standards are expected to be deployed.

Patrick J. Gannon
President & CEO
OASIS Open
Patrick.gannon@oasis-open.org

ACKNOWLEDGMENTS

Thanks to Tracy and her team at McGraw-Hill/Osborne for chasing chapters while I was in between Barcelona, Boston, Dublin, and California. Thanks to Ed at XMLSec, Inc., for his expert technical review and comments. Thanks to the other authors for their excellent contributions. Thanks to everyone at Vordel for the privilege of tapping into their knowledge and hard work.

—Mark O'Neill

I would like to thank the W3C XML Key Management Working Group for its work on the XKMS protocol and the VeriSign Web Services Engineering team, in particular Scott Lurndal for providing the original code on which the examples in the text were based.

—Phillip Hallam-Baker

Thanks to Tracy Dunkelberger at McGraw Hill/Osborne for organizing everything; to Elizabeth Seymour and Dennis Weaver at McGraw Hill/Osborne for their comments; to Ed Simon at XMLSec, Inc., for his technical comments; to Colin Larkin at Ericsson and in particular to Mark O'Neill, Andrew White, Tony Palmer, Karl Nesbitt, and the technical team at Vordel Limited for answering questions since 1999.

—Seán Mac Cann

Thanks to Paul Madsen of Entrust for his technical review of the Liberty Alliance Project chapter. It was a pleasure working with Mark (the lead author) and Tracy and her team at McGraw-Hill/Osborne.

—Ed Simon

To everyone at my agency, Studio B, thanks for your past and continued support. To Neil Salkind, my agent, thanks for your wisdom and pragmatic advice. To Bill Moffitt, at Sun Microsystems, thanks for your continued support of my publishing efforts. Finally, thanks to my family, especially my wife Maya, for always being there, through good times and tough times.

—Paul A. Watters

INTRODUCTION

This book describes how the world of Web Services and the world of information security are coming together. Web Services and security make a compelling match, because Web Services need security in order to enjoy widespread deployment, and security technologies need the ease of deployment provided by Web Services. In theory at least, this is a win-win situation. The downside, though, is that the technologies can be complex and difficult to understand. This book will help you understand Web Services security by explaining the technologies in plain English, using practical programming examples.

We start out by introducing Web Services. Web Services is an important new technology, one which is distinguished by its cross-industry support. IBM, HP, Oracle, Microsoft, Novell, and Sun all offer Web Services frameworks. Gartner predicts that in 2004, Web Services will dominate deployment of new application solutions for Fortune 2000 companies (Gartner, Inc., 2002). Security concepts such as authentication, authorization, and data integrity are referenced throughout this book. These security concepts are given their own chapter to set the scene for later chapters where they are related to Web Services. A common thread running through this book is that Web Services security relies on these established security concepts and technologies, which have not changed or been made obsolete by Web Services.

These two introductory chapters set the scene for a chapter discussing the gamut of security protocols and procedures relevant to Web security. This chapter discusses not only the *how* of Web Services security, but also the *why*. Web Services security technologies such as SAML and WS-Security operate at the application layer, but even so, it is important to keep the *entire security context* of the Web Service in mind. This includes properly configured firewalls, the use of patched and locked-down Web servers, and (especially if digital certificates are used) the use of an adequate security policy document. It would be foolish to address just the new security challenges posed by Web Services and leave a system open to attack through more traditional channels. Therefore, as well as covering the theory of Web Services security, this book is intended to be a practical guide to deploying secure Web Services. This might sound like a lot of work, but once you're familiar with the basic concepts, it all starts to make sense.

Next, the new security initiatives addressing Web Services are dealt with chapter by chapter. These are XML Signature, XML Encryption, SAML, XACML, XKMS, and WS-Security. If you already know the basics of XML, Web Services, and information security, you can skip directly to these chapters. In addition to these vendor-neutral technologies, vendor-led initiatives such as Microsoft's .NET myServices and Project Liberty are discussed as well.

The area of UDDI security is still somewhat hypothetical and a matter for debate, but there is a great deal of interest in this debate. Therefore, the application of initiatives such as XML Signature and XML Encryption to UDDI is allotted a chapter. ebXML may be considered as an alternative to Web Services. However, it includes many technologies that overlap with Web Services—XML, of course, and SOAP also. In addition, ebXML has a security model that makes use of technologies such as XML Signature and XML Encryption. Therefore, it deserves a place in the book.

Unusually, perhaps, for a technical book, a chapter is dedicated to the legal aspects of Web Services security. These legal aspects include the digital signature laws as they apply to XML Signature, privacy issues when implementing SAML, and the legal questions arising from application-to-application transactions. Legal considerations are catching up on all aspects of information technology, and Web Services is no exception. Questions like, "When an application connects to another application to make a fraudulent transaction, who is to blame?" and "Is nonrepudiation realistic?" are answered in this chapter.

Although this book is about securing Web Services, we frequently look at the flip side of securing Web Services—attacking Web Services. This is largely speculative, but it is not difficult to look at the techniques used to attack Web applications and extrapolate them to Web Services. The future of Web Services security will depend not only on what attacks are developed against Web Services, but also on which attacks are publicized. As in all walks of life, it is important to "know your enemy." This book is designed to provide all the information needed to protect Web Services from attack.

The case studies appendix takes the Web Services topics that are covered in the main body of the book and presents them in a real-life context. Each opens with a statement of a problem, and then lists the appropriate Web Services security technologies to be used in the solution. Remember that the entire security context of the Web Service must be taken into account—firewalls, patched and locked-down Web servers, and (for some solutions) the use of either a secure channel (SSL, VPN) or message-level security.

INTENDED AUDIENCE FOR THIS BOOK

Programmers and architects charged with deploying Web Services require knowledge of the security implications of this new technology. In addition, network security professionals require knowledge of the new application-layer security challenges posed by Web Services, and the new security standards that address these challenges. These two groups—security professionals in companies that are rolling out Web Services, and the application professionals actually rolling out these Web Services—are the audience for this book.

Primary Audiences

The primary audiences for this book are software developers and architects who are rolling out XML Web Services.

Secondary Audiences

The secondary audiences for this book include information security professionals who wish to know how to address the security vulnerabilities exposed by the use of XML Web Services.

The book is written in a direct manner, using simple examples where feasible, so it is hoped that the general nontechnical reader can also learn about this exciting new area.

PART I

Introduction

CHAPTER 1

Presenting Web Services

It is a significant gesture when the entire computer industry agrees on a new technology. Such is the case with Web Services. Leading industry players such as IBM, HP, Oracle, Microsoft, Novell, and Sun support Web Services, not only in marketing terms but also by releasing Web Services products. In addition, many existing products are incorporating Web Services functionality into their feature sets. All this activity means that there is now a plethora of Web Services platforms and Web Services development tools available. A cynic might point out that all that is missing are the actual Web Services themselves! These services are appearing, however. Web Services look set to dominate the deployment of new application solutions over the next few years.

Many aspects of Web Services present challenges for security. These challenges are being addressed by the initiatives that are presented in this book—initiatives such as WS-Security, SAML, and XKMS. This chapter introduces Web Services. Web Services depend on XML, so an overview of XML is provided. This includes XML Schema, which is important to know since many of the Web Services security specifications include XML Schema definitions.

Readers who are already familiar with Web Services may wish to skip over this chapter. But beware if you have a hazy notion of Web Services. The first trap for the newcomer who wishes to understand Web Services is the name "Web Services" itself. To take the approach of looking at the name "Web Services" and guessing, not unreasonably, that it must refer to "services on the Web" is a mistake. The fact is that both the "Web" and the "Services" words in the term "Web Services" are misleading. Let's examine why.

Defining Web Services

IBM's definition of Web Services states that "Web Services are self-contained, modular applications that can be described, published, located, and invoked over a network, generally, the World Wide Web." When the definition refers to Web Services being invoked over the World Wide Web, it means that they use HTTP as the transport layer and an XML-based message layer. However, Web Services do not actually require HTTP—XML-formatted data can be sent over other transport protocols (message queuing, for example), which may be more suited to mission-critical transactions. In addition, the World Wide Web is associated in the public mind with hypertext (HTML in particular, of course), rather than XML. If (and when) Web Services migrate from HTTP to other transport protocols, then "Web Services" will be less concerned with the World Wide Web as we know it, but will presumably still carry the word "Web" in its name. Web Services connotes producing a "web" of functionality, so the word "web" may still be applicable.

Navigating Firewalls

Web Services generally uses the HTTP and SSL ports (TCP ports 80 and 443, respectively) in order to pass through firewalls. In the early days of "Web Services," vendors would say that their products were "firewall compliant." This meant that firewalls would not block the Web Services traffic, whereas CORBA traffic attempting to use CORBA-specific ports may be blocked. Web Services make it easier to deploy distributed computing without having to open firewall ports, or having to "punch a hole in the firewall" as network administrators like to say. This "under the radar" deployment has serious security implications. Most firewalls are unable to distinguish Web Services traffic, traveling over HTTP and SSL ports, from Web browser traffic. With some firewalls it is possible to block Web Services traffic altogether, but not possible to set up different rules for separate Web Services. Chapter 3 discusses these issues in depth.

Service-Oriented Architecture: Publish, Find, and Bind

The word "Services" in Web Services refers to a Service-Oriented Architecture (SOA). SOA is a recent development in distributed computing, in which applications call functionality from other applications over a network. In an SOA, functionality is "published" on a network where two important capabilities are provided— "discovery," the ability to find the functionality, and "binding," the ability to connect to the functionality. In the Web Services architecture, these activities correspond to three roles: Web Service provider, Web Service requester, and Web Service broker, which correspond to the "publish," "find," and "bind" aspects of a Service-Oriented Architecture.

Web Services use what is termed *dynamic binding*. This means that applications that make use of Web Services can be dynamically composed, with the the client binding to the server at runtime. The programming language used for the Web Service itself is immaterial; implementations of various pieces of functionality published as Web Services can be platform- and programming language-neutral. If a publisher wishes to radically change the way in which they implement functionality, or publish new functionality that can be found ("discovered") by Web Service requesters, the Web Services architecture provides this capability. Before Web Services, static binding was traditional for application communication. Static binding meant that application integration was less flexible, because the communicating applications (and by extension their IT departments) would have to agree on which object types and programming languages to use.

Previous initiatives, such as CORBA, DCOM, Distributed Smalltalk, and Java RMI, required more agreement and shared context among business systems. Frequently, the functionality that was exposed was linked directly to the software objects used to implement the functionality. This does not mean that these technologies are not useful, just that the coarser-grained integration of Web Services may be more appropriate for distributed computing over the open Internet. Many of the Web Services technologies introduced in this chapter—UDDI, WSDL, and SOAP—were created in order to enable an SOA to run on the open Internet.

That's enough theory for now. Let's look at the factors that enable this new technology. The SOA publish/find/bind functionality in Web Services depends on XML. So, let's start with XML.

Introducing the XML Family

Although XML stands for eXtensible Markup Language, the acronym "XML" is mostly used to describe not only XML itself, but also the ever-growing family of related technologies. The core XML specification itself is relatively simple. In fact, it is so simple that many people, when looking at XML for the first time, find it difficult to understand why such a simple technology could be feted with such world-changing powers. The trick is not just to look at the language, which is a syntax for presenting data in a structured manner, but to also look at the surrounding technologies that act on XML in order to define it, transform it, transmit it, and secure it. This collection of technologies surrounding the core XML specification represents the real power of XML.

XML: A Syntax to Define Markup Languages

XML is a specification, defined by the W3C (World Wide Web Consortium), which defines a syntax used to define markup languages. This may seem like a roundabout definition. XML defines a syntax to structure a document, using *markup*. Documents used for specific purposes (for example, legal agreements defined by the LegalXML group) are examples of documents that have been *marked up* using XML. Because they use XML, they can be manipulated by the great quantity of XML-enabled applications available. To see the advantages of XML, let's look at a before-and-after example.

Structured Documents

It is sometimes said that every single document is an example of a structured document, because every document has some internal logic that can be leveraged in order to break it into parts, or to translate it into another format. The problem, though, is finding this structure. This takes time and effort. In the past, it was common practice for applications to define their own unique structural markup, but today applications must share their data as easily as possible and so it makes sense to standardize a structural markup language—and that is the reason for XML.

Various methods of structuring data have been proposed over the past 30 years. Many of these have found their way into commercial use. EDI (Electronic Document Interchange) documents, for example, mainly use the offset distance from the left of the page as a means of structuring documents. The following line, taken from a UN/EDIFACT EDI purchase order, contains the name and address of a supplier:

```
NAD SU  JOE BLOGGS INC         101 SOME STREET          BOSTON, MA 12345      US
```

The structural rules for this EDI document state that the first three characters specify the type of data in the line. By examining the specification for this particular type of EDI document, we find that NAD means Name and Address. The characters in the fifth and sixth positions identify the role of the entity whose name and address we are viewing—in this case, it's a supplier (SU stands for Supplier). The rest of the line contains the name and address itself, in fixed blocks for each line of the address, along with a state, ZIP code, and country code. Information about the structure of EDI documents is contained in lengthy specification documents. These documents explain what the various codes mean, and the offsets to use to pick information out of the EDI file.

The disadvantages for the EDI approach were that the *semantic* information about the data was missing. The information about what NAD and SU actually mean is contained in a specification document. This is also a problem for comma-separated files. Name-value pairs, such as those used in Windows initialization files and Java configuration files, provide the semantic information, but are too unsophisticated to be used for complex, nested information.

XML defines a new method of structuring documents, based on SGML. The same EDI fragment could be rendered in XML, as shown here in Listing 1-1.

Listing 1-1

```
<NameAndAddress Role="Supplier">
<CompanyName>Joe Bloggs Inc</CompanyName >
<AddressLine>101 SOME STREET</AddressLine>
<AddressLine>BOSTON</AddressLine>
<AddressLine>MA</AddressLine>
<ZipCode>12345</ZipCode>
<CountryCode>US</CountryCode>
</NameAndAddress>
```

This XML fragment contains the same raw data as the corresponding EDI fragment, but it adds descriptive information about the data. This descriptive information is contained in elements, sometimes called tags, which are surrounded by angle brackets. "NameAndAddress" is one element in the example, and AddressLine is another. Where additional information relating to an element is required, this can be added as an attribute. The role information relates specifically to the NameAndAddress, because it is the name and address of a supplier. The lines of the address are nested under the NameAndAddress element.

Verbosity

As you can see from the example, XML is quite verbose. The W3C (World Wide Web Consortium) recommends that XML elements and attribute names not be abbreviated. Therefore, NameAndAddress is used instead of NAD. The meaning of the data is more obvious than for the EDI file. This means, of course, that the XML documents are larger than other types of structured documents, even though they may convey the same meaning. This book is about Web Services, and Web Services involve computer-to-computer communication. Therefore, it is tempting to imagine that there is a trade-off between the human readability of XML and the compactness of the data.

The argument goes: "This data is being sent from one computer to another computer. No humans are reading it, so why does it have to be human readable? Surely it would be better for the data to be more compact and quicker to send." This argument sounds convincing, but it neglects the full context of XML communication. Compression is available at lower layers of the communications stack. XML documents generally compress very well because they contain many repeating strings of text in element and attribute names. Chapter 5 shows how a compression algorithm can be used in conjunction with a digital signature, so that a document can be compressed before or after being signed.

TIP Don't give in to the temptation to cut down on the size of XML element and attribute names. Instead, ensure that compression is implemented at lower layers of your Web Services rollout.

Document Type Definitions and XML Schema

XML that follows the syntax rules defined by the W3C XML specification is called *well formed* XML. These syntax rules include the requirements:

- The start tag and the end tag should be the same.
- There should be no "overlapping" tags.
- Element and attribute names must be surrounded by quotes.

The extensible nature of XML means that anybody can create an XML document, providing that it is well formed. However, if the XML document is not understood by anyone else, it has limited use because one of the goals of XML is to facilitate the sharing of information. That is why consortia such as OASIS (Organization for the Advancement of Structured Information Standards) and industry-specific groups such as RosettaNet (for the electronics procurement industry) provide central points for organizations to agree on XML definitions. Many of the security specifications discussed in this book include definitions of permitted XML syntax (for example, to define a SAML assertion or an XML Signature). Let's take a look at what it means to define the structure of XML.

XML is based on SGML (Standardized General Markup Language), a metalanguage that predates the World Wide Web. SGML includes a means of defining which particular elements and attributes are used to define meaning in an XML document. These definition files are called DTDs—Document Type Definitions. DTDs allow organizations to standardize their use of XML so that each organization can understand the other's documents. Remember that the XML specification defines only syntax, so if two organizations decide they're just going to communicate "using XML," that doesn't mean very much. The question is, what type of XML?

Let's have a look at an example of a DTD. Listing 1-2 shows a DTD that defines the XML from Listing 1-1.

Listing 1-2

```
<?xml version="1.0"?>
<!DOCTYPE AddressingInfo [
<!ELEMENT NameAndAddress (CompanyName, AddressLine+, CountryCode)>
<!ELEMENT CountryCode (#PCDATA)>>
<!ELEMENT CompanyName (#PCDATA)>
<!ELEMENT AddressLine (#PCDATA)>
```

```
<!ELEMENT ZipCode (#PCDATA)>
<!ATTLIST NameAndAddress Role CDATA #REQUIRED>
]>
```

This DTD opens with a line to state which XML version it supports. Then, the DOCTYPE directive states that this defines a piece of data called AddressingInfo. This means that a document that is governed by this DTD can refer to this fact by referring to the DTD, also using the DOCTYPE directive:

```
<!DOCTYPE AddressingInfo SYSTEM http://www.example.com/AddressingInfo.dtd>
```

This line tells an XML processor to validate the document against the AddressingInfo DTD. If the document conforms to the DTD, it is said to be a *valid* document.

The next line tells us that the NameAndAddress contains three subelements (or "children"): CompanyName, AddressLine, and CountryCode. These are defined on the next three lines as PCDATA. PCDATA means "parsed character data," meaning that they are to contain textual data that can be parsed by a text parser. After the elements comes the attribute. NameAndAddress has only a single attribute, Role.

As is apparent from Listing 1-2, DTDs define XML documents but do not actually use XML themselves. This is a disadvantage, because it means another language for the XML implementer to learn.

This is not the only disadvantage of DTDs. DTDs are limited in the extent to which fine-grained constraints can be placed on XML data. Simple constraints are possible—declaring an element to be mandatory, for example—but the rules for element contents are limited. For example, if an element called MusicalNote is intended to contain a musical note that may only be *A* through *G*, then DTDs provided no way to enforce that rule. A document would still be valid (that is, conforming to the DTD) even if it contained a nonexistent *H* note.

XML Schema, an alternative to DTDs, was created to address these deficiencies. More complex rules about XML documents can be created than were possible in DTDs, and these rules are themselves written in XML. However, XML Schema has proven to be a mixed success. Many argue that it is overly complex and difficult to learn. However, most of the XML and Web Services security specifications described in this book contain XML Schema definitions. The basics of XML Schema are simple, and in fact are no more difficult to understand than DTDs.

Keeping with our example, the XML Schema defining the XML in Listing 1-1 is shown in Listing 1-3.

Listing 1-3

```
<?xml version="1.0" encoding="UTF-8" ?>
<xs:schema xmlns:xs="http://www.w3.org/2001/XMLSchema">

<xs:complexType name="NameAndAddress">
  <xs:sequence>
    <xs:element name="CompanyName" type="xs:string" use="required"/>
```

```
        <xs:element name="AddressLine" maxOccurs="unbounded" type="xs:string"/>
        <xs:element name="CountryCode" type="countryCodeType"/>
        <xs:element name="ZipCode" type="zipCodeType"/>
    </xs:sequence>
    <xs:attribute name="Role" type="xs:string" use="required"/>
</xs:complexType>

<xs:simpleType name="zipCodeType">
    <xs:restriction base="xs:string">
        <xs:pattern value="[0-9]{5}"/>
    </xs:restriction>
</xs:simpleType>

<xs:simpleType name="countryCodeType">
    <xs:restriction base="xs:string">
        <xs:pattern value="[A-Z]{2}"/>
    </xs:restriction>
</xs:simpleType>

</xs:schema>
```

When the DTD (see Listing1-2) and the XML Schema are compared, it is apparent that the XML Schema is more complex and allows for more constraints on the XML to be defined. In addition, XML Schema allows data types to be defined. In Listing 1-3, a data type called zipCodeType is defined to mean a five-character data string that is composed of integers from 0 through 9. Similarly, in the Schema, a two-character restriction is placed on the data contained in the CountryCode element.

Security specifications require a great deal of accuracy. Differences between the implementations of security recommendations have dogged the information security industry over the past 10 years. Therefore, XML Schema is an important tool used to define Web Services security technologies, and we will see that XML Signature, XML Encryption, WS-Security, and others all make use of XML Schema.

XPath

XPath is another XML-related specification that is used in Web Services security. XPath defines a syntax to pinpoint just a portion of an XML document. This is useful if just part of an XML document is to be encrypted or digitally signed, or if an access control decision is being made based on the contents of an XML document. If we wish to just sign the contents of the CompanyName element in Listing 1-1, it would be specified using the following XPath syntax:

```
/NameAndAddress/CompanyName
```

This pinpoints the CompanyName element, which is located underneath the NameAndAddress element. XPath gets much more complicated than this, of course, but this information is not immediately relevant for an understanding of how XPath is used in Web Services security.

XML for Communication

It was realized quite early on in the history of XML that it could be used to act as an envelope for information as it passed between different computing systems, which otherwise would be unable to communicate. This required the definition of an XML-based enveloping technology. Simple Object Access Protocol (SOAP) was defined by Microsoft and DevelopMentor to provide this functionality. Seen in terms of a service-oriented architecture, SOAP allows for applications to bind to other applications in order to make use of their functionality. SOAP has since been submitted to the W3C and is a W3C recommendation. Visit the W3C site (http://www.w3c.org) for more details on the specification.

SOAP is used to send data from one application to another application, so it is sometimes seen as a messaging protocol as well as a means of using functionality that is published by a remote application. These two aspects of SOAP—messaging and remote procedure calls (RPCs)—are both important.

Other technologies have been developed in order to fill out the vision of an XML-based service-oriented architecture. Web Services Definition Language (WSDL) enables an organization to define a Web service so that a Web Service broker can formulate a SOAP message to bind to it. Universal Description, Discovery, and Integration (UDDI) allows a Web Service provider to publish information about a Web Service so that a Web Service requester can find that Web Service. In a moment we'll look at how these technologies work together, but first let's look at where these new technologies fit in the history of Web-based applications.

SOAP: Third Generation of Web-based Applications

This use of XML for application integration represents the third generation of Web-based applications. The first generation of Web-based applications involved Web servers running CGI applications for dynamic content and people using Web browsers to interact with Web sites. This enabled the B2C (Business To Consumer) revolution. The second generation of Web-based applications also involved Web browsers interacting with Web servers. However, the Web servers now existed as part of a multiple-tier architecture, using an application server in the background, which may in turn connect to an organization's internal systems. This enabled businesses to connect their supply-chain management (SCM) and enterprise resource planning (ERP) software to the Internet. This was intended to create a B2B (Business To Business) revolution to rival the B2C revolution seen some years before.

TIP SOAP's main advantage is loose coupling. SOAP can either be used for Remote Procedure Calls (called "RPC SOAP") or for messaging between applications (called "Document-based SOAP"). In most cases, messaging is preferable to RPC, since it means that applications do not have to share an object model, or rely on a synchronous always-on connection. When thinking about SOAP, try not to think of it as "glue between applications," but rather as "e-mail between applications."

The bad news, though, was that the deployment of Web-based B2B projects did not turn out to be as dramatic as expected. The reason for this was that most B2B communications are machine to machine, not person to machine. The second generation of Web-based applications still involved people connecting to Web servers using Web browsers. B2B communication between machines, with no people involved, has been around for a long time. EDI networks have been used for many years to send large quantities of information between businesses. But, as we saw earlier in this chapter, EDI is not an ideal solution. Now that SOAP is defined as an enveloping protocol, with XML generally acknowledged as the de facto means of representing structured data, EDI may be implemented using XML. This holds the promise to finally enable the B2B revolution to take off, by allowing software across organizations to communicate using a flexible, open framework. The business-level aspects of EDI, which involve "choreographing" the flow of documents to match a business process, are being addressed by groups such as ebXML (www.ebXML.org).

At this stage, it should be obvious that the prospect of software from different companies communicating together, while powerful, is fraught with security concerns. In fact, without a convincing security model, the Web Services framework we've outlined would be next to useless.

An Example Web Services Scenario

Let's look at a typical Web Services scenario. We'll use the well-worn stock-ordering example, which is something of a "hello world" for Web Services. The initial scenario is shown in Figure 1-1.

UDDI

In Figure 1-1, company A wishes to make use of the stock ordering system that is provided by company B. The first step in a services-oriented architecture is for company A to find out about company B's Web Services. This is achieved in this case by using UDDI. Later, in a dedicated chapter, we will discuss UDDI security. UDDI sometimes gets a bad reputation. There is a perception that it is used to publish services to the entire world, allowing anybody to connect to the UDDI registry, find a Web Service published by a previously unknown company, and bind to it. This clearly

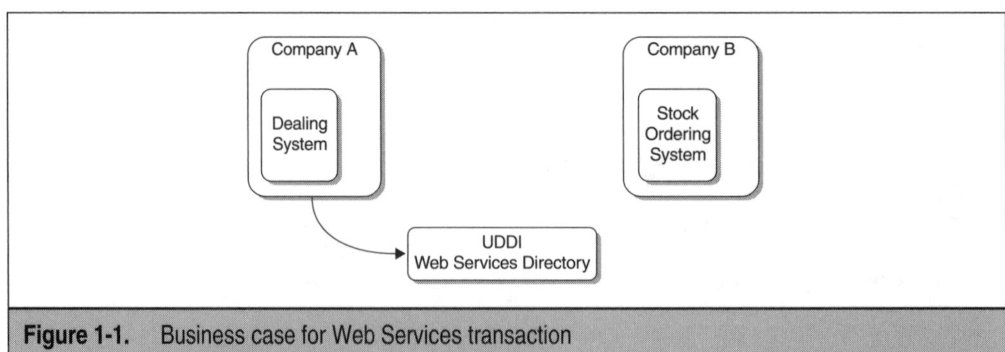

Figure 1-1. Business case for Web Services transaction

does not match real-world business scenarios, in which business is rarely done between complete strangers—especially in the absence of credential checks such as credit worthiness. But this view does UDDI a disservice. Most uses of UDDI involve cases where the transacting parties already know each other. It provides a way to publish information about newly available Web Services, or to provide information about a Web Service whose interface has changed. In addition, UDDI is useful inside an organization (that is, "behind the firewall") in order to publish information used by internal applications to bind to each other using SOAP. UDDI security is discussed in Chapter 13.

An example UDDI enquiry is shown in Listing 1-4.

Listing 1-4

```
<find_business generic='1.0' xmlns='urn:uddi-org:api'>
     <name>Company B</name>
</find_business>
```

Continuing with our example, Figure 1-2 shows company A retrieving a document from company B that lists the Web Services provided by company B.

To keep this example simple, let's assume that company B only has one Web Service. Therefore, the response from the UDDI repository will look like Listing 1-5.

Listing 1-5

```
<businessList generic="1.0" operator="Company B" truncated="false" xmlns="urn:uddi-org:api">
   <businessInfos>
      <businessInfo businessKey="cbfa05fb-277d-4b7e-a101-e6925b376c18">
         <name>Company B</name>
         <description xml:lang="en"> A leading provider of financial services
         </description>
      <serviceInfos>
          <serviceInfo serviceKey="5f73eff6-7a85-41cf-99d9-66cda3a82e63"
 businessKey="cbca05fb-277d-4b7e-a101-e6925b376c18">
           <name>Stock Ordering Service</name>
         </serviceInfo>
      </serviceInfos>
    </businessInfo>
  </businessInfos>
</businessList>
```

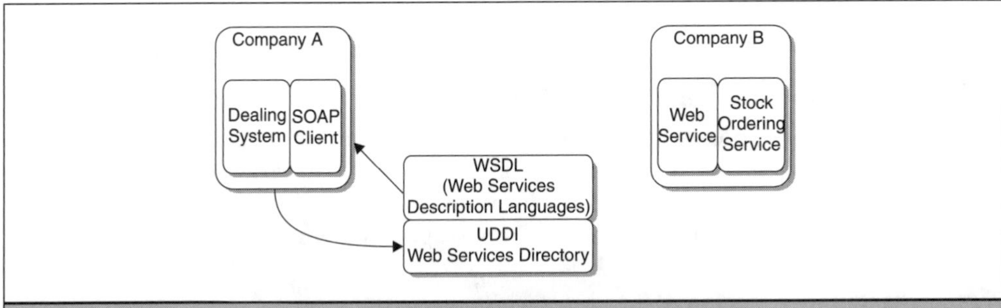

Figure 1-2. Company A retrieves WSDL data for company B's Web Service

In Listing 1-5, we can see the serviceKey value for the stock ordering service. Company A can now use this serviceKey value to perform a query to get the binding information about the stock ordering service, using the XML in Listing 1-6.

Listing 1-6

```
<get_serviceDetail generic='1.0' xmlns='urn:uddi-org:api'>
   <serviceKey>5f73eff6-7a85-41cf-99d9-66cda3a82e63</serviceKey>
</get_serviceDetail>
```

The binding information retrieved from this get_serviceDetail message is shown in Listing 1-7.

Listing 1-7

```
<serviceDetail generic="1.0" operator="Company B" truncated="false"
 xmlns="urn:uddi-org:api">
   <businessService serviceKey="be1a0b34-e2f1-4f4b-dae6-258c338ae358"
 businessKey="cbea05fb-277d-4b7e-a101-e6925b376c18">
   <name>Stock Ordering Service</name>
   <description xml:lang="en">NYSE and Nasdaq Stock Ordering Service.</
description>
   <bindingTemplates>
      <bindingTemplate serviceKey="be1a0b34-e2f1-4f4b-aae6-258c338ae358"
 bindingKey="00cbd2b2-2333-4f85-b144-369be3d95f7c">
        <description xml:lang="en">NASDAQ and NYSE Stock Ordering Service with
 real-time trades.</description>
        <accessPoint URLType="https">https://www.stockorder.com/Stock</
accessPoint>
        <tModelInstanceDetails>
          <tModelInstanceInfo
tModelKey="uuid:64c756d1-3374-4e00-ae83-ee12e38fae63">
            <description xml:lang="en">Stock Ordering Service.</description>
          </tModelInstanceInfo>
        </tModelInstanceDetails>
      </bindingTemplate>
<categoryBag>
      <keyedReference tModelKey="uuid:a035a07c-f362-44dd-8f95-e2b134bf43b4"
keyName="KEYWORD" keyValue="STOCK"></keyedReference>
    </categoryBag>
  </businessService>
</serviceDetail>
```

WSDL: Web Service Definition Language

Now company A is in possession of enough information to retrieve the WSDL information from company B, in order to construct a SOAP message to send to company B's stock ordering service. The location of the Web Service can now be seen in the accessPoint element. The WSDL message is shown in Listing 1-8.

Listing 1-8

```
<?xml version="1.0"?>
<definitions name="StockQuote"
             targetNamespace="http://stockorder.com/stockorder.wsdl"
```

```
            xmlns:tns="http://stockorder.com/stockquote.wsdl"
            xmlns:xsd1="http://stockorder.com/stockquote.xsd"
            xmlns:soap="http://schemas.xmlsoap.org/wsdl/soap"
            xmlns:wsdl="http://schemas.xmlsoap.org/wsdl/">
    <wsdl:types>
       <xsd:schema targetNamespace="https://www.stockorder.com/Stock"
             xmlns:xsd="http://www.w3.org/2000/10/XMLSchema">
          <xsd:element name="StockOrderRequest">
             <xsd:complexType>
                 <xsd:all>
                    <xsd:element name="tickerSymbol" type="string"/>
                    <xsd:element name="quantity" type="string"/>
                    <xsd:element name="market" type="string"/>
                 </xsd:all>
             </xsd:complexType>
          </xsd:element>
       </xsd:schema>
    </wsdl:types>
    <!-- request StockOrder is of type StockOrderRequest -->
    <wsdl:message name="GetLastTradePriceInput">
        <wsdl:part name="body" element="xsd1:TradePriceRequest"/>
    </wsdl:message>
      <wsdl:portType name="StockOrderPortType">
        <wsdl:operation name="StockOrder">
           <wsdl:input message="tns:StockOrderRequest"/>
           <wsdl:output message="tns:StockOrderRequest"/>
        </wsdl:operation>
    </wsdl:portType>
    <wsdl:binding name="StockOrderSoapBinding"
                 type="tns:StockOrderPortType">
        <soap:binding style="document" transport="http://
schemas.xmlsoap.org/soap/http"/>
        <wsdl:operation name="GetLastTradePrice">
           <soap:operation soapAction="http://www.stockquote.com/
StockOrder"/>
            <wsdl:input>
               <soap:body use="literal"/>
           </wsdl:input>
           <wsdl:output>
               <soap:body use="literal"/>
           </wsdl:output>
        </wsdl:operation>
    </wsdl:binding>
</wsdl:definitions>
```

As can be see in Listing 1-8, WSDL isn't a language designed for general human comprehension. However, it gives a Web Services broker all the information necessary to construct a SOAP message. We see at the top of the message that it refers to the XML Schema for the Web Service. We also see at the top of the WSDL message that a number of *namespaces* are used. These namespaces are used so that there is no confusion caused by XML elements and attributes from different contexts having the same names. This would occur if, for example, the XML Schema for the StockQuote service had element names in common with the XML Schema for SOAP. Namespaces avoid this problem, and are familiar to software developers as a common feature of modern programming languages.

Examining a SOAP Message

At this stage, a SOAP message can be sent from company A to company B. This action is illustrated in Figure 1-3.

Let's have a look at the actual SOAP message that is sent. Listing 1-9 shows the SOAP message itself.

Listing 1-9

```
<SOAP-ENV:Envelope xmlns:SOAP-ENV="http://schemas.xmlsoap.org/soap/envelope/">
<SOAP-ENV:Header>
</SOAP-ENV:Header>
<SOAP-ENV:Body
<StockOrder:StockOrder xmlns:StockOrder="https://www.stockorder.com/Stock">
<StockOrder:symbol>SGP</StockOrder:symbol>
<StockOrder:quantity>2000</StockOrder:quantity>
<StockOrder:market>New York</StockOrder:market>
</order:buy>
</SOAP-ENV:Body>
</SOAP-ENV:Envelope>
```

The SOAP message in Listing 1-9 is quite a simple message, because all the parameters are basic SOAP string types. Note also that although Figure 1-3 shows security data included in the SOAP message. We've omitted it from the SOAP listing. We'll see later in the book how WS-Security allows security information to be placed into SOAP messages. This security data can include security tokens to indicate the identity of the sender, and digital signatures to ensure that the SOAP message hasn't changed since it was digitally signed. Note again the use of namespaces to protect against "collisions" in the data caused by identical element and attribute names across different XML Schemas.

Listing 1-9 also shows that SOAP messages have a *header* and a *body*. Information in the header concerns processing of the message. The payload of the message is contained in the body. Here we see that the header portion of the SOAP message is empty. This is because we've omitted the security data (for now). Because it is an XML-based language, SOAP is extensible. Many security initiatives have chosen to insert security information into the SOAP header. The SOAP body is more suited to payload data, and as we'll see in the next section, this payload can be divided up if it is intended for more than one SOAP actor.

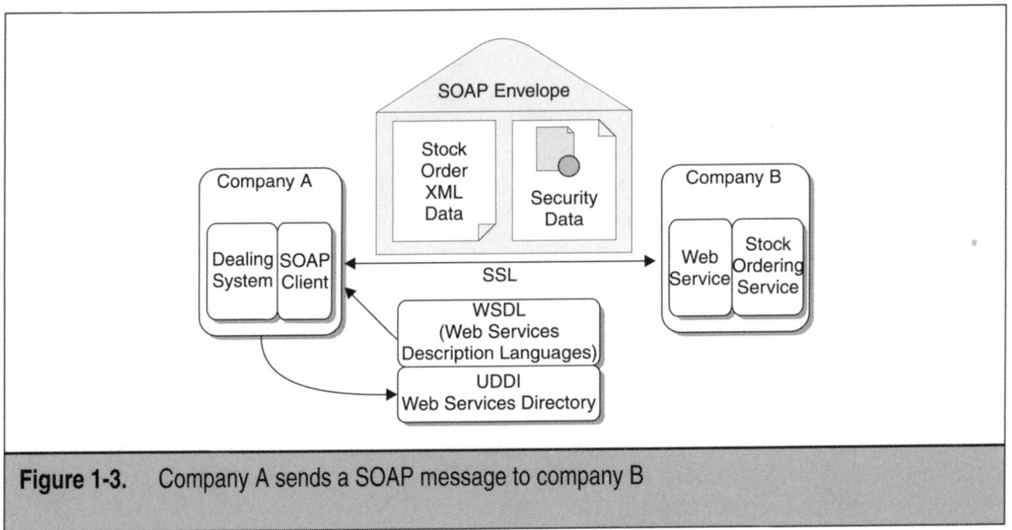

Figure 1-3. Company A sends a SOAP message to company B

SOAP With Attachments (SWA) allows SOAP messages to include binary attachments, expressed using the same Multipart Internet Message Exchange (MIME) syntax as is used for e-mail. This addresses one of the early criticisms of SOAP, namely that it wasn't suitable for binary information. ebXML makes use of SWA, as we'll see in Chapter 13.

Routing SOAP Among Multiple Parties

In our simple example, company A sends a SOAP message directly to company B in order to bind to stock ordering functionality that has been published by company B. However, company A may wish to use additional services, all in the context of this one transaction. For example, company A may also want to use a Stockquote service, which may be published by a third party, prior to using the stock ordering service. Another scenario would be where company A wishes to run a portfolio update service after running the stock order service. This single SOAP message may be routed between more than one SOAP "actor" (note that in the SOAP 1.2 specification, "Actor" is replaced by "Role"—this is somewhat confusing for security, since "role" already has a definition in role-based access control). Each Web Service is responsible for certain portions of the message. If a certain actor must process certain elements in the header of the SOAP message (for example, a digital signature), the mustUnderstand attribute is set to true for these elements.

Note that the SOAP 1.1 specification from the W3C does not include information about how to route a SOAP message. More recent specifications, such as WS-Routing from Microsoft, address the area of routing, as does ebXML's messaging specification. SOAP does, however, allow for portions of a SOAP message to be flagged as being appropriate for certain SOAP services. SOAP 1.2 incorporates routing, based on

WS-Routing. This has implications for XML Proxies and XML Firewall applications, which may be required to honor routing information in SOAP messages. We will encounter XML Firewall functionality in the third case study in the Appendix.

Because SOAP messages can be routed between multiple SOAP roles, it is important that there are mechanisms to ensure that certain information cannot be seen (or manipulated) by intermediate roles before reaching their intended destination. That is why persistent security in the SOAP message itself is required.

SOAP Fault

After sending this SOAP message, company A's Web Service broker will either receive a SOAP message in response, with content to indicate that the stock order was successful, or it will receive a SOAP Fault message. A SOAP Fault indicates that a problem occurred in the processing of the SOAP message.

A SOAP fault uses the Fault element, defined in SOAP 1.2 within the SOAP envelope namespace ("http://www.w3.org/2002/06/soap-envelope"), and defines the following five child elements:

- **Code (mandatory)** This element contains a subelement called "Value" that must include one of the SOAP fault codes defined at http://www.w3.org/TR/2002/WD-soap12-part1-20020626/#faultcodes. These are
  - *VersionMismatch:* This error code indicates that this version of SOAP is not supported. This error is appropriate if a Web Service only supports SOAP 1.2, and is sent a SOAP 1.1 message.
  - *MustUnderstand:* A SOAP header item was flagged as "MustUnderstand," but the Web Service was not able to process the element.
  - *DataEncodingUnknown:* This error indicates that the Web Service was unable to deserialize the SOAP message.
  - *Sender:* This means that the data sent to the Web Service was incorrectly formed, or did not contain the appropriate information. This is the SOAP fault code that should be returned for a SOAP message that, for example, does not contain the appropriate security information.
  - *Receiver:* The message could not be processed for reasons attributable to the processing of the message rather than to the contents of the message itself. The error may be due to the failure of an upstream processor, such as an XML database which had run out of disk space.
- **Reason** This element expresses an error in human-readable text. All fault elements must include a Reason element. It is important that this text be useful and not something like "A fault occurred." However, in the scenario where a message was blocked due to a security issue, it is important that this field does not give away information to an intruder that could be useful to attack the Web Service (for example, "username OK, password wrong" would be helpful for an attacker).

- **Node (optional)** SOAP messages can be routed among a number of SOAP nodes. The Node field indicates which of the SOAP applications along the message path notified the fault.
- **Role (optional)** The Role element information item identifies the role the node was operating in at the point the fault occurred.
- **Detail** This element is mandatory when part or all of the SOAP body could not be processed. This element is not intended for information about difficulties in processing information contained in the SOAP header.

Since this book focuses on Web Services security, Listing 1-10 shows an example of a SOAP Fault generated by an authentication failure on the part of the Web Services broker.

Listing 1-10

```
<?xml version="1.0" ?>
<env:Envelope xmlns:env="http://www.w3.org/2002/06/soap-envelope">
 <env:Header>
  <upg:Upgrade xmlns:upg="http://www.w3.org/2002/06/soap-upgrade">
   <envelope qname="ns1:Envelope"
             xmlns:ns1="http://www.w3.org/2002/06/soap-envelope"/>
   <envelope qname="ns2:Envelope"
             xmlns:ns2="http://schemas.xmlsoap.org/soap/envelope/"/>
  </upg:Upgrade>
 </env:Header>
 <env:Body>
  <env:Fault>
   <env:Code><env:Value>env:Server</env:Value></env:Code>
    <env:Reason>Not authenticated</env:Reason>
   </env:Fault>
 </env:Body>
</env:Envelope>
```

The Reason element portion is included in the Fault element because the error relates to the Body element.

Practical Tools

We've been looking at raw SOAP, UDDI, and WSDL messages. You might be glad to hear that there are many vendor and open-source tools available for Web Services that insulate a programmer from raw XML. Web Services are for distributed computing, and there is no guarantee that the messages sent by computers to other computers will be readily understandable. The SOAP message we saw in Listing 1-9 was very simple. If more complex objects, rather than basic strings, need to be sent in a SOAP message, then a SOAP platform is certainly required.

Tools for XML Processing

XMLSpy is a very useful and highly regarded tool for manipulating XML, XML Schema, and WSDL, amongst other formats. It is available at www.altova.com. JAX (Java API for XML) allows XML processing to take place in Java programs. IDEs such as Visual Studio.NET may be used to manipulate XML also. We will see these tools used extensively in later chapters.

Availability of Tools for Web Services

The major application servers all support Web Services. In Chapter 10, we'll see how Microsoft .NET leverages Web Services for application integration across the full battery of .NET servers. Pure-play Web Services companies such as Cape Clear also produce Web Services development and deployment tools, including tools for UDDI.

A number of script-based tools are available also, including Perl's SOAP::Lite module.

CHAPTER 2

Presenting Security

It is traditional for texts on information security to begin with a description of a perfectly secure system—generally a sealed vault in an underground bunker—and then to consider how this tight security renders the contents of the vault useless because they cannot be examined, changed, or traded. In order to make the contents of the vault useful, some access to the vault must be granted. However, granting this access involves compromises that make the vault less secure. This analogy takes physical security and maps it to Internet security with a simple lesson to learn—the more access, the less security. We saw in the previous chapter that Web Services is about increasing access to functionality—using a services-oriented architecture to publish, find, and bind. If the physical security analogy is followed, then Web Services inevitably involves a trade-off of security for ease of access. Though valid, the physical security analogy is limited. The information security techniques we'll be learning about in this chapter deal with securing the access to information.

Information on the Internet is in one of two states: in storage or in transit. When information is in storage, the locked vault analogy is apt. However, when it is in transit, a more appropriate analogy may be that of an armed escort who accompanies the information to make certain that it arrives intact at its destination. The escort ensures not only that the data is protected, but that it travels intact from the sender to the recipient and that the recipient knows who sent the data. This ensures that not only the data is secure, but the *process* is secure also. Comparing Web Services to a locked vault is always going to provide a negative view of security, because Web Services security is about making a process (not an entity) secure. We've seen that Web Services provides important new efficiencies by exposing functionality using a service-oriented architecture. The challenge is to leverage these efficiencies while taking the appropriate precautions that they will not be misused.

Security can be seen in either a positive or a negative sense. The positive aspect is when security acts as an enabler for a solution—for example, partner or supplier integration. The negative sense is when security acts as a blockade to stop unwanted access to resources. This is the contrast between "letting the good guys in" and "keeping the bad guys out." Web Services security involves both. Different technologies are used for each aspect, with some overlap. But this does not mean that a mishmash of security technologies is used. Information security (sometimes shortened to "infosec") can be sliced and diced into a set of logical components. In this chapter, we'll examine these components, which form the basis for Web Services security.

The goal of this chapter is for you to start thinking like an information security professional, keeping in mind the logical components of information security. So, rather than first thinking "we need to use XML Signature for this project," you should first think "we need to ensure data integrity in this project" before beginning to think about the specific technology that will be used to ensure data integrity.

THE BUILDING BLOCKS OF SECURITY

The division of information security into logical components makes it easier to understand, and therefore easier to deploy. These logical components are confidentiality, authentication, authorization, integrity, nonrepudiation, privacy, and availability. These are the check boxes that need to be kept in mind when designing a secure system. If only some of the boxes are checked, security loopholes exist.

Confidentiality

We've seen that data in a networked system is either in transit or at rest. In the world of information security, the term *confidentiality* is used to refer to the requirement for data in transit between two communicating parties not to be available to third parties that may try to snoop on the communication. There are two broad approaches to confidentiality. One approach is to use a private connection between the two parties—either a dedicated line or a virtual private network (VPN). Another approach, used when data is being sent over an untrusted network such as the Internet, is to use encryption.

Introducing Encryption

In the public mind, encryption is often seen as synonymous with computer security. It would be easy to write an introduction to computer security that focused only on encryption. This heightened public awareness of encryption is due in part to the success of SSL (Secure Sockets Layer) for business-to-consumer (B2C) e-commerce. One of the features of SSL is the encryption of data as it passes between a Web browser and a Web server. The Padlock icon on Web browsers provides a neat graphical reminder that encryption is occurring (it also indicates that the Web site was authenticated; we'll see what that means later). It indicates that eavesdroppers cannot read the data being submitted to a Web site, or requested from a Web site.

Encryption is undoubtedly important, both for confidentiality and as the basis of other security technologies such as digital signatures. However, it is not a kind of magical fairy dust that can be added to a system in order to make it secure. Remember, it is just one of the components of security. A Web-based system is not "secure" simply because it uses SSL for confidentiality; the other security check boxes mentioned earlier must also be ticked.

TIP Don't think of "security" and "cryptography" as synonymous. Much security does not depend on encryption technologies, but rather on content-filtering, caution, and plain common sense. Adding encryption doesn't make a system "secure" if encrypted traffic can access a system which is not supposed to be publicly available.

The Terminology of Encryption

Cryptography is a branch of mathematics, and as such it includes a lot of specialized terminology. A number of pieces of encryption terminology are required to understand this book. In the terminology of encryption, *plaintext* refers to unencrypted data, while *ciphertext* refers to encrypted data. An encryption algorithm is used to take plaintext and convert it into ciphertext. This algorithm is a combination of mathematical functions that jumble the plaintext, making ciphertext.

However, the algorithm alone isn't enough to perform the encryption operation. If that were the case, then when the details of the algorithm were discovered, the ciphertext could be decrypted. The answer to this problem might seem obvious: just keep the algorithm secret. This approach is called "security through obscurity" and does not hold much water, because a secret algorithm that is kept secret and not subject to examination by the world's cryptography experts is likely to have security flaws. In addition, an imposter could use the algorithm to decrypt data even if the inner workings of the algorithm (for example, source code of a cryptography toolkit) were kept secret. Therefore, algorithms have keys, in order to add a variable element to the algorithm which is only known by the parties who are exchanging confidential data. This means that the algorithm can be public, subject to examination by cryptography experts, but relies on a secret key each time it is used. The key is fed into the algorithm, along with the plaintext, and ciphertext is created.

TIP Avoiding "Security through obscurity" goes further than the avoidance of obscure and secret encryption algorithms. It also extends to practices like using obscure, hard-to-guess names for resources. These are all to be avoided.

An *initialization vector* is used to add another element of variability to the encryption. This is required because if two parties agree on an algorithm and on a key, but don't use an initialization vector, then the source data will be identical to the ciphertext. For example, if the message "Yes, I can do that" happens to be repeated, then the ciphertext will be the same, and that is a security risk. We will see in the chapter on XML Encryption (Chapter 4) how initialization vectors (IVs), keys, and encrypted keys are expressed in XML format.

Cryptanalysis is the name given to the examination of a cryptographic system with a view to discovering the decryption key. In cryptanalysis, other aspects of the system may be known—the plaintext and the ciphertext, and the encryption algorithm itself—but the key is secret. If the key can be found, then other ciphertext encrypted using the same key can be decrypted.

It is important to realize that the use of strong encryption does not provide absolute certainty that encrypted data will not be decrypted and read. All strong cryptography can do is to make it extremely difficult to decrypt the data. In practice, this means that the timescale and computing power required to break the encryption make the exercise unattractive. Since cryptanalysis of the encryption algorithms in popular use has shown that they do not have known "backdoors" for discovering the key, the attacker is limited to a "brute force" attack. This means guesswork (repeatedly attempting to decrypt the data using a series of decryption keys), which takes time. If it is known that the decryption key is eight characters long, and each character can be any 8-bit ASCII character, there are more than 10^{19} possible keys to try. The number of possible keys is known as the *keyspace*. On average, a brute force attacker will have to traverse through half of the keyspace before they get lucky and find the decryption key. The time required to traverse through the keyspace can be reduced by using dedicated hardware or multiple machines, but this costs money. A "back-of-the-envelope" calculation can be used to find out whether the cost of breaking the encryption is greater than the value of the data itself. If it is, then that means that a potential attacker may not bother attempting a brute force attack on the encrypted data.

There are two types of encryption in general use for Web Services security: symmetric encryption and asymmetric encryption. In symmetric encryption, the decryption key is the same as the encryption key, as shown here. In asymmetric encryption, the decryption key is not the same as the encryption key. Let's look at both of these in turn.

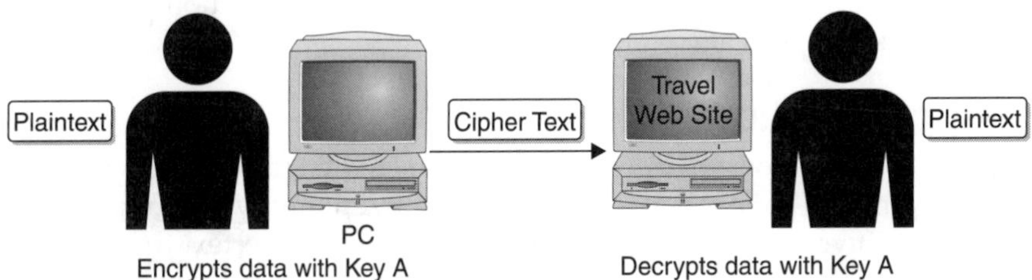

Symmetric Encryption

Symmetric encryption involves the use of the same key for encryption as for decryption. Looking at the preceding illustration, we can see why it is known as "symmetric" encryption—the illustration is symmetric horizontally because encryption and decryption use the same key. Examples of symmetric key algorithms are DES (Data Encryption Standard), which has been in use for over 20 years as a recommendation of the U.S. government, and AES (Advanced Encryption Standard), which replaces DES.

Because in symmetric encryption the one-and-only key is also used for decryption, it must be kept secret. Otherwise, the confidentiality requirement isn't met. If a brute force attack is successful and the key becomes known, all ciphertext encrypted using that key can be decrypted. This is important for Web Services because we are dealing with information in transit. The data is being sent to a recipient, and since it is encrypted, it is confidential. The problem, therefore, is how to send the key safely to the recipient of the data so that only that recipient can read the data. It is obvious that the key cannot be sent in the clear with the data, because that would defeat the purpose of using encryption in the first place. (If the key could be "sniffed" as it is sent to the recipient, there would be no need for a brute force attack at all.)

There are two options for sending the key. Option one is to use a separate communication channel to send the key. For example, the encryption key could be communicated to the recipient over the phone. This is known as sending the key "out of band." This is feasible for infrequent communications since a DES key, for example, is only eight characters long and could be conveyed in a phone call. However, for Web Services security, this approach is out of the question because the overhead of sending the key out of band would cancel out the integration advantages offered by a service-oriented architecture. All the advantages of publish, find, and bind that we discussed in Chapter 1 would be lost. Also, since Web Services are software talking to other software, the concept of a human being "picking up the phone" isn't applicable. Of course, the out-of-band communication does not have to be a phone call, and can be another method. However, unless it is a trusted channel, it cannot be guaranteed that the key won't be "sniffed."

The second option is to encrypt the key itself, which means that it can be sent using the same communications channel (even in the same message) as the encrypted document. However, if the key is also encrypted using symmetric encryption, we've just introduced the problem of how to send the new key that is used to decrypt the first key—and we are back to square one. We'll see in the next section how asymmetric encryption solves this problem.

Asymmetric Encryption

In the following illustration, we can see how asymmetric encryption gets its name. Two different keys are used so that the diagram is not horizontally symmetric. This may seem counterintuitive. How can one key be used to create ciphertext from plaintext, and then a completely different key be used to convert the ciphertext back into the original plaintext? That answer to this question involves some fairly complex mathematics. The most famous and widely used asymmetric algorithm is the RSA algorithm (named after its creators: Rivest, Shamir, and Adleman), which uses prime number arithmetic. Luckily, we don't have to concern ourselves with mathematics in this chapter, and so we are more interested in the overall reason why it exists. Asymmetric encryption removes the need to send the decryption key to the recipient of encrypted data.

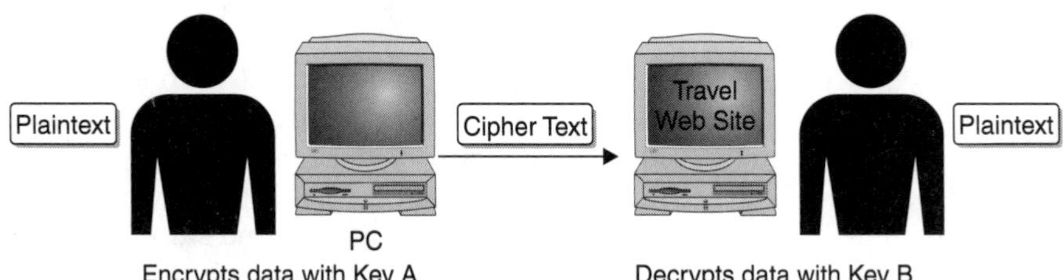

Recall that we suggested encrypting the symmetric key and sending it to the intended reader of the data, but this seemed to land us back at square one – how is the key itself encrypted? Actually, that problem applies only if symmetric encryption is used to encrypt the key. If asymmetric encryption is used to encrypt the key, the only requirement is that the reader of the data holds the key to be used to decrypt the data—that is, the corresponding key of the key pair. It is this second key that must be kept private; hence the term "private key." Notice that we don't call it a "decryption key." That is because it can be used for more than decryption, as we'll see later when we discuss digital signatures. Similarly, the key that is used for encryption is not only an "encryption key," but can also be used in the context of digital signatures. Therefore, the term "public key" is more appropriate for this key, because the key should be available to any party that is encrypting data to be sent to the holder of the private key.

At this stage, some questions might present themselves. These are

1. Since asymmetric encryption is such a good solution for encrypting a key, why not use it for encrypting all the data and not bother using symmetric encryption at all?
2. How does the reader of the data get their private key in the first place; how could such a sensitive item be sent to them?
3. How does the entity encrypting the data know that they are using the appropriate public key?

The answer to the first question is easy. Symmetric encryption is much faster than asymmetric encryption, so it makes sense to use symmetric encryption to encrypt the data and only use the slower asymmetric encryption to encrypt the key itself. The answer to the second question is also relatively straightforward. The private key is generated by the reader of the data on their computer, and it never leaves their computer. Better still: the private key can be generated on a hardware token such as a smartcard, and never leave the smartcard. The answer to the third question is slightly more complex. We'll see in the nonrepudiation section that public keys are rarely distributed alone. They are contained in something called a "digital certificate." A public key alone does not contain identity information, but a digital certificate does. Digital certificates ensure that the correct public key is used for encryption.

This completes our discussion of confidentiality. Let's look at the next information security requirement: integrity.

Integrity

In the field of information security, integrity has a special meaning. It does not mean that information cannot be tampered with. It means that if information is tampered with, this tampering can be detected. In an untrusted network, it may be impossible to ensure that the data is tamper-proof when it is in transit to its destination. So, knowledge about the fact that tampering has occurred is the next best thing.

Data integrity relies on mathematical algorithms known as hashing algorithms. A hashing algorithm takes a block of data as input and produces a much smaller piece of data as output. This output is sometimes called a "digest" of the data. If the data is a message, it is called a "message digest." The digest is bound to the original data in the following way: if the original data changes, however slightly, and the hashing algorithm is rerun, the resulting digest will also be different. Examples of hashing algorithms include SHA-1.

Digital Signatures

A hashing algorithm alone cannot ensure integrity. Think about the scenario where a digest is added to the end of a message before it is sent to a recipient. An attacker who tampers with the message could simply construct a new digest and append it to the message instead. In this case, the tampering would be undetected, and so the integrity requirement would not be met.

This section follows the section on confidentiality for a reason, because encryption is also used for integrity. Specifically, asymmetric encryption is used. Recall that it isn't appropriate to call the public key the "encryption key" or to call the private key the "decryption key," even if those names accurately define their roles when they are used to fulfill the confidentiality requirement. The reason is that the process can be run in reverse: the private key can be used for encryption and the public key can be used for decryption. This might seem counterintuitive: if data can be decrypted using a public key, it isn't confidential at all, is it? The answer is that only the digest of the data is encrypted using the private key, and only the holder of the private key can perform this encryption operation. The corresponding public key is then used by the reader of the data to decrypt the encrypted digest. If the hashing algorithm is rerun, and the resulting digest is found to be the same as the decrypted digest, this verifies the integrity of the data.

This encrypted digest bears some similarity to a handwritten signature, so it is called a "digital signature." However, the way in which a digital signature (that is, an encrypted digest) ensures the integrity of data is not similar to a handwritten signature, because handwritten signatures do not ensure the integrity of a signed document. For example, a ten-page paper document could be signed and one of the middle pages replaced, and the signature could not be used to indicate that anything is amiss. Therefore, it is important to understand that digital signatures are not the same as handwritten signatures.

In this book, we will concentrate on XML Signature, which is a means (but not the only means) of rendering a digital signature in XML format. PKCS#7 was an earlier specification that described how a digital signature could be rendered. Later, we will see how WS-Security allows an XML Signature to be embedded in a SOAP message.

TIP Don't confuse digital signatures with other types of electronic signatures. "Electronic signature" is a loose term that is used to describe signing technologies that involve electronics. Digital signatures are a type of electronic signature. Other types of electronic signatures include stylus pads on which a person can electronically pen their handwritten signature (sometimes called a "digitized signature"). These are used by document delivery companies and at credit card payment terminals.

Recall the third question posed at the end of the section on confidentiality. To refresh your memory, here it is again: How does the entity encrypting the data know that they are using the appropriate public key? For integrity, we have a similar question:

How can the entity processing a digital signature be sure that they are using the appropriate public key? This question is answered in the next section.

Nonrepudiation

Nonrepudiation literally means that the originator of a message cannot claim *not* to have sent a given message. We saw in the preceding two sections on confidentiality and integrity that it is important that the appropriate public key is used. If the wrong public key is used for encrypting a document, or to verify a digital signature, the results can be disastrous. Any doubt about the authenticity of the public key throws integrity and confidentiality into question. A public key must be somehow bound to the identity of the party who is digitally signing the data, or decrypting the data. This binding to an identity also helps to deliver nonrepudiation. We will see in this section, however, that nonrepudiation is an elusive goal that requires a combination of technologies.

Digital Certificates

When a private key is generated, the corresponding public key is generated at the same time. Recall that the public key is used to encrypt information that is intended for the holder of the corresponding private key. If the wrong public key is used, the results are either bad or disastrous. They are bad if the intended reader cannot decrypt the data. They are disastrous if an imposter has somehow substituted his or her own public key and now holds the private key, which can be used to decrypt the data. Therefore, it is vitally important that the public key can be bound to the identity of the holder of the private key.

By looking at a public key alone, there is no way of ensuring the identity of the holder of the private key. A key is, after all, just a string of bytes. Digital certificates were invented to solve this problem. A digital certificate typically includes identity information (for example, name, location, and country) about the entity holding the corresponding private key, a serial number and expiry date, and, of course, the public key itself. The X.509 specification is used to format the information in a digital certificate. X.509 is fully extensible, meaning that any additional identity attributes can be added to the digital certificate.

Public Key Infrastructure

A digital certificate is issued by a certificate authority (CA). A digital certificate is bound to the CA that issues the certificate. This binding is performed using a digital signature, which ensures the integrity of the digital certificate. In practice, this means that the operator of the CA is vouching for the identity of the entity that is described by the digital certificate. In order to be able to vouch for this identity, an identification verification procedure must be performed. The identification verification procedure depends on the policy of the CA, and can range from a simple e-mail exchange to a face-to-face passport submission.

While a CA is used for issuing digital certificates, the identification verification is performed by a registration authority (RA). An RA and CA work in lockstep. When an identity is verified, the RA instructs the CA to issue a digital certificate. The RA may be operated by the same organization that provides the CA, or the RA function may be performed by another party such as a regional affiliate.

Once issued, a digital certificate may be required to be publicly available. If so, a popular method for publishing digital certificates is to use an X.500 directory. An X.500 directory is a hierarchical (that is, tree-like) storage mechanism. Lightweight Directory Access Protocol (LDAP) is typically used to request and retrieve X.509 certificates from an X.500 directory.

As we've seen, the most important part of an X.509 certificate is the public key. The public key has a corresponding private key. It is obviously important that this private key should not be available to anybody except for the entity who initially created the key pair. If this key is compromised (meaning that if there is any chance at all that it has been exposed to a third party), this means that data should no longer be encrypted with the corresponding public key. In addition, data that is digitally signed using the corresponding private key should not be trusted. This is a powerful reason why it is recommended that different public key pairs be used for encryption and signing.

It is vital that potential users of the corresponding public key be made aware if the private key is compromised, or is even suspected of being compromised. In this scenario, the digital certificate is revoked, meaning that the CA issuer has indicated that it is no longer valid. Information about revoked digital certificates is contained in a certificate revocation list (CRL). Like digital certificates themselves, a CRL can be stored in a directory and accessed using LDAP.

Together, CAs, RAs, and X.500 directories are known as a public key infrastructure (PKI). By linking public keys to actual identities using digital certificates, and by ensuring that a compromised private key results in swift revocation of a digital certificate, a PKI fulfils the nonrepudiation requirement. In Figure 2-1, you can see how PKI can be used for a Web Services transaction.

TIP Although digital certificates and PKI may be used to enable trust between a SOAP requester and a Web Service, this does not mean that end users must use digital certificates to authenticate to a system which uses Web Services. PKI is a notoriously difficult technology to deliver to end users. It is more practical for end users to authenticate using a username/password combination. However, WS-Security can then be used to embed information about the end user in a security token, for example, an X.509 certificate or a SAML Assertion, in a SOAP message.

Four steps are outlined in the diagram. Step 1 is to generate a key pair and register the public key with a registration authority. This ensures that the certificate authority issues a digital certificate containing the public key. XKMS is the XML specification that can be used to provide PKI services over the Web. Note that XKMS is key-centric

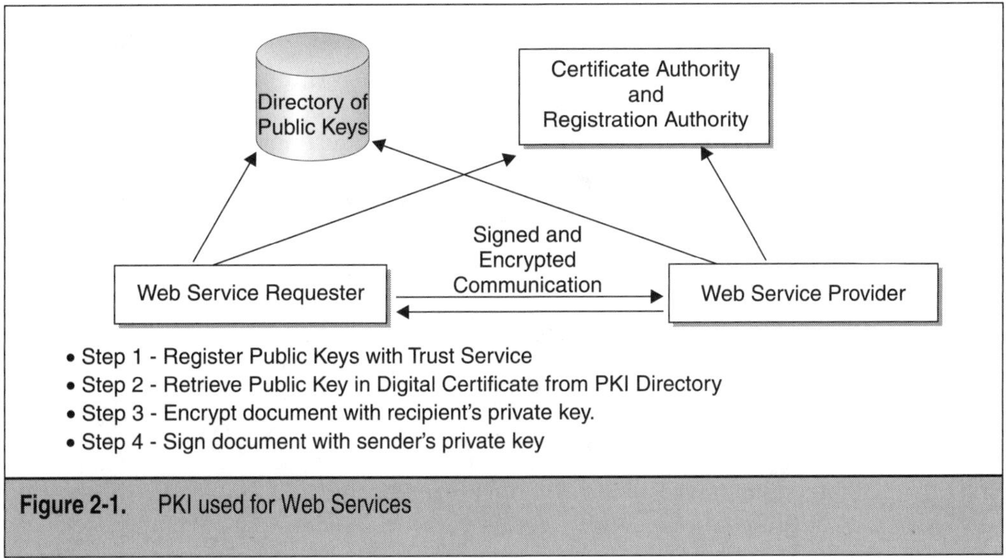

Figure 2-1. PKI used for Web Services

not certificate-centric, because it can be used without any certificates at all. In the diagram, both the Web Service requester and the Web Service provider register their keys using XKMS, and then their keys are held in a publicly available directory. If the requirement is only for the Web Services provider to be authenticated, then only they need to register their public key.

The public key can then be used to send encrypted data to the Web Service. Step 2 shows a Web Service requester retrieving the public key of the Web Service from a PKI directory. LDAP or Directory Services Markup Language (DSML) can be used for this step. Specific protocols such as SSL allow a Web Service provider to expose their public key to requesters, without the requirement to look up the key in a public directory; however, a public service may still be required in order to ensure that the key is valid. When a public key is enclosed in a digital certificate, the issuer of the certificate (sometimes called a "trusted third party" or "TTP") signs both the key and the identity information of the key holder, thus binding them together and vouching for the identity of the key holder.

Step 3 shows secure communication between the Web Service provider and the Web Service requester. This data may be encrypted using the Web Service provider's public key, with the public key's validity checked using XKMS. XML Encryption can be used to encrypt a portion of the SOAP message, or SSL can be used at a lower communication layer to encrypt the session. XML Signature can be used for message integrity and nonrepudiation. As we can see from this diagram, many of the XML Web Services security specifications take existing procedures and apply an XML interface.

Authentication

In the previous section, we saw how the mathematical algorithms of asymmetric encryption can be linked with an identity-checking registration process and a directory server in order to deliver nonrepudiation. This same PKI technology can also be used for authentication—that is, to establish the identity of a communicating party. However, other methods are available for authentication, including biometrics, passwords, and hardware devices that issue one-time passwords. What these have in common is that a token is in the possession of the entity that is authenticated. In the case of a smartcard, the token is hardware-based; and in the case of a private key on a hard drive, the token is software-based. At a theoretical level, however, they are both tokens.

This book is about Web Services security, which adds a new twist on authentication. While a human user may authenticate directly to their systems, they will not be running Web Services directly. As we saw in the previous chapter, Web Services is software talking to other software. However, Web Services may well be run on behalf of a human user who has authenticated using a human-to-machine authentication technique (for example, a password). For example, a currency trader may authenticate to their dealing terminal at 8:00 A.M., and then press a button to perform a trade at 8:15 A.M. The processing of this trade may involve Web Services being run, perhaps both inside the dealer's company and at a third-party settlement company. It may be a requirement for the Web Services to be called on behalf of the trader. Therefore, information about the dealer's authentication status must be carried in the Web Service communication. This scenario, which is essential for Web Services, is enabled by SAML. SAML defines an XML syntax used for exchanging information about authentication and authorization.

Public Key Infrastructure for Authentication

We've seen that digital certificates bind a public key to the identity of the holder of the corresponding private key. When a digital certificate is used for authentication, it must be accompanied with proof-of-possession (POP) of the corresponding private key. After all, if this wasn't required, anybody could retrieve digital certificates from an online directory and use them for authentication. A common way to implement proof-of-possession is to digitally sign a piece of data and send the digital certificate as part of the digital signature.

It is important when digital signatures are used for authentication to avoid the possibility of a replay attack. A replay attack involves intercepting data and then sending it again. In the case of an authentication request, a successful replay attack would result in an imposter assuming another person's identity. It is important, therefore, that the signed data include a random element. This can be achieved using a challenge-response algorithm, whereby the entity that wishes to authenticate is presented with a piece of data they must digitally sign. The digital signature, possibly including the digital certificate, is then returned. If the signature is valid, the user has been authenticated.

The most popular application of digital certificates for authentication is Secure Sockets Layer (SSL), which uses asymmetric cryptography to perform authentication over HTTP. A requester (for example, a Web browser) issues a random challenge to a Web server and examines the response to ensure that the Web server holds the private key that corresponds to the public key in their digital certificate.

We learned in Chapter 1 that Web Services does not rely on HTTP, so SSL is not always an option for message authentication. WS-SecureConversation, part of the Microsoft Global XML Web Services Architecture (GXA) re-creates the functionality of SSL at the SOAP layer. In addition, the Web Services Development Kit (WSDK) supports XML Signature over a Timestamp element in a SOAP header. This functionality guards against a replay attack, since the SOAP message is only valid between the "Created" and "Expired" times contained within the Timestamp element.

TIP Be careful not to confuse replay attacks with denial of service attacks. If a single message is sent 1000 times to a Web Service, with a view to bringing the Web Service to its knees, that's a denial of service attack. If a single message, containing authentication information, is detected and replayed in order to obtain illegal access to the Web Service, that's a replay attack.

An example of a timestamp is shown in Listing 2-1. This conforms to the WS-Security specification. A digital signature over this timestamp binds it to the identity of the signer, and limits the possibility of a replay attack.

Listing 2-1

```
<wsu:Timestamp xmlns:wsu="http://schemas.xmlsoap.org/ws/2002/07/utility">
<wsu:Created wsu:Id="Id-76810165-4de7-4e51-9674-583326995c88">
2002-08-14T17:33:27Z
</wsu:Created>
<wsu:Expires wsu:Id="Id-d3e1d6f4-9986-474d-9706-9ab7ffe785dd">
2002-08-14T17:38:27Z
</wsu:Expires>
</wsu:Timestamp>
```

TIP Ensure that the time period between the creation and expiration of a timestamp is short enough to limit the window of opportunity for a replay attack.

Smartcards

The word "smartcard" is a relatively loose term, and refers to any credit-card-sized device that contains a microchip. Smartcards can be used to store private keys for use in asymmetric encryption. Recall that when a public and private key pair is generated, and a smartcard is used, the private key never leaves the smartcard. This makes for a very secure solution. Of course, if the smartcard is somehow compromised or lost, the corresponding public key should not be used and its digital certificate should be entered into its PKI's certificate revocation list.

If the smartcard stores a private key, the process used for authentication is similar to the process when the private key is not on a smartcard. However, the overall security of the system is enhanced because smartcard-based authentication is "two-factor" rather than "one-factor." Here, "two-factor" refers to "something you have" (the smartcard) and "something you know" (the password to use the private key on the smartcard). When the private key is not on a smartcard and is instead resident on the hard drive, the authentication is "one-factor"—just "something you know" (the password required to use the private key on the hard drive).

Two-factor authentication can also be used without asymmetric encryption. This is the approach used by tools such as RSA Security's SecurID cards. These tokens present one-time keys on an LCD screen. "One-time keys" are so-called because they do not repeat. The user may have a password that they must enter into the device to retrieve a one-time key (called a "one-time pad"), or the key may simply be presented onscreen. If the user is required to use a password, that is two-factor authentication (something you know, something you have). If there is no password, it is only one-factor authentication (something you have). These one-time key devices interact with a server that verifies the keys. One-time key devices are extremely secure, especially when two-factor authentication is used. However, they are not particularly applicable to Web Services since Web Services involves software communicating with other software, which means there may be literally nobody around to read the display on the one-time key card and enter it into a dialog box. If an end user has authenticated using a smartcard, then this fact may be conveyed in a SAML Authentication Assertion, which "asserts" that the end user used a hardware token to authenticate.

Biometrics

Biometrics presents an excellent authentication solution, but they are not directly applicable for Web Services security. They are indirectly applicable when a user authenticates to a system using biometrics, and then information about their authentication action is used as part of a "single sign-in" system.

Username and Password

Username and password is perhaps the most common form of authentication on the Internet. The WS-Security Addendum, published in August 2002, describes a means to include a username and password combination as a "security token" in a SOAP message. The password may be sent in clear text, or alternatively a digest of the password may be sent.

Because end users rarely authenticate directly to a Web Service, SAML can be used to construct an assertion to indicate that a user has authenticated using username and password. Then, the SOAP message sent on the user's behalf can include this SAML assertion but not the actual username or password.

Authorization

Authorization is an information security requirement that is sometimes linked with authentication, and it is important to see the difference between the two. While authentication is about "who you are," authorization is about "what you are allowed to do." Just because a user is authenticated doesn't mean that they are authorized. Authentication is necessary for authorization, however. Authorization software allows an administrator to manage a policy for access control to services. It also typically provides the provisioning of access control rights to users. Authorization software, from vendors such as Netegrity and Oblix, can make use of users and groups that have already been configured in corporate directories. Users may be assigned to groups and roles.

The principal motivation of role-based access control (RBAC) is to map security management to an organization's structure. Traditionally, managing security has required mapping an organization's security policy to a relatively low-level set of controls, typically access control lists (ACLs). With RBAC, each user's role may be based on the user's job responsibilities in the organization. Each role is assigned one or more privileges (for example, access to certain information). It is a user's membership in defined roles that determines the privileges the user is permitted.

When looking at authentication software, we saw that single sign-on technologies such as SAML may be used to convey information about an authentication event that has occurred. Similarly, we will see how a SOAP profile of SAML may provide a means for an authorization event to be conveyed to a Web Service. When multiple Web Services are being run in quick succession, and time is of the essence, it is important that the overhead of authorization not occur each time another Web Service is being run.

Policy Enforcement Points and Policy Decision Points

One of the important architectural features of authorization software is that the location where the authorization decision is made be separated from the location where the policy is enforced. These two locations are known as the policy decision point (PDP) and the policy enforcement point (PEP), respectively. The PEP is at the location where potential users present their credentials—for example, at a Web server. The PDP is not located on this system, but is on another system that is not exposed to users. This distinction is important because the PDP must be kept safe from tampering. It must not be exposed to the outside world. If it was on the Web server, which is an untrusted system, there would be the chance that it could be compromised and the policy changed. When we encounter SAML, we will see this distinction between the PDP and PEP expressed in the form of the SAML Protocol.

Availability

Availability may not strike the reader as being an obvious security requirement. However, if critical information is not available when needed, that is costly for any business. As well as the Web Service itself, security services themselves require availability. For example, a certificate revocation list is used for nonrepudiation. If this is not available, the nonrepudiation feature is lost.

Denial of Service Attacks

One of the means of denying availability is to mount a denial of service (DoS) attack. A DoS attack aims to use up all the resources of a service so that it is unavailable to legitimate users. DoS attacks have evolved over the past few years, and the corresponding defensive technologies have also evolved. One of the chief innovations was the distributed denial of service (DDoS) attack. This involves gaining unauthorized access to many computers and installing DoS software on these compromised computers. Some compromised computers act as "handlers" that each orchestrate large numbers of "agents," which are the computers that perform the actual DoS attack. DDoS attacks can be very destructive in terms of limiting availability to services.

Privacy

Like availability, privacy is a requirement that might not come immediately to mind when information security is discussed. Sometimes privacy is mistaken for confidentiality. We've seen that confidentiality is the requirement that data that is in transit is not available to eavesdroppers. The privacy requirement concerns the privacy rights of the subject of the data.

Many privacy protection laws are now in force worldwide, requiring that private data not be disclosed without consent from the subject of the data. Many of the publicized Internet security breaches are privacy breaches. When credit card data is stolen on the Internet, it is rarely a breach of confidentiality for transport-level security, because strong encryption is almost universally used for data in transit on the Internet. However, when credit card data is in storage at a Web site, for example, it may well *not* be encrypted. If there are any back doors in the Web application, or a direct database connection is available, the credit card data may be stolen. When this happens, it is both a breach of confidentiality (at the server) *and* a breach of the privacy because the data was supposed to remain private.

Other privacy violations are possible if authorization solutions are misconfigured, or not applied at all. Web Services offers a whole new means of accessing information, and, therefore, a new means of violating privacy if security is not correctly applied.

TIP Privacy rules vary from country to country. In particular, data protection rules vary by country. Consult your national government web site to determine what the requirements are in your jurisdiction.

PEELING BACK THE LAYERS OF SECURITY

In the previous section we looked at the building blocks of security: confidentiality, integrity, nonrepudiation, authorization, authentication, and availability. If we think of that as a horizontal view of security, looking across all of the available tools, then in this section we are looking vertically, down through the communications layers on which the building blocks of security stand.

Table 2-1 shows the seven layers of the Open System Interconnect (OSI) stack.

Though we will see in Chapter 3 that Web Services security has specific implications for layer 7, the application layer, the security at other levels of the OSI stack is also important. Let's look some of the OSI layers, examining how they are vulnerable to security breaches. A common thread emerges—by sending an application data that it doesn't expect, vulnerabilities can be probed and exploited. We'll see how this was possible at lower layers of communication, and in the next chapter we'll see how it now occurs at the application layer.

Network Layer

Security options at the network layer are largely unchanged from the time before Web Services existed. Firewalls continue to be vital, even if new vulnerabilities and challenges have opened up at higher layers of the OSI stack.

Choosing and Configuring a Firewall

The network layer is protected by firewalls. Firewalls examine IP packets coming into and leaving an organization. They ensure that suspicious or malicious packets are not allowed to pass through. Routers also perform packet filtering. One of the major debates in information security concerns the ongoing importance of firewalls. Historically, firewalls were used to block unwanted protocols by blocking the TCP ports that they

Layer Number	Layer Name	Example of Technology that Uses this Layer
Layer 7	Application	E-mail, directory services
Layer 6	Presentation	Encrypted data, compressed data POP/SMTP
Layer 5	Session	POP/25, SSL
Layer 4	Transport	TCP, UDP
Layer 3	Network	Packets IP, ARP
Layer 2	Data Link	PPP, 802.11
Layer 1	Physical	ADSL, ATM

Table 2-1. OSI Stack

used. However, the ports for Web browsing would be left open. Consequently, many application vendors adapted their product to use the Web ports—that is, ports 80 and 443 (for SSL). This had the effect of bypassing firewalls. However, that does not mean that firewalls are no longer useful. Firewalls continue to guard against lower layers of communication.

Next, we will examine one of these attacks: the so-called "ping of death."

Example: Blocking the "Ping of Death"

The evocatively named "ping of death" attack involved pinging a computer with a packet greater than 65,536 bytes (as opposed to the default 64 bytes). It struck in the late 1990s, and found vulnerabilities in UNIX, MacOS, Netware, printers, and routers. An IP datagram of 65,536 bytes is illegal. However, the design of IP packets meant that it was possible to create such a datagram by exploiting the method by which packets are fragmented. When the packet is reassembled, it can overflow the buffer, causing unpredictable results.

This targeting of a buffer overflow is a common attack method that we will see in the next chapter. Web Services is not as vulnerable to buffer overflow attacks as earlier integration technologies were. However, it is still important to learn the lesson of the "ping of death" and not take it for granted that the input to a system will be as expected. "Never trust your input" is a useful rule to keep in mind.

Session and Transport Layers

The session and transport layers also have specific security technologies. These are not superseded by Web Services security. They are still very useful in order to secure network communications at layers under the application layer. In particular, they remain important for ensuring the confidentiality of SOAP communications.

SSL

SSL provides both confidentiality (through encryption) and authentication (using digital certificates) for HTTP traffic. The use of SSL for confidentiality is phenomenally successful. It is the de facto means of encrypting information traveling from a Web browser to a Web server. The use of SSL for authentication of Web sites is successful also. Using SSL, a user of a Web browser can ensure that the Web site they are visiting is authentic. Companies such as VeriSign issue digital certificates to Web sites so that Web sites can prove their identity to potential customers. SSL provides for authentication in the reverse direction also—that is, for a user of a Web browser to prove his or her identity to a Web site. This aspect of SSL is not as successful, however. That is because the overhead of generating a public and private key pair, and then registering this with a PKI, is unattractive for most Web browser users. Consequently, on the B2C Internet, consumers can be sure of the identity of the authenticated online stores with which they transact, but the stores typically cannot be 100 percent sure of the identity of their customers.

Application Layer: S/MIME

S/MIME is a solution for confidentiality, integrity, and nonrepudiation for e-mail messages. It uses encryption for confidentiality, and digital signatures for integrity and nonrepudiation. Note that the provision of nonrepudiation relies on the existence of a PKI.

A SOAP message may, in time, be sent using SMTP (Simple Mail Transport Protocol) and when that happens S/MIME will be a useful technology for security. The type of digital signature used in S/MIME is a PKCS#7 signature. This has been superseded to some extent by XML Signature.

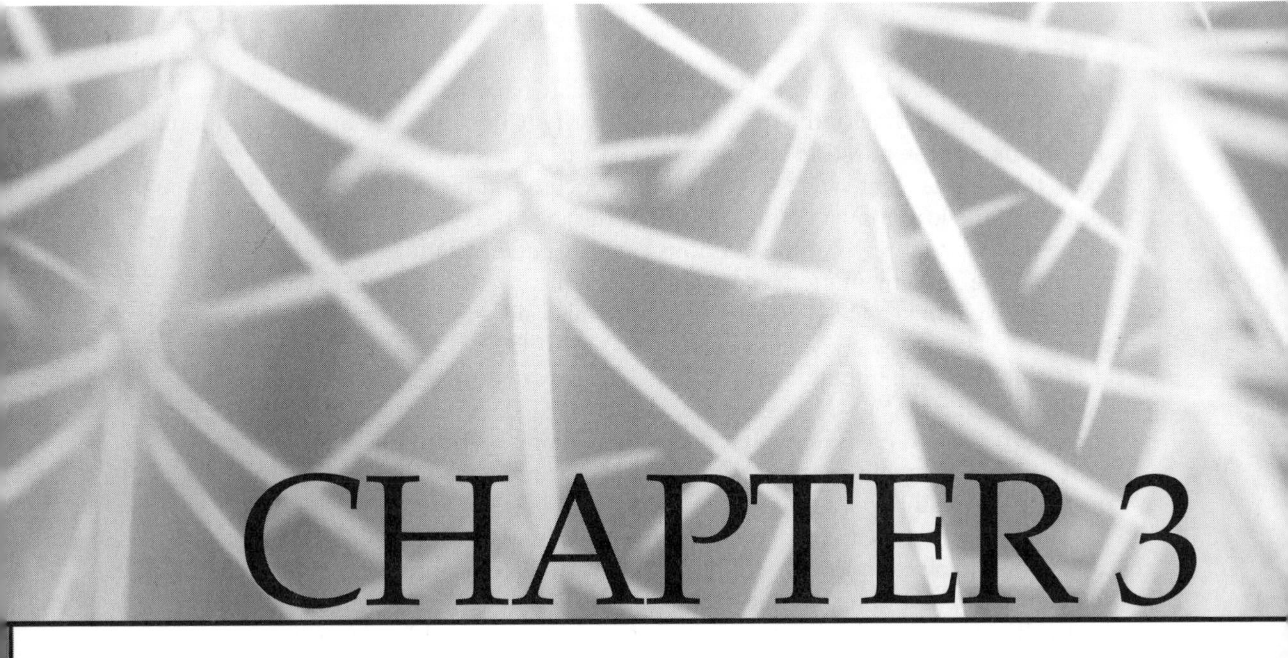

CHAPTER 3

New Challenges and New Threats

Now that we know what Web Services are (Chapter 1) and have at least a basic understanding of the principles of security (Chapter 2), we are in a position to answer the question "what kind of security does Web Services need?" We will see in this chapter that Web Services security focuses on the application layer, although security at the lower layers remains important. The principles of security are the same as those we encountered in the previous chapter: authentication, authorization, and so forth. The implementation technologies on which we focus are HTTP and SOAP, although we will keep SMTP security in mind also since SOAP can be bound to SMTP as well as HTTP.

It may not seem immediately obvious why security for SOAP presents such a challenge. After all, SOAP is generally bound to HTTP, which already has SSL for authentication and confidentiality. In addition, many Web authorization tools already exist. It is a reasonable question to ask why these aren't enough, and the answer is made up of a number of reasons.

The first reason is that, although frequently bound to HTTP, SOAP is independent of the underlying communications layers. Many different communications technologies can be used in the context of one multihop SOAP message; for example, using HTTP for the first leg, then SMTP for the next leg, and so forth. End-to-end security cannot therefore rely on a security technology that presupposes one particular communications technology. Even in the case of a single SOAP message targeted at a Web Service, transport-level security only deals with the originator of the SOAP request. SOAP requests are generated by machines, not by people. If the Web Service wishes to perform security based on the end user, it must have access to authentication and/or authorization information about the end user on whose behalf the SOAP request is being sent. This is the second reason for Web Services security.

This information is not available in the transport layer, which deals only with the originator of the SOAP request. When SOAP messages are routed between Web Services, the same problem applies. The security context spans multiple connections, meaning the principles of security such as integrity and confidentiality must also apply across these multiple connections. These challenges are met by persisting security information inside the SOAP message. This chapter introduces WS-Security, a framework for including security information as XML in SOAP messages. Next, the specifications for expressing security information (digital signatures, encryption, authentication, and authorization data) in XML are introduced.

If confidentiality, integrity, and identity-based security can be viewed as the positive aspects of security, then protecting against hacker attacks is the negative aspect. Hacker attacks are a fact of life when computers connect to the Internet. These attacks tend to follow the path of least resistance; that is, by circumventing security, not tackling it head-on. A sophisticated authentication system is useless if it requires people to "play by the rules" and these rules can be bypassed. Now that many of the vulnerabilities at lower layers of the network have been addressed, the playing field has moved to the application layer. In this chapter, we'll see how these attacks share many characteristics with the older, more traditional attacks at lower layers of the communications stack.

Web Services presents both a security challenge and a security threat. The challenge is to implement the principles of security at the application layer. The threat is that

Web Services presents a new avenue of attack into enterprise systems, one that is not addressed by current security infrastructure (including firewalls). This chapter examines the new technologies that address these challenges and threats.

WEB SERVICES SECURITY CHALLENGES

In Chapter 2, we were introduced to the layers of the OSI stack. Table 3-1 shows us how the OSI layers apply to Web Services.

Notice that SOAP is in layer 7, together with HTTP and SMTP. However, SOAP travels over HTTP or SMTP. This does not mean that SOAP belongs in a new layer, a layer 8. On the contrary, the seven-layer communications stack still applies for *each individual communication* from a SOAP requester to a Web Service. However, one SOAP-based communication is not the full story. Web Services security presents three challenges:

- The challenge of security based on the end user of a Web Service
- The challenge of maintaining security while routing between multiple Web Services
- The challenge of abstracting security from the underlying network

Let's examine each of these challenges.

The Challenge of Security Based on the End User of a Web Service

SOAP is a technology used to enable software to talk to other software much easier than was previously possible. End users (that is, humans) do not make SOAP messages themselves. However, if access to the Web Service is to be decided based on the information about the end user, the Web Service must have access to the information that allows it to make this authorization decision. This information does not have to include the end user's actual identity. Consider Figure 3-1.

Layer Number	Layer Name	Web Services Technology
Layer 7	Application	HTTP, SMTP, SOAP
Layer 6	Presentation	Encrypted data, Compressed data
Layer 5	Session	POP/25, SSL
Layer 4	Transport	TCP, UDP
Layer 3	Network	IP Packets
Layer 2	Data Link	PPP, 802.11, etc.
Layer 1	Physical	ADSL, ATM, etc.

Table 3-1. OSI Layers

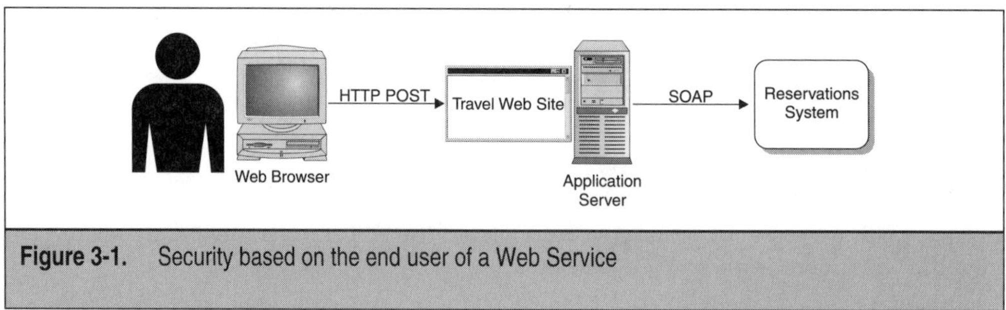

Figure 3-1. Security based on the end user of a Web Service

The end user in Figure 3-1 is accessing a travel Web site and making a reservation. The reservation is made, on the user's behalf, on a third-party system accessed using SOAP. The end user may have authenticated to the travel Web site, perhaps using a username and password. Because of the successful authentication, the user may have been shown personalized content. Information about the user's identity, as well as attributes of the end user such as their travel preferences and previous bookings, are known to the Web site. However, in Figure 3-1, we see that the Web Service only has visibility of the travel Web site, not the end user.

How can this information about the end user be conveyed to the Web Service? Session layer or transport layer security between the application server and the Web Service doesn't convey information about the identity of the end user of the Web Service. It merely conveys information about the application server that is sending the SOAP message. It may be the case that many of the requests to the Web Service originate from that application server.

This challenge is addressed by including security information about the end user in the SOAP message itself. This information may concern the end user's identity, attributes of the end user, or simply an indication that this user has already been authenticated and/or authorized by the Web server. This information allows the Web Service to make an informed authorization decision.

This scenario is likely to be widespread where many Web Services are used to implement functionality "behind the scenes." It shouldn't be the case that the end user has to reauthenticate each time a SOAP request must be sent on their behalf. The challenge of providing this functionality is sometimes called "single sign-on" or "federated trust."

End-User Access to a Web Service: A Practical Example

This example uses the ASP.NET Web Matrix tool, freely downloadable from http://www.asp.net. ASP.NET Web Matrix in turn requires the .NET Framework to be installed. The .NET Framework can be downloaded from the following URL: http://msdn.microsoft.com/netframework. Please ensure that you download the latest service pack for the .NET Framework.

Simple "Add" and "Subtract" Web Services

When ASP.NET Matrix is opened, it displays the dialog box seen in Figure 3-2.

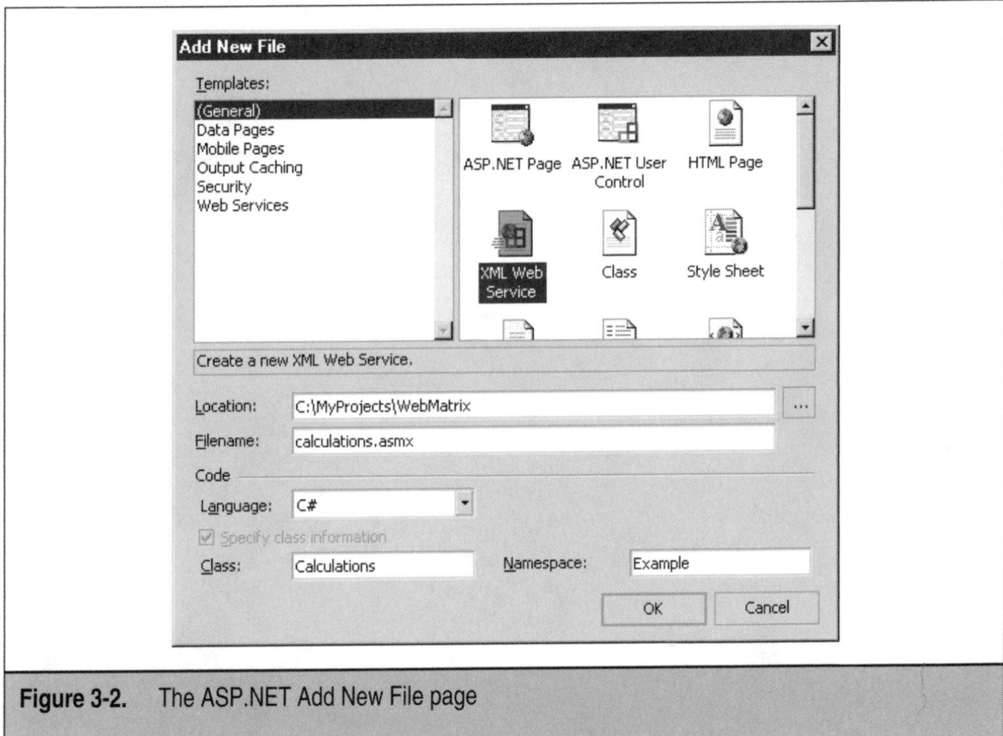

Figure 3-2. The ASP.NET Add New File page

Enter **calculations.asmx** in the Filename text box, **Calculations** in the Class text box, and **Example** in the Namespace text box. Choose C# as the language. Now click OK. You will be presented with the screen shown in Figure 3-3.

Conveniently, for our example, the code for an example Add Web Service is already provided. Now add a "Subtract" method so that the code listing onscreen is identical to the following code:

```
<%@ WebService language="C#" class="Calculations" %>
using System;
using System.Web.Services;
using System.Xml.Serialization;
public class Calculations {
    [WebMethod]
    public int Add(int a, int b) {
        return a + b;
    }

    [WebMethod]
    public int Subtract(int a, int b) {
        return a - b;
    }
}
```

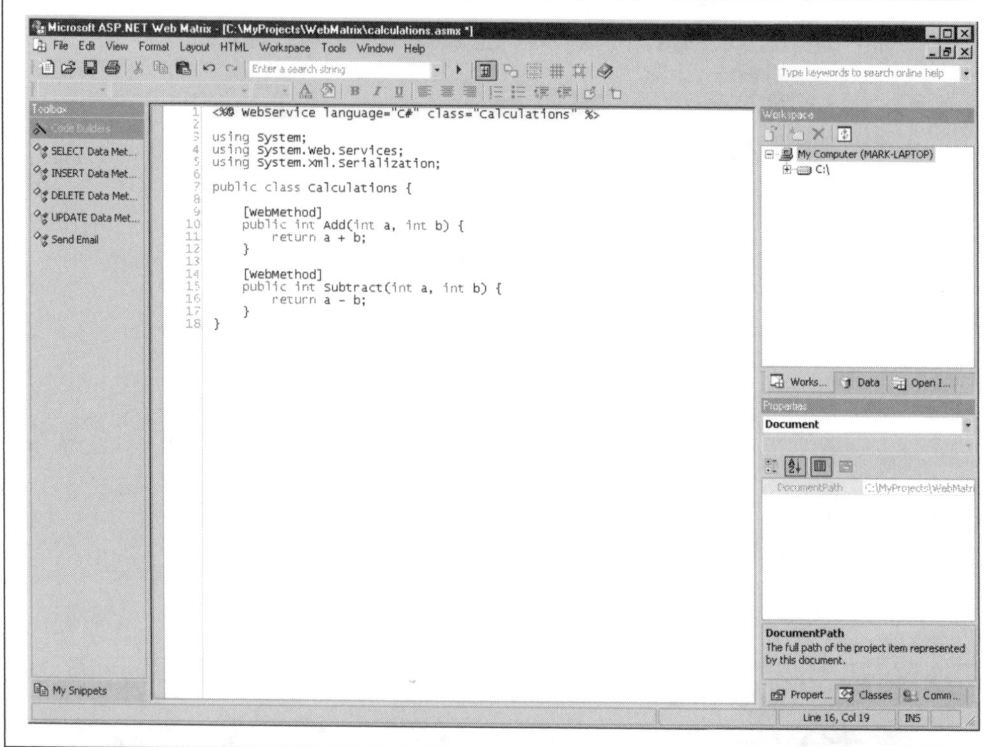

Figure 3-3. ASP.NET development environment

Click the Save button and then click the Run icon (the right-facing triangle on the toolbar). You will be prompted with the dialog box seen in Figure 3-4.

Click the Start button to start the ASP.NET local Web server. Now open a Web browser and navigate to http://localhost:8080/calculations.asmx . A Web form is automatically created in order to pass data to the calculation Web Services. In order to see the WDSL descriptors for the Web Service, navigate to http://localhost:8080/calculations.asmx?WDSL.

From the main Calculations Web Service page, click the Add link. The resulting page shows a Web form that can be used to submit data to the Web Service, and examples of SOAP messages that can be targeted to the Web Service.

It is important to note the distinction between the user calling the Web Service directly, using the form, and the scenario where SOAP is sent on the user's behalf. This distinction is shown in Figure 3-5.

When the data from the form is submitted to the Web Service, the user's browser is making a direct connection to the Web Service, using HTTP GET or HTTP POST. SSL, or cookies can be used to secure the connection between the Web Service and the user's

Start Web Application

Start Web Application

Start a Web application at the selected application directory.

Application Directory: C:\MyProjects\WebMatrix

Use ASP.NET Web Matrix Server

Application Port: 8080

Use or create an IIS Virtual Root

Application Name:

Enable Directory Browsing

Start Cancel

Figure 3-4. The ASP.NET Web Services deployment dialog box

browser. However, when SOAP is used—meaning that one of the example SOAP messages is submitted to the Web Service—the user is one step away from the communication. The application sending the SOAP message on the user's behalf may use cookies or SSL, but that would only secure the connection between the application and the Web Service. If the user has connected to a Web site that uses the calculation Web Service on their behalf, then the Web Service will only have visibility of the Web

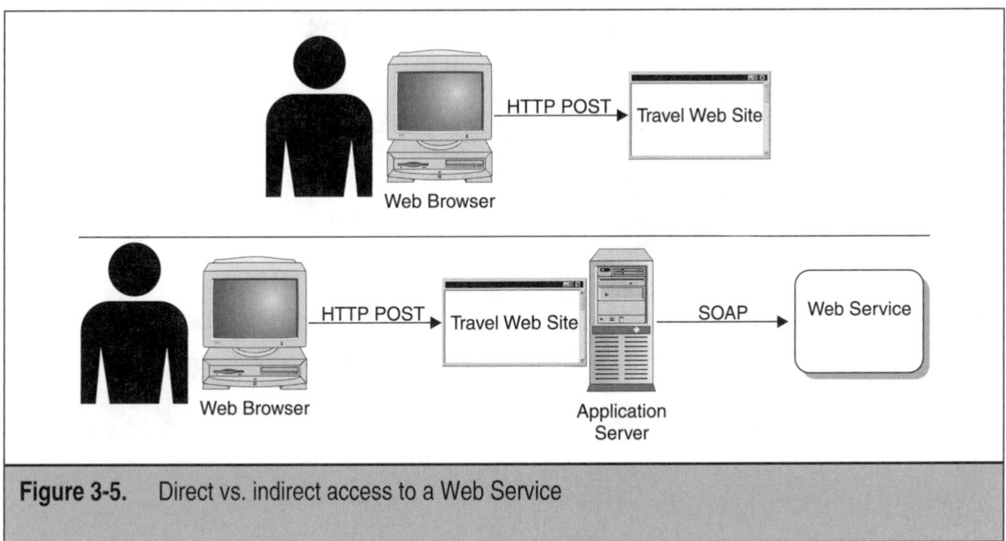

Figure 3-5. Direct vs. indirect access to a Web Service

site that is sending the SOAP message, not of the end user on whose behalf the message is being sent.

The problem is that there are two security contexts in play. These are spelled out in Figure 3-6.

In our trivial calculation example, it may not seem important who is running the Web Service. But imagine that the end user is a currency dealer who connects to a local portal in order to execute a trade. If a Web Service is run on that dealer's behalf, the provider of the Web Service must know not only what portal is sending the SOAP request to it, but *who the dealer is*. The solution to this problem, as we will see, is to include information about the end user in the SOAP message itself.

The Challenge of Maintaining Security While Routing Between Multiple Web Services

Although SOAP routing is not in the scope of SOAP 1.1 or SOAP 1.2, it has been proposed as part of Microsoft's GXA (Global XML Web Services Architecture). WS-Routing provides a means for SOAP messages to route between multiple Web Services. WS-Routing defines how to insert routing information into the header of a SOAP message. This routing information can be thought of as equivalent to routing tables that operate at lower layers of the OSI stack for routing IP packets.

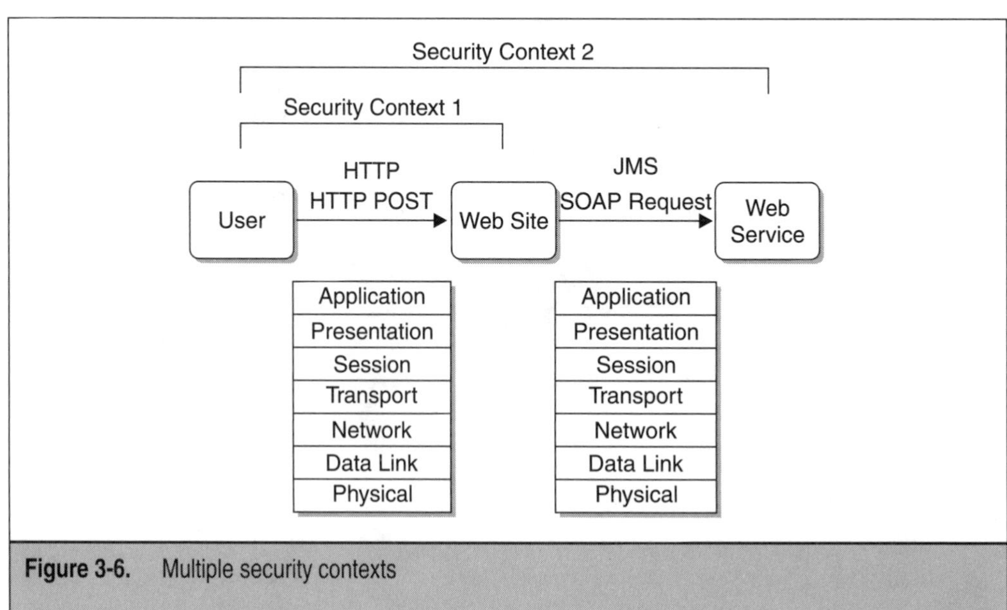

Figure 3-6. Multiple security contexts

WS-Routing means that one SOAP message may traverse multiple SOAP "hops" between the originator and the endpoint. The systems that implement these hops may have nothing in common apart from the ability to parse and route a SOAP message.

The following code listing is an example of a SOAP message that uses WS-Routing in order to route between Web Services. It routes from the originator, via an intermediary, to an endpoint. It is targeted at the Calc Web Service, familiar from the previous example in this chapter.

```
<?xml version="1.0" encoding="UTF-8"?>
<SOAP-ENV:Envelope
   xmlns:SOAP-ENV="http://schemas.xmlsoap.org/soap/envelope/"
   xmlns:SOAP-ENC="http://schemas.xmlsoap.org/soap/encoding/"
   xmlns:xsd="http://www.w3.org/2001/XMLSchema"
   xmlns:xsi="http://www.w3.org/2001/XMLSchema-instance">
   <SOAP-ENV:Header>
      <h:path xmlns:h="http://schemas.xmlsoap.org/rp/"
      SOAP-ENV:actor="http://schemas.xmlsoap.org/soap/actor/next"
      SOAP-ENV:mustUnderstand="1">
         <rp:action xmlns:rp="http://schemas.xmlsoap.org/rp/">
              Addition
         </rp:action>
         <rp:to xmlns:rp="http://schemas.xmlsoap.org/rp/">
              http://www.example.com/Calc
         </rp:to>
         <rp:fwd xmlns:rp="http://schemas.xmlsoap.org/rp/">
            <rp:via>http://wwww.intermediary.com/webservice</rp:via>
         </rp:fwd>
         <rp:rev xmlns:rp="http://schemas.xmlsoap.org/rp/">
            <rp:via/>
         </rp:rev>
         <rp:from xmlns:rp="http://schemas.xmlsoap.org/rp/">
            originator@example.com
         </rp:from>
         <rp:id xmlns:rp="http://schemas.xmlsoap.org/rp/">
            uuid:EC823E93-BE2B-F9DC-8BB7-CD54B16C6EC1
         </rp:id>
      </h:path>
   </SOAP-ENV:Header>
   <SOAP-ENV:Body>
     <SOAPSDK1:Add xmlns:SOAPSDK1="http://tempuri.org/message/">
     <A>1</A><B>2</B>
     </SOAPSDK1:Add>
   </SOAP-ENV:Body>
</SOAP-ENV:Envelope>
```

Figure 3-7 illustrates how this routing scenario involves more than one security context.

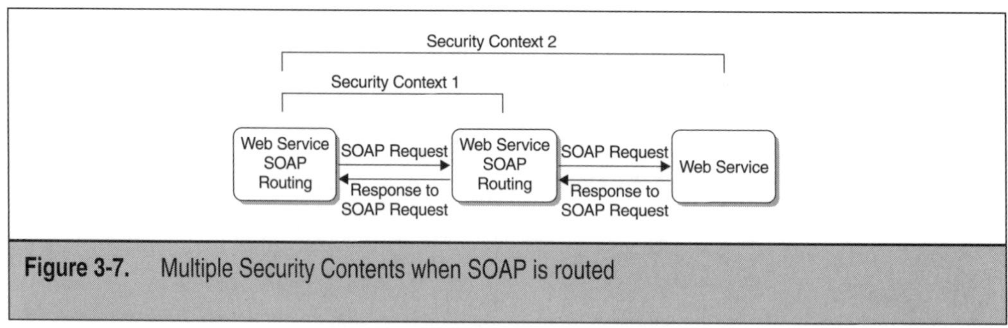

Figure 3-7. Multiple Security Contents when SOAP is routed

SOAP routing does not have to depend on routing information in the SOAP message itself. Routing can be performed for a number of reasons, including scaling a Web Services infrastructure between multiple SOAP servers, bridging between two different networking protocols, or transforming message content from one format to another. All of these scenarios extend the security context beyond a single SOAP request/response.

When routing between Web Services, the requirement for confidentiality can apply from the originator through to the final SOAP endpoint. It may be a requirement that information be kept secret from SOAP intermediaries. There may be a chance that intermediaries may disclose the information either deliberately or through leaving "gaps" between one transport-level security session and the next. While the data is decrypted, it is vulnerable. This is the same problem that plagued the first release of the Wireless Access Protocol (WAP), in which data was decrypted in between the wireless encryption session and encryption on the fixed wire. This so-called "WAP gap" caused a loss of confidence in WAP security and was addressed in later releases of the WAP specification. Implementing encryption only at the transport level makes a "SOAP gap."

It is often noted that most security breaches happen not while data is in transit, but while data is in storage. This is the principle of least resistance—attempting to decrypt eavesdropped encrypted data from an SSL session is much more difficult than simply testing if a Web site maintainer has remembered to block direct access to the database where the credit card numbers are stored. If decrypted data is stolen from a database, the consequences are no less dramatic. Once data has reached its final destination, it must be stored in a secure state. Confidentiality for a SOAP transaction should not involve simply chaining instances of confidentiality together, since "SOAP gaps" of unencrypted data are available between each decryption and encryption.

The Challenge of Abstracting Security from the Underlying Network

As we saw in Chapter 1, the term "Web" Services is misleading. "Services" is somewhat redeemable since it indicates a services-oriented architecture (SOA).

However "Web" points squarely at the World Wide Web. However, Web Services is not reliant on HTTP. "Net Services" would have been a better term, but it is too late to change the name now. Just as Web Services is not reliant on the Web, Web Services security cannot rely on Web security. This does not mean that Web security can be ignored. We'll see later in this chapter that Web server security can be the "soft underbelly" of an HTTP-based SOAP service and may well afford the path of least resistance to an attacker.

SSL is the obvious choice for confidentiality and authentication (one-way or two-way) for the single connection between a SOAP requester and a Web Service over HTTP. First-generation Web Services are almost unanimously using HTTP, so for the implementer, the reasons to use SSL are compelling. However, second-generation Web Services are likely to move beyond HTTP to reliable messaging frameworks such as HTTPR and SonicXQ, and peer-to-peer technologies such as Jabber.

SSL: A Pragmatic Solution

The challenge of HTTP independence is one that faces standards groups as they are generating Web Services security specifications. A more mundane challenge faces the architect charged with implementing Web Services for their organization: to get secure services up and running as soon as possible. SSL provides for confidentiality between the SOAP requester and the Web Service itself, as well as authentication. If this is all that is required, with no possibility that end-user security or SOAP routing will be introduced to the solution in the future, then this is a pragmatic solution. Chapter 2 explained that it is the high-level principles of security that must be implemented, and just because SOAP is used, it doesn't follow that SOAP security must be used. SSL is available in all Web servers, and with the vast majority of first-generation Web Services using HTTP, it is a useful and pragmatic solution.

MEETING THE CHALLENGES: NEW TECHNOLOGIES FOR WEB SERVICES SECURITY

At this point, we've seen the requirement for new Web Services security specifications. Let's look at how this requirement is being met by introducing new security specifications, which will be explored in greater detail in subsequent chapters.

Persistent Security

The three security challenges we've seen have one thing in common. The principles of security must apply to a security context that includes more than a single request/response SOAP message. The solution to this problem is to *persist* security data in the SOAP message itself. The security data therefore is not lost after one SOAP communication has ended. Confidential information in a SOAP message should remain confidential over the course of a number of SOAP hops.

A number of industry specifications have been developed for this purpose. These specifications can be organized into two distinct categories:

1. A standardized framework to include XML-formatted security data into SOAP messages.
2. Standards for expressing security data in XML format. This security information should be used for the high-level principles of security: confidentiality, authentication, authorization, integrity, and so forth.

Including XML-Formatted Security Data in SOAP Messages: Introducing WS-Security

WS-Security has emerged as the de facto method of inserting security data into SOAP messages. Work on WS-Security began in 2001, was published by Microsoft, VeriSign, and IBM in April 2002, and was then submitted in June 2002 to the OASIS standards body in order to be made into an industry standard. WS-Security defines placeholders in the SOAP header in order to insert security data. It defines how to add encryption and digital signatures to SOAP messages, and then a general mechanism for inserting arbitrary security tokens. WS-Security is "tight" enough to present the definitive means of including security data into SOAP messages, but is "loose" enough to not place limits on what that security data can be.

Confidentiality for Web Services: Introducing XML Encryption

XML Encryption is a specification from the W3C. It provides not only a way of encrypting portions of XML documents, but also a means of encrypting any data and rendering the encrypted data in XML format. XML Encryption makes encryption functionality easier to deploy.

XML Encryption is not a replacement for SSL. SSL is still the de facto choice for confidentiality between two entities that are communicating using HTTP. However, if the security context extends beyond this individual HTTP connection, XML Encryption is ideal for confidentiality. The capability to encrypt XML is nothing new, because XML is just text after all. However, the ability to *selectively encrypt* XML data is what makes XML Encryption so useful for Web Services. Encrypting an entire SOAP message is counterproductive, because the SOAP message must include enough information to be useful—routing information, for example. Selectively encrypting data in the SOAP message is useful, however. Certain information may be hidden from SOAP intermediaries as it travels from the originator to the destination Web Service.

XML Encryption does not introduce any new cryptography algorithms or techniques. Triple-DES or RSA encryption may still be used for the actual encryption. XML Encryption provides a way to format the meta-information about which algorithm was used, and when the encryption occurred. This aids the Web Service in decrypting the data, provided the decryption key is available to it. This is important, because prior to XML

Encryption the only standardization of encryption data was for e-mail messages (that is, S/MIME). If an organization wished to send encrypted data to another organization, both organizations would have to agree on the format of the encrypted data, how and which algorithms to use, and possibly also how to send an encrypted key. Now that information can be contained in an XML Encryption block. Chapter 5 explores XML Encryption in detail, including code examples in C# and Java.

WS-Security defines how XML Signature data can be included in a SOAP message. This provides *persistent confidentiality* beyond a single SOAP communication.

Integrity for Web Services: Introducing XML Signature

XML Signature is a specification produced jointly by the W3C and the Internet Engineering Task Force (IETF). Like XML Encryption, it does not only apply to XML. As well as explaining how to digitally sign portions of an XML document, XML Signature also explains how to express the digital signature of any data as XML. As such, it is an "XML-aware digital signature." PKCS#7 is a means of rendering encrypted data, and signed data, which predates XML Signature and XML Encryption. Rather than using XML, it uses Abstract Syntax Notation number 1 (ASN.1). ASN.1 is a binary format, renowned for its complexity. Producing or verifying a PKCS#7 signature requires not just cryptography software, but also an ASN.1 interpreter. XML Signature also requires cryptography software, of course, but an XML DOM replaces the ASN.1 interpreter.

The power of XML Signature for Web Services is the ability to selectively sign XML data. For example, a single SOAP parameter passed to a method of a Web Service may be signed. If the SOAP request passes through intermediaries en route to the destination Web Service, XML Signature ensures end-to-end integrity.

WS-Security describes how to include XML Signature data in a SOAP message. An important feature of XML Signature is that it can be very selective about what data in an XML instance is signed. This feature is particularly useful for Web Services. For example, if a single SOAP parameter needs to be signed but the SOAP message's header needs to be changed during routing, an XML Signature can be used that only signs the parameter in question and excludes other parts of the SOAP message. Doing so ensures end-to-end integrity for the SOAP parameter while permitting changes to the SOAP's header information. Chapter 4 explores XML Signature in detail, including code examples in C# and Java.

Web Services Authentication and Authorization: Introducing SAML, XACML, Passport, and Liberty

Single sign-on (SSO) is one of the "hard" problems in information technology. As seen in Figure 3-5, if a user signs on to a Web site and then a SOAP request is produced on the user's behalf, the destination Web Service may require information about the end user in order to make an authorization decision. Otherwise, the destination Web Service only has visibility of the machine that is creating the SOAP request. There are two approaches to this requirement. The first approach is to include the information in the SOAP message itself. The second approach is to request this information from a central repository.

Security Assertions Markup Language (SAML) provides a means of expressing information about authentication and authorization, as well as attributes of an end user (for example, a credit limit) in XML format. SAML data may be inserted into a SOAP message using the WS-Security framework. SAML is used to express information about an act of authentication or authorization that has occurred in the past. It does not provide authentication, but can express information about an authentication event that has occurred in the past; for example, "User X authenticated using a password at time Y." If an entity is authorized based on the fact that they were previously authorized by another system, this is called "portable trust." SAML is important to address the challenge of multihop SOAP messages also, because separate authentication to each Web Service is often out of the question. By authenticating once, being authorized, and effectively reusing that authorization for subsequent Web Services, single sign-on for Web Services can be achieved.

Note that this information in a SAML assertion may not indicate the end user's identity. The user may have authenticated using a username and password, and the administrator of the Web site may have no idea of the user's actual identity. It may simply be an indication that the user presented credentials and was authenticated and authorized. SAML allows information to be placed into a SOAP message to say "this person was authorized according to a certain security policy at a certain time." If the recipient of this SOAP message trusts the issuer of the SAML data, the end user can also be authorized for the Web Service. This SAML data is known as an "assertion" because the issuer is *asserting* information about the end user. The concept of security assertions has existed before SAML, and is already widely used in existing software.

XML Access Control Markup Language (XACML) is designed to express access control rules in XML format. Although the two technologies are not explicitly linked, XACML may be used in conjunction with SAML. An authorization decision expressed in a SAML assertion may have been based on rules expressed in XACML.

Microsoft's Passport technology takes a different approach to single sign-on. The user authenticates to the passport infrastructure, either directly through www.passport.com or through an affiliate site that makes use of functionality provided by passport.com. Once the user is authenticated and authorized by Passport, their authentication status is also available to other Web Services that use Passport. Like SAML, this provides single sign-on. However, the model is different, relying on a central point of authentication rather than SAML's architecture where authentication happens at an individual Web Service. By being implemented at the site of the Web Service itself, SAML authentication and authorization information may be based on *role-based security*. Role-based security means that access to resources is based on the user's organizational role; for example, in a medical setting doctors may have access to certain information while nurses have access to different information.

Another industry proposal for the SSO on the Web is the Liberty Alliance Project, championed by Sun. The Liberty Alliance Project aims to enable a noncentralized approach to SSO, termed a "federated network identity." At the time of this writing, it appears the Passport proposal by Microsoft may be taking a similar tack to the Liberty Alliance Project.

PKI for Web Services: Introducing XKMS

As you may recall from Chapter 2, PKI is a system that allows public key keys to be trusted by providing key signing and key validation services. Although accepted as an important, even vital, technology, PKI has a reputation for being notoriously difficult to implement. The benefits of XML and Web Services apply quite naturally to PKI: addressing interoperability and integration issues. The XML Key Management specification (XKMS) enables PKI services such as trustworthily registering, locating, and validating keys through XML-encoded messages. Because XKMS is service-oriented and uses XML messages, it is only natural that it be implemented as a SOAP-based Web Service giving it the distinction of not only being useful for securing Web Services, but also being available as a Web Service itself. By leveraging the benefits of XML and by learning from past experiences with pre-XML PKI architectures, XKMS makes PKI practical for common use.

Like XML Signature, XKMS eliminates the need for ASN.1 functionality in software that deals with digital certificates. It goes further, however, and can allow XML software to use digital certificates and PKI without the need to implement cryptography algorithms. This is useful for software developers, many of whom may not have the time or inclination to delve into cryptography or employ cryptography toolkits.

WEB SERVICES SECURITY THREATS

We've seen the positive side of Web Services security: the industry cooperation on new specifications and frameworks. Now let's investigate the negative side. The new specifications that implement the principles of security for Web Services are useless if the user is required to "play by the rules." A sophisticated authorization system using SAML and WS-Security is useless if the Web Service on which it runs can be disabled by a CodeRed attack. (CodeRed is a worm program that attacks IIS Web servers.)

Some of these "new threats" are, in fact, old threats, such as buffer overflow and attempts to exploit other programming errors, but the avenue of attack—SOAP—is new.

Firewalls have traditionally addressed vulnerabilities at the lower layers of the OSI stack. Firewall functionality has progressively moved up the OSI stack to reach the application layer. However, they are not yet "SOAP-intelligent."

The following section examines these aspects of Web Services security.

Web Application Security

Application layer security existed long before SOAP. Application layer security for Web servers involves securing both the Web server itself and Web applications that use the Web server as their platform. A Web application is a CGI-based application with which the user interacts using a Web browser. Attacks on Web applications initially focused on attacking the platform itself, exploiting security holes in the Web server. These frequently took the form of buffer overflow attacks. Like the "ping of death" attack we saw at the network layer in Chapter 2, buffer overflow attacks on a Web server presented more data than the Web server expected. This data would be written to memory, and could find its way into the execution stream. This allows arbitrary commands to be executed on the server.

It is difficult and time-consuming to produce a buffer overflow attack, but once produced, the attack can be packaged into a scriptable tool that so-called "script kiddies" can use. Script kiddies use existing techniques and programs or scripts to search for and exploit weaknesses in computers on the Internet. The derogatory nature of the term refers to the fact that the use of such scripts or widely known techniques does not require any deep knowledge of computer security.

Gradually, buffer overflow attacks on HTTP implementations were addressed in patches to Web servers. At that stage, attacks began to exploit the extra features bundled with certain Web servers, features often installed whether users wanted them or not. These extra features included indexing engines and example scripts. After these holes were patched, it became more difficult for hackers to construct attacks on Web server software. This is when application layer hacking attacks progressed to attacking Web applications, rather than the platforms on which the Web applications run. These are not across-the-board attacks that can be packaged and used against thousands of Web servers by script kiddies. These attacks are specific to individual Web applications. However, they can be put into categories, including the following:

- **SQL attacks** Inserting SQL statements into Web forms in order to force a database to return inappropriate data, or to produce an error that reveals database access information. For Web Services, this category of attack translates to manipulating data in a SOAP message to include SQL statements that will be interpreted by a back-end database.
- **Directory traversal attacks** Attempts to bypass hyperlinks by attempting to directly access resources. For example:
  - If a URL is http://www.example.com/documents/sales.htm, what happens if http://www.example.com/documents/ is requested?
  - Does a directory called /test/ exist?

For Web Services, this category of attack translates to attempting to detect other SOAP services which are not explicitly offered.

- **URL string attacks** Manipulating CGI name/value pairs in the URL string; for example, changing "maxResults=10" to "maxResults=1000" to return more information from a database. For Web Services, this translates to circumventing the rules on SOAP parameters (for example, if a search SOAP service takes an integer between 1 and 10 as a SOAP parameter, what if the number 1000 is submitted?).

Many of these attacks can be avoided by implementing careful programming practices and by cleaning up resources that are not required on the Web server. However, it is often the case that no matter how much care is taken; vulnerabilities can slip through the net.

TIP In order to guard against the possibility of attacks on application vulnerabilities, consider the use of an XML firewall or XML proxy to filter SOAP requests before they reach your application.

When bound to HTTP, SOAP itself can be seen as a Web application, albeit a more standardized and formalized application than what has gone before. It is likely that initial SOAP implementations will be vulnerable to attacks based on invalid data such as buffer overflow attacks or attacks based on SOAP routing that attempt to create SOAP "worms." This vulnerability is not necessarily due to carelessness but, rather, due to the fact that all security bases cannot be covered in initial versions of any software. The lesson from the history of Web server attacks is that once the platform is secured, the playing field shifts to the applications implemented on that platform. These attacks are potentially more dangerous than in the case of CGI applications; because of the nature of the business processes implemented using SOAP.

The Role of Firewalls for Web Services

"SOAP bypasses firewalls." This phrase is frequently heard. Let's examine what it means. The first question to ask is: What is a firewall? The answer is that different categories of firewalls apply to different layers of the OSI stack.

Packet-Filtering Firewalls

The lowest layer at which a firewall works is layer 3. At this level, the firewall checks if the information packets are from a trusted source and is not concerned with the content of the packets. These are called "packet-filtering firewalls" and are usually part of a router. IP packets are compared to a set of criteria and dropped or forwarded accordingly. These criteria can be source and destination IP address, source and destination port number, the protocol used, and the format of the IP packet.

The "ping of death" that we encountered in the previous chapter applies at the network layer and is protected by packet-filtering firewalls. Much of this functionality is now built into operating systems and routers.

Circuit-Level Firewalls

At layer 4, firewalls filter traffic based on more sophisticated criteria. TCP layer firewalls are known as "circuit-level firewalls." These firewalls monitor TCP handshaking to determine a session's legitimacy. Information about the protected network they are protecting is hidden, because packets appear to originate from the firewall and not from an address inside the protected network. These firewalls do not filter individual packets; rather, filtering is based on the rules of the TCP session, including who initiated the session and at what time.

Circuit-level firewalls prevent "session hijacking"—sending an IP packed that is intended to appear as if it belongs to a trusted session. It also hides an internal network from an attacker who wishes to scan it for vulnerabilities.

Application-Level Gateways

Application-level gateways filter packets at the application layer. They are aware of what traffic meant for specific applications should look like. For example, it knows the difference between Web traffic and telnet traffic, even though both use TCP/IP. Application-specific commands and user activity can be logged. These firewalls are relatively processor-intensive.

An application-level gateway will know that if it is protecting an e-mail POP server, the command "USER" is allowed, and takes one parameter (that is, the username). Anything else is not allowed. For example, traffic that looks like telnet traffic directed to the POP server will be blocked.

Stateful-Inspection Firewalls

Stateful-inspection firewalls operate at multiple levels and include much of the functionality of packet-filtering firewalls, circuit-level firewalls, and application-level gateways. These are complex and powerful, but tend to be difficult to configure. When not properly configured, they may contain security holes.

Application Layer Firewalls

Many firewalls have been configured to only allow Web (HTTP, SSL) and e-mail (POP, SMTP) traffic to pass. Other TCP/IP ports, and other protocols, are routinely blocked. It has become standard practice to "tunnel" other applications through the Web ports (80 for HTTP, 443 for SSL), effectively disguised as normal Web traffic. This is generally not done for malicious reasons, but rather for pragmatic reasons, because all other ports are blocked. In particular, SOAP is very frequently bound to HTTP. It provides a standardized means for applications to communicate over the Web ports. One of the lessons of computer industry history is that standards drive usage and SOAP promises to enable the explosive growth of application communication over the Web ports.

When a firewall examines a SOAP request received over HTTP, it might conclude that this is valid HTTP traffic and let it pass. Firewalls tend to be all or nothing when it comes to SOAP. A SOAP-level firewall should be able to:

- Identify whether the incoming SOAP request is targeted at a Web Service that is intended to be available.
- Identify whether the content of the SOAP message is valid. This is analogous to what happens at the network layer, where IP packet contents are examined. However, at the application layer it requires knowledge of what data the Web Service expects.

Content-Filtering Security at the Application Layer

Web Services present a new avenue of attack into the enterprise. Even so, some of the tactics are familiar: feeding unexpected data to an application in order to confuse it, or disable it. In Chapter 2 we saw how the "ping of death" was an attack that operated at the network level to provide unexpected data in an Internet Protocol (IP) packet. Web Services present details of their interface in WSDL files, which effectively say, "Here are the details of the data that I expect." This invites a hacker to send it inappropriate data in order to see what happens.

A WSDL file may contain the following line:

```
<xsd:element name="tickerSymbol" type="string"/>
```

This indicates that one of the parameters expected by the Web Service is a string, called "tickerSymbol." The options for a speculative attack on this Web Service would include sending it a number instead of a string, or sending it a very large string designed to overload the Web Service. It is important, therefore, that "sanity checks" are performed on incoming data directed to Web Services. This may take the form of checking SOAP parameters against an XML Schema. However, XML Schema validation is processor-intensive. In addition, certain portions of a SOAP message may be *volatile*, meaning that they change while in transit between the SOAP requester and the Web Service. Volatile portions of a SOAP message include the header, which may contain routing information that changes as the message is routed. Therefore, it is more appropriate to use XPath to narrow down the data validation to nonvolatile portions of the SOAP message.

Another aspect of content filtering is ensuring that only valid Web Services are called. Firewalls must be able to distinguish SOAP requests from invalid requests. A valid request and an invalid request may differ only on the basis of the SOAP method called. The following code listing shows a valid SOAP request to a method called "GetTime" that takes a time zone as a parameter:

```
<SOAP-ENV:Envelope
 SOAP-ENV:encodingStyle="http://schemas.xmlsoap.org/soap/encoding/"
 xmlns:SOAP-ENV="http://schemas.xmlsoap.org/soap/envelope/">
<SOAP-ENV:Header></SOAP-ENV:Header>
<SOAP-ENV:Body>
<SOAPAPP:GetTime xmlns:SOAPAPP="http://tempuri.org/message/">
<TimeZone>GMT</TimeZone>
</SOAPAPP:GetTime>
</SOAP-ENV:Body>
</SOAP-ENV:Envelope>
```

The following code listing shows a SOAP request that targets another Web Service method, called "ResetComputer":

```
<SOAP-ENV:Envelope
 SOAP-ENV:encodingStyle="http://schemas.xmlsoap.org/soap/encoding/"
 xmlns:SOAP-ENV="http://schemas.xmlsoap.org/soap/envelope/">
<SOAP-ENV:Header>
</SOAP-ENV:Header>
<SOAP-ENV:Body>
<SOAPAPP:ResetComputer xmlns:SOAPAPP="http://tempuri.org/message/">
```

```
</SOAPAPP:ResetComputer>
</SOAP-ENV:Body>
</SOAP-ENV:Envelope>
```

The challenge for firewalls is how to allow the first SOAP message, targeting a valid method of a Web Service, and to block the second one. There are analogies with firewall functionality at lower layers of the OSI stack. Filtering on the targeted SOAP method is only the first step, however.

Filtering on the data that is provided to a Web Service is more complicated. The details of each Web Service are specific. Consider a Web Service that takes a ZIP code as a parameter. The valid input is a five-character string. If the Web Service receives 5,000 characters as input, this may indicate that an attacker is testing for vulnerability to a buffer overflow attack. In order to block this sort of attack, a firewall must be aware of what type of data is valid for the Web Service.

The Next Steps for Firewalls

Application layer security began by ensuring that connecting entities played by the rules for applications that ran over TCP/IP; then, they progressed to patching holes in Web servers; and now it has moved to blocking attacks on Web applications. A SOAP implementation bound to HTTP may be seen as a Web application itself, and therefore the next step is to prevent SOAP implementations from attack. After protecting the SOAP implementation, the final step is to protect Web Services that use that SOAP implementation.

The challenge is to ensure that the firewall rules are in sync with the Web Services themselves—and it seems obvious that UDDI and WSDL should be used for this purpose. UDDI, after all, is used to return a list of deployed services. A dynamic updating firewall could query this list using a UDDI query such as we encountered in Chapter 1, and use this to ensure that only legal traffic passes through.

The next challenge is to ensure that only permitted traffic travels *out* of the network to third-party Web Services. A number of organizations are investigating the establishment of two-way Web Services gateways that act as "choke points" for SOAP traffic. This ensures that only valid SOAP traffic comes into the enterprise, and only valid SOAP traffic leaves the enterprise.

This is the natural evolution of firewall functionality, which began at the network layer and has been "climbing the ladder" of the OSI stack ever since.

Hint: When choosing a firewall product, check if the vendor supports SOAP filtering. A firewall should be capable of blocking SOAP messages based on target (endpoint) and based on the payload of the SOAP message, validated against an XML Schema.

This is the end of Part I. We have seen what Web Services are, what the high-level principles of security are, and how security is applied to Web Services. Part II looks at the implementation technologies in-depth.

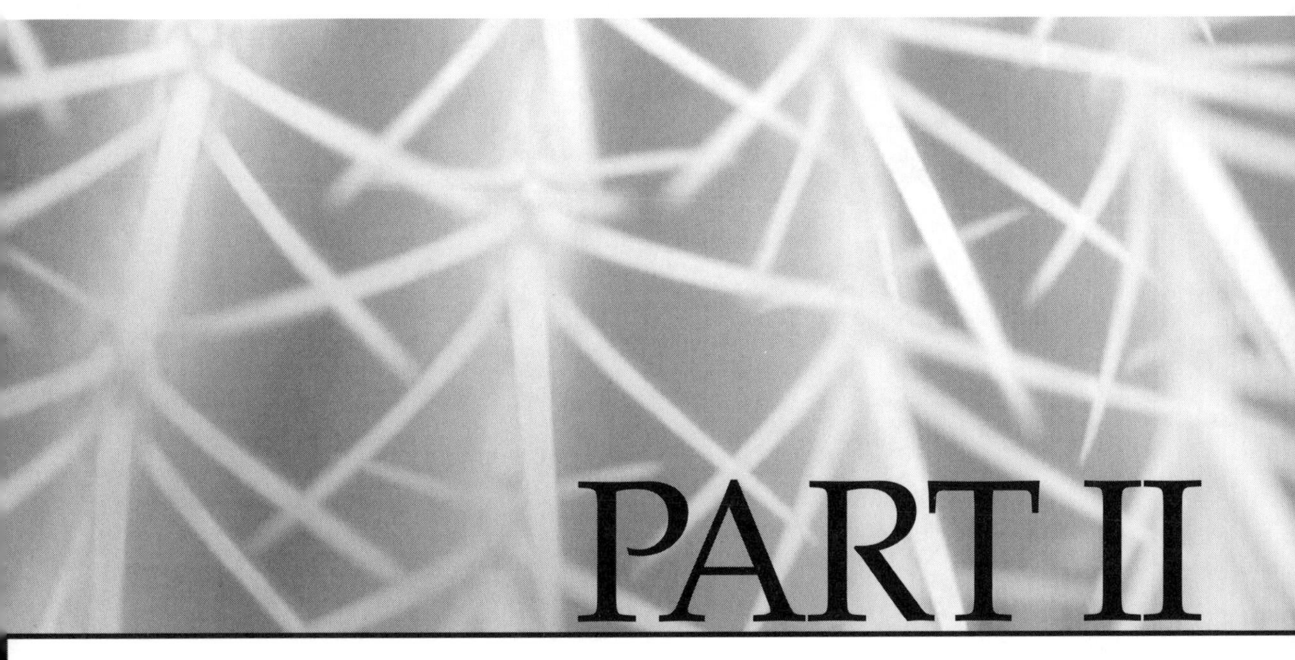

PART II

XML Security

CHAPTER 4

XML Signature

It's no accident that XML Signature was the first XML security standard to reach recommendation status. Although not a Web Services security technology itself, XML Signature is a building block for many Web Services security technologies such as XKMS and WS-Security. Without XML Signature, these would not exist. Just as XML forms the basis of Web Services, XML security (XML Signature and XML Encryption) forms the basis of Web Services security.

We saw in Chapter 2 that in the world of security, digital signatures are highly versatile. When tied to the identity of the signing party, digital signatures are used to provide nonrepudiation. When a digital signature indicates proof of possession of a signing token such as a private key or a smartcard, they can also be used for authentication. Used alone, digital signatures provide data integrity. This is useful not only to provide integrity for data being passed in a SOAP message, but also to provide integrity for security tokens in the SOAP message. In Chapter 6 (SAML) and Chapter 4 (XML Encryption), we will see how XML Signature is used in conjunction with other XML security and Web Services security technologies.

One of the central themes of this book is that security should be considered in terms of high-level requirements first, before dropping down to the implementation technology. This means that rather than first thinking "I need XML Signature for my Web Services," a security architect should think "I need to ensure the integrity of the data I am receiving through my Web Services, so how best can I enforce that?" XML Signature is one of the ways, but there are others (SSL enforces integrity for data while the SSL session occurs, and IPSec also enforces integrity while data is in transit). Thinking in terms of high-level security principles is not only less confusing, it's also safer than the low-level approach of throwing brand new security specifications at a problem, without thinking about the problems which they are meant to solve. Simply adding a certain technology to the mix is rarely enough.

On its own, XML Signature provides integrity for data. XML Signature is also important for authentication and nonrepudiation, but it does not provide these functions on its own. For these, it must exist in the context of identity-based security. WS-Security describes how XML Signature can be used to bind a security token to a SOAP message, and, by extension, bind the identity of the signer to a SOAP message.

In a similar vein, XML Signature is a technology that must be implemented correctly if it is to be a valid security tool. It is important to know what is being signed. Conversely, if a signature is being verified, it's important that the signature is over the appropriate data. Imagine the scenario where a signed SOAP message is received, but the signature is over a meaningless portion of the SOAP message. The signature would still verify correctly, and as a result the data may be wrongly trusted.

When XML Signature is performed as a result of a human decision to sign (for example, when a user sees some data onscreen and presses a "sign" button), there are implications also. The user is making the signing decision based on visual data, but the user may not actually see the underlying XML, which is what is signed. This would raise doubt about the signature's validity.

XML Signature may also be used for integrity and nonrepudiation of WSDL files also, so that a definition of a Web Service can be published and later trusted to *not* have been tampered with, or been forged by a third party. XML Signature also finds uses in ebXML, which we will see later.

Used alone, XML Signature provides a useful means of expressing a digital signature over XML data. This is important, but it requires a SOAP binding to be useful for Web Services—in other words, a formal definition of how an XML Signature can be placed into a SOAP message, in order to express a digital signature over an XML payload, or over a security token such as an X.509 certificate. WS-Security provides this SOAP binding for XML Signature.

MAKING SENSE OF XML SIGNATURE

The XML Signature specification, developed by the W3C and IETF, expresses the structure of an XML Signature as follows:

Listing 4-1

```
<Signature>
     <SignedInfo>
       (CanonicalizationMethod)
       (SignatureMethod)
       (<Reference (URI=)? >
         (Transforms)?
         (DigestMethod)
         (DigestValue)
       </Reference>)+
     </SignedInfo>
     (SignatureValue)
    (KeyInfo)?
    (Object)*
   </Signature>
```

In the preceding code listing, elements ending in a plus sign may be present multiple times, and elements ending in a question mark are not mandatory. In this section, the various parts of an XML Signature will be encountered and explained. Let's look at what XML signature is, and what it isn't.

An XML Signature Is a Digital Signature Expressed in XML

XML Signature isn't a new way of performing a digital signature. The asymmetric encryption and hashing technologies that we learned about in Chapter 2 are still used to make the actual digital signature.

When evaluating a new technology, it's frequently useful to compare it with what has gone before. This sets the new technology in context, and we can see why it is useful. Sometimes new XML formats have been said to be "XML for the sake of XML," and that the addition of angle brackets to a document format is not useful. This is sometimes the case, but not for XML Signature. Let's see why it is necessary.

Before XML Signature: PKCS#7 Signature and S/MIME

Digital signature technologies existed prior to XML Signature, the most common being PKCS#7 Signature. Public Key Cryptography Standards (PKCS) is a voluntary standard created by RSA Data Security and other information security industry organizations.

Before the advent of XML Signature, it was possible to digitally sign an XML document, treating it just the same as any digital document, using PKCS#7 Signature. However, it wasn't possible to express the signature in a standardized XML format. Also, it wasn't possible to sign *just part* of an XML document, and leave other parts of the document unsigned.

Bindings for digital signatures already existed. In particular, Secure Multipurpose Internet Mail Extensions (S/MIME) provides a means of attaching a digital signature to an e-mail message in such a way that the recipient can verify the integrity and (providing the user's identity is linked to the signature) nonrepudiation of the signer.

An example of a digitally signed XML document, expressed as an S/MIME message with the signature expressed in PKCS#7 format, is shown here:

Listing 4-2

```
MIME-Version: 1.0
Content-Type: multipart/signed; protocol="application/x-pkcs7-signature";
micalg=sha1; boundary="----4566B95511D40A079BBB73F773CC7C0D"

This is an S/MIME signed message

------4566B95511D40A079BBB73F773CC7C0D
<?xml version="1.0" encoding="UTF-8"?>
<bookOrder>
  <item>
    <title>Developing Web Applications with string and cardboard</title>
    <isbn>0-123-45678-9</isbn>
    <quantity>1</quantity>
    <price unit="USD">39.95</price>
  </item>
  <payment>
    <billedTo>John Smith</billedTo>
    <amount currency="USD">39.95</amount>
    <dueDate>1 January 2003</dueDate>
    <cardInfo>
      <cardNumber>1234 5678 9012 3456</cardNumber>
      <cardExpiration>08/2006</cardExpiration>
    </cardInfo>
  </payment>
</bookOrder>
------4566B95511D40A079BBB73F773CC7C0D
Content-Type: application/x-pkcs7-signature; name="smime.p7s"
Content-Transfer-Encoding: base64
```

```
Content-Disposition: attachment; filename="smime.p7s"
MIIG6wYJKoZIhvcNAQcCoIIG3DCCBtgCAQExCzAJBgUrDgMCGgUAMAsGCSqGSIb3
DQEHAaCCBFkwggRVMIIDPaADAgECAgEBMA0GCSqGSIb3DQEBBAUAMHoxCzAJBgNV
BAYTAklFMQ8wDQYDVQQIEwZEdWJsaW4xETAPBgNVBAcTCER1YmxpbiA0MRQwEgYD
VQQKEwtWb3JkZWwgTHRkLjEMMAoGA1UECxQDUiZEMSMwIQYDVQQDExpWb3JkZWwg
U2VsZiBTaWduZWQgQ0EgUm9vdDAeFw0wMjA0MTkxMjA0NDRaFw0wMzA0MTkxMjA0
NDRaMGkxCzAJBgNVBAYTAklFMQ8wDQYDVQQIEwZEdWJsaW4xETAPBgNVBAcTCER1

[20 lines omitted for brevity]

TC51wSeO+Fi0ieZ3+r1XPAQRbq7FVptkOzbTBCOyZhaklyNIXUs9nBr/lJ5aiHho
LRhXwmHbWM/BgJMA2TIV143R5xhGFwTfrR7jRb3OjipkOgTPenaO7+wWdrhvIQ4=

------4566B95511D40A079BBB73F773CC7C0D--
```


Listing 4-2 shows a digitally signed XML document, where XML Signature is not used. Let's look at the same-signed XML document, this time with the signature expressed in XML Signature format:

Listing 4-3

```
<bookOrder>
  <item>
    <title>Developing Web Applications with string and cardboard</title>
    <isbn>0-123-45678-9</isbn>
    <quantity>1</quantity>
    <price unit="USD">39.95</price>
  </item>
  <payment>
    <billedTo>John Smith</billedTo>
    <amount currency="USD">39.95</amount>
    <dueDate>1 January 2003</dueDate>
    <cardInfo>
      <cardNumber>1234 5678 9012 3456</cardNumber>
      <cardExpiration>08/2006</cardExpiration>
    </cardInfo>
  </payment>
  <dsig:Signature Id="" xmlns:dsig="http://www.w3.org/2000/09/xmldsig#">
  <dsig:SignedInfo>
  <dsig:CanonicalizationMethod
   Algorithm="http://www.w3.org/2001/10/xml-exc-c14n">
  </dsig:CanonicalizationMethod>
  <dsig:SignatureMethod
   Algorithm="http://www.w3.org/2000/09/xmldsig#rsa-sha1">
  </dsig:SignatureMethod>
  <dsig:Reference URI="">
  <dsig:Transforms>
  <dsig:Transform Algorithm=
  "http://www.w3.org/2000/09/xmldsig#enveloped-  signature">
  </dsig:Transform>
  </dsig:Transforms>
```

```
  <dsig:DigestMethod Algorithm="http://www.w3.org/2000/09/xmldsig#sha1">
  </dsig:DigestMethod>
  <dsig:DigestValue>eyaOpi/dmWGQuHlDj6YtFwGFf6g=</dsig:DigestValue>
  </dsig:Reference>
  </dsig:SignedInfo>
  <dsig:SignatureValue>
  RhiKxqYUw50KtWlKPAxdzfXhPg5vDL/Pvt8VCIs6Ek1UO/1ljeyTkOzI0TEW32+PKvANCrCCpwgb
…
  WIQCIBeXMuHF2gsLd9AW6JNFkkhMh3OHfT4anQ==
  </dsig:SignatureValue>
  <dsig:KeyInfo>
  <dsig:X509Data>
  <dsig:X509SubjectName>
  CN=Joe User,OU=Human Resources,O=Company X,L=New York City,ST=NY,C=US
  </dsig:X509SubjectName>
  <dsig:X509Certificate>
  MIIEVTCCAz2gAwIBAgIBATANBgkqhkiG9w0BAQQFADB6MQswCQYDVQQGEwJJRTEPMA0GA1UECBMG

  [20 lines omitted for brevity]
  </dsig:X509Certificate>
  </dsig:X509Data>
  </dsig:KeyInfo>
  </dsig:Signature>
</bookOrder>
```

With XML Signature, the same cryptographic algorithms may be used. In particular, RSA or DSA and the same message digest algorithm (SHA-1 in this case) can be used. That means that, cryptographically speaking, the digital signature is the same. In terms of the high-level principles of security, both PKCS#7 and XML Signature amount to the same thing. On their own, they provide integrity for data, and when the signer's identity can be linked to the signature (through an X.509 certificate in this case), they provide nonrepudiation also. In the right circumstances, digital signatures can also be used for authentication.

Replacing ASN.1 Encoding with XML

Look again at the XML Signature example, and compare it to the PKCS#7 signature. In the XML Signature example, the various components of the signature are much more obvious. This is the well-known human-readability advantage of XML. Although people may not look at XML Signature, or indeed any type of XML directly, it is useful for people designing and monitoring systems that use digital signatures. An XML processor (for example, a DOM implementation) is used to parse the XML Signature. In the case of a PKCS#7 signature, ASN.1 was used. ASN.1 is optimized for size and for machine-readability, meaning that a document which uses ASN.1, like a PKCS#7 signature, is unintelligible to humans.

Abstract Syntax Notation 1 (ASN.1) was invented in 1984 and published jointly by the International Standards Organization, the International Electrotechnical Commission, and the International Telecommunications Union. ASN.1 is a collection of techniques and notations for specifying data structures in a machine-independent manner. Token sets defined using ASN.1 can be used in combination with standardized encoding rules such as the basic encoding rules (BER) and the packed encoding rules (PER). ASN.1 is supported by mature tools for encoding and decoding binary information into and out of BER and PER format, as well as to other proprietary encoding formats. ASN.1 is widely deployed in the wireless and fixed-line communications industry as an enabling technology for cell phone messages, radio paging, free and premium phone services, and ISDN telephony. In addition, ASN.1 is used for streaming audio and video over the Internet, and is fundamental to ISO security and messaging standards, including X.509 digital certificates and X.400 e-mail.

Because of its use for X.509 digital certificates, which bind a person's identity to a public key, ASN.1 continues to be relevant for Web Services security.

Data Transformation

Data transformation is a common feature in XML processing. Interoperability between various XML-enabled systems frequently depends on the existence of an intermediary system that will format the data such that it can be understood by both parties. In the case of XML Signature, it takes on a special significance. As well as being transformed for interoperability between XML systems, signed data may require transformation for the following reasons:

- The data has been encrypted after being signed, in which case it must be "transformed" using decryption in to the original plaintext before the signature can be verified.
- The data is large and has been compressed prior to transmission, in which case it must be "transformed" using decompression into the original data.
- Transformations provide the ability to selectively sign data (for example, "sign all <update> elements") or ignore certain data (for example, "sign everything except the <Log> elements").

There is another reason, too, which we will examine in the following section.

Canonicalization

Canonicalization is an arcane word, and its use in Web Services security is made more confusing by the fact that it is often abbreviated to "C14N" (meaning a word beginning with *C*, ending in *N*, with 14 letters; this is the same reason why "Internationalization" is sometimes abbreviated to "I18N"). In computer science, the "canonical" way of performing an action is the widely accepted "correct" way of performing that action. The fact that it's "correct" is only based on consensus, and there may be no particular reason why another method is not used instead, except that the variation would cause confusion and incompatibility. Eric Raymond's *The New Hacker's Dictionary* explains that the word derives from the Greek and Latin word for "reed," because a particular length of reed was widely accepted as a standard measure.

How does this relate to Web Services? Remember that a digital signature breaks if any change, however minor, occurs to the signed data. XML can change and still be valid XML. Indeed, if an XML process "cleans up" XML by removing useless data such as blank space between XML elements, that breaks the signature. The following lines of XML are both valid for a schema that accepts white space between elements:

```
<BookOrder> <Title>Hillwalking in Spain</Title> </BookOrder>
<BookOrder><Title>Hillwalking in Spain</Title></BookOrder>
```

An XML processor may have "helpfully" removed the unnecessary white space between the XML elements. This may happen automatically if the XML is inputted by a DOM parser into memory, and then later rendered as XML output. There are many other "helpful" changes that can occur to XML as it travels between XML-processing systems. For example, attributes may be reordered into alphabetical order, line breaks may be added, or the format of line breaks may change. All of these changes break the signature, and it may appear that the data had been maliciously tampered with. Canonicalization addresses this type of false alarm.

Canonicalization involves changing the XML into a canonical format prior to passing it into the digest algorithm, and then changing it into this canonical format prior to recalculating the digest in order to verify the signature. The original algorithm for canonicalization was inclusive canonicalization, referenced by the following URI:

```
http://www.w3.org/TR/2001/REC-xml-c14n-20010315
```

The problem with inclusive canonicalization concerns namespaces. If an XML document is digitally signed using XML Signature, namespace declarations in that document are signed also. If the signed document is inserted into another XML document that has new namespaces that are not in the original signed XML document, canonicalization includes these new namespaces in the data that is fed into the digest algorithm used to verify the signature. The namespaces "bleed" into the signed data. The inclusion of these extra namespaces breaks the signature, even though the XML itself is the same.

This problem may sound quite esoteric until we consider SOAP. If signed data is packaged into a SOAP message, the SOAP namespace declarations find their way into the canonicalized XML. This breaks the signature. A subsequent canonicalization method called "exclusive canonicalization" fixes this problem. It is highly recommended that exclusive canonicalization be used in SOAP rather than inclusive canonicalization, for this reason.

Canonicalization was not needed in PKCS#7 signatures because there was not a possibility that ASN.1 data could change and still be valid (except for detached PKCS#7 signatures). Consequently, the PKCS#7 signature previously shown does not use canonicalization.

An XML Signature May Be Placed Inside an XML Document

Looking again at the PKCS#7 signature and the XML Signature, we can see that the XML Signature example inserts the signature into the data itself. This is only one option. In fact, there are three ways in which an XML Signature can relate to the data that is signed. These are enveloped, enveloping, and detached.

Enveloped XML Signature

Enveloped XML Signature means that the signature is contained within the signed document itself. The example we saw earlier in this chapter is an example of an enveloped XML Signature. It is important that the entity verifying the signature uses a transform to remove the signature from the signed document, before feeding the document into the digest algorithm. Otherwise, the signature would break since it obviously did not contain an XML Signature before it was signed.

The transform that is used to remove the XML Signature from the signed data is identified using the following URI: http://www.w3.org/2000/09/xmldsig#enveloped-signature. The functionality of the enveloped signature transform is equivalent to the following XPath statement:

```
<XPath xmlns:dsig="&dsig;">
   count(ancestor-or-self::dsig:Signature |
   here()/ancestor::dsig:Signature[1]) >
   count(ancestor-or-self::dsig:Signature)
</XPath>
```

As you can see, it is easier to reference the transform than to construct this XPath transform!

An enveloped signature is a useful form of XML Signature for Web Services. That is because it allows for signed data to be inserted into SOAP messages, now that the problem of inclusive canonicalization has been cleared up.

It goes without saying that an enveloped signature is only useful for signing XML data, because it requires an XPath transform for validation.

Enveloping XML Signature

With an enveloping XML Signature, the signed data is contained within the XML signature structure itself. An Object tag is used to encapsulate the signed data (which may be XML data or not). Notice in the following example that the Res0 identifier is used in the Reference element in order to point at the Object data that is being signed. Being an enveloping signature, everything is located within the Signature block.

```
<Signature xmlns="http://www.w3.org/2000/09/xmldsig#">
  <SignedInfo>
    <CanonicalizationMethod
    Algorithm="http://www.w3.org/TR/2001/REC-xml-c14n20010315">
    </CanonicalizationMethod>
```

```
    <SignatureMethod Algorithm="http://www.w3.org/2000/09/xmldsig#rsa-sha1">
    </SignatureMethod>
    <Reference URI="#Res0">
      <DigestMethod Algorithm="http://www.w3.org/2000/09/xmldsig#sha1">
      </DigestMethod>
      <DigestValue>SytlSLP6mn+BB4gPF+nyHc4n4Xo=</DigestValue>
    </Reference>
  </SignedInfo>
  <SignatureValue>
    O9wByjog8R7yhJqaU46PGey7JqEgZ6Azfe9ShaXnRY8jJXEWDMhEBW73gMgYxy+mxDJ9tDZV
    QohNuKUtJBhsqKl+M/fDEXYUgtfzNjz7WwbjUE/YbNjqyEDFhmwLMb/Iy7gw+tBIM2AqyBoO
    BciwiLTyP4yEtXAv2oIqadh181g=
  </SignatureValue>
  <KeyInfo>
    <KeyValue>
      <RSAKeyValue>
        <Modulus>
          czG5DqYFMKxINCLVurHW6gHdUxRLf11ikpRMI7+5LGhtyM/QsgMhmX3UNjbG9TtgEO
          uYBnJCDXJ0364z4gof1oO0OlpNNcaqJ0N1uCqiz1QInQymHL5emzaYVtAiTMa6M5e2
          88G8XoY6d4Rbozm/AM7m+6EwLxBpzzYGl/CgtDk=
        </Modulus>
        <Exponent>AQAB</Exponent>
      </RSAKeyValue>
    </KeyValue>
    <X509Data>
      <X509IssuerSerial>
        <X509IssuerName>CN=John Smith (RSA),OU=TRL,O=IBM,C=JP</X509IssuerName>
        <X509SerialNumber>1019448261</X509SerialNumber></X509IssuerSerial>
      <X509SubjectName>CN=John Smith (RSA),OU=TRL,O=IBM,C=JP</X509SubjectName>
      <X509Certificate>
MIIB+TCCAWICBDzDi8UwDQYJKoZIhvcNAQEEBQAwRDELMAkGA1UEBhMCSlAxDDAKBgNVBAoTA0lC
[ 8 lines omitted for brevity ]
bPpHnYtbdrS1R+aNrBNkjexNzm/dnvp77+zyfI8jn0r5Gx4hcqnu7185i4wUwzQDWgEqKXI=
      </X509Certificate>
    </X509Data>
  </KeyInfo>
<dsig:Object xmlns="" xmlns:dsig="http://www.w3.org/2000/09/xmldsig#" Id="Res0">
<bookOrder>
  <item>
    <title>XML and Java: Developing Web Applications, Second Edition</title>
    <isbn>0-201-77004-0</isbn>
    <quantity>1</quantity>
    <price unit="USD">49.99</price>
  </item>
  <payment>
    <billedTo>John Smith</billedTo>
    <amount unit="USD">49.99</amount>
    <dueDate>3 June 2002</dueDate>
```

```
    <cardInfo>
      <cardNumber>1234 5678 9012 3456</cardNumber>
      <cardExpiration>08/2008</cardExpiration>
    </cardInfo>
  </payment>
</bookOrder>
  </dsig:Object>
</Signature>
```

Because an XML instance's root element typically determines the processing of that data, it would not be sensible to bury a SOAP message inside an enveloping XML Signature. Enveloping XML Signatures can, however, be very useful inside SOAP messages.

Detached Signature

A detached signature is a signature that is separate from the signed entities or entities. This means that the signed data need not be XML at all. Indeed, as the XML Signature specification points out, it can be "any digital content." An interesting corollary of detached signature processing is that if the URI cannot be dereferenced, meaning that the signed resource is no longer available, then the signature breaks. This means that detached XML Signature may find uses in guaranteeing the integrity of online resources (such as Web pages) against tampering and defacement. This signed data can be referenced using a URI, meaning that it can be located online and is not limited to data that is available locally in files. Looking at the Reference element in the following example, we can see that the W3C XSL specification is being signed:

```
<Signature xmlns="http://www.w3.org/2000/09/xmldsig#">
  <SignedInfo>
    <CanonicalizationMethod
    Algorithm="http://www.w3.org/TR/2001/REC-xml-c14n-20010315">
    </CanonicalizationMethod>
    <SignatureMethod Algorithm="http://www.w3.org/2000/09/xmldsig#rsa-sha1">
    </SignatureMethod>
    <Reference URI="http://www.w3.org/TR/xml-stylesheet">
      <DigestMethod Algorithm="http://www.w3.org/2000/09/xmldsig#sha1">
      </DigestMethod>
      <DigestValue>60NvZvtdTB+7UnlLp/H24p7h4bs=</DigestValue>
    </Reference>
  </SignedInfo>
  <SignatureValue>
    JkWOVRLbGmvvOOBCckzEprh34sN5EvSfGsJYZapqBIbY2AShKVXApADl5UKhEdF4Fey8RVzo
    4jOQAFpKwI86NVc3nRtsxj3SfQjpoL1Waf54E4AB04NUi3NvaN2KZb8Yz/3AD7H98fUn/8BB
    AiLNa0YX1E9yrdl4rayzPqlECdc=
  </SignatureValue>
  <KeyInfo>
    <KeyValue>
      <RSAKeyValue>
```

```
        <Modulus>
          czG5DqYFMKxINCLVurHW6gHdUxRLf11ikpRMI7+5LGhtyM/QsgMhmX3UNjbG9TtgEO
          uYBnJCDXJ0364z4gof1oO0OlpNNcaqJ0N1uCqiz1QInQymHL5emzaYVtAiTMa6M5e2
          88G8XoY6d4Rbozm/AM7m+6EwLxBpzzYGl/CgtDk=
        </Modulus>
        <Exponent>AQAB</Exponent>
      </RSAKeyValue>
    </KeyValue>
    <X509Data>
      <X509IssuerSerial>
        <X509IssuerName>CN=John Smith (RSA),OU=TRL,O=IBM,C=JP</X509IssuerName>
        <X509SerialNumber>1019448261</X509SerialNumber></X509IssuerSerial>
      <X509SubjectName>CN=John Smith (RSA),OU=TRL,O=IBM,C=JP</X509SubjectName>
      <X509Certificate>
MIIB+TCCAWICBDzDi8UwDQYJKoZIhvcNAQEEBQAwRDELMAkGA1UEBhMCSlAxDDAKBgNVBAoTA0lC
TTEMMAoGA1UECxMDVFJMMRkwFwYDVQQDExBKb2huIFNtaXRoIChSU0EpMB4XDTAyMDQyMjA0MDQy
MVoXDTAyMDcyMTA0MDQyMVowRDELMAkGA1UEBhMCSlAxDDAKBgNVBAoTA0lCTTEMMAoGA1UECxMD
VFJMMRkwFwYDVQQDExBKb2huIFNtaXRoIChSU0EpMIGeMA0GCSqGSIb3DQEBAQUAA4GMADCBiAKB
gHMxuQ6mBTCsSDQi1bqx1uoB3VMUS39dYpKUTCO/uSxobcjP0LIDIZl91DY2xvU7YBDrmAZyQg1y
dN+uM+IKH9aDtDpaTTXGqidDdbgqos9UCJ0Mphy+Xps2mFbQIkzGuj0XtvPBvF6GOneEW6M5vwDO
5vuhMC8Qac82BpfwoLQ5AgMBAAEwDQYJKoZIhvcNAQEEBQADgYEAIUoHZxUdL2/o08/NdJ0wc+6p
X7P4lviATr2vIogLY4QiuLJ8g30EC7JMxYoMuGDwFvIWfX+pBvUweoncoQ/WTuPfwjodvR1u9mu7
bPpHnYtbdrS1R+aNrBNkjexNzm/dnvp77+zyfI8jn0r5Gx4hcqnu7185i4wUwzQDWgEqKXI=
      </X509Certificate>
    </X509Data>
  </KeyInfo>
</Signature>
```


XML Signature Allows Multiple Documents to Be Signed

S/MIME allowed for multiple documents, all digitally signed using PKCS#7, to be linked together in one single document. XML Signature goes one step further. Multiple documents can be signed with one single XML Signature. How is this possible? The answer is through the use of references.

Multiple Reference Elements in One SignedInfo Element

The way in which an XML Signature is constructed is clever and efficient. The most processor-intensive aspect of signature generation and signature verification is the use of asymmetric encryption—the RSA and DSA algorithms. By contrast, the calculation of a digest from a piece of data is not as processor-intensive. Therefore, it makes sense to perform asymmetric encryption over as small a portion of data as possible. This extends to the scenario where multiple documents must be signed at once.

The SignedInfo portion of an XML Signature, as the name suggests, contains information about each resource being signed. Each portion of signed data is referred to in a separate Reference. Each Reference includes (1) the digest of the data itself in a DigestValue element, (2) information about what algorithm was used to construct the digest contained in a DigestMethod element, and (3) what transforms, if any, must be performed on the data prior to verifying the digest. Multiple References may be in a single SignedInfo XML element in a digital signature. The computationally intensive asymmetric encryption only takes place over the SignedInfo section.

It is worth noting that information about which signature and canonicalization algorithms are used is also contained in the SignedInfo section. This is important to know, since if this information was subject to undetectable change, this would break the signature. For example, if it were possible to change to the algorithm information in an XML Signature produced by the DSA signing algorithm such that it appeared that the RSA signature algorithm was used instead, the signature would be in dispute.

The various items listed as references may be detached from, enveloped by, or envelope the XML Signature. Because one XML Signature can cover multiple references, a single XML Signature can be, at once, enveloping, enveloped, and detached.

XML Signature Is "XML-Aware Signature"

As we saw in the enveloped signature and enveloping signature examples, XML Signature allows for just a portion of an XML document to be signed. The Reference element can use an XPath transform to point to the signed data. In addition to the basic XPath transform, a second expanded form of the XPath transform, called XML-Signature XPath Filter 2.0, has been developed to increase the usability and efficiency of XML Signature XPath transforms. It can also be used for transforms inexpressible with a basic XPath such as adding a second enveloped signature to a document.

XML Signature is particularly useful for Web Services since it can be used to sign just a single SOAP parameter, for example, and leave volatile (that is, changeable) portions of the SOAP message unsigned. When data is being routed between different services, XML Signature provides a way to ensure that data intended for one service (called an "Actor" in SOAP 1.1 and a "Role" in SOAP 1.2) is not changed by another service.

USES OF XML SIGNATURE FOR WEB SERVICES SECURITY

XML Signature finds multiple uses for Web Services security. When used alone, it provides data integrity. When linked to the signer's identity, it provides nonrepudiation of data content. In addition, it can be used for authentication. When SOAP routing occurs, it can be used for workflow.

Persistent Integrity

Digital signatures ensure data integrity, meaning that if a document changes, then no matter how slight the change, it can be detected. In a Web Services communication, data integrity may also be present at lower layers of the OSI stack (for example, using SSL or IPSec). However, when integrity is implemented only in the course of the SOAP communication, it is not persistent integrity. If the document changes after reaching the Web Service, then the change is undetectable.

This persistent integrity is particularly useful where a document may be composed of portions that are authored by different entities—for example, in a workflow scenario. XML Signature guarantees the integrity of certain portions of a document, but allows participants in a workflow system to edit other unsigned portions of the document.

Nonrepudiation: How Useful Is the KeyInfo Element?

Nonrepudiation extends integrity to link the signature to the identity of the signer so that the signer cannot deny signing the data. The KeyInfo section of signature can be used to reference the public key of the signer. However, this is not enough, because nonrepudiation is achieved by proving that a particular private key, however discovered, was used to create the signature. The <KeyInfo> element may provide hints about the discovery of the private key (often very good hints), but it is optional (and is not necessarily signed). In Chapter 2, we learned that the way in which a certificate authority binds a public key to a person's identity is by issuing a digital certificate. As well as the use of a certificate authority, nonrepudiation may also involve the use of a timestamping service in order to guarantee the time in which the signature was created.

Nonrepudiation is a feature not provided by session layer or transport layer security. With the use of SSL for B2C (business to consumer) commerce, nonrepudiation was not such an important requirement due to the low value of the transactions involved. The picture is different for the kind of B2B transactions likely to be performed using Web Services, where a small percentage of deniable fraud cannot be tolerated.

Certificate Verification

An additional aspect of nonrepudiation is signature validation.

XKMS provides a means to verify a digital certificate without requiring the use of an ASN.1 processor. The KeyInfo section of an XML Signature is packaged into a SOAP message and sent to an XKMS trust service. See Chapter 10 (XKMS) for more details.

Certificate verification is important since although a signature may verify correctly, the signer's digital certificate may no longer be valid. This may have occurred because they lost their smartcard, because their password was stolen, or simply because their certificate has expired. A check against an XKMS trust service, or a non-XML system such as a certificate revocation list (CRL) or an Online Certificate Status Protocol (OCSP) responder verifies the current status of the digital certificate.

Authentication

A document that has been signed using XML Signature authenticates the signer, provided that the information in the KeyInfo section of the XML Signature can be tied to the signer's identity using a digital certificate. If this information is used to authenticate, care should be taken to avoid replay attacks. The next section examines what a replay attack is, and how it can be avoided.

Replay Attacks

If message authentication is required, it is important to avoid a replay attack. Authentication at the session or transport layers involves the use of "choreography" of messages – a challenge, followed by a response – in order to negotiate a secret key.

SOAP-SEC was superseded by WS-Security, but the discussion of replay attacks is useful because it is simple and succinct:

> "Digital signatures alone do not provide message authentication. One can record a signed message and resend it (replay attack). To prevent this type of attack, digital signatures must be combined with an appropriate means to ensure the uniqueness of the message, such as nonces or time stamps."
>
> *from SOAP-SEC specification, published on the World-Wide Web Consortium web site (http://www.w3.org/TR/SOAP-dsig/)*

Sending the message a second time does not break the integrity of the message, nor does it break the link between the signer of the message and the signed data. It is for these reasons that the replay attack is powerful. It is the equivalent of finding a hand-signed paper document beside a fax machine and resending it. If the document says "Please transfer $1000 into my checking account," and an imposter sends it again—thus transferring another $1000 into the account—that's a replay attack.

There are two possible solutions to this problem. One is to separate sender authentication from document authentication. This can be achieved in an HTTP-based Web Services environment by combining client-side SSL with XML Signature in a SOAP message. This ensures that if a duplicate document is received, the sender has been authenticated.

The second solution is to ensure that the digital signature is over data which changes for each message. This type of changing data would include an incremental counter, a nonce, or a timestamp. Returning to the analogy with the re-sent fax, this would be the equivalent of including a printout of the current time in the fax. If a duplicate document was received containing the same time, that would be suspicious.

CREATING AND VALIDATING AN XML SIGNATURE

Let's get down to practicalities and see how XML Signatures are created and validated.

Creating an XML Signature

Here are the high-level steps used to create an XML Signature. See the XML Signature specification (www.w3c.org/Signature) or an XML Signature Toolkit's documentation for complete information.

Step-by-Step

1. List the URIs of the resources that are to be signed. These resources may be external resources on the Web, a local file, or an XML fragment in the same document as the signature.
2. Feed each resource into a digest algorithm to produce a digest.
3. Package each digest into a Reference element, along with information about the digest that was used, which algorithms were used, and which transforms were used.
4. Construct the SignedInfo section, combining the content in Reference elements with information about what signature algorithm and canonicalized algorithm are to be used.
5. Canonicalize the SignedInfo data.
6. Calculate the digest of the SignedInfo data.
7. Calculate the signature of the SignedInfo digest.
8. Insert the signature value into the SignatureValue element.
9. Optional step: Create a KeyInfo section in the XML Signature.
10. Place the SignedInfo, SignatureValue, and KeyInfo sections into a Signature element.

Java Code Example

The IBM XML Security Suite includes an example Java program that implements XML Signature. The SampleSign2 Java application can be found in the dsig folder, which is under the samples folder.

The XML Security Suite provides many useful Java classes that take the hard work out of implementing the ten steps for creating an XML Signature. A TemplateGenerator object creates the structure of an XML Signature, in which the various components (SignedInfo, KeyInfo, and so forth) can be inserted. This TemplateGenerator object takes a generic document class, plus information about the algorithms to be used (signature algorithm, canonicalization algorithm, digest algorithm), as input. Methods such as addTransform and addReference allow referenced documents to be obtained (for example, from the file system or from a URI) and put into Reference elements within an XML Signature template. Once this is done, we reach the actual signing stage. Here is some example code for signing—the com.ibm.xml.dsig.* and java.security.* namespaces are required.

```
KeyStore keystore = KeyStore.getInstance("JKS");
keystore.load(new FileInputStream(keystorepath), storepass);
X509Certificate cert = (X509Certificate)keystore.getCertificate(alias);
Key key = keystore.getKey(alias, keypass); // a private key
if (key == null) {
    System.err.println("Could not get a key: "+alias);
    System.exit(1);
```

```
}
KeyInfo keyInfo = dsig.SignatureUtil.createKeyInfo(cert);
Element signatureElement = signatureGen.getSignatureElement();
keyInfo.insertTo(signatureElement, prefix);
//
// Sign
//
SignatureContext sigContext = new SignatureContext();
sigContext.setIDResolver(idg);
sigContext.sign(signatureElement, key);
doc.appendChild(signatureElement);
dsig.SignatureUtil.printDocument(doc, System.out);
```

Firstly, the signing (that is, private) key and the public key certificate are obtained from a Java keystore. The signatureGen object is an instance of the TemplateGenerator class and it returns the actual SignatureValue element that is loaded with the value obtained when the "sign" method of the SignatureContext object is run.

The programmer is shielded from much of the intricacy of XML Signature, and certainly does not need to know the inner workings of cryptographic or canonicalization algorithms.

Note that XML Signature is not part of the JDK at the moment, but may enter the JDK in the future through the work of the JSR (Java Specification Requests) 105 group, sponsored by Sun.

Validating an XML Signature

The validation of an XML Signature follows many of the same steps as the creation of the signature. The reason for this is simple: in order to ensure that the signed data hasn't changed, the digest of the data must be recalculated and compared with the original. If a signature contained *only* a digest, then it would be equivalent to a checksum. If that were the case, an imposter could simply change the digest as well as changing the signed data, to conceal the change. That is why the SignatureValue contains a version of the digest which has been encrypted using the private key of the signer. The corresponding public key is used (step 5 in the following Step-by-Step exercise) to obtain the digest. If this matches the digest of the signed data, that means that the data has not changed since it was signed.

Step-by-Step

1. Use the SignatureMethod element to obtain the information about what signature algorithm and digest method were used to create the signature.
2. Canonicalize the SignedInfo section using the canonicalization algorithm listed in the SignedInfo section.
3. Recalculate the digest using the canonicalized SignedInfo section as input.
4. Obtain the signature itself from the SignatureValue element.

5. Use the signer's public key and the Signature to obtain the original SignedInfo digest value, and compare this with the digest value obtained in step 3.
6. At this stage, we've passed "core validation" of the XML Signature. We know that the SignedInfo section has not changed if the digests match. To complete "full validation," we must obtain the original documents that are referred to in the Reference elements and ensure that the digests of these documents match the values in the DigestValue elements in their Reference elements.

C# Code Example

For the signature creation, we used Java. So let's use C# and the .NET CLR (Common Language Runtime) for the signature validation. Of course, XML Signature is language independent so a signature created with one language should always verify using another language, providing, of course, that the signed data has not changed.

The following namespace definitions are required for the .NET example:

```
using System;
using System.IO;
using System.Security.Cryptography.Xml;
using System.Security.Cryptography;
using System.Xml;
```

The SignedXML class in the .NET Framework includes a number of high-level methods used for XML Signature, such as the following:

- **SigningKey** Specifies the key that signs the XML data
- **AddReference** Adds a signed resource as a Reference to the XML Signature
- **SigningKey** Specifies the key used to perform the signature
- **ComputeSignature** Calculates the signature, using the signing key
- **CheckSignature** Verifies a signature

In this example, the XML document is loaded, and then the CheckSignature() function is run:

```
// Load the XML.
XmlDocument xmlDocument = new XmlDocument();
xmlDocument.PreserveWhitespace = true;
XmlTextReader r = new XmlTextReader(fileName);
xmlDocument.Load(r);
r.Close();

SignedXml signedXml = new SignedXml(xmlDocument);

// asssume there is only one <ds:Signature>
```

```
XmlNodeList nodeList = xmlDocument.GetElementsByTagName("Signature",
"http://www.w3.org/2000/09/xmldsig#");
signedXml.LoadXml((XmlElement)nodeList[0]);

if (signedXml.CheckSignature()) {
            Console.WriteLine("Signature check OK");
        } else {
            Console.WriteLine("Signature check FAILED");
        }
```

CHECKLIST

- ☐ Ensure that you understand how XML Signature differs from other forms of electronic signatures.
- ☐ Know what canonicalization is, and why it's important.
- ☐ When choosing an XML security or Web Services security product, ensure that the product supports Exclusive Canonicalization.
- ☐ For applications which require the creation and validation of large volumes of XML Signature data, consider the use of hardware acceleration.
- ☐ Refer to the WS-Security chapter to understand how XML Signature is used in the WS-Security framework to ensure the integrity of security tokens in SOAP messages.

CHAPTER 5

XML Encryption

Question: What does it mean when a computer is termed "secure?" Simson Garfinkel and Gene Spafford write in their book, *Practical UNIX & Internet Security*, that "a computer is secure if you can depend on it and its software to behave as you expect." This is a neat definition that gets across an important point that is sometimes forgotten in the information security industry: that security is implemented in the context of a system, not just for its own sake. That's the definition from industry experts. Now, ask a person on the street what it means when a computer is "secure." Chances are, you will hear an answer that mentions encryption—"it's secure if the files on it are encrypted." Ask what else is involved in making the computer secure and you will probably get a blank look.

This tight link between security and encryption in the public mind might be because of science-fiction novels and movies involving code breaking, or real-life characters such as the code breakers of World War II. In any case, we have seen that there is more to security than encryption. In fact, there is more to *cryptography* than encryption. In Chapter 4, we saw how cryptography is used for the high-level security principles of integrity and nonrepudiation, using XML Signature. In Chapter 2 we saw what encryption is, and how it can be divided into symmetric (one key) and asymmetric (two keys) encryption. We saw how it is one option for satisfying the high-level security principle of confidentiality. The other option is to impose tight access control over the data, or use an air gap to keep the data totally separate from a network.

This chapter builds on Chapter 2 to explain what XML Encryption is, and what it isn't. We'll see what it is used for in the world of Web Services. Finally, we'll see some code examples. At no point do we need to drop down into the actual cryptography, but some knowledge of the cryptographic principles from Chapter 2 is certainly useful.

INTRODUCTION TO XML ENCRYPTION

This is a Web Services security book, so let's jump ahead a little bit and put XML Encryption into a Web Services context.

Persistent Encryption for Web Services Transactions

Confidentiality means that information at rest and in transit cannot be accessed by unauthorized parties. When information is at rest, as in a database, a strong access control policy may be used for confidentiality, as may an "air gap" between the protected data and the network. When information is in transit, encryption is often the most appropriate means of ensuring confidentiality. There are multiple confidentiality options available at various levels of the OSI stack. Remember, it is not the technology that is used, but the security principle that is to be implemented. The question should be "how do I get confidentiality into my communication?" not "how do I get XML

Encryption into my communication?" SSL may be used if the SOAP request is bound to HTTP, or IPSec may be used at the network layer.

When is XML Encryption useful for Web Services? The chief importance of XML Encryption for Web Services is that it allows the security principle of confidentiality to be satisfied across more than just the context of a single SOAP request. This capability finds a number of applications in Web Services, because the security context of a SOAP message often extends beyond a single SOAP request. One obvious scenario is if information in a SOAP message must be kept confidential while it is sent over a multihop SOAP transaction. In this scenario, if SSL alone is used, a gap exists at each SOAP endpoint, where the sensitive data would be temporarily in the clear.

Additionally, if information in a SOAP message must be kept encrypted after the SOAP message has been processed by a Web Service, XML Encryption is also useful. This scenario would apply if encrypted information is being submitted into a database via a Web Service.

These scenarios have one thing in common: *persistent encryption.* This contrasts with session encryption. The encryption is not linked to the point-to-point SOAP exchange, so it does not end when the message reaches a SOAP endpoint.

Now that we've seen where XML Encryption fits into the picture for Web Services, let's take a closer look at what it is and how it works.

XML-Aware Encryption

XML Encryption is a W3C Recommendation. Its functionality boils down to two themes:

1. Encrypted data can be expressed using XML.
2. Portions of an XML document can be selectively encrypted.

Note that XML Encryption is not a new type of encryption. The same tried-and-trusted encryption algorithms—DES, Triple-DES, AES—are used for XML Encryption. It isn't just a way of encrypting XML documents; that could be done before, because encrypting an entire XML document is no different than encrypting any other type of digital document. *Selective encryption* of an XML document is something new, which couldn't be done before XML Encryption.

Expressing Encrypted Data Using XML

This capability may seem mundane, and perhaps it is. Expressing data as XML is not so exciting now that the world is moving to expressing many types of structured data in XML. However, the general advantages of XML apply. Enclosing encrypted data in XML is an advantage to the consumer of the encrypted data, since an XML DOM can be used to extract the ciphertext and feed it into an algorithm (along with a key of course) for decryption.

What Information Is Expressed Using XML Encryption?

It is not only the encrypted data that may be expressed in XML using XML Encryption. Optional items include

- Details of the data type of the encrypted document (for example, JPEG, XML, HTML, and so forth)
- An encrypted key (for example, symmetric key)
- Information about how the encrypted key was agreed on (for example, Diffie-Hellman)
- Reference to the encrypted data, if it is not in the EncryptedData XML fragment itself
- The encryption method that was used (for example, RSA for encrypting a symmetric key, AES for data)

To express some of these items, XML Encryption "borrows" some XML elements from XML Signature, namely the KeyInfo block. If a public key is to be transported in XML and there already exists a method for doing this, defined in the XML Signature specification, then it makes sense to use these elements in XML Encryption also. We will see later that two extra subelements were added to KeyInfo in order to cater for encrypted keys.

In the shorthand rendering of XML Encryption below, we can see the XML Signature elements, distinguished by their "ds" namespace (note that a question mark denotes an optional element):

```
<EncryptedData Id? Type?>
    <EncryptionMethod/>?
    <ds:KeyInfo>
      <EncryptedKey>?
      <AgreementMethod>?
      <ds:KeyName>?
      <ds:RetrievalMethod>?
      <ds:*>?
    </ds:KeyInfo>?
    <CipherData>
      <CipherValue>?
      <CipherReference URI?>?
    </CipherData>
    <EncryptionProperties>?
  </EncryptedData>
```

ENCRYPTION SCENARIOS

XML Encryption may be applied in three broad cases:

1. Encryption of an XML element and its contents
2. Encryption of the contents of an XML element
3. Encryption of arbitrary data (which may be XML)

We will examine each of these three cases, using this example piece of XML as plaintext:.

```
<?xml version='1.0'?>
  <PaymentInfo xmlns='http://foo.org/details'>
    <Name>Joe User</Name>
    <CreditCard Limit='12,000' Currency='EUR'>
      <Number>1234 5678 9012 3456</Number>
      <Issuer>Local Bank</Issuer>
      <Expiration>12/06</Expiration>
    </CreditCard>
  </PaymentInfo>
```

Note that this example is not a SOAP message. We will see in the WS-Security chapter how XML Encryption is applied to a SOAP message using WS-Security. WS-Security defines a *SOAP binding* for XML Encryption that identifies encrypted information through a new Confidentiality element.However, the syntax and concepts from this chapter are as relevant for XML Encryption in SOAP as for any other context.

Encrypting an XML Element and Its Contents

Consider the scenario where only the credit card number must be encrypted. The following example illustrates this case:

```
<?xml version='1.0'?>
  <PaymentInfo xmlns='http://foo.org/details'>
    <Name>Joe User</Name>
    <EncryptedData Type='http://www.w3.org/2001/04/xmlenc#Element'
     xmlns='http://www.w3.org/2001/04/xmlenc#'>
      <CipherData>
        <CipherValue>A23B45C56</CipherValue>
      </CipherData>
    </EncryptedData>
  </PaymentInfo>
```

Notice that the CreditCard element and its contents are gone, and are replaced by an EncrypedData block. The elements below the CreditCard element (that is, Number. ExpirationDate, and so forth) and their contents are encrypted also. The actual encrypted data is contained in the CipherValue element.

The "Element" Type

In the preceding example, we saw that EncryptedData contains an attribute called Type, which is a value of http://www.w3.org/2001/04/xmlenc#Element. This value indicates that an XML element, including its content and subelements and attributes, was encrypted. If the data type was not specified, the encrypted XML element could be decrypted and treated as plaintext that just happens to include angle brackets and look like XML. The use of this type identifier ensures that this doesn't happen.

Encrypting the Content of an XML Element

This scenario involves the CreditCard element being left unencrypted, while the contents are encrypted and contained in the CipherValue element:

```
<?xml version='1.0'?>
  < PaymentInfo xmlns='http://foo.org/details'>
    <Name>Joe User</Name>
    <CreditCard Limit='12,000' Currency='EUR'>
      <EncryptedData xmlns='http://www.w3.org/2001/04/xmlenc#'
       Type='http://www.w3.org/2001/04/xmlenc#Content'>
        <CipherData>
          <CipherValue>A23B45C56</CipherValue>
        </CipherData>
      </EncryptedData>
    </CreditCard>
  </PaymentInfo>
```

The Content Type

Another type defined by the XML Encryption specification, and which we see in the example above, is http://www.w3.org/2001/04/xmlenc#Content. This indicates that the *contents* of an XML element—not the element itself—were encrypted. The contents include all child nodes whether they be elements, text, or comments.

Encrypting Arbitrary Data (Including XML)

Remember we learned that the IANA data identifiers may be used to identify the format of the plaintext. These are particularly useful when arbitrary data is encrypted. An example of an encrypted JPEG file is shown here:

```
<?xml version='1.0' ?>
<EncryptedData xmlns='http://www.w3.org/2001/04/xmlenc#'
```

```
       Type='http://www.isi.edu/in-notes/iana/assignments/media-types/
jpeg'>
      <CipherData>
            <CipherValue>GEwsRe234f</CipherValue>
       </CipherData>
</EncryptedData>
```

Type Information for Arbitrary Data

Apart from the Element and Content data types, XML Encryption does not denote any particular way to define other data types. This is not a problem, though, because there are already standardized names for data types. For example, the official type definitions supplied by the Internet Assigned Numbers Authority (IANA) may be used. These cover an enormous variety of data types, including familiar types such as PDF and JPEG. The IANA definitions are available at the following URL: http://www.isi.edu/in-notes/iana/assignments/media-types/media-types. The IANA data type for XML is the following: http://www.isi.edu/innotes/iana/assignments/media-types/text/xml. In addition to IANA, any proprietary or vertical industry-specific data type can be used. These may be specified using a DTD or an XML schema definition.

The EncryptedData element also contains optional attributes of MimeType (for the MIME-type—for example, image/png) and Encoding (for example, base64).

If no Type, MimeType, or Encoding are provided in the EncryptedData element, this does not mean that the data cannot be decrypted. The data format may be understood at the application context—that is, the decrypting application knows what type of data to expect, and requires no information in the XML Encryption block to tell it what the data type is.

CipherValue and CipherReference

In the three examples cited previously, the ciphertext was included in the CipherValue element. What if one wanted to encrypt a very large data source such as an MPEG file? In this scenario, where the encrypted data is large, it may be preferable to put it into a file of its own. The CipherReference element can be used to point to the encrypted data. The CipherReference location is expressed in the form of a URI, which should be dereferenced (that is, followed so as to pull down the data) in order to obtain the data for decryption.

It is optional to include transforms under the CipherReference element. In the following example, a transform is used to base64-decode the data:

```
<CipherReference URI="http://www.example.com/MyEncryptedData.xml">
    <Transforms>
      <ds:Transform Algorithm="http://www.w3.org/2000/09/xmldsig#base64"/>
    </Transforms>
  </CipherReference>
```

XML Encryption Uses Transforms Differently than XML Signature

You might notice that the URI and transforms are similar to elements used in XML Signature, but there are differences in the way they are used. In XML Signature, the transforms are applied in the same order by both the signature generator and validator. In XML Encryption, the transforms specified are solely intended for the decryptor and are often the reverse of what the encryptor did. For example, an encryptor might encrypt an MP3 file, base64 the octets, and store the ciphertext in a database. On the decryption side, the decryptor will retrieve the ciphertext from the database, de-base64 it, and then decrypt it.

ENCRYPTION STEPS

After seeing the three broad scenarios in which XML Encryption can be applied, let's look at exactly what steps are involved in encrypting data.

Step 1: Choose an Encryption Algorithm

In the XML Signature chapter, we learned that symmetric encryption is faster than asymmetric encryption. However, symmetric encryption uses a secret key, which must be conveyed to the recipient. We will see later in the chapter that this can be performed by encrypting the secret key and putting it into an EncryptedKey structure.

Two block-cipher algorithms, Triple-DES and AES, are explicitly supported by XML Encryption. Block ciphers encrypt data block by block, and can be compared with stream ciphers. DES (that is, "single" DES, not Triple-DES) is not supported by XML Encryption. For XML Encryption, AES and Triple-DES are mandated to use Cipher Block Chaining (CBC).

Before going further, we'll look in depth at what some of the terms in the preceding two paragraphs mean.

Symmetric Encryption: Triple-DES

Triple DES is ANSI standard number X9.52. It specifies the use of three DES operations. It is a block encryption algorithm, meaning that the plaintext is encrypted in fixed-size blocks. Similarly, decryption takes the ciphertext in blocks. If the data is not conveniently divisible into the appropriately sized blocks, "padding" can be used to pad the data out into a multiple of the block size.

As the name suggests, three 64-bit keys are used for Triple-DES, along with a 64-bit initialization vector (IV). The first key encrypts the data to produce ciphertext. The second key is used to "decrypt" this ciphertext. The word *decrypt* is in inverted commas since the decryption operation doesn't produce the plaintext, but rather produces more ciphertext. The third key is then used to further encrypt this ciphertext. Note that this is just one mode of Triple-DES encryption—the other modes use different ordering of the encryption and decryption steps.

Note that while the input key for DES is 64 bits long, the actual key used by DES is only 56 bits in length. The least significant (rightmost) bit in each byte is a parity bit, and for cryptographic reasons should be set so that there are always an odd number of 1s in every byte. These parity bits are ignored, so only the seven most significant bits of each byte are used, resulting in a key length of 56 bits. However, this does not mean that Triple-DES has a strength of 168 bits (56 multiplied by 3). The strengths of Triple-DES vary according to the mode; for example, its estimated strength is 112 bits when the first and last keys are equal. So, this means that although Triple-DES uses three times the key length, it isn't three times the strength of DES.

Ciphertext produced using Triple DES is prefixed by the initialization vector. This ciphertext needs to be base64 encoded if it is to be enclosed in an XML Encryption <CipherValue> element.

Symmetric Encryption: Advanced Encryption Standard (AES)

In October 2000, following extensive analysis by cryptographers worldwide, the Rijndael algorithm was selected by the United States National Institute of Standards and Technology (NIST) to replace DES. Rijndael, which was submitted by two Belgian cryptographers, Joan Daemen and Vincent Rijmen, became the Advanced Encryption Standard (AES). Like DES, AES is a symmetric algorithm that uses block encryption (a block cipher)—that is, the plaintext and ciphertext are broken up into blocks to be sequentially fed into the algorithm. Padding is used to ensure that the data is filled out to be a multiple of the block size, which for AES is 128 bits.

Cipher Block Chaining (CBC) for Symmetric Encryption Block Ciphers

When a block cipher symmetric algorithm (such as Triple-DES or AES) is used in CBC mode, it has the property that the decryption of a block of ciphertext depends on the preceding ciphertext blocks. This means that if a change is made to one block of ciphertext, this affects the decryption not just of that block but of all blocks that follow it in the ciphertext. The dependency on previous blocks also means that if the blocks of ciphertext are rearranged, decryption with the appropriate key will not produce the plaintext. An initialization vector (IV) is used with CBC mode in order to ensure that the same plaintext encrypted with the same key will not produce the same ciphertext.

CBC is preferred to the other mode that can be used for block ciphers—Electronic Code Book (ECB) mode—since it makes attacks based on plaintext patterns less practical.

The Use of an Initialization Vector (IV)

The IV adds a "seed" to the encryption, which mitigates against the fact that characteristics of the plaintext may be known. However, one problem with an IV is that if it is changed, the decrypted plaintext changes also. But think about this for a moment in the context of the high-level security principles of confidentiality and integrity. XML Encryption is not supposed to be used for integrity of data. It is for confidentiality. If the plaintext can be changed by changing the IV, then this affects the integrity of the data. In such cases, the XML Encryption specification recommends "This attack can be avoided by securing the integrity of the plaintext data, for example by signing it." The lesson is that signing, not encryption, should be used for integrity.

Step 2: Obtain and (Optionally) Represent the Encryption Key

Decryption, obviously enough, requires a decryption key. There are a number of ways to ensure that the entity performing the decryption has the appropriate key.

Rely on the Application Context and Include No Key with the Ciphertext

It is not mandatory to include a key, or any information about a key, into an XML Encryption block. If the choice of which key to use for decryption is already known by the decrypting entity, there is no need to include this information with the encrypted data.

Using KeyName

The next-simplest scenario is where the decrypter has a number of decryption keys to choose from. In this case, the keys can be referred to by name, providing that the same names are used by the encrypting party and the decrypting party. Let's say that the name of the key is "Image decryption key." The KeyName element, borrowed from the XML Signature specification, is used to convey this information.

```
<EncryptedData xmlns='http://www.w3.org/2001/04/xmlenc#'
        Type='http://www.w3.org/2001/04/xmlenc#Element'/>
   <EncryptionMethod
          Algorithm='http://www.w3.org/2001/04/xmlenc#3des-cbc'/>
   <ds:KeyInfo xmlns:ds='http://www.w3.org/2000/09/xmldsig#'>
     <ds:KeyName>Image decryption key</ds:KeyName>
   </ds:KeyInfo>
   <CipherData><CipherValue>ni320jas2</CipherValue></CipherData>
 </EncryptedData>
```

The assumption is that the decryptor is able to use the name "Image decryption key" to choose the actual decryption key.

Key Transport: Sending a Symmetric Key, Encrypted, in an EncryptedKey Structure

"Key transport" is the name given to the process of encrypting the symmetric key in order to safely send it to the decrypting entity. It may seem like this just creates a new problem—how do you send the key that was used to encrypt the symmetric key? But remember how asymmetric encryption works. Effectively, the decryption key is the private key of the recipient. By using asymmetric encryption for confidentiality of the symmetric key, it means that only the holder of the private key can obtain the symmetric key and use it to decrypt the data. This may beg the question, "why not just use asymmetric encryption for all of the data?" The answer is that asymmetric encryption is much slower than asymmetric encryption, so it makes sense to only use symmetric encryption for the encrypted data. To recap, here are the steps:

1. Generate a random symmetric key (for example, a Triple-DES key).
2. Use the symmetric key to encrypt the plaintext.
3. Encrypt the symmetric key using the public key of the recipient.
4. Put the encrypted symmetric key into an EncryptedKey structure.
5. Send the EncryptedKey data to the recipient, either in the same XML document as the EncryptedData block or separately.

The following example shows an EncryptedData structure that indicates that the data in the CipherValue element was encrypted using 128-bit AES encryption. Notice the KeyInfo section from the XML Signature is used.

```
<EncryptedData Id='EData'
      xmlns='http://www.w3.org/2001/04/xmlenc#'>
  <EncryptionMethod
      Algorithm='http://www.w3.org/2001/04/xmlenc#aes128-cbc'/>
     <ds:KeyInfo xmlns:ds='http://www.w3.org/2000/09/xmldsig#'>
        <ds:RetrievalMethod URI='#EKey'
           Type="http://www.w3.org/2001/04/xmlenc#EncryptedKey">
        <ds:KeyName>SymmetricKey</ds:KeyName>
     </ds:KeyInfo>
     <CipherData><CipherValue>fj4io2sa23fF</CipherValue></CipherData>
</EncryptedData>
```

Notice that the RetrievalMethod for the key points to an element using the ID EKey and indicating in the Type attribute that the encrypted key is held in an EncryptedKey structure. The EKey structure is shown here:

```
<EncryptedKey Id='EKey' xmlns='http://www.w3.org/2001/04/xmlenc#'>
   <EncryptionMethod
         Algorithm="http://www.w3.org/2001/04/xmlenc#rsa-1_5"/>
   <ds:KeyInfo xmlns:ds='http://www.w3.org/2000/09/xmldsig#'>
     <ds:KeyName>Joe's Private Key</ds:KeyName>
   </ds:KeyInfo>
   <CipherData><CipherValue>j230fw</CipherValue></CipherData>
   <ReferenceList>
     <DataReference URI='#EData'/>
   </ReferenceList>
   <CarriedKeyName>TheEncryptedKey</CarriedKeyName>
 </EncryptedKey>
```

The EncryptedKey structure looks similar to the EncryptedData structure, with the important difference that the CipherValue includes an encrypted 128-bit AES key rather than encrypted plaintext. The algorithm that was used to encrypt the key is indicated by the Algorithm attribute of the EncryptionMethod element. The KeyName indicates which key is used to decrypt the AES key.

CarriedKeyName is used to provide information about the original symmetric key. It may be that encrypted data is being sent to a number of different recipients. In this case, the same symmetric key would be used, but each time it is encrypted using a different public key and put into a separate EncryptedKey block. By giving each AES key the same value for the CarriedKeyName, it conveys the fact that the key is the same. The ReferenceList refers to the data which was encrypted using the symmetric key.

Using Diffie-Hellman Key Agreement

Diffie-Hellman key agreement is used to create a shared secret random number that can then be used as a symmetric algorithm's secret key. The XML Encryption specification defines how Diffie-Hellman parameters may be enclosed in an AgreementMethod element.

Step 3: Serialize the Data into UTF-8 Encoding

This step only applies to XML plaintext, which must be converted into UTF-8 prior to encryption. UTF-8 (UTF stands for a Unicode Transformation Format) maps Unicode characters (plaintext) into octets—that is, a sequence of bytes. Octets are what encryption algorithms expect as data input. If only a portion of an XML document is to be encrypted, identified using XPath, then this XPath step must be performed prior to the UTF-8 processing.

Step 4: Perform the Encryption

At this stage, we have the octets, we've chosen our algorithm, and we have our key. The encryption that is performed is not specific to XML Encryption. Indeed, one of the main purposes of XML Encryption is to marshall arbitrary data (including XML) into the octets that are required by encryption algorithms.

Step 5: Specify the Data Type

The data type is conveyed using the Type, MimeType, and Encoding attributes we encountered in the three examples at the start of this chapter. Specifying the data type is not mandatory, although it is important that the decrypting entity knows the data type.

Process the EncryptedData Structure

In the XML Encryption schema, EncryptedType is the abstract type from which both EncryptedData and EncryptedKey are derived. Think of it like an interface in Java or a virtual data type in C++. It is not used as an element itself, but it has properties that are implemented by elements that are actually used.

The EncryptedData structure includes information about the encrypted data as well as the CipherData element, which includes either the encrypted data itself in a CipherValue element or a pointer to the encrypted data (in a CipherReference element).

If the data to be encrypted is either an element or content (that is, the contents of an XML element), it should be placed into the original XML document, replacing the unencrypted element or content. If the encrypted data was not XML, return the resulting EncryptedData element to the application for further processing.

DECRYPTION STEPS

Decryption essentially involves reversing the encryption steps.

Step 1: Determine the Algorithm, Parameters, and ds:KeyInfot

Because none of these items are mandatory, they may be omitted from the EncryptedType structure if they are already known by the decrypting entity. If they are not already known to the decryptor, the parameters are to be found in the EncryptedData structure (see step 2 of the encryption steps for a sample EncryptedData structure).

Step 2: Locate the Key

The key may be located using the ds:KeyInfo structure. If the key is encrypted and contained in an EncryptedKey structure, it must be decrypted using the decrypting party's private key.

Alternatively, if the key is referenced by its name in a KeyName element, the key should be retrieved from the local key store using the name, or a binding between this name and the name of the key. The key can be held locally or, alternatively, it could be the key name for an XKMS query.

Step 3: Decrypt the Data

If the data is obtained from a CipherValue element, the text must be base64 decoded to obtain the encryped octet sequence that the encryption algorithm expects. If the data is obtained by dereferencing a URI from a CipherReference element, any transforms specified must be performed on the data in order to retrieve the encrypted octet sequence. Decrypt the octet sequence according to the algorithm and key determined earlier.

Step 4: Process XML Elements or XML Element Content

At this stage, we have obtained UTF-8 encoded data. This must be placed into the original XML data in place of the EncryptedData structure. If the data is not an XML element or the content of an XML element, then skip to step 5.

Step 5: Process Data that Is Not an XML Element or XML Element Content

If the decrypted data is not an XML element or data in an XML element, then we pass it back to the application, which must know what to do with it. This is where the type information is essential. If it is not included with the encrypted data, it must be already known by the decrypting application.

CODE EXAMPLES

The IBM XML Security Suite ships with a number of example programs that implement XML Encryption. Java source code is provided.

Let's walk through the encryption process using the Java classes provided by the XML Security Suite. These classes take over the work of creating the XML structures we've encountered in this chapter. The cryptography is performed by an implementation of the java.security classes. Remember, there is nothing new about the cryptography used for XML Encryption, so any java.security implementation can be used.

Encrypting an XML Element Using Triple-DES

The first step is to create an EncryptedData structure into which the ciphertext and the key information will go.

Step 1: Create a Generic EncryptedData Structure

```
EncryptionMethod em = new EncryptionMethod();
em.setAlgorithm(EncryptionMethod.TRIPLE_DES_CBC);
KeyName kn = new KeyName();
kn.setValue("key");
KeyInfo ki = new KeyInfo();
ki.addKeyId(kn);
EncryptedData ed = new EncryptedData();
ed.setType(EncryptedData.ELEMENT);
ed.setEncryptionMethod(em);
ed.setKeyInfo(ki);
Element encData = ed.createElement(elem.getOwnerDocument());
```

As we can see in the preceding code, we are using Triple-DES with cipher block chaining. The key will be referenced using the name "key," and the encrypted data is an XML element (as opposed to element content, or arbitrary data).

The next step is to use a com.ibm.xml.enc.EncryptionContext object to load our XML element, our key, and an algorithm factory into the EncryptedData structure that we've made. The XML element we are encrypting is contained in an org.w3c .dom.Element object. The key is contained in a java.security.Key object. A factory for encryption algorithm implementations uses a com.ibm.xml.end .AlgorithmFactory object.

Step 2: Create and Populate a com.ibm.xml.enc.EncryptionContext Object

The EncryptionContext object has many methods that are useful for encryption. Here, we load it up with our element, the EncryptedData structure, and our key:

```
EncryptionContext encCont = new EncryptionContext();
encCont.setData(elem);
context.setEncryptedType(encData.getDocumentElement () null, null, null);
encCont.setKey(key);
encCont.setAlgorithmFactory(algFac);
```

At this stage, we have everything in place that we need for encryption.

Step 3: Perform Encryption

These two lines populate the EncryptedData structure with the CipherValue, and replace the unencrypted element with the new EncryptedData structure:

```
encCont.encrypt();
encCont.replace();
```

The EncryptedData structure is shown here:

```
<EncryptedData
xmlns="http://www.w3.org/2001/04/xmlenc#"
  Type="http://www.w3.org/2001/04/xmlenc#Element">
  <EncryptionMethod
    Algorithm="http://www.w3.org/2001/04/xmlenc#3des-cbc" />
  <KeyInfo
    xmlns="http://www.w3.org/2000/09/xmldsig#">
    <KeyName>key</KeyName>
  </KeyInfo>
<CipherData>
   <CipherValue>jp2so32</CipherValue>
  </CipherData>
</EncryptedData>
```

Decrypting Using the IBM XML Security Suite DecryptionContext

We saw in the encryption code that the EncryptionContext object is very useful. Similarly, the DecryptionContext object does a lot of work for decryption.

```
DecryptionContext decCont = new DecryptionContext();
KeyInfoResolver kiRes = new KeyInfoResolver();
decCont.addEncryptedData(encData);
decCont.setKeyInfoResolver(kiRes);
decCont.setAlgorithmFactory(algFac);
decCont.decrypt();
```

The KeyInfoResolver object is used to retrieve the key from the ds:KeyInfo structure. An AlgorithmFactory object is again used to obtain an implementation of the appropriate encryption algorithm.

THE OVERLAP WITH XML SIGNATURE

Encryption does not guarantee the integrity of data. We saw earlier in this chapter that if the initialization vector (IV) for a symmetric algorithm is manipulated, the ciphertext will not decrypt to the original plaintext.

We have also seen that the KeyInfo structure from XML Signature is reused in XML Encryption. In addition, asymmetric encryption algorithms, used for XML Signature, are used in XML Encryption for key transport—sending a secret key.

Let's look at the two cases when XML Encryption and XML Signature are used together on the same document.

Using XML Encryption on a Signed Document

If a document has a digital signature expressed using XML Signature, and it is to be encrypted, then certain caveats must be kept in mind. If a document is digitally signed, that means a digest of the document is enclosed in the digital signature. In an XML Signature structure, this digest is located in the DigestValue element. If the signed data is encrypted, the digest value is valuable information for an attacker who wishes to guess it. The attacker can use the digest algorithm as a tool for guessing the plaintext. Once the attacker obtains a digest that matches the digest in the digital signature, the encryption is broken.

This back door can be blocked by encrypting the digital signature as well as the plaintext. The disadvantage of this approach is that there may be no way of knowing that the data was digitally signed, because the signature is encrypted. An alternative approach, which avoids this problem, is to encrypt only the digest value of the signature.

Using XML Signature on an Encrypted Document

The problem with signing an encrypted document revolves around the question, "What are you signing?" Signing ciphertext is not the same as signing the original plaintext, even though the two are linked by the encryption process. Therefore, the signing of ciphertext has no value as a tool to implement nonrepudiation. However, digital signatures are also used to implement integrity, and in this case they can be used to ensure that the XML Encryption data has not changed. This is useful to deter attacks that change the IV, for example.

Sign-Encrypt-Sign

"Sign-encrypt-sign" (that is, sign first, then encrypt, then sign the encrypted signature) is a useful strategy. The first signature signs the plaintext (since signing ciphertext has no value for nonrepudiation). The encryption step hides the signature from prying eyes, and also encrypts the plaintext. The final signature step ensures that if the ciphertext is changed (maliciously or by accident) as it is sent, this tampering will be noticed.

CHECKLIST

- ☐ Know when XML Encryption is appropriate, and when it is not needed. XML Encryption is useful when a portion of an XML document must be encrypted, and other parts left unencrypted. XML Encryption is also useful when XML data must be *persistently encrypted*.
- ☐ Remember that key management is vital for XML Encryption. Do not store keys on the file system of an untrusted machine, for example a server located in a DMZ. Unlike XML Signature, where a signature can be verified without the use of a private key, XML Encryption requires a private key for decryption. The safety of this private key is vitally important.

CHAPTER 6

SAML

Blending the S2ML and AuthML specifications, the Secure Assertion Markup Language (SAML) is a complex specification developed through OASIS, and currently has "OASIS Open Standard" status. This chapter will explain SAML 1.0 in the context of use cases. SAML, almost by definition, is designed to work in the background and be invisible to the user; therefore, it can be difficult to understand such a "hands-off" technology. You are probably already familiar with the concept of single sign-on, and Kerberos in particular. In addition, you have read about the need to separate security policy decision making from security policy enforcement—these are important bedrocks of the SAML specification.

HOW SAML ENABLES "PORTABLE TRUST"

The OASIS SAML specification allows trust assertions to be specified using XML. These assertions can concern authorizations, authentications, and attributes of specific entities, whether these be individuals or computer systems. These entities must be identifiable within a specific security context, such as a human who is a member of a workgroup or a computer that is part of a network domain. An assertion can be defined as a claim, statement, or declaration. This means that assertions can only be accepted as true subject to the integrity and authenticity of the entity making the assertion. That's why the authorities for attributes and for authentication play a key role in the SAML model. Essentially, if you can trust the authority making the assertion, the assertion can be accepted as true with the same level of certainty as any other certification authority can be trusted.

In addition to assertions, the SAML specification also defines a client/server protocol for exchanging XML message requests and responses. As with all Web Services, the underlying transport protocol is not mandated, with SOAP running over HTTP being the most likely configuration. SAML data can be identified in XML documents by two prefixes: saml: specifies an assertion, while samlp: indicates usage of the SAML client/server protocol.

SAML enables "portable trust" by supporting the assertion of authentication of single principals between different (and potentially multiple) domains. Why is this an important goal for Web Services? In cooperative B2B e-commerce systems involving a number of different companies where there is an aggregation of services offered through a single intermediary, all participants (customers, partners, staff, and systems) need to be authenticated in the same way across the entire virtual system. This model relies upon authoritative systems for each organization being capable of authentication for all subjects within their home domain, in order to allow seamless and secure execution of remote services, as shown in Figure 6-1. Here, two businesses (A and B) have their own security and authentication domains (domain A and domain B, respectively). Normally, a service offered within domain A or domain B is only available to principals (users and systems) that have been authenticated by a server in their own domain. Thus, users and systems in domain A can access a service in domain A because the authentication server - domain A has authenticated them. However, what if principals from domain A wish to invoke services in domain B?

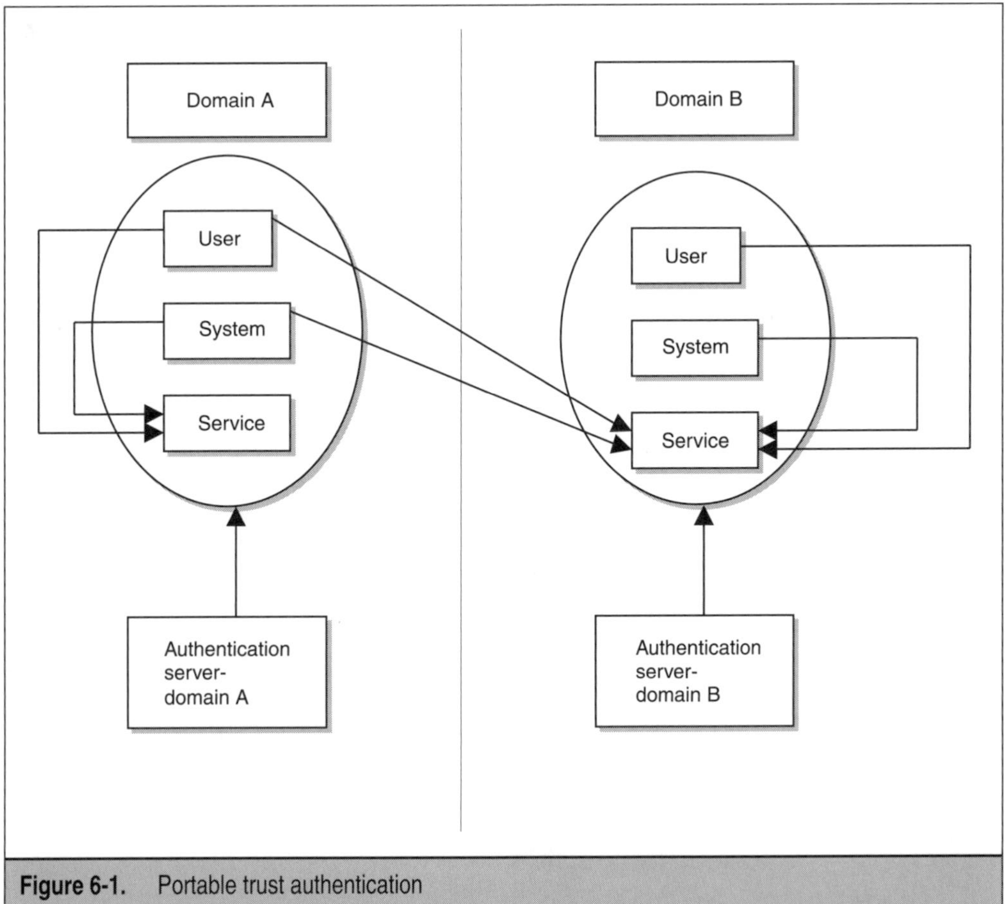

Figure 6-1. Portable trust authentication

This model prevents two very difficult scenarios from occurring. First, one organization would have to take on the responsibility for authenticating all foreign principals. Not only would this introduce a heavy administrative burden on the authenticating organization, it would be unacceptable to the other participants in the enterprise. For example, a bank is not going to hand over its authentication data to an external party just so that party can invoke a service from the bank, and vice versa. Returning to our Figure 6-1 example, authentication for domain A would now have to be undertaken by the authentication server - domain B. This solution, as shown in Figure 6-2, would not be palatable by the administrators of domain A!

Setting up a central authentication registry for every partnership that an organization has developed would be necessary if principals from both organizations were able to invoke each other's services. This approach requires setting up and maintaining a new authentication registry for every partnership, which would be very costly. Allowing all

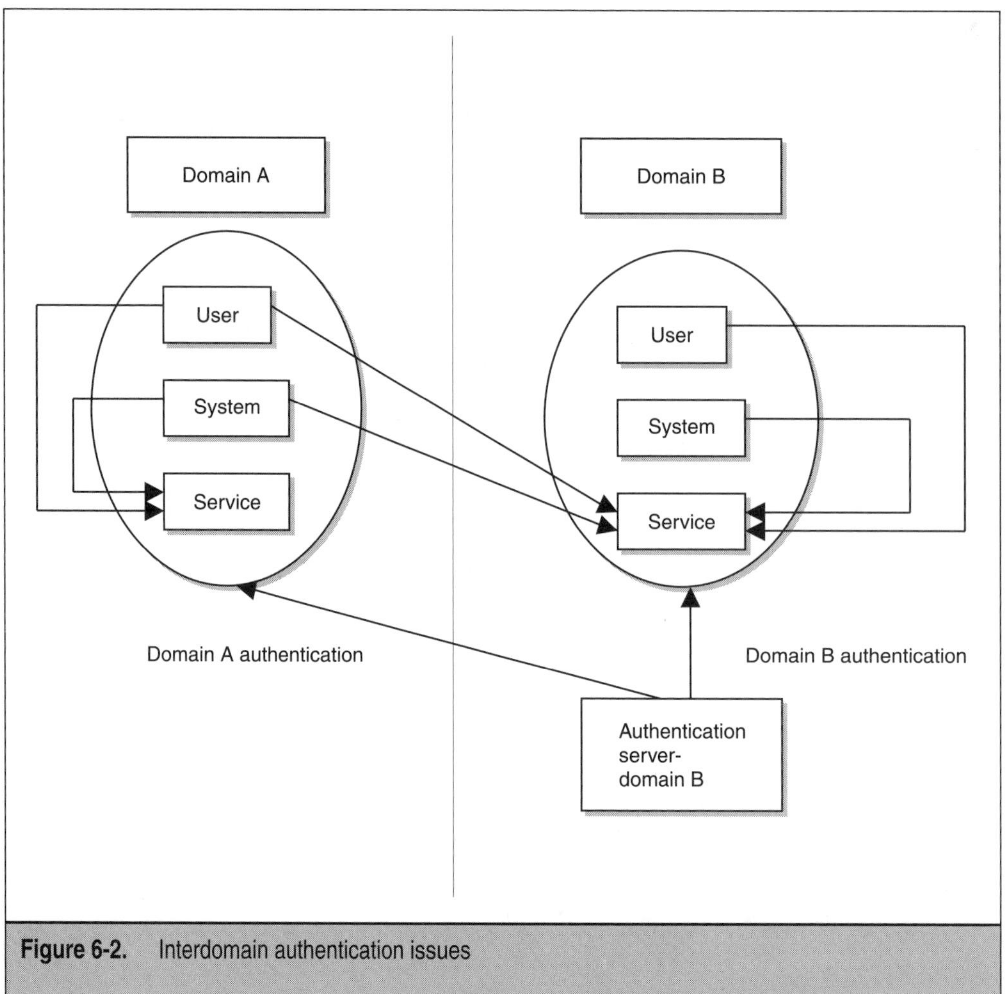

Figure 6-2. Interdomain authentication issues

parties in a transaction to accept each other's authentication tokens as valid prevents reauthentication to the viral-like distribution of credentials. Returning to the example shown in Figure 6-1, a new server called authentication server – domain C would have to be created in order to allow the sharing of credentials between domain A and domain B, into a new "super" domain C, as shown in Figure 6-3. The questions of who maintains and pays for this new service, who manages it, and how to handle crossover of confidential information between the servers are not easily resolved.

Clearly, allowing individual domains to retain their own internal authentication systems provides the best solution to the proliferation of authentication systems and

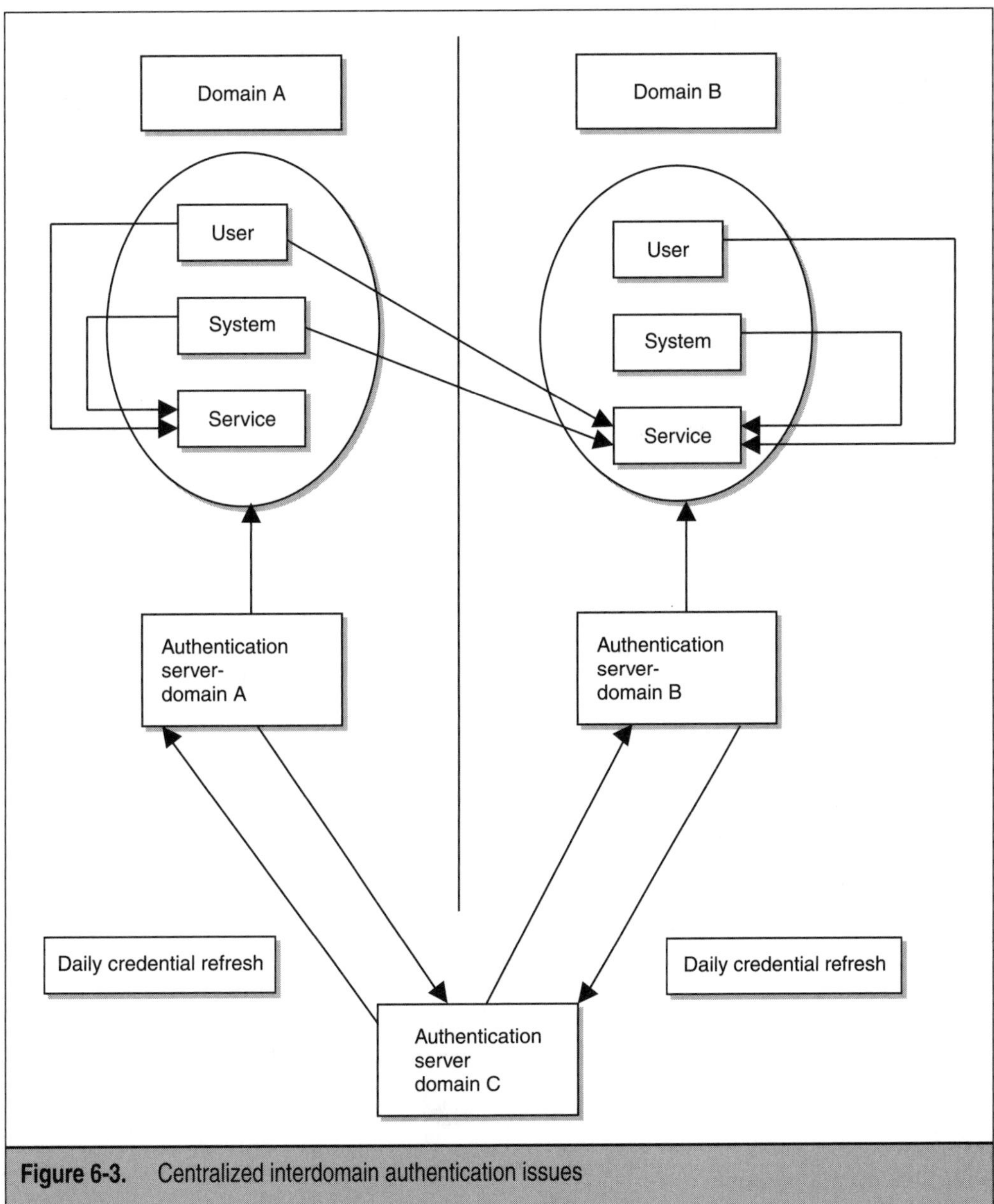

Figure 6-3. Centralized interdomain authentication issues

related issues such as the integrity of credentials if they are distributed. This provides the "loose coupling" of authentication systems, by means of assertions, that are provided in other Web Services, such as the decoupling of message format from transport type. Removing the brittleness from the authentication process makes it infinitely more flexible. However, in order to allow principals from one domain to invoke services in another domain, assertions must be made about an authenticated principal after the single sign-on has occurred and a trust relationship has been established.

Introducing the Three Types of Assertions

From a client perspective, being able to have a single sign-on also reduces the difficulties involved in accessing multiple services from multiple providers—after a principal has been authenticated once, an assertion about that authentication can be made each time an authentication point is reached in a business process. For example, in a B2C e-commerce application, a client can use the same authentication assertion to access a bank account as well as a merchant's shopping basket. However, it's important to note that assertions are not limited to authentication—they also include attributes and authorizations. For example, if the client has $1,000 available credit, the bank may authorize a withdrawal of that amount with respect to the purchase from the merchant. Rather than having to pass credit card details to the merchant, the merchant accepts the assurance from the bank that the client can pay for the goods ordered.

A set of assertions is known as a profile. A principal's profile can comprise assertions made by different organizations, which is acceptable as long as the entities trust each other. For example, computer records in different government departments could be combined together to form a "citizen" profile, which might contain authorizations like the following:

- Can reside in the country without restrictions
- Can drive a motor vehicle
- Can pay taxes
- Can claim social security
- Can travel internationally with a valid passport

Each of these authorizations may be granted by a different department, even within different jurisdictions, but a profile can nonetheless be constructed and data exchanged by using SOAP. The profile can potentially be shared by all of the parties involved in administering authorizations. Of course, the citizen might want to control just what information is shared. Just because the technology makes it possible, doesn't mean it should happen unfettered.

Profiles are used in real-world applications to authorize specific types of activities, based on policies. For example, in order to authorize a claim for social security, a citizen may need to have the authorizations "Can reside in the country without restrictions" and "Can pay taxes," while "Can drive a motor vehicle" would not be relevant.
The exception would be where the primary key for identifying principals (such as a driver's license number) was used in other domains, as occurs frequently in government

(for example, social security numbers). Each of the business logic decisions would be encapsulated in the relevant policy.

In the following sections, we will examine each type of assertion in detail.

Explanation of the Concept of an "Assertion"

SAML provides three types of assertions: authentication assertion, authorization decision assertion, and attribute assertion. Each type of assertion can have its own policies, profiles, and attributes. It can be very confusing to discuss the attributes of the attribute assertion, but the correct type can usually be identified from context. The following elements are common to all assertions:

- **<Advice>** Contains additional evidence relating to the assertion.
- **<Assertion>** Contains the data elements for all assertion types.
- **<AssertionIDReference>** Refers to a SAML assertion.
- **<Audience>** Contains the URI for the intended audience.
- **<AudienceRestrictionCondition>** Restricts the potential audience of an assertion.
- **<Conditions>** Specifies logical conditions that the assertion is subject to.

An <Assertion> is specified using an AssertionType, which is comprised of the following elements:

- **<AttributeStatement>** Statement relating to an attribute.
- **<AuthenticationStatement>** Statement relating to authentication.
- **<AuthorizationDecisionStatement>** Decision relating to authorization.
- **<ds:signature>** XML digital signature for authentication.
- **<Statement>** General extension schema statement for external applications.
- **<SubjectStatement>** Extension schema statement relating a principal.
- **AssertionID** Unique ID of IDType.
- **IssueInstant** Time when the assertion was made.
- **Issuer** Name of the assertion issuer.
- **MajorVersion** The assertion's major version.
- **MinorVersion** The assertion's minor version.

In addition to assertions, the following common statements are supported:

- **<Statement>** General extension schema statement for external applications.
- **<SubjectStatement>** Extension schema statement relating a principal.
- **<Subject>** Defines a principal related to a statement.

- **<NameIdentifier>** Defines a principal by using a NameQualifier, a name, and a specific format.
- **<SubjectConfirmation>** Specifies an authentication protocol to authenticate a principal using a specific <ConfirmationMethod> and any additional data in <SubjectConfirmationData>.
- **<AuthenticationStatement>** Specifies that a principal was authenticated by an external authority at a specific date and time.
- **<SubjectLocality>** Contains the IP address and DNS name of the authenticated system.
- **<AuthorityBinding>** Specifies details about a SAML authority.
- **<AuthorizationDecisionStatement>** URI that states a decision concerning an authorization based on a set of evidence.

Authentication Assertion

The authentication authority receives a set of credentials from the credentials collector, and processes them according to a specific policy. An authentication assertion can then be made with respect to the two other assertions (authorization decision assertion and attribute assertion), if the authority determines that the credentials are valid. The assertion defines several authentication elements such as the identity of the issuer and the principal, the time the authentication was granted, and how long the authentication is valid for. The assertion clearly indicates that a principal was authenticated by a specific system at a specific point in time—unlike, say, traditional UNIX authentication, which is all or nothing.

The <AuthenticationStatement> is generated after authentication and contains the method by which the principal was authenticated, the time it occurred, and where it occurred. The <SubjectLocality> element specifies the DNS name and IP address of an authenticating system, while the <AuthorityBinding> element indicates that additional data concerning a principal may be available.

The following authentication methods are supported:

- Passwords
- Kerberos
- Secure Remote Password (SRP)
- Hardware token
- Certificate-based client authentication (SSL/TLS)
- X.509 public key
- Pretty Good Privacy (PGP) public key
- SPKI public key
- XKMS public key
- XML digital signature

Attribute Assertion

An attribute assertion begins with an attribute authority accepting an authentication assertion and using a policy to determine the privileges of a principal. The attribute assertion can be passed to a policy decision point (PDP) for authorization.

The <AttributeStatement> contains <Subject>, <Attribute>, <NameIdentifier>, <SubjectConfirmation>, <ConfirmationMethod>, and <SubjectConfirmationData> elements. The <AttributeDesignator> element defines the attributes involved in a request with respect to a specific namespace, and includes the <AttributeName> and associated <AttributeNamespace> elements. The <Attribute> element itself contains the attribute value <AttributeValue>, related to the underlying assertion.

Authorization Decision Assertion

An authorization decision assertion involves making a decision about whether or not a principal can access a specific resource, given an authentication assertion and an attribute assertion. It involves two entities: the policy decision point (PDP) and the policy enforcement point (PEP). According to a policy, the PDP and PEP make and enforce authorization decisions, respectively. Obviously, requests for authorization to access resources can be accepted (Permit), can be denied (Deny), or cannot be determined (Indeterminate); hence, the importance of an authority's decision-making process.

The <AuthorizationDecisionStatement> specifies what decision was made with respect to an authorization decision assertion request. The <AuthorizationDecision Statement> contains a resource URI, which identifies the resource that the principal is attempting to access; a decision, which states whether access is granted or denied; an action, specifying what the principal is authorized to do; and optionally the evidence upon which the decision was taken.

SAML Architecture

Fundamentally, SAML is concerned with access control for authenticated principals based on a set of policies. The applications and environment that can potentially use SAML are quite varied, from simple browser-based applications running over HTTP to full-blown J2EE applications supporting *n*-tier architectures. There are two actions that must be performed with respect to access control in any enterprise system: making decisions about access control based on a set of policies, and enforcing those decisions at the system level. The SAML architecture provides two roles for performing these actions: the policy decision point (PDP) and the policy enforcement point (PEP), respectively. If a PDP is external to the system, it will need to have access to a policy retrieval point (PRP) in order to retrieve policies relevant to decisions being made. This connection should use a secure transport; otherwise, details of policies may become public.

A PDP makes decisions concerning access control based on one or more parameters and/or their logical combination. This means that simple types of access can be granted, such as whether or not a user is using a secure transport layer like HTTPS. Or, more complex types of access can be granted, such as whether a specific group member is attempting access at a specific time on a specific day. For example, a commodities trader should only be able to trade stocks within certain time periods during the day, so access will be denied outside of those times. The parameters that can be used to make decisions about access control include the following:

- Whether a user has exceeded a limit on the number of accesses to a specific service
- Whether a user is a member of a specific group
- Whether a user is a member of an organization
- Whether the client can establish a secure connection
- Whether the client can supply an authentication credential
- Whether the client's hostname or IP address is valid
- Whether the current day lies within the boundaries defined as legal
- Whether the current time lies within the boundaries defined as legal

In order to prevent denial of service attacks, it would also be useful to log all access attempts and to block incoming connections from a specific client if they persist in requesting a resource to which they have no access. This could potentially be achieved in combination with an XML firewall.

PEPs and PDPs

The IETF/DMTF policy framework (http://www.ietf.org/html.charters/policy-charter.html) specifies that a policy repository should store the different policies that can be applied to services on a specific server, and that a policy management tool can be used to set specific policies. Where a single management tool can be used to centralize administration of common policies across many systems, the administrative burden required to manage access control policies can be greatly reduced. Policy management tools, at a minimum, need to provide a user-friendly interface to discover resources, encapsulate transformational logic for ensuring the consistency of sets of policies applied to the same principals, and provide a reliable method for distributing policies around the network. Policies can be evaluated in real time or at the time of creation for boundary error conditions, logical relation satisfaction, policies that will never be satisfied under any situation, and whether a set of policies delivers a desirable outcome. The framework also defines the activities of PEPs and PDPs with respect to policy processing. When an enforcement decision is required, a PEP makes a connection to the appropriate PDP for the decision. The policy function is evaluated with data supplied from the PEP to the PDP. Clients make their connections to SAML authorities by using the SAML client/server protocol, where a <Request> is always answered with a specific <Response>.

Imagine a set of four policies with the following parameters in a share-trading environment of a financial institution:

- Members of group Clients can access the service BuyStocksConsumer.
- Members of group Brokers cannot access the service BuyStocksConsumer.
- Members of group Clients cannot access the service BuyStocksStaff.
- Members of group Brokers can access the service BuyStocksStaff.

The purpose of these policies is to allow clients to buy stocks using the consumer interface, while brokers cannot use the same interface. Instead, they must use a special staff interface that is not available to consumers. Now, when the PEP passes a decision request for access control to the PDP, the PDP must logically evaluate the inputs it receives with respect to these rules. If these rules are consistent, the processing is trivial, and if a match is made against any policy, it will be returned positively. For example, if Joe.Bloggs@iBuyStocks.com is a member of Clients, a match will be made against the first policy and access will be granted to BuyStocksConsumer. However, what happens if Joe.Bloggs is both a member of Clients and Brokers? Clearly, the first and second policies are inconsistent in this case, and the PDP policy evaluation engine must be able to detect the mismatch, and not just return a positive evaluation of Joe.Bloggs after processing only the first policy. This suggests that $O(p^2)$ time is required to cross-check each set of policies for consistency, where p is the number of applicable policies.

Example Architecture

Let's examine a simple application at this point to show how the decision process actually works in an authentication scenario. In the following example, Joe.Bloggs is the principal, and the SecurityDomain is iBuyStocks.com. The AttributeName is the username, the AttributeNamespace is the same as the SecurityDomain, and the request is an AttributeQuery, which should return the appropriate attributes for the user involved, as shown in the following example request code:

```
<samlp: Request>
      <samlp: AttributeQuery>
            <saml: Subject>
                  <saml: NameIdentifier
SecurityDomain="iBuyStocks.com" Name="joe.bloggs"/>
            </ saml: Subject>
            <saml: AttributeDesignator AttributeName="username"
AttributeNamespace="iBuyStocks.com">
            </ saml: AttributeDesignator>
      </ samlp: AttributeQuery>
</ samlp: Request>
```

The response is shown next, where the authentication is validated against a previous Kerberos authentication of the principal. Some key characteristics of the authentication are displayed, including the time period for which it is valid, the time at which it was granted, and the method used.

```
<samlp: Response
MajorVersion="2"
MinorVersion="1"
RequestID="192.168.203.16.98765574"
InResponseTo="192.192.208.64.77645543"
StatusCode="Success">
      <saml: Assertion
MajorVersion="1"
MinorVersion="0"
AssertionID="192.192.208.64.77645543"
Issuer="iBuyStocks.com"
IssueInstant="2002-11-16T10: 00: 23Z">
            <saml: Conditions
NotBefore="2002-11-16T10:01:00Z"
NotOnOrAfter="2002-11-23T10:01:00Z" />
            <saml: AuthenticationStatement
AuthenticationMethod="Kerberos"
AuthenticationInstant="2002-11-16T10:00:00Z">
                  <saml: Subject>
                        <saml: NameIdentifier
SecurityDomain="iBuyStocks.com"
Name="joe.bloggs" />
                  </ saml: Subject>
              </ saml: AuthenticationStatement>
      </ saml: Assertion>
</ samlp: Response>
```

Access Control

One of the useful features of SAML is the ability to map access control elements to those used by the most common systems. This means that developers do not need to implement their own systems for access control. The control types covered in the following subsection are supported.

Read, Write, Execute, Delete, Control These controls are the standard ones found on most operating systems:

- **Read** Principal can read data.
- **Write** Principal can write data.
- **Execute** Principal can execute the application.
- **Delete** Principal can delete data.
- **Control** Principal is allowed to stipulate access control policies.

The URI for this action is "urn:oasis:names:tc:SAML:1.0: action:rwedc". An alternative is read, write, execute, delete, control, negation, which allows all or any of the access controls to be specifically denied. The URI for this alternative action is "urn:oasis:names:tc:SAML:1.0: action:rwedc-negation."

Get, Head, Put, Post These actions correspond to the HTTP operations of the same name, with Get and Head reading data from a server, and Put and Post writing data to a server. The URI for the action is urn:oasis:names:tc:SAML:1.0: action:ghpp.

UNIX Permissions UNIX permissions can be set using either symbolic or octal codes. For example, the attribute "+rwx" would grant read, write, and execute permissions on a file using symbolic codes, while 0777 would be the octal equivalent. The URI for this action is urn:oasis:names:tc:SAML:1.0:action:unix.

DEPLOYING SAML

Commercial products using SAML have been slow to appear. The following systems currently support SAML in production:

- Entegrity's AssureAccess
- Entrust's GetAccess portal
- Netegrity's AffiliateMinder
- Securant's RSA Cleartrust
- Sun's iPlanet Directory Server with Access Management
- Sun's ONE Network Identity
- Systinet's WASP Secure Identity

A number of companies now provide toolkits to work with SAML and develop applications based on the single sign-on model. These include the Netegrity JSAML toolkit, and VeriSign's Trust Services Integration Kit. These toolkits use their own APIs to implement SAML operations defined in the specification. However, there is currently a proposal for standardizing the APIs for Java, with the development of JSR 155: Web Services Security Assertions, through the Java Community Process (JCP). JSR 155 will implement all of the assertion operations defined in the specification, as well as provide guidance in the area of patterns for using SAML to develop applications. At the time of writing, JSR 155 is still under discussion and its recommendations have not been made public.

It also remains to be seen to what extent Microsoft will implement SAML in its products, because they already have a successful single sign-on technology called Passport. Although it is targeted at client/server Web-based applications, the success of Passport can be judged by the number of sites that now support its single sign-on authentication. These issues are not meant to dampen your enthusiasm for SAML—it's just that as a developer, you need to be aware of the rapidly changing nature of Web Services!

VeriSign's Trust Services Integration Kit

One of the more complete toolkits for working with SAML is the VeriSign Trust Services Integration Kit (TSIK). The TSIK is unique in that it provides a platform for creating trusted services and client/server applications, especially those that use Web Services. It provides access to many of the mandatory components required to support PKI, payments processing, XML digital signatures, XML messaging, and XML encryption. In addition, it now provides support for SAML to assert authentication and authorizations between security domains. The FAQ for the TSIK is at http://www.xmltrustcenter.org/developer/verisign/tsik/faq.htm, and a developer's forum is at http://www.xmltrustcenter.org/developer/verisign/tsik/forum.htm.

The Java API provided with TSIK defines five major factory classes that can be used to process assertions:

- **SOAPAssertionProviderFactory** Produces AssertionProvider objects that connect to assertion authorities to retrieve Assertion objects, using SOAP.
- **XMLAssertionGeneratorFactory** Provides AssertionGenerator translator objects that map Assertion objects from XML.
- **XMLRequestGeneratorFactory** Provides RequestGenerator translator objects that map Request objects from XML.
- **XMLResponseGeneratorFactory** Provides ResponseGenerator translator objects that map Response objects from XML.
- **XMLSecurityParameters** Configures parameters for XML security.

Of the classes created by the factory classes, the AssertionProvider is probably the most significant, so an AssertionProvider example is examined in the next section.

Creating an AssertionProvider

An AssertionProvider is either an authentication authority (AuthNStatementProvider), attribute authority (AttributeStatementProvider), or PDP (AuthZDecisionStatement Provider). Each of these classes is specific to the provider type. In the more generic case, creating an AssertionProvider using the SOAPAssertionProviderFactory class is shown in the following Java code:

```
KeyStore k = KeyStore.getInstance(KeyStore.getDefaultType());
X509Certificate c = (X509Certificate) k.getCertificate("username");
PrivateKey pk = (PrivateKey) k.getKey("username", "password".toCharArray());
SOAPAssertionProviderFactory f = new SOAPAssertionProviderFactory(new
URL("https://treefrog-onsite-fe.bbtest.net:8081/vspts/SamlResponder"));
f.setSigningKey(new RSASigningKey(pk));
f.setVerifyingKey(new RSAVerifyingKey(c));
AssertionProvider p = f.newAssertionProvider();
```

In this example, a new KeyStore object is initialized and the X.509 certificate for the appropriate user is retrieved. The private key for the user is also retrieved when the appropriate password is supplied. The private key and certificate-embedded public key allow for signing and verifying, respectively. Next, a SOAPAssertionProviderFactory is instantiated, with a test URL in this instance. Next, the factory object is signed and verified, and a new AssertionProvider object *p* is created by invoking the newAssertionProvider() method.

Authentication

To create a query for authentication using Kerberos, the AuthNQuery class is instantiated as shown in the following example:

```
NameIdentifier n = new NameIdentifier("joe.bloggs@iBuyStocks.com");
SubjectConfirmation c = new
 SubjectConfirmation(Identifiers.AUTHN_METHOD_KERBEROS);
Subject s = new Subject(n, c);
Query q = new AuthNQuery(s, Identifiers.AUTHN_METHOD_KERBEROS);
```

Here, the NameIdentifier specifies a principal to be authenticated and the SubjectConfirmation class specifies how the authentication is to be undertaken (in this case, Kerberos is used). The Subject class combines elements of the NameIdentifier and SubjectConfirmation classes, in a form suitable for creating a new AuthNQuery object. The query can then be used in conjunction with an AssertionProvider to return the set of appropriate assertions from the server. To establish the authenticity of the authentication request, an Authenticity object is retrieved from the list of assertions by calling the isAuthentic() method. If required, an AuthNStatement object can be instantiated to retrieve the relevant details of the principal using the getSubject() and getNameIdentifier() methods.

Making an Attribute Query

A sample SAML AttributeQuery XML request is shown here, using Kerberos as the authentication method:

```
<samlp:AttributeQuery>
      <saml:Subject xmlns:saml="urn:oasis:names:tc:SAML:1.0:assertion">
            <saml:NameIdentifier Format=""

      NameQualifier="verisign.com/ams">joe.bloggs</saml:NameIdentifier>
            <saml:SubjectConfirmation>
            <saml:ConfirmationMethod>urn:ietf:rfc:1510
            </saml:ConfirmationMethod>
            <saml:SubjectConfirmationData>password
            </saml:SubjectConfirmationData>
            </saml:SubjectConfirmation>
      </saml:Subject>
<saml:AttributeDesignator AttributeName="//verisign.com/core/attr/
email" AttributeNamespace="verisign.com/ams/namespace/common"
```

```
 xmlns:saml="urn:oasis:names:tc:SAML:1.0:assertion"/>
</samlp:AttributeQuery>
```

Here, we can see that the AttributeQuery contains several elements, such as NameIdentifier and SubjectConfirmation, that help to identify the principal to whom the attribute request relates. SubjectConfirmation also contains elements like ConfirmationMethod, which in this instance specifies Kerberos (urn:ietf:rfc:1510). The following XML response would be provided from a server responding to this request:

```
<samlp:Status>
      <samlp:StatusCode Value="samlp:Success"/>
</samlp:Status>
```

Here, we can see that the request was successful. However, it's also possible that a number of error codes could be returned, including the following:

- **VersionMismatch** Client and server are running different software versions.
- **Requester** There was an error on the client side.
- **Responder** There was an error on the server side.
- **RequestVersionTooHigh** Client's protocol version is too new for the server to process correctly.
- **RequestVersionTooLow** Client's protocol version is too old for the server to process correctly.
- **RequestVersionDeprecated** Client's protocol version is no longer supported at all.
- **TooManyResponses** Maximum of possible returned elements has been exceeded.
- **RequestDenied** Request has been understood by the server but has been refused, possibly because of security concerns.
- **ResourceNotRecognized** Attribute query requested is not supported or it is invalid.

After the successful status has been returned in this example, the following authentication data is returned:

```
<saml:AuthenticationStatement AuthenticationInstant="2002-11-16T13:32:31Z"
AuthenticationMethod="Kerberos">
      <saml:Subject>
            <saml:NameIdentifier
NameQualifier="verisign.com/ams">jbloggs</saml:NameIdentifier>
      </saml:Subject>
</saml:AuthenticationStatement>
```

Here, we can see that the NameIdentifier for jbloggs has been returned. Now the AttributeData is returned:

```
<saml:AttributeStatement>
      <saml:Subject>
      <saml:NameIdentifier
NameQualifier="verisign.com/ams">jbloggs</saml:NameIdentifier>
       </saml:Subject>
     <saml:Attribute AttributeName="//verisign.com/xas/attr/
contactInfo" AttributeNamespace="verisign.com/ams/namespace/common">
      <saml:AttributeValue>
me>
<lastName>Bloggs</lastName>
<emailAddress>joe.bloggs@iBuyStocks.com</emailAddress>
</contactInfo>
      </saml:AttributeValue>
</saml:Attribute>
</saml:AttributeStatement>
</saml:Assertion>
```

Here, we can see in the raw XML the various tokens associated with this principal's AttributeValue, including the contactInfo element, with the tokens firstName, lastName, emailAddress, and telephoneNumber.

Let's look at the client code required to process the response. The AttributeStatement object is instantiated, which contains specific attributes for the principal, and even their Role-Based Access Control (RBAC) authorizations. By invoking the getAttributes() method of an AttributeStatement object, when the attributes are returned in the response from the server, they can be displayed by calling the getAttributeName()and getAttributeValues() methods of the Attribute class in a display like this:

```
Name 1: //verisign.com/core/attr/first_name
Value 1: Joe
Name 2: //verisign.com/core/attr/last_name
Value 2: Bloggs
Name 3: //verisign.com/core/attr/email
Value 3: joe.bloggs@iBuyStocks.com
Name 4: //verisign.com/core/attr/phone_number
Value 4: 02-9999-8888
Name 5: //verisign.com/core/attr/organization_name
Value 5: iBuyStocks.com
Name 6: //verisign.com/core/attr/department
Value 6: Consumer
Name 7: //acme.com/role
Value 7: Client
```

In this example, seven names and values were returned.

CHECKLIST

- ☐ How does SAML enable portable trust?
- ☐ What interdomain authentication issues arise for foreign principals?
- ☐ What's the difference between a policy enforcement point (PEP) and a policy decision point (PDP)?
- ☐ What is an AttributeQuery?

CHAPTER 7

XACML

The previous chapter described how SAML is used to convey information about authorization, authentication, and attributes in XML-formatted assertions. These authorization decisions are based on configurable rules. XACML (pronounced "zac-mull" and standing for "eXtensible Access Control Markup Language") is being produced by the OASIS standards body to define an XML vocabulary to express the rules on which access control decisions are made.

XACML defines rules to allow access to resources (read, write, execute, and so forth) based on characteristics of the requester ("only members of the Human Resources department can access this document"), characteristics of the request protocol (for example, "SSL must be used to access this document"), and the authentication context (such as "a digital certificate must be used for authentication if this document is to be read").

As well as defining the format of the rules themselves, XACML defines conditions for creating rules ("rules for making rules"), how rules may be combined, and how rules are processed to perform decisions. Policy statements may be created by collecting XACML-expressed rules together.

INTRODUCTION TO XACML

Before we launch into the "how" of XACML, let's ask the "why" question. It may not be immediately obvious what problem XACML is attempting to solve. In the case of SAML, information is being sent between different parties and therefore the parties must agree on a format for that data. If two companies disagree on how they will describe authentication and authorization events, then single sign-on is impossible because the companies are unable to express information about the security status of a user to each other. However, if these same two companies express their authorization rules differently, the picture is not so bad because these rules are generally not sent on the network, but are used in the background to express policy. Why, then, spend time producing a common XML format for authorization rules?

The answer is that XACML is useful as a policy exchange format, in order for systems to exchange or share authorization policies—even if the policies are translated into a proprietary or native policy language prior to the actual execution of the policy. XACML means that access control policies do not have to be tightly linked to the systems that they govern, but can be enterprise-wide across many different resources, including XML documents, non-XML documents, relational databases, and application servers. It's another example of the advantages of XML being applied to security. Indeed, it can be argued that like XKMS, XACML is more about applying XML to security, rather than about applying security to XML. The documents accessed using a policy expressed in XACML do not have to be XML documents at all—and in the majority of cases they will not be XML.

XACML can best be understood in terms of the architecture of SAML. In the SAML chapter, we encountered the SAML protocol, using an authorization decision query to request a decision on authorization. In addition, an attribute query can be performed in order to find out information used to make an authorization decision. The information used to make these decisions can be expressed in XACML.

Basic Concepts of Access Control

In order to understand XACML, it's important to understand the concepts of access control. There are two basic access control models that apply to systems on the Internet: access control lists (ACLs, sometimes pronounced "ack-els"), and, more recently, Role-Based Access Control (RBAC).

Access Control Lists (ACL)

In ACL, each username is mapped to a separate permission set for particular resources. This permission set includes the Read, Write, Execute, and Change permissions. This arrangement is sometimes called an "access matrix." Examples of ACLs are found in UNIX and Microsoft Windows.

Role-Based Access Control

Role-Based Access Control (RBAC) has gained popularity in recent years, mainly because it allows access control to be performed by taking the context of users into account. Users can be put into groups, and assigned to "roles." These roles can reflect organizational structure. For example, a user with a role of "doctor" can view certain documents, and another user with a role of "nurse" can view other documents. It is the roles that have the permission sets, not the users. A role can be created by inheriting one or more properties from other roles, which is reminiscent of the use of multiple inheritance (and interfaces, in the case of Java) in object-oriented programming.

Rules can also depend on factors such as time of day, so that a rule can be assigned to a user that links together the "doctor" and the "weekday access" roles. RBAC is less complex than ACLs because the size of the rule base increases in proportion to the number of roles and resources, not in proportion to the number of users. Therefore, it is generally believed that RBAC-based systems scale better than ACL-based systems.

As a side note, it is somewhat unfortunate that the use of the word "role" in SOAP 1.2 in place of "actor" has added another meaning to the word "role." Role-Based Access Control focuses on the role of the user, not the role of the service processing a message. If the use of the phrase "SOAP role" gathers currency, it could spread confusion.

RULES IN XACML

XACML uses a lot of terminology, and often the meaning of English language words in XACML is not exactly the same as their use in the vernacular. We will start with the definition of a rule and work from there.

Definition of a Rule in XACML: Target, Effect, and Conditions

A rule in XACML is defined as "A *target*, an *effect*, and a *set of conditions*." To understand this definition, we have to understand the specific meanings of "target," "effect," and "conditions." A target is defined as the space of decision requests that refer to actions on resources (documents, services, or systems) by subjects (people or computers). An example target would be "Read access to documents in the C Drive by Marketing Personnel." An effect is either "permit" or "deny." Because it is often inappropriate to have a rule fixed to always be enforced the same way, "conditions" can be applied to the rule, which can make the rule dynamic. These conditions involve the calculation of "attributes" of either the subject (if the subject has a management role), the resource (if the document is a PDF document), the action (if a local copy of the file must be made), or the environment (if it is after 5.30 P.M.).

By using this definition of rules, XACML can accommodate complex scenarios involving access to widely different resources by people or machines, depending on aspects of not just the requestor and the resource in question, but also of other conditions. The ability to query an attribute is called a "predicate" of a rule. All of this fits with the architecture of SAML, because the ability to issue an authorization decision assertion may depend on the content of certain attribute assertions. This can be mapped to the situation in XACML where the predicate of a rule is the evaluation of an attribute (such as the time of day or the role of a user).

An Example Rule

Consider the following rule adapted from the XACML draft specification. This rule grants read access to patient medical records on the example.com site only if the requestor (that is, the SAML *subject*) is the patient:

```
<?xml version="1.0" encoding="UTF-8"?>
<Rule RuleId="//medico.com/rules/rule1" Effect="Permit"
xmlns="urn:oasis:names:tc:xacml:0.15i:policy"
xmlns:function="urn:oasis:names:tc:xacml:0.15i:function"
xmlns:identifier="urn:oasis:names:tc:xacml:0.15i:identifier"
xmlns:saml="urn:oasis:names:tc:SAML:1.0:assertion"
xmlns:xsi="http://www.w3.org/2001/XMLSchema-instance"
xsi:schemaLocation="urn:oasis:names:tc:xacml:0.15i:policy
http://www.oasis-open.org/tc/xacml/v15/
draft-xacml-schema-policy-15i.xsd">
<Description>A person may read any record for which he or she is the
designated patient</Description>
<Target>
<Subjects MatchId="function:rfc822Name-equal" DataType="xs:boolean">
<AttributeDesignator Designator=
"//xacmlContext/Request/Subject/Attribute
[@DataType='identifier:rfc822Name']"DataType="identifier:rfc822Name"/>
```

```
<Attribute DataType="identifier:rfc822Name">@</Attribute>
</Subjects>
<Resources MatchId="function:string-match" DataType="xs:boolean">
<AttributeDesignator Designator=
"//xacmlContext/Request/Resource/@ResourceURI" DataType="xs:anyURI"/>
<Attribute DataType="xs:anyURI">//example.com/record.*</Attribute>
</Resources>
<Actions MatchId="function:subset" DataType="xs:boolean">
<AttributeDesignator Designator="//xacmlContext/Action[@Namespace=]"
DataType="xs:string"/>
<Attribute DataType="xs:string">read</Attribute>
</Actions>
</Target>
<Condition FunctionId="function:string-equal" DataType="xs:boolean">
<AttributeDesignator Designator=
"//xacmlContext/Request/Subject/SubjectId" DataType="xs:string"/>
<AttributeDesignator Designator=
"//xacmlContext/Request/Resource/patientName" DataType="xs:string"/>
</Condition>
</Rule>
```

Look at the preceding example rule. You can see that it has a target, effect, and conditions, which is the definition of a rule in XACML. The effect of the rule is "permit"—meaning that if the rule is granted, the access (defined as an action on a resource) is permitted. The other type of effect would be "deny."

The target of the rule is identified by the RFC 822 name of the domain "example.com". This is the site where the medical records are being stored in this hypothetical example. Further down the rule, we see the *condition* of the rule. The condition states that the SubjectId and the patientName must be *equal*; that is, people can only access their own medical records.

Use of Functions in Rule Conditions

XACML has formalized the use of mathematic statements for rules processing. Notice the condition in the following rule, which uses the function:date-subtract operation to ensure that the age of the requestor is greater than 16:

```
<Condition FunctionId="function:and" DataType="xs:boolean">
<Function FunctionId="function:string-equal" DataType="xs:boolean">
<AttributeDesignator Designator=
"//xacmlContext/Request/Subject/SubjectId" DataType="xs:string"/>
<AttributeDesignator Designator=
"//xacmlContext/Request/Resource/guardianName" DataType="xs:string"/>
</Function>
<Function FunctionId="function:dayTimeDuration-greater-than"
```

```
DataType="xs:boolean">
<Function FunctionId="function:date-subtract"
DataType="xs:dayTimeDuration">
<AttributeDesignator Designator=
"//xacmlContext/Other/OtherAttribute/Attribute
[@DataType='identifier:today'sDate']" DataType="xs:date"/>
<AttributeDesignator
Designator="//xacmlContext/Request/Resource/patient/patientDoB"
DataType="xs:date"/>
</Function>
<Attribute DataType="xs:dayTimeDuration">16-0-0</Attribute>
</Function>
</Condition>
```

XACML includes definition of arithmetical operations (add, subtract, multiply, and divide) on integers, decimal numbers, and dates, rounding, greater than/less than, and matching. Together, these allow for complex rules to be constructed.

An Obligation in a Rule

The following example, when included in an XACML rule, indicates that the enforcer of the rule must send an e-mail to the subject of the decision when permission to the protected resource is granted:

```
<Obligations>
<Obligation ObligationId="//example.com/emailer" FulfilOn="Permit">
<AttributeDesignator Designator="//xacmlContext/Request/Resource/patient/email"
DataType="xs:string"/>
<AttributeAssignment DataType="xs:string" AttributeId="//medico.com/text">
Your medical record has been accessed by:</AttributeAssignment>
<AttributeDesignator Designator="//xacmlContext/Request/Subject/SubjectId"
DataType="xs:string"/>
</Obligation>
</Obligations>
```

Note that the implementation of the e-mail is dependent on the environment that is implementing the policy decision.

An Example of a "Deny" Rule

So far, we have seen rules that, if granted, allow access. Let's look at the converse, a rule whose effect is "deny" for the assigned target. The target of this rule is administrator read/write access to patient records. Again, we see that the target includes the subject's role (administrator), the resource (identified by the XPath "//example.com/record/medical.*"), and the action (read or write). Notice the use of a function (function:string-match) to match the name "administrator" to the subject of the requestor. If a SAML authentication assertion is being used to identify the subject, an XSL transformation can be used to convert from the SAML syntax to the XACML "//xacmlContext/Request/Subject/Attribute[@DataType='identifier:role']" syntax.

```
<?xml version="1.0" encoding="UTF-8"?>
<Rule RuleId="//example.com/rules/rule4" Effect="Deny"
xmlns="urn:oasis:names:tc:xacml:0.15i:policy"
xmlns:function="urn:oasis:names:tc:xacml:0.15i:function"
xmlns:identifier="urn:oasis:names:tc:xacml:0.15i:identifier"
xmlns:saml="urn:oasis:names:tc:SAML:1.0:assertion"
xmlns:xsi="http://www.w3.org/2001/XMLSchema-instance"
xsi:schemaLocation="urn:oasis:names:tc:xacml:0.15i:policy
http://www.oasis-open.org/tc/xacml/v15/draft-xacml-schema-policy-15i.xsd">
<Description>An administrator shall not be permitted to read
or write medical elements of a patient record</Description>
<Target>
<Subjects MatchId="function:string-match" DataType="xs:boolean">
<AttributeDesignator Designator="//xacmlContext/Request/Subject/Attribute
[@DataType='identifier:role']" DataType="xs:string"/>
<Attribute DataType="xs:string">administrator</Attribute>
</Subjects>
<Resources MatchId="function:anyURI-equal" DataType="xs:boolean">
<AttributeDesignator Designator=
"//xacmlContext/Request/Resource/@ResourceURI" DataType="xs:anyURI"/>
<Attribute DataType="xs:anyURI">//example.com/record/medical.*
</Attribute>
</Resources>
<Actions MatchId="function:subset" DataType="xs:boolean">
<AttributeDesignator Designator="//xacmlContext/Action[@Namespace=]"
DataType="xs:string"/>
<Attribute DataType="xs:string">read write</Attribute>
</Actions>
</Target>
</Rule>
```

A "Policy" in XACML

The definition of policy in XACML is perhaps the most important aspect of the specification. It means that an organization can use a single policy to enforce access to many different devices and systems. XACML uses the element name "policyStatement" to express information about a policy in XML format. A policyStatement element includes the following content:

- PolicyID
- MetaPolicy
- Effect
- Target

- Rules
- Rule-combining algorithm
- Obligations

Each policy may reference one or more rules, linked together using a rule-combining algorithm. XACML formalizes the algorithms used to link rules together to make policies, and, as we'll see later, the algorithms to link together policies to make metapolicy. The target of a policy statement is used by the PDP to determine where the policy is applicable for a particular request. If the target is already identified in the rules, it does not need to be included in the policy statement. An *obligation* is defined as an action to be performed once the authorization decision is complete. An example of an obligation would be the creation of a digitally signed record each time a person's medical records are accessed.

The following is an example of a policy that includes the four rules we saw in the rules section of this chapter. Each rule is referenced in a <RuleDesignator> element. Notice that two of the rules are referenced by their RuleID value, one is included as a base64-encoded digest, and one rule is included in its entirety.

The target of the policy is defined in the subelements of the <Target> element. The target specifies the subjects (who), resources (what), and actions (for example, read, write) of the policy. Because the individual rules that make up the policy will already have subjects, resources, and actions, a decision must be made about how to combine these into a target space for an overall policy.

The target of a policy must include all the decision requests that it is intended to evaluate. The target may be declared by the writer of the policy or computed from the targets of its component rules.

If the target of the policy statement is to be determined from the targets of the component rules, two approaches are allowed:

- The target of the policy may be the union of the target definitions for resource, subject, and action that are contained in the component rules.
- The target of the policy may be the intersection of the target definitions for resource, subject, and action that are contained in the component rules.

The rule-combining algorithm, specified by the RuleCombiningAlgId identifier, indicates the algorithm by which the results of evaluating the component rules are combined when evaluating the policy. In the case of the following example, "denyOverrides" means that a deny decision from a rule overrides a permit decision from another rule. The alternative would be "permitOverrides."

```
<?xml version="1.0" encoding="UTF-8"?>
<PolicyStatement PolicyId="//medico.com/rules/policy5" RuleCombiningAlgId=
"urn:oasis:names:tc:XACML:identifier:ruleCombiningAlgorithms:denyOverrides"
xmlns="urn:oasis:names:tc:xacml:0.15i:policy"
xmlns:function="urn:oasis:names:tc:xacml:0.15i:function"
```

```
xmlns:saml="urn:oasis:names:tc:SAML:1.0:assertion"
xmlns:xsi="http://www.w3.org/2001/XMLSchema-instance" xsi:schemaLocation=
"urn:oasis:names:tc:xacml:0.15i:policy draft-xacml-schema-policy-15i.xsd">
<Target>
<Subjects MatchId="function:superset" DataType="xs:boolean">
<AttributeDesignator Designator=
"//xacmlContext/Request/Subject/Attribute[@DataType='identifier:role']"
DataType="xs:string"/>
<Attribute DataType="xs:string"></Attribute>
</Subjects>
<Resources MatchId="function:anyURI-equal" DataType="xs:boolean">
<AttributeDesignator Designator=
"//xacmlContext/Request/Resource/@ResourceURI" DataType="xs:anyURI"/>
<Attribute DataType="xs:anyURI">//example.com/record/medical.*
</Attribute>
</Resources>
<Actions MatchId="function:subset" DataType="xs:boolean">
<AttributeDesignator Designator="//xacmlContext/Action[@Namespace=]"
DataType="xs:string"/>
<Attribute DataType="xs:string">read</Attribute>
</Actions>
</Target>
<RuleSet>
<RuleDesignator>
<RuleId>//example.com/rules/rule1</RuleId>
</RuleDesignator>
<RuleDesignator>
<RuleDigest Base64Digest="H7jiE0+jwkn63k/JhB3+D9aI4V3J9z/o0"/>
</RuleDesignator>
<Rule RuleId="//example.com/rules/rule3" Effect="Permit">
<Description>A physician may write any medical element for
which he or she is the designated primary care physician</Description>
<Condition FunctionId="function:and" DataType="xs:boolean">
<Function FunctionId="function:string-equal" DataType="xs:boolean">
<AttributeDesignator Designator=
"//xacmlContext/Request/Subject/SubjectId" DataType="xs:string"/>
<AttributeDesignator Designator=
"//xacmlContext/Request/Resource/physicianName" DataType="xs:string"/>
</Function>
<Function FunctionId="function:present" DataType="xs:boolean">
<AttributeDesignator Designator=
"//xacmlContext/Request/Resource/patient/email" DataType="xs:string"/>
</Function>
</Condition>
</Rule>
<RuleDesignator>
<RuleId>//example.com/rules/rule4</RuleId>
</RuleDesignator>
</RuleSet>
```

```
<Obligations>
<Obligation ObligationId="//example.com/emailer" FulfilOn="Permit">
<AttributeDesignator Designator=
"//xacmlContext/Request/Resource/patient/email" DataType="xs:string"/>
<AttributeAssignment DataType="xs:string" AttributeId=
"//medico.com/text">Your medical record has been accessed
by:</AttributeAssignment>
<AttributeDesignator Designator=
"//xacmlContext/Request/Subject/SubjectId" DataType="xs:string"/>
</Obligation>
</Obligations>
</PolicyStatement>
```

The Definition of Metapolicy in XACML

As we've seen, a policy can refer to a *metapolicy*. A metapolicy combines policies and allows for a hierarchy-based resolution of policy conflicts (for example, if two policies differ on their decision). When policies are combined, similar rule-combining algorithms (for example, "DenyOverrides" or "PermitOverrides") are used to determine the composite policy. When multiple policies are used, multiple policy administration points (PAPs) may be in operation. Metapolicies are important new features that were impossible before XACML.

XACML Architecture: PIPs, PEPs, PRPs, PAPs, and PDPs

XACML shares architectural concepts and jargon with SAML. There are many entities whose three-letter acronyms begin with a *P* and end with a *P*. The first *P* always stands for *policy*, which is a set of rules that may be combined. The third *P* always stands for *point*, and indicates that this XACML component occupies a place in the XACML architecture. Note that although each of these entities is called a "point," there is no reason why they all have to be on different computers.

Figure 7-1 shows an XACML architectural diagram. This chain of XACML entities shown in the diagram uses the context of a Web Service request. A SOAP request is received and intercepted by a policy enforcement point, and the allow/deny decision involves the collaboration of many other XACML entities. The response of the Web Service depends on the results of XACML policy effect.

The steps in Figure 7-1 are numbered in the order of execution. Information from the incoming SOAP request is intercepted by the policy enforcement point (PEP) in step 1 and used to construct a SAML authorization decision query. The results of this query determine if the request is to be granted access to the Web Service. The authorization decision query sends details of the resource requested (that is, the Web Service) to the policy decision point (PDP), along with details of the identity of the requestor. The identity information is taken from the Web Service request. This identity information may come from an X.509 certificate used for SSL authentication or contained in the SOAP message itself (for example, a WS-Security BinarySecurityToken element), or from the NameIdentifier element in a SAML authentication assertion.

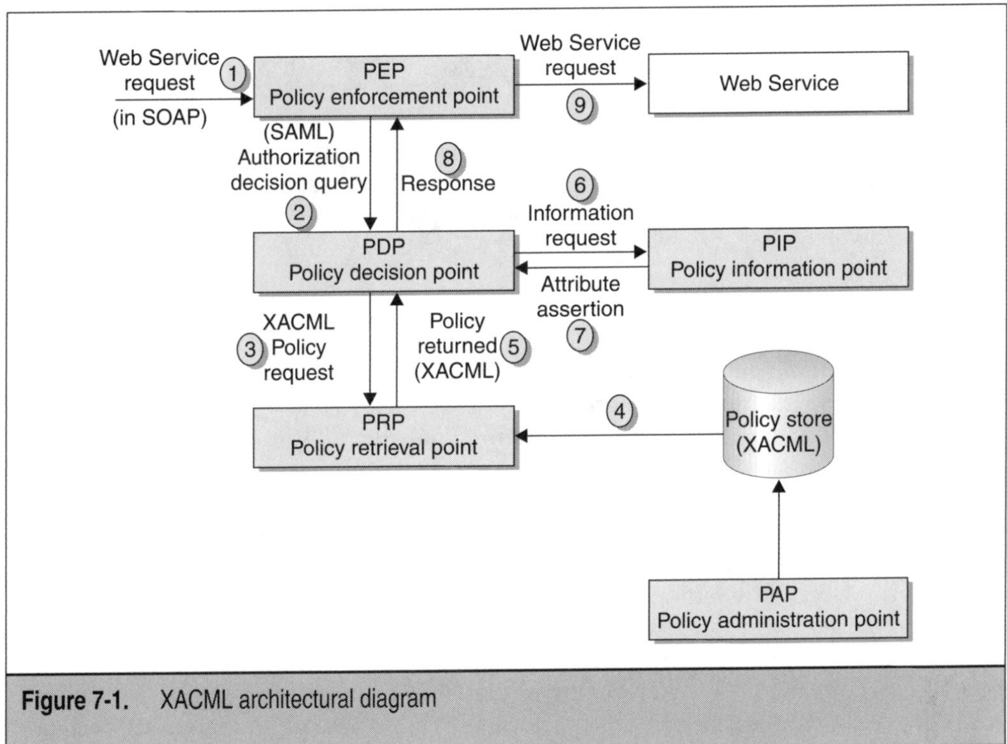

Figure 7-1. XACML architectural diagram

TIP Although Figure 7-1 shows a single PEP talking to the PDP, when multiple SOAP endpoints must be protected, it is more efficient to distribute the XACML architecture so that multiple PEPs talk to one PDP. A distributed architecture means that a policy can be enforced across multiple XML gateways into an organization. It also has clear benefits for policy version control, because multiple policies do not have to be synchronized between multiple PDPs.

The policy is retrieved by the PDP from the policy retrieval point (PRP). This is shown in steps 3 and 5. In most cases, the PRP will be located on the same physical machine as the PDP, meaning that the policy request (step 3) does not have to travel across the network and be subjected to network latency. The PDP may cache the policy information that it receives (step 5) from the policy retrieval point.

If the policy information for the resource is not available at the PRP, it may be retrieved from a policy store. That situation would occur if the resource has never been accessed before, or if the policy is being refreshed. The policy store is shown on the right in Figure 7-1. It must be capable of importing or exporting XACML. Rules are combined into policies by an administrator using a policy administration point (PAP). This would generally take the form of a console that allows the administrator to create rules, tying together subjects (users or computers that require access), resources (data and systems to which access will be required), and attributes (predicates for rules). These rules may then be combined together. Rules may also be imported or exported as XACML.

Although XACML may be used to import and export rules, it is not a requirement that the policies actually are stored as XACML in the policy store. An XML database, such as Software AG's Tamino, may be used for storage of XACML in its native format. Alternatively, a relational database with an XML interface—for example, Oracle 9i or Microsoft SQL Server 2000—may be used.

Steps 6 and 7 show a policy information point being used to calculate a *predicate* of a rule. Remember that a predicate in XACML is defined as "the ability to query an attribute." The attribute may be an attribute of the subject or an "environmental" attribute. An example of an attribute of the subject would be their role in a Role-Based Access Control (RBAC) system. An example environmental attribute would be the time of day (for example, access to a service may only be allowed during normal working hours). The attribute information is returned as a SAML attribute assertion (step 7).

Once the PDP has received all the information it needs in order to make a decision, it evaluates the rule and, if the result is that access is granted, then it returns a SAML authorization decision assertion to the PEP. This may be inserted into the SOAP message that is forwarded to the target Web Service (step 9).

Rules are enforced by a policy enforcement point (PEP). An example of a PEP would be a Web Service that receives incoming requests for resources and connects to a PDP in order to query authorization decisions for these resources. Although the authorization decision may be made elsewhere (that is, at the PDP), the rule is enforced at the Web Service that is receiving the request.

TIP Although a policy enforcement point must, by definition, be capable of receiving incoming SOAP requests, it is important that other pieces of SAML and XACML architecture are not exposed to untrusted communications. For example, the policy administration point should not be contactable from the "outside world," which would carry the danger that an intruder could change the policy or launch a denial of service attack on the policy store. It is recommended that the only portion of the XACML architecture to sit outside the firewall should be the policy enforcement point.

Let's look at an example of an authorization decision query that is sent by a PEP to a PDP, referencing the resource where access is being attempted. For the purposes of this example, we will assume that the SOAP message indicates to the Web Services whose medical records are being requested by using an XPath expression. For example, the records of Joe User may be requested by passing the following XML fragment in a SOAP message:

```
<RequestedPatientDetails>//medicalRecord/patient/Joe User
...
</RequestedPatientDetails>
```

Note that an XML-style hierarchical structure is used to represent the information. This does not mean that XACML can only be used for access control to XML-based information. The hierarchical structure can be applied to other data—for example, the contents of a file system.

The PEP searches the incoming SOAP message for this element and constructs an authorization decision query targeted at the PDP. The authorization decision query might look like the following:

```
<AuthorizationDecisionQuery Resource="//medicalRecord/patient/Joe
User">
</AuthorizationDecisionQuery>
```

A policy retrieval point (PRP) receives the policy for a particular decision request. The PDP connects to the PRP to retrieve the policy for a particular decision request.

Combining these together, the PDP issues an authorization decision—the decision is based on the policy rules, such as the "patient name = name of the requester" rule that we've discussed, and may also depend on a PIP (say, to query the role of a patient). Policy is configured by a PAP, and retrieved by the PDP from a PRP. If a rule has no *predicate*, meaning that no attributes need to be queried for this rule (for example, " no access whatsoever is allowed to this resource"), no information request to a PIP is necessary.

If the outcome of the decision is to permit access to the patient medical records, the following authorization decision statement would be sent back to the PEP:

```
<Response xmlns:="urn:oasis:names:tc:SAML:1.0:protocol"
xmlns:saml="urn:oasis:names:tc:SAML:1.0:assertion">
<saml:Assertion>
<saml:AuthorizationDecisionStatement Resource=
"//medicalRecord/patient/Joe User" Decision="Permit">
<saml:Subject>
<saml:NameIdentifier SecurityDomain="example.com"
Name="MedicalRecords"/>
</saml:Subject>
<saml:Actions>
<saml:Action>Read</saml:Action>
</saml:Actions>
</saml:AuthorizationDecisionStatment>
</saml:Assertion>
</Response>
```

Processing SOAP Requests

We see in Figure 7-1 that our example rule applies to access to a Web Service, and the rule is enforced by a PEP. The PEP receives SOAP requests and makes an authorization decision query to a PDP. In this scenario, we need to enforce the rule that states that the identity of the party requesting the medical records must be the same as the identity of the subject of the medical records. Therefore, we need to find out the identity of the person on whose behalf the SOAP request is being made, so that we can check this against the name of the person whose medical records are being accessed.

Using a SAML Attribute in an Authorization Decision Request

Recall from Chapter 3 that the identity of the SOAP requestor is not necessarily the same as the identity of the end user on whose behalf the SOAP request is being made. To find out who is actually running the Web Service, we can look into the SOAP request to find a security token. An example of a security token is a SAML authorization assertion. This contains information about the authentication act of the end user (for example, "Joe User authenticated using a password at 9 A.M. on December 1"). In addition, an attribute assertion in the SOAP message can indicate attributes of the end user—for example, their role as defined in an RBAC system.

The following is an example of an authorization decision request to a PDP that uses a SAML authentication assertion and also a SAML attribute assertion:

```
<?xml version="1.0" encoding="UTF-8"?>
<Request xmlns="urn:oasis:names:tc:xacml:0.15i:context"
xmlns:ds="http://www.w3.org/2000/09/xmldsig#"
xmlns:identifier="urn:oasis:names:tc:xacml:identifier"
xmlns:xacml="urn:oasis:names:tc:xacml:0.15i:policy"
xmlns:xsi="http://www.w3.org/2001/XMLSchema-instance"
xsi:schemaLocation="urn:oasis:names:tc:xacml:0.15i:context
http://www.oasis-open.org/tc/xacml/v15/draft-xacml-schema-context-15i.xsd">
<Subject>
 <SubjectId Format="xsi:string">Joe User</SubjectId>
</Subject>
<Resource>
<ResourceSpecifier Format="xsi:anyURI" Scope="Descendants"
ResourceId="/record/patient/Joe User"/>
</Resource>
<Action Namespace="">read</Action>
<Environment>
<EnvironmentAttribute AttributeId=
"urn:oasis:names:tc:SAML:1.0:Assertion" DataType="xsi:string">
<saml:Assertion AssertionID="64578390"
Issuer="example.com" IssueInstant="2002-03-08T08:23:47-05:00"
MajorVersion="0" MinorVersion="28"
xmlns="urn:oasis:names:tc:SAML:1.0:assertion"
xmlns:ds="http://www.w3.org/2000/09/xmldsig#"
xmlns:xsi="http://www.w3.org/2001/XMLSchema-instance" xsi:schemaLocation=
"http://www.oasis-open.org/committees/security/docs/
cs-sstc-schema-assertion-01.xsd">
<saml:AuthenticationStatement AuthenticationInstant=
```

```
"2002-03-08T08:23:45-05:00" AuthenticationMethod="http://www.oasis-
open.org/committees/security/docs/draft-sstc-core-28/password-sha1">
<saml:Subject>
<saml:NameIdentifier NameQualifier="\\medico.com">
Joe User
</saml:NameIdentifier>
<saml:SubjectConfirmation>
<saml:ConfirmationMethod>
http://www.oasis-open.org/committees/security/docs/
draft-sstc-core-24/artifact
</saml:ConfirmationMethod>
</saml:SubjectConfirmation>
</saml:Subject>
<saml:SubjectLocality IPAddress="1.2.3.4"/>
</saml:AuthenticationStatement>
</saml:Assertion>
</EnvironmentAttribute>
<EnvironmentAttribute AttributeId="urn:oasis:names:tc:SAML:1.0:Assertion"
DataType="xsi:string">
<saml:Assertion MajorVersion="0"
MinorVersion="28" AssertionID="68938960"
Issuer="example.com" IssueInstant="2000-06-15T15:02:39-05:00"
xmlns="urn:oasis:names:tc:SAML:1.0:assertion"
xmlns:ds="http://www.w3.org/2000/09/xmldsig#"
xmlns:xsi="http://www.w3.org/2001/XMLSchema-instance" xsi:schemaLocation=
"http://www.oasis-open.org/committees/security/docs/
cs-sstc-schema-assertion-01.xsd">
<saml:AttributeStatement>
<saml:Subject>
 <saml:NameIdentifier NameQualifier=
"\\example.com">Joe User</saml:NameIdentifier>
</saml:Subject>
<saml:Attribute AttributeName="role"
AttributeNamespace="//example.com">
<saml:AttributeValue>Patient</saml:AttributeValue>
</saml:Attribute>
</saml:AttributeStatement>
</saml:Assertion>
</EnvironmentAttribute>
</Environment>
</Request>
```

In this example, we can see that Joe User authenticated using a password credential, which was verified against a SHA-1 digest. We can also see when Joe User authenticated.

Below the authentication assertion, we see the attribute assertion. This indicates that Joe User has the role of Patient. All of this information is used by the PDP to produce an authorization decision assertion.

Digital Rights Management

Digital Rights Management (DRM) provides a compelling use case for XACML. DRM distinguishes between the *content provider, content clearinghouse, customer,* and *content distributor*. In DRM, content distributors make digital works available over the Internet. Customers purchase rights to these works—for example, the right to download and view them. The customer must be authenticated, so that the customer pays. Payment is handled by a content clearinghouse. This may be the same entity as the content provider, or they may be separate entities. The content provider is the owner of the legal rights to the work. An example of a content provider is a record company, which owns the legal rights to songs.

DRM Policy Using XACML

We have seen how XACML allows the creation of rules, which are consolidated into policies. In the case of DRM, it is a useful exercise to think about how access control rules for online content can be expressed, taking into account that the content provider must be paid.

The payment of the content provider maps to the use of *obligations* in XACML. If the content provider is also acting as a content clearinghouse, then after the work is issued to the customer, the PEP must execute payment to the content provider. If the content provider and content clearinghouse are not the same entity, an obligation can be defined such that the PEP must notify the content clearinghouse of the purchase.

The authentication of the end user is important if payment enforcement requires information about the end user. However, the policy may require that the information about the content provider is also required. This would be required if it must be proved that the content provider is indeed legally allowed to confer rights to this work. An example would be a video-on-demand service, which must be able to prove that it is allowed, by the movie publisher, to offer a movie for download.

DRM policy may be required to be dynamic, in which case information requests from a PIP to a PEP can be used to find out attributes of the work (such as the number of downloads permissible).

Security Considerations When Using XACML

XACML, as we have seen, is a powerful method for defining rules, policies, and metapolicies. The architecture of XACML with PEPs, PDPs, and so forth has important security requirements that influence implementation decisions. XACML applies the advantages of XML to access control, but the XML communications involved in a XACML architecture must also be secure. As with all security discussions in this book, we will concentrate on the high-level principles of security and see how they apply.

Authentication

It is important for a PEP to authenticate the identity of the PDP to which it sends decision requests. Furthermore, the PDP must trust the identity of PIPs to which it sends information requests.

It is equally important for a PDP to authenticate the identity of its clients and assess the level of trust to determine what, if any, sensitive data should be passed.

The authentication techniques that we encountered in Chapter 2 may be used to provide this authentication, including signature-based authentication, transport-level or session-level authentication, or the use of a private network.

Confidentiality

In Chapter 3, we saw that confidentiality means that the contents of a message can be read only by the desired recipients and not by anyone else who intercepts the message while it is in transit. There are two areas in which confidentiality should be considered: one is confidentiality during transmission, and the other is confidentiality within a <policyStatement> itself. Confidentiality during transmission can be achieved by using encryption on the transport that is used—say, a VPN or IPSec. Confidentiality within the policy statement can be used, for example, to hide details of payment amounts that are to be enforced as an obligation of a rule. When the policy is being stored, or sent, the payment details can be selectively encrypted using XML Encryption (see Chapter 5 for details on how this can be achieved).

Integrity

Because processing of policy statement documents by a PDP is at the core of the XACML architecture, it is important that these documents cannot be changed without detection. In many cases, this can be achieved at the system level by ensuring the integrity of the systems, including PAPs and PRPs, and implementing confidentiality between parties.

However, when policy is distributed between organizations to be acted on at a later time, or when the policy travels with data, it is appropriate to have a digital signature of the policy included with the policy statements. XML Signature is the ideal candidate to provide this (see Chapter 4 for more information about XML Signature).

Trust Model

Although beyond the scope of XACML, a trust model must be in place for a XACML architecture to be enabled. The use of keys for digital signatures and encryption assumes that the identity of an entity can be linked to the keys. Various forms of a trust model can be used, including PKI (hierarchical trust) and PGP (a web of trust).

Privacy

XACML enables access control, but ironically the system itself requires access control for various reasons, including privacy. Information about the role of a user (for example, their membership in a certain group or their credit status) is private information and should not be disclosed to third parties. This means that when the information is stored, processed, or sent, it should be kept confidential.

CHECKLIST

- ☐ Remember that XACML defines both architecture and syntax. The syntax is a means of defining access control rules, policies, and metapolicies. The architecture defines how various entities process these XACML documents to perform access control.
- ☐ Ensure that a XACML architecture only exposes the policy enforcement point (PEP) to incoming XML traffic.
- ☐ Consider organizing non-XML data into a hierarchical XML-like structure.
- ☐ When choosing a SAML or XACML product, ensure that the product can support policy enforcement at multiple entry points into the organization, but with centralized policy administration.

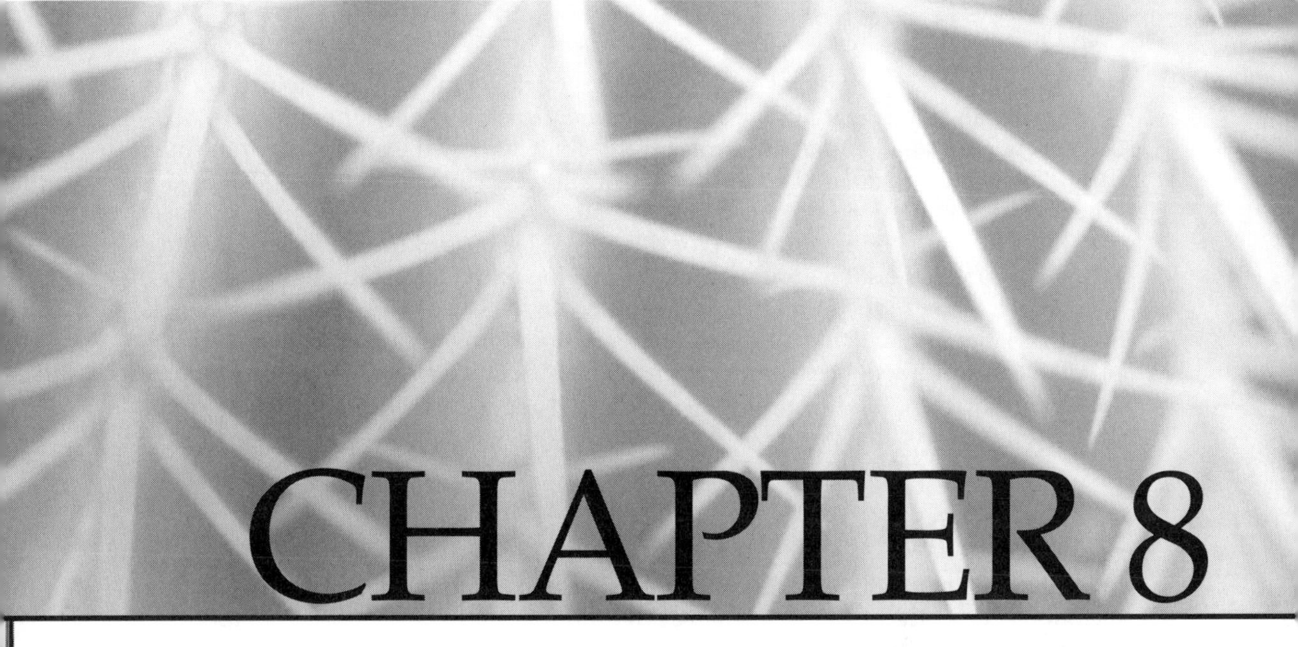

CHAPTER 8

XML Key Management Specification (XKMS)

In previous chapters, we have seen how cryptography may be used to protect the integrity and confidentiality of XML documents using XML Signature and XML Encryption, provided that the sender and recipient know the public key of the other party. This need is addressed by the XML Key Management Specification (XKMS), a Web Service that supports management of public keys.

XKMS 1.0 was submitted to the World Wide Web Consortium as a technical note in March 2001 and a working group formed to develop a standard. Although a number of vendors released products and prototypes based on the 1.0 specification, a number of minor variations were made during interoperability testing—leading to an unofficial XKMS 1.1 specification. Because no commercial products currently in use are based on the 1.0 specification, this chapter is based on the XKMS 2.0 specification currently being finalized by the working group.

PUBLIC KEY INFRASTRUCTURE

Public key technology is an exceptionally flexible and adaptable technology. Knowing the public key of the other party enables the confidentiality and integrity of any message or document to be protected. If the number of parties is small, this task is comparatively easy: the users can simply get together in a room and read out their public keys. However, once the number of users is too large for everyone to meet in the same room at the same time, the problem of distributing public keys becomes much harder.

Public Key Infrastructure (PKI) addresses this problem. In his original paper proposing the idea of public key cryptography, Whitfield Diffie proposed that public keys might be listed in a directory in much the same way that telephone numbers are. In order to send a message to Bob, Alice would look up his public key in the directory. This model has the advantage of simplicity, but at the time that it was proposed the Internet was neither ubiquitous nor reliable. This problem led Lauren Kohnfelder to propose that the individual entries should be signed by the maintainer to create a *certificate*. The certificate could then be distributed independently of the directory.

Over the years many PKIs have been proposed that have enjoyed varying degrees of success, most of which have been based on some form of digital certificate. A list of commonly cited PKIs is given in Table 8-1. Although the concepts behind PKI are

PKI Name	Comments
X.509	X.509 began as a certificate format for use with protocols in the Open Systems Interconnect (OSI) family. Despite the limited success of OSI protocols, X.509 certificates are the basis of the most widely used PKIs.
PKIX	Public Key Infrastructure X.509 (PKIX) began as a profile of the X.509 specification describing the use of X.509 certificates with IETF protocols such as SSL, S/MIME, and IPSEC. Since then, the PKIX group has defined extensions to the X.509 to the extent that PKI is often referenced as a PKI model in its own right.

Table 8-1. Commonly Cited Public Key Infrastructures

PKI Name	Comments
PGP	Pretty Good Privacy (PGP) was designed by Phil Zimmerman in a reaction to what he saw as the unnecessarily complex and authoritarian procedures required to manage an X.509 certification authority. In the PGP model, any key holder may issue a certificate (in the PGP model, it is called a key signing). Over time the key signings created by a community of PGP users form a "web of trust."
SPKI	Simple Public Key Infrastructure has many similarities to PGP—any user may be a certificate issuer. Unlike PGP, however, the names used in SPKI are relative so that if Alice issues a certificate for 'Alice's Bob' that might or might not refer to a completely different person to 'Carol's Bob'. Because of this, SPKI has been called the first postmodern PKI. Although SPKI has been designated an "experimental" (that is, non-standards track) protocol by the IETF, the ideas behind SPKI have influenced other important work, in particular the design of aspects of the Microsoft .NET security framework.
DNSSEC	DNS Security is a special-purpose PKI designed to secure the Internet Domain Name System (DNS), which translates DNS names (for example, abc.com) into Internet addresses (for example, 10.23.0.4). Future extensions may permit DNSSEC to be used to secure applications, provided that DNSSEC itself has been successfully deployed.

Table 8-1. Commonly Cited Public Key Infrastructures *(continued)*

relatively simple, applying these ideas to solve real-world problems has proven to be far from simple. Providing even a summary of the full features of X.509 alone would take an entire chapter, and a description comprehensive enough to serve as a guide for a programmer would take an entire book.

PKI in Five Easy Points

Fortunately, it is possible to describe XKMS without explaining how any of these PKIs work. In fact, the whole objective of XKMS is to allow a programmer to use a PKI despite knowing only a little of what the PKI does and nothing of how the PKI does it. For the purposes of understanding this chapter it suffices to know the following five points:

1. A PKI manages credentials.
2. A credential states the name of the holder of the private key corresponding to a public key.
3. A name may be the name of a person or company or a network name such as an e-mail address.
4. Before issuing a credential the credential issuer should authenticate the request to ensure that the party requesting the credential is both
   a. the legitimate user of the specified name, and
   b. the actual holder of the private key associated with the specified public key

5. Once issued, credentials may in certain circumstances be revoked, for example if
   a. the private key is compromised in some way (lost, accidentally disclosed)
   b. information in the credential is found to be invalid
   c. the key holder has broken the issuer's terms of use

XKMS AND PKI

PKI is complex because the issues it deals with are complex. PKI provides a means of linking an identity in the physical world with an online identity. The concept of identity in the physical world is very complex. A given name may correspond to many people and a single person may use many names. Naming of corporations is even more complex. The name Rolls Royce is for most people synonymous with luxury automobiles, but Rolls Royce Plc., which owns the Rolls Royce trademark actually makes aircraft engines.

Attempts to produce a "simple" PKI have invariably ended up merely transferring complexity from one place to another, often increasing the difficulty of the task in the process. For this reason, XKMS does not attempt to eliminate the complexity of PKI; instead it allows that complexity to be transferred from a place where it is hard to manage (the application client) to a managed service that can specialize in PKI management.

XKMS is a Web Service that provides an interface to a PKI. An application accessing a PKI through an XKMS service is shielded from the complexities of the underlying PKI (see the following illustration). In effect, the complexity of the PKI is transferred from the client to the XKMS service.

TIP One of the most difficult to implement parts of a PKI is the user interface. Shielding the application from the complexity of PKI allows the user to be likewise shielded from complex configuration panels.

Moving the complexity of PKI management from the application to the XKMS service has many advantages. It is worth spending some time on these advantages because the problems of PKI deployment addressed by XKMS are common to a great many e-commerce applications, and the advantages of XKMS are in many cases the advantages of the Web Services architecture.

Reduced Client Complexity

One of the original design goals for XKMS was to allow handheld devices such as the then planned Microsoft Pocket PC to have full access to PKI functionality, despite limited memory and user interface capabilities. An XKMS client interface library may be coded in a few thousand lines of code on a machine that already provides the necessary XML and SOAP support. Even a partial implementation of the PKIX specification is likely to involve a hundred times that amount of code.

Ease of Coding

Traditional PKIs became so complex that the ease of coding ceased to be a major concern in their design. It was assumed that application developers would use some form of toolkit or operating system layer to support PKI functions. This approach had many disadvantages, not least the fact that the PKI toolkits tended to be developed by PKI vendors—and consequently tended to be rather better at interconnecting to PKI products sold by the vendor that wrote it than being a strictly correct implementation of the PKIX standard. Another disadvantage is that toolkits only eliminate the need to implement complex functionality; the need to test remains as does the need to provide a user interface. In many cases, these tasks are made more difficult as the toolkit implementation may be more complex than is strictly necessary for the implementation.

Although we present examples in this chapter of using the VeriSign Trust Service Integration Kit (TSIK), a full-featured XKMS client implementation may be written and tested in under a week if necessary.

The Client Deployment Problem

As the use of PKI has grown, the sophistication of the PKIX specification has increased considerably. Application support for these more sophisticated features has progressed at a much slower rate. One of the reasons for this slow pace of adoption has been that a PKI feature has little value until it is widely deployed, because any client that relies upon support for that feature will only be able to communicate within a very narrow circle. This creates a vicious circle—the feature has no value until it is widely supported, and application developers are understandably reluctant to add complex features to their programs that have little immediate value.

Even after a developer agrees to add support for a feature, there is a considerable delay before deployment becomes widespread. The product cycles of the major application vendors typically introduce a minimum delay of two years between adding a feature to the product requirements and the product reaching the market. There is then a further delay as the new products gradually replace the old. The cumulative effect of these delays is that deployment of a new PKI feature will typically take about ten years from initial design to the point where deployment is widespread enough for applications to rely on support.

XKMS removes the complexity of PKI from the client and transfers it to a trust service. This allows new PKI features to be deployed without making modifications to already deployed clients.

TIP XKMS is an ideal solution if some form of PKI support is required in an embedded device such as a router for a virtual private network. Such devices are required to be "install and forget" since customers do not want to have to regularly upgrade or replace them to keep up with developments in PKI technology.

Centralized Trust Management

Next to the problem of deploying PKI clients with the necessary features, the most common complaint from enterprises attempting to deploy (particularly) large PKIs is the complexity of configuring the clients to apply the enterprise security policy. XKMS allows PKI configuration to be managed as an enterprise resource rather than being left to individual user preferences. This is frequently essential if the PKI is going to be successful, because the preference of many end users is frequently to disable security altogether.

This feature of XKMS has drawn some criticism. One of the core doctrines of modern security protocol design is the *end-to-end* principle pioneered by MIT. That is, if Alice sends an e-mail message to Bob, the cryptography protecting the message should be applied in the device that Alice uses to generate the message (the sending end) and only removed in the device Bob uses to receive the message (the receiving end). According to the end-to-end principle, Alice and Bob should rely on the cryptography they control rather than the network to provide security.

The end-to-end principle has traditionally treated PKI as if it were simply another processing step and therefore something the end users should configure for themselves in each device they own. This first came into question in enterprise deployments, where the PKI is intended to implement the enterprise security policy rather than the personal preferences of individual employees. The "ends" of the communication may be in the devices, but the ends of the trust relationships are the enterprises that employ Alice and Bob rather than Alice and Bob themselves.

As devices with embedded PKI features start to become ubiquitous, the need for some form of centralized PKI management is becoming apparent even in consumer applications. Most consumers are likely to opt to have their PKI management performed for them by a specialist—in most cases as a service delivered through their network provider. The few consumers who have the inclination and necessary expertise to configure their own PKI can achieve full control through their own XKMS services.

TIP Consider adding XKMS support to an application even if you intend to provide comprehensive native support for PKIX/X.509. Doing so will allow your customers to make their own choices with respect to PKI configuration rather than rely on the choices you make for them.

THE XKMS PROTOCOL

The XKMS specification defines two Web Services. The XML Key Registration Service Specification supports operations that manage the life cycle of public key credentials. The XML Key Information Service Specification (X-KISS) supports query operations that obtain and validate public key credentials. An XKMS service may support X-KRSS operations, X-KISS operations, or both.

Before discussing how X-KRSS and X-KISS allow public key credentials to be obtained and managed, we first consider the credentials themselves. XKMS is designed to provide an interface to any form of PKI. As such, the credentials managed by the PKI might have the form of X.509 certificates, PGP key signings, or possibly some new form of credential yet to be defined. In order to avoid committing XKMS to the design decisions of any one PKI, a new PKI credential is defined: the key binding association.

Key Binding Association

A key binding association is an assertion that the holder of the private key corresponding to a specified public key is associated with one or more identities and Internet protocol addresses.

This somewhat abstract definition is best explained by way of an example. If Bob holds the private key corresponding to the public key X, a key binding association might be created to state that fact. For the purposes of communicating with Internet users, a key binding association linking a public key to a real-world name is rather less useful than one that links the public key to an e-mail address, online chat service, or other form of Internet address.

For example, the following example of a key binding states that a particular set of RSA public key parameters (a modulus and exponent value) may be used with the protocol S/MIME (described in RFC 2633) for e-mail sent to or received from the e-mail address bob@bobcorp.test:

```
<KeyBinding>
    <KeyInfo>
        <ds:KeyValue>
            <ds:RSAKeyValue>
                <ds:Modulus>4i0BEhQ8Jc4tjwZYbvtMyYfBrIGOMx34K4Cdo2pAzo
GnV679FLmGHWnQy2cSj39hf5D1mIaPyD3j/33TdfglTaaKqp7IPf6ei754f0uI/r1HpX7uq
sw+j9LC4Z7GnG3yoY/eBJOZ8TRwMnx+MkwmopXPVLvhMWRyiUOcO3SEkTE=</ds:Modulus>
                <ds:Exponent>AQAB</ds:Exponent>
            </ds:RSAKeyValue>
        </ds:KeyValue>
    <UseKeyWith Application="urn:ietf:rfc:2633" Identifier="bob@bobcorp.test" />
</KeyBinding>
```

The XKMS key-binding element makes use of the KeyInfo element defined in XML Signature to specify the public key credentials. In this particular case, the public key credentials consist of the actual RSA public key parameters that an e-mail client would use to send encrypted e-mail to Bob. In the general case, however, the key binding may include any of the credentials supported by the XML Signature KeyInfo element—for example:

- An X.509 certificate
- A PGP key
- A SPKI certificate
- The actual cryptographic parameters of the key
- A new public key credential type
- A location from which any of the above may be obtained

The key binding associates the public key credential with additional information that allows an application to use it—for example:

- The cryptographic functions allowed for use with the credential: signature, encryption, and key exchange
- The application protocols that the credential may be used with such as S/MIME secure e-mail, SSL transport layer security, or IPSEC
- The earliest time the key binding information is valid and the time at which it has expired
- The status of the key binding information

XKMS defines four elements that define either an actual instance of a key binding or a request for a key binding to be found or created:

- **KeyBinding** A key binding instance issued by a trusted source that has been validated by that issuer
- **UnverifiedKeyBinding** A key binding instance issued by an untrusted source that requires verification
- **QueryKeyBinding** A template used to request a key binding instance using query by example
- **PrototypeKeyBinding** A template specifying the requested parameters of a key binding to be registered

Table 8-2 describes the members of the KeyBinding element.

Item	Description
Id@	A unique identifier for the key binding
Status	The key binding status
Status/StatusValue@	A QName that specifies the status of the key binding. Allowable values are xkms:Valid, xkms:Invalid, and xkms:Indeterminate
Status/ValidReason Status/InvalidReason Status/IndeterminateReason	Optional elements that specify the aspects of the key binding status that were determined to be valid, invalid, and indeterminate
ValidityInterval	The validity interval in which the particular instance of the key binding has the specified validity
ValidityInterval/NotBefore@	The time instant at which the validity interval begins
ValidityInterval/NotOnOrAfter@	The time instant at which the validity interval has ended
KeyInfo	The public key credentials to which the key binding association relates. The credentials may be specified as an actual key value, an X.509 certificate, PGP key signing, or any other form of public key credential supported by the XML Signature specification
KeyUsage	A QName that specifies the cryptographic key uses for which the key may be used. Allowable values are xkms:Encryption, xksm:Signature, and xkms:Exchange
UseKeyWith	The UseKeyWith element specifies a particular application and identifier with which the credentials specified in the key binding may be used
UseKeyWith/Application	A URI that specifies the application protocol with which the credential may be used. The specification defines values to be used for commonly used security protocols such as S/MIME, SSL, and IPSEC; other protocols may be specified by defining an appropriate URI
UseKeyWith/Identifier	Specifies the subject to which the credential corresponds within the specified application protocol
PolicyIdentifier/Policy@	A URI identifying the issuance policy

Table 8-2. Members of the KeyBinding Element

XKMS Protocol

The XKMS protocol is essentially a request-response protocol layered on SOAP, with optional embellishments described at the end of the chapter.

The request and result messages used in the individual XKMS operations share a common format. These common members are defined in Table 8-3.

Item	Description
Id@	A unique identifier for the message
Service@	The service URI of the XKMS service
Nonce@	Randomly generated information that is used in the extended protocol processing options to defeat replay and denial of service attacks
ds:Signature	An enveloped XML Signature that authenticates the XKMS message
OpaqueClientData	Optional information supplied by the client in a request that is returned unmodified in the response

Table 8-3. Members Common to Request and Result Elements

Additional members are defined for request messages, allowing the client to specify the protocol options it supports, the types of and maximum quantity of information to be provided in the response, and additional information used in the extended protocol options. These additional members are described in Table 8-4.

Additional members are defined for request messages, allowing the service to specify the result of the operation (success, failure, and so on) and binding the request to the response by means of the request Id. These additional members are described in Table 8-5.

Item	Description
ResponseMechanism	Specifies any extended protocol options supported by the client for this request, such as asynchronous processing or the two-phase protocol. Multiple ResponseMechanism values may be specified
RespondWith	Specifies a data type that the client requests be present in the response, such as a key value, an X.509 certificate, or a certificate chain. Multiple RespondWith values may be specified
PendingNotification	Optionally specifies a means of notifying completion of the operation when asynchronous processing is used
OriginalRequestID@	This attribute is used in the extended protocol to specify the Id attribute of the initial request in a multistage request
ResponseLimit@	The maximum number of key binding elements that the service should return in a response

Table 8-4. Members of the Request Element

Item	Description
ResultMajor	The principal result code of the XKMS operation
ResultMinor	The secondary result code of the XKMS operation, giving additional information such as a reason for the result
RequestId	The Id attribute of the corresponding request

Table 8-5. Members of the Response Element

XML KEY INFORMATION SERVICE SPECIFICATION

The X-KISS protocol supports two services, *locate* and *validate*. Both services answer queries of the form "What are the public key credentials that I should to communicate with X using protocol Y?" The difference between the services is that the locate service may return information that has not been validated as trustworthy by the service. A validate service must only return information that is considered trustworthy in accordance with a specific trust policy.

Locate

A locate service functions like a directory. It is the responsibility of the client to validate all information returned by the locate service. A locate service may filter the information it returns to ensure that only information that is trustworthy is returned, but it is not required to do so. A locate service may be operated in a trustworthy manner, but a client using the service must not rely on the machine operating the service being secure.

As a result of these restrictions, a locate service is typically used for distributing signed credentials such as X.509 certificates or PGP key signing information that are authenticated by a third party.

A locate request contains one QueryKeyBinding that identifies the key binding for which information is request.If the locate operation is successful the response contains one or more UnverifiedKeyBinding elements. These elements are shown in Table 8-6.

Request Element	Description
QueryKeyBinding	Template that identifies the key binding requested
Response Element	**Description**
UnverifiedKeyBinding	Key binding information returned by the locate service

Table 8-6. Request and Response Elements of the Locate Service

TIP The XKMS locate function was designed as a replacement for the directory services traditionally associated with PKIs. The XKMS locate function is designed to support the exact query functionality required by a PKI-enabled application and as a result is considerably simpler to implement than configuring an LDAP or X.500 directory for the same purpose.

CAUTION Information provided by locate should not be relied on without first verifying it. This may be done by either forwarding the response data to a trusted XKMS validate service or by performing the appropriate certificate chain validation rules.

Example 8-1: Sending an Encrypted E-mail Alice wants to send an encrypted e-mail to Bob whose e-mail address is bob@xyz.newcorp.com. To do this, she must find Bob's certificate. Her e-mail client makes an XKMS locate request for Bob's e-mail encryption certificate to the XKMS locate service of Bob's company (don't worry about how Alice finds this service; we will discuss this later on). The e-mail client then performs PKIX certificate chain validation to decide whether Bob's certificate is trustworthy and, if this is the case, sends the encrypted e-mail to Bob. This is shown in the illustration.

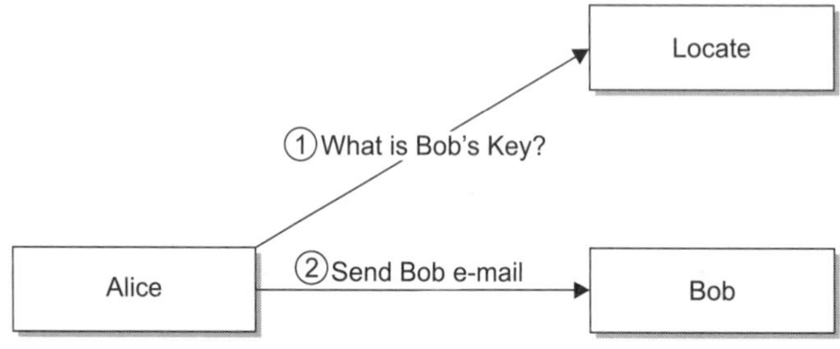

NOTE In XKMS 2.0, the e-mail application identifies the security protocol (S/MIME) and e-mail address explicitly. In the XKMS 1.0 specification, the e-mail address is specified as a URL (mailto:bob@xyz,newcorp.com), which required the service to try to guess which security protocol the client intended to use.

Example 8-2: Building Trust Paths in a Complex PKI Delegating the problem of finding trust paths to an XKMS service allows a simple client to access the functions of a very complex and sophisticated PKI—for example, the federal bridge CA currently being established by the U.S. federal government. Initial proposals for a PKI to support the U.S. government agencies ran into interminable political arguments as various agencies argued over who should be "in charge." This led to a proposal for a "bridge CA" that allows the various agencies to communicate securely without ceding authority or recognition to another agency. Each agency is the "root of trust" for its own PKI. The individual agencies each recognize and are recognized by the bridge CA as a peer.

The following illustration shows a (somewhat simplified) example of using the bridge CA. Alice works for the Executive Office of the President (EOP) while Bob works for the National Security Agency (NSA). Alice and Bob both regard the agency they work for as their root of trust. So to send an encrypted e-mail to Bob, Alice's e-mail client must find the trust path from the EOP CA through the bridge CA, and the NSA CA to Bob (shown in bold arrows). To send an encrypted reply, Bob's e-mail client must find the trust path from the NSA root through the bridge CA, to the EOP CA, and then to Alice.

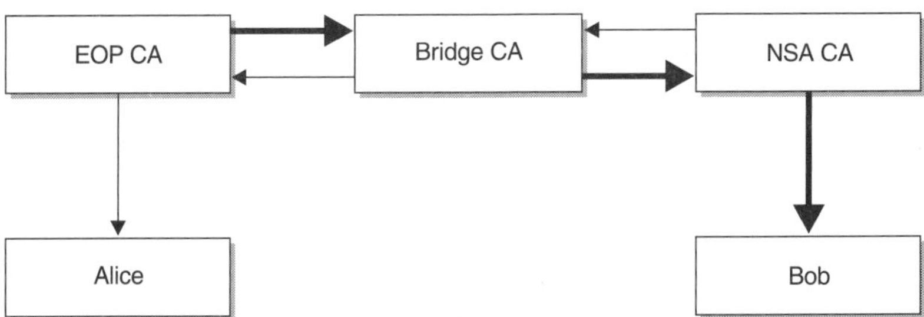

This process becomes complex, especially when considering the larger problem of bridging the U.S. government PKI to the PKIs maintained by other governments (for example, allies in NATO), universities, suppliers, and so forth. XKMS hides this complexity from the application, allowing the application programmer to ignore the issue of how to navigate the various bridges to discover the trust path necessary to allow the communication to be secured.

Validate

A locate service does not provide any assurance that the key binding information it returns is trustworthy. A service of this type is useful for locating signed credentials such as certificates but still requires the client to do a substantial amount of work to check that the credential is valid and trustworthy.

The validate service provides all the functions of locate but returns a *trusted* key binding that has been validated in accordance with the policy of the validate service.

A validate request contains one QueryKeyBinding that identifies the key binding for which information is requested. If the operation is successful, the response contains one or more KeyBinding elements.

These elements are shown in Table 8-7.

Request Element	Description
QueryKeyBinding	Template that identifies the key binding requested
Response Element	**Description**
KeyBinding	Key binding information returned by the validate service

Table 8-7. Request and Response Elements of the Validate Service

The illustration shows an example of using a validation service in a corporate supply chain application. The Web Services administered by the sales and support departments both receive signed requests from customers that must be verified before the operations requested are performed. The sales and support machines forward the credentials provided in the request signatures to a local validate service that decides whether they are valid with respect to the corporate trust policy.

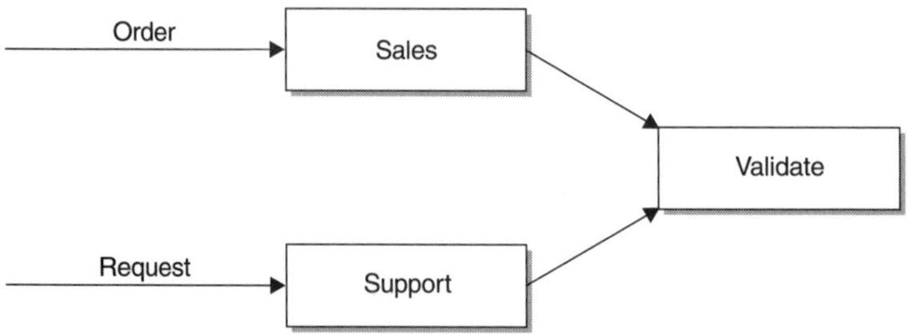

Centralizing the credential validation in this way allows the management of this task to be separated from the management of the sales and support functions. This might allow the sales or support functions to be outsourced to a service provider while still allowing the enterprise full control over the criteria used to evaluate credentials. Management of the XKMS validate service might also be outsourced to another third party, which might provide additional services such as insuring the individual transactions against fraudulent credential use.

A validate service is a trusted service. In computer security terms, a service is trusted if compromise of the trusted service could result in harm to the users or applications that rely upon it.

A trusted system is not necessarily a *trustworthy* system. A bank vault is a *trusted* system if it is used to store large quantities of money; however, it is not a trustworthy system if the combination lock is set to an easily guessed combination such as 1234. The steps required to make a system trustworthy depend on the degree of harm that could result from a compromise. Compromise of a PKI is likely to result in a very considerable degree of harm, so an XKMS validate service is likely to require a very substantial degree of physical security, network security, and operational security.

NOTE The need for particular care when returning trusted information is the reason that XKMS defines two separate services. Applications using a locate serve are required to validate the information returned before they rely on it. Because of this, a locate service may be operated in environments which lack the physical and information security precautions essential to the validate service.

CAUTION An application should only trust information from a validate service if the validate service has previously been identified as trustworthy.

Using the VeriSign TSIK to Perform Locate and Validate

The locate and validate services may be used from a Java program, using the VeriSign TSIK as follows:

- Create an XMLTransportSOAP object for the URL of the service
- Create an instance of the XKMSLocate or XKMSValidate object
- Send the request to the XKMS object using the send() method
- Process the response

The following code fragment shows an example of using the TSIK to locate the certificate corresponding to the specified key name using the VeriSign test service:

```
public static void Locate (String keyName, KeyPair signingKey)
      throws IOException, XKMSException, NoSuchAlgorithmException,
            InvalidKeySpecException, Exception
      {
      service = "http://interop-xkms.verisign.com/xkms/Acceptor.nano";
      XmlTransport transport = new XmlTransportSOAP(new URL(service));

      String responses[] = {XKMSLocate.KeyName, XKMSLocate.X509Cert};

      XKMSLocate locate = new XKMSLocate(keyName, responses, signingKey);
      XKMSLocateResponse response = locate.send(transport);

      System.out.println("Response status is " + response.getStatus());
      if (response.getStatus()) {
            System.out.println("KeyInfos is " + response.getXKMSKeyInfos());
            }
      }
```

Configuration Options

XKMS locate and validate services may be used in combination. A credential may be obtained from any number of untrusted locate services and then presented to a validate service for verification.

XKMS services may be combined in a referral configuration or a chained configuration. In the referral configuration, the client first makes a query to a locate service and then forwards the information to the validate service itself (see the following illustration).

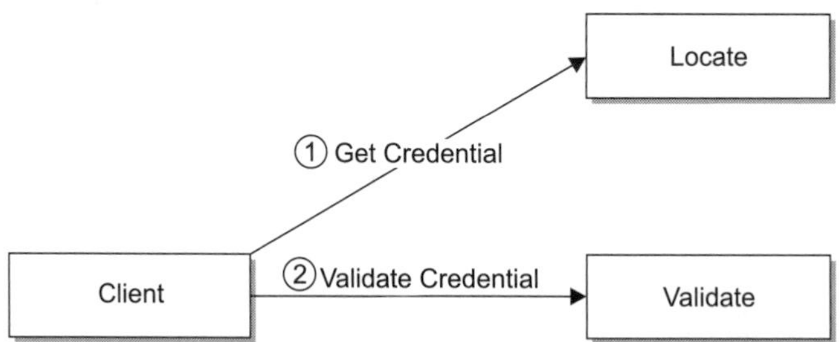

In the chained service model, the validate service performs the locate query on behalf of the client (see the following illustration). The chained service model moves all the decision-making tasks from the client and is therefore more generally applicable.

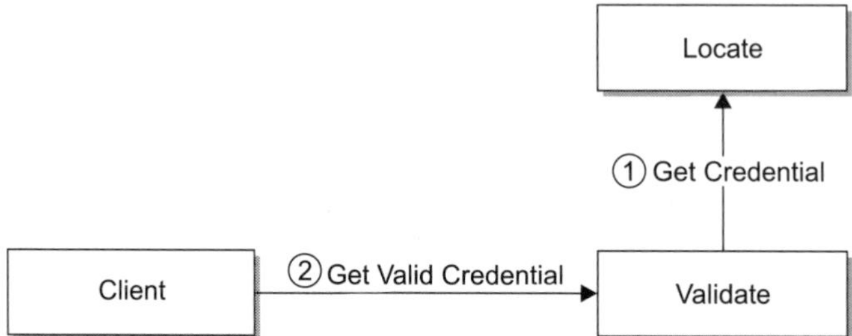

Locating X-KISS Locate Services So far we have discussed the use of X-KISS services to locate untrusted key binding information and hinted at the fact that there are likely to be many locate services in use. How, then, is a client meant to find the right locate service to direct a particular query to?

A possible solution would be to use a Web Services directory such as UDDI. This only postpones the issue, however, because it is very likely that there will be multiple UDDI services.

What is really needed is a way to use the Domain Name System (DNS) to translate Internet names into addresses, to advertise the existence of an XKMS service for a DNS domain. A recently defined extension to DNS called the SRV record does just that.

CAUTION The DNS system as currently deployed is insecure and so an application should not place any significant degree of trust in information received from DNS, including SRV records. The security of DNS will be greatly improved when the DNS Security specification being developed by the IETF is widely deployed.

The following illustration shows an example of using the SRV record to locate an XKMS service. In order to send a message to bob@xyzcorp.com, Alice's e-mail client first uses the DNS system to look up the SRV record that specifies the address of the XKMS service for XYZ Corp, which in this case is pki1.xyzcorp.com.

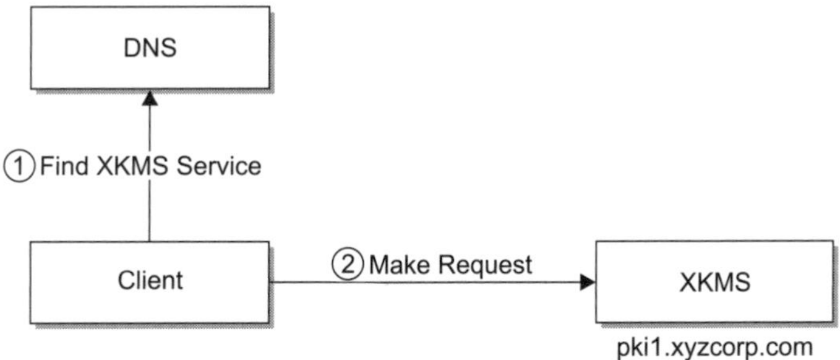

Trusting X-KISS Validate Services A validate service is a trusted service. In order to rely on the information supplied by the validate service, it must be authenticated in some way. This leads to the question of how the client validates the authentication key of the validate service.

At present, the deployed XKMS services typically use an X.509 certificate to authenticate messages from the service. This solution is clearly not optimal, however, because one of the objectives of XKMS is to allow clients to make use of a PKI without having to manage X.509 certificates.

At present, there is no standards group addressing this problem; however, a research paper outlining a possible solution has been published, and it is likely that a working group will be formed as soon as the XKMS 2.0 specification is completed.

XML Key Registration Service Specification

The X-KRSS protocol is used to establish and manage public key credentials. X-KRSS supports four services—register, recover, reissue, and revoke—which together allow the lifecycle of the public key credential to be managed from initial creation through to expiry or revocation.

Just as the X-KISS service allows applications to issue queries for any type of PKI credential through the abstract XKMS key binding concept, X-KRSS allows an application to manage any type of credential through the same key binding concept. Managing key bindings rather than the credentials themselves allows the application to be independent of the underlying PKI.

For example an e-mail client might register a public key to be used with S/MIME secure e-mail. The register service might then, in turn, create a certificate so that other S/MIME users could send encrypted mail to the user but the client itself need not be aware that this took place.

Authentication

Management of public keys requires a strong means of identifying the party requesting the particular operation. If Bob is going to trust the information registered with the service as Alice's public key, the service had better provide some degree of assurance that the key really does belong to Alice. Similarly if a service receives a request from "Alice" requesting that her information be modified in some way, or possibly revoked, the service had better first check that "Alice" really is the Alice intended.

This type of authentication problem is, of course, precisely the type of application for which PKI would normally be the solution. There is a problem however, Alice cannot be expected to use a public key to authenticate her first request for a public key. For this reason X-KRSS provides two basic means of authenticating requests, by means of a digital signature and by means of a one time use pass phrase. A digital signature is used for all requests made by operators or administrators who are managing another user's keys. The one time use pass phrase is used to identify the user in circumstances such as initial registration, where the user does not yet have a public key established.

A one time use pass phrase is similar to a password except that, as the name implies, it is intended to be used only once. As such it does not matter whether it is easy to remember or not. The one time use pass phrase is issued "out of band", that is outside the channels that are described by the XKMS specification. The security of the out of band communication method will largely determine the strength of authentication achieved.

The strongest form of authentication for normal use would be for the administrator of the register service to meet the applicant in person and verify their identity by means of government-issued documents such as a driver's license and passport. This level of authentication is not usually practical, however, and so in large enterprises where "in-person" authentication is required, the task of authentication is typically delegated to either managers or secretaries.

In many applications, however, it is perfectly acceptable to simply send the pass phrase to the registrant by e-mail. While the e-mail might be intercepted and read on its way to the intended user, knowing the pass phrase would only allow the attacker to register a bogus key pair for the user, it would not allow the attacker to fool the user into using the bogus key pair, nor would it allow the attacker to obtain the private key. It is very likely that the attack will be quickly discovered since the legitimate recipient of the pass phrase will be unable to register a key.

In addition the revoke service has its own additional form of authentication which is used exclusively for revocation operations.

Register

The first step in the life cycle of a key binding is registration. The client specifies the information it wants to bind to a public key. The client may ask the register service to generate the public key pair to be registered or cause the public key pair to be generated itself.

For example, Alice wants to use S/MIME to secure her e-mail. She meets the administrator of the register service in person and is handed a one time use pass phrase in a sealed envelope. When she returns to her desk, she tells her client to register a new key pair and enters the pass phrase for authentication. The register service verifies that the pass code is the same one that the administrator issued to Alice, and if the match is correct, the key binding is generated and registered.

TIP When designing an authentication mechanism for an XKMS register service, consider how the user might be authenticated with the minimum of inconvenience.

Client Key Generation Client-side key generation avoids the need for the private key to be disclosed to the register service and is therefore to be preferred whenever possible. Client-side key generation is particularly desirable in applications where the user is going to use the private key to sign documents and might be tempted to claim that a service that had access to the key during registration had secretly copied the key and then used it to make unauthorized signatures.

Service Key Generation In some cases client-side key generation is impossible or impractical. Increasingly, private keys are being embedded in hardware devices such as smartcards, network interface devices, and CPUs during manufacture. Most devices are not capable of generating public key pairs in a time short enough to be acceptable to the operators of the assembly lines.

TIP Many PKI applications use separate keys for signing and encryption even though public key algorithms such as RSA allow the same key to serve both purposes. Separating the cryptographic uses of the key allows the encryption key to be escrowed without requiring the signing key to be escrowed. It is also good cryptographic practice, providing protection against certain types of cryptographic protocol attack.

Using the Register Service A register request contains a prototype for the key binding to be issued, an authentication element and in the case of a client-side generated key pair, a proof of possession element. The proof of possession element prevents an attacker from registering another person's public key in their name, which would allow them to claim that documents signed by the genuine key holder were theirs. If the register operation is successful, the response contains the key binding(s) that resulted, and in the case of a service-generated key pair, the encrypted private key. These elements are shown in Table 8-8.

Request Element	Description
PrototypeKeyBinding	Specifies the key binding to be registered
Authentication	Additional information used to authenticate the request
ProofOfPossession	Proof that the request was authorized by the party that holds the private key corresponding to the specified public key
Response Element	**Description**
KeyBinding	A key binding resulting from or changed by the requested operation
PrivateKey	Encrypted private key parameters of a service-generated key pair

Table 8-8. Request and Response Elements of the Register Service

The register service may be used from a Java program using the VeriSign TSIK as follows:

1. If the key generation is client-side, generate the public key pair.
2. Create an XMLTransportSOAP object for the URL of the service.
3. Create an instance of the XKMSRegister object.
4. Send the request to the XKMS object using the send method.
5. Process the response.

The following code fragment shows an example of using the TSIK to locate the certificate corresponding to the specified key name using the VeriSign test service:

```
public static void RegisterServiceKey(String keyName, String authCode,
            String revocationCode)
      throws IOException, XKMSException, NoSuchAlgorithmException,
            InvalidKeySpecException, Exception
      {
      service = "http://interop-xkms.verisign.com/xkms/Acceptor.nano";
      XmlTransport transport = new XmlTransportSOAP(new URL(service));
      XKMSKeyData data = new XKMSKeyData(new XKMSKeyName(keyName));
      XKMSAuthInfo authInfo = new XKMSAuthInfo(revocationCode, authCode);
      XKMSRegister register = new XKMSRegister(data, authInfo);

      XKMSRegisterResponse response = register.send(transport);

      System.out.println("Response status is " + response.getStatus());
      if (response.getStatus()) {
          System.out.println("The key name is " + response.getKeyName());
          System.out.println("The public key is " + response.getPublicKey());
          System.out.println("The private key is " + response.getPrivateKey());
           }
      }
```

Recover

PKI allows the confidentiality of data to be protected using ciphers so strong that it would take millions of years to decrypt it using the most powerful techniques in the public cryptanalytic literature. This creates something of a problem if an important data file is encrypted and the private key required to decrypt it is lost for any reason. A key recovery system stores a copy of the private key with a *key escrow agent* during registration so that it can be recovered if necessary.

TIP Even if you do not intend to support the use of a key recovery system in your application, you should carefully consider the consequences of losing a private key and if necessary provide the user with some other means of backing up their private key by themselves such as by storing it on a floppy disk.

In practice, there are many reasons why recovery of a private key may be necessary. The private key may have been stored in a smartcard or other hardware device that has become lost or broken. The private key may have been encrypted using a pass phrase that the user has forgotten, or the user may have died or been incapacitated for some reason, or the user might withhold the pass phrase out of malice or for purposes of extortion.

Governments in some countries have also promoted mandatory use of key recovery systems in which the key escrow agent is either the government itself or a contractor acting on behalf of the government. Proposals of this nature have raised many questions as to the trustworthiness, in this respect, of governments in general and certain governments in particular. While such public policy considerations are outside the scope of this book, it is important to consider that the civil liberties issues raised by government-mandated key escrow do not eliminate the need for some form of key recovery in PKI deployments intended to support encryption of stored data.

The X-KRSS recover service can only recover private keys if they have been previously escrowed. The necessary key escrow would typically be performed by an X-KRSS register service using the service-generated key option. XKMS does not provide a mechanism for escrow of client-generated keys.

Using the Recover Service The recover service is very similar to the register service except that the request is made with respect to a preexisting key binding association rather than creating a new one. The user sends an authenticated request to the recover service, which then returns either a refusal or an encrypted private key.

A recover request specifies the key pair to be recovered by means of a key binding element and contains an authentication element. If the recovery operation is successful, the response contains the key binding(s) whose status was changed by the revoke operation and the recovered private key in an encrypted form. These elements are shown in Table 8-9.

Request Element	Description
KeyBinding	Specifies the key binding to be issued or reissued
Authentication	Additional information used to authenticate the request
Response Element	**Description**
KeyBinding	A key binding resulting from or changed by the requested operation
PrivateKey	Encrypted private key parameters of a service-generated key pair

Table 8-9. Request and Response Elements of the Recover Service

Reissue

Once a key binding is registered, it may require periodic updating from time to time. This function is supported by the X-KRSS reissue operation.

Although the key binding associations used by XKMS have no predetermined lifespan, the credentials issued by the underlying PKI may. For example, all X.509 certificates contain two date fields—notBefore and notAfter—which define the validity interval of the certificate. An XKMS client that needs access to the renewed certificate may obtain it by means of the reissue request.

Using the Reissue Service The reissue service is very similar to the register service except that the request is made with respect to a preexisting key binding association rather than creating a new one. The user sends an authenticated request to the reissue service, which returns either a refusal or the reissued key binding information.

A reissue request contains the same information that is provided in a register request, the key binding to be reissued, an authentication element, and a proof of possession for the private key. If the operation is successful, the response contains the reissued key binding. These elements are shown in Table 8-10.

Revoke

The X-KRSS revoke service revokes a previously registered key binding association and any cryptographic credentials that are associated with it. Revoking a key binding

Request Element	Description
KeyBinding	Specifies the key binding to be reissued
Authentication	Additional information used to authenticate the request
ProofOfPossession	Proof that the request was authorized by the party that holds the private key corresponding to the specified public key
Response Element	**Description**
KeyBinding	A key binding resulting from or changed by the requested operation

Table 8-10. Request and Response Elements of the Reissue Service

association means that it is no longer considered trustworthy and that it should no longer be relied upon by applications.

A key binding association may be revoked for many reasons: the private key may have been disclosed or otherwise compromised, it may be discovered that a mistake was made during the authentication process and the credential was issued to an impostor, or the user may simply have changed jobs so that the statements made in the credential are no longer valid.

Using the Revoke Service To use the revoke request, the client sends a revoke request that identifies the key bindings to be revoked. The service must determine whether the request comes from a party authorized to revoke the key binding.

In most cases, the key holder is one of the parties authorized to revoke their key binding in case they compromise the private key by disclosing it or losing a hardware token it might be stored on. This raises the same problem we saw in the registration service—how to authenticate a user who has lost control of their private key.

XKMS addresses this problem by allowing the user to specify a special revocation identifier when the key binding is registered. The revocation request is then authenticated using the corresponding revocation code. The revocation code and revocation code identifier are generated using a one-way hash function so that the revocation code identifier can be calculated from the revocation code, but not vice versa.

For example, if the original revocation pass phrase was "Have A Banana," the revocation code would be H_1 ("haveabanana") and the revocation code identifier would be H_2 (H_1("haveabanana")) where H_1 and H_2 are both one-way functions.

In addition, there would usually be other parties authorized to revoke a key binding, such as a system administrator. In these cases, the revocation request would typically be authenticated by means of a digital signature created using the private key of the party requesting the revoke operation.

A revoke request specifies the key binding to be revoked and contains either an authentication element or a revocation code. If the revoke operation is successful, the response contains one or more key bindings that reflect the changed status. These elements are shown in Table 8-11.

Request Element	Description
KeyBinding	Specifies the key binding to be reissued
Authentication	Additional information used to authenticate the request
RevocationCode	The revocation code value that generates the revocation code identifier value specified during registration
Response Element	**Description**
KeyBinding	A key binding resulting from or changed by the requested operation

Table 8-11. Request and Response Elements of the Recover Service

ADVANCED PROTOCOL FEATURES OF XKMS 2.0

In XKMS 1.1, all operations consisted of a single request message followed by a single response. XKMS 2.0 specifies additional protocol options that allow a client to make multiple XKMS requests simultaneously, allow an XKMS service to queue XKMS requests for later processing, and make it possible to defend against denial of service attacks.

NOTE XKMS was one of the first Web Services to be designed. It is likely that some, possibly all, of the "advanced features" of the XKMS protocol will eventually find their way into the SOAP specification itself or one of the associated security specifications at a future date.

Compound Requests

A compound request allows a client to make multiple XKMS requests in a single request message. This allows for faster processing than would be possible if the client had to make each request individually, waiting for the result to be returned before making the next request.

Compound requests were only supported in XKMS 1.0 for the register operation and only as a separate specification called X-Bulk, which was intended to support issuing of public key pairs and certificates to smartcards and other embedded devices.

During the design of XKMS 2.0, it was argued that the ability to make multiple requests at the same time is useful in many other cases. In particular, an e-mail client sending an encrypted message to 25 recipients is likely to be unacceptably slow if the public key of every recipient has to be retrieved individually. Compound requests were introduced to fill this need.

Asynchronous Processing

In some situations, an XKMS service may not be able to respond to a request immediately.

Asynchronous processing may be required because some form of operator intervention is required to complete an operation. For example, a registration procedure might require some form of offline authentication procedure to be completed before a credential is issued. Manual intervention is frequently required in key recovery operations; in some cases, a key recovery procedure may require authorization by more than one administrator.

Asynchronous processing is also desirable in cases where the request may take a long time to complete. For example, a manufacturer of smartcards might make a compound request to register 10,000 service-generated public key pairs at a time. Generating such a large number of keys is likely to take a significant amount of time. If the client has to wait for the service to complete processing the request before a result of any kind is returned, it might be waiting 20 minutes or more—the client has no way to know if the service is simply slow or has failed. Such long delays are likely to result in unreliable behavior due to dropped connections, timeouts, and other network issues that cause unexpected behaviors.

Asynchronous processing involves two separate request/response pairs (see the illustration). The client makes the first request specifying the ResponseMechanism type xkms:Asynchronous. The service may return the actual response immediately or signal that the response will be returned asynchronously using the ResultMajor code xkms:Pending. Once the service has completed processing the request, the client obtains the result by issuing a pending request message.

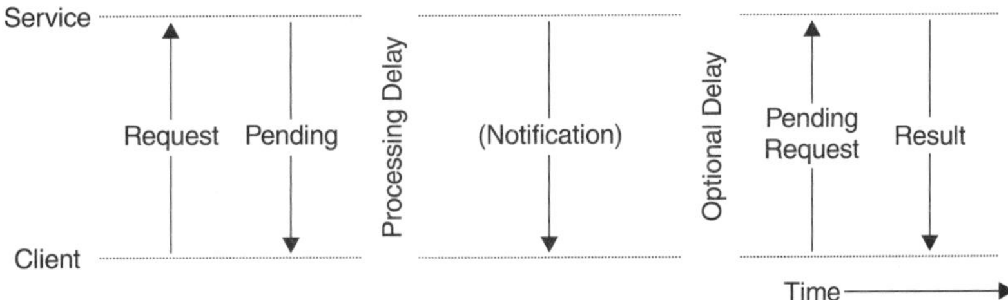

The means by which the client determines that the service has completed processing the request is outside the scope of the XKMS specification. A client may suggest a notification mechanism to the service in the original request, which the service may choose to support or ignore. Alternatively, the client may poll the service to determine whether processing has completed.

Two-Phase Request Protocol

A successful denial of service attack against an XKMS service may result in the services that rely upon it becoming unavailable. It is important, therefore, that an XKMS service is able to protect itself against a denial of service attack by refusing spurious requests.

Rejecting spurious requests is difficult, however, because an attacker may forge the source address of the IP packets containing the request. If the XKMS service simply refused service after an unacceptable number of spurious requests, the denial of service measures intended to protect the service would instead make it easier for the attacker to deny service to users. Moreover, the attacker could choose to deny service to individual users of the XKMS service without causing a complete loss of service likely to attract wider attention.

The two-phase protocol provides protection against denial of service attacks by checking that the requestor can read IP packets sent to the purported source of the request.

The client sends an initial request to the service. Unless the service has reason to believe that the request is part of a denial of service attack, the service may respond with an immediate result.

If, however, the service has determined that it is under a denial of service attack and the request may be a part of that attack, it returns a response with the ResultMajor code xkms:Represent that contains a *nonce* value. The term "nonce" is used in the description of cryptographic protocols to refer to an apparently random value that is hard for another party to guess. In order for the service to act on the request, the client must represent the request together with the previously issued nonce value (see the illustration). The ability to present the nonce demonstrates that the request comes from a source that can read messages sent to the purported source IP address, thus providing a very high degree of confidence that the purported source address is genuine. The service may therefore distinguish between requests that actually originate from that address and packets forged to appear to originate from that address.

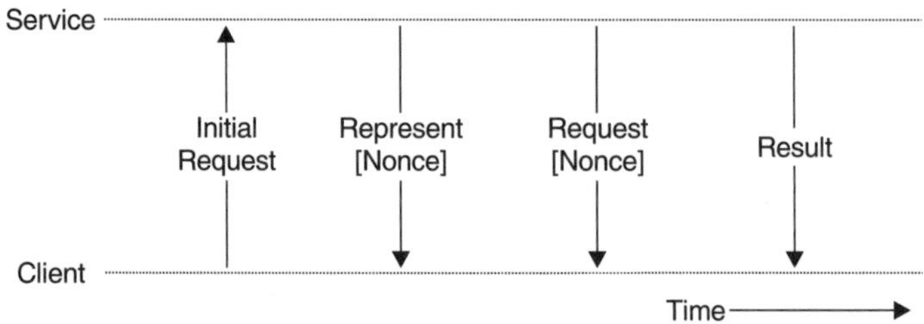

CHECKLIST

- ☐ What is a PKI? What does it do?
- ☐ What problems of PKI deployment does XKMS address?
- ☐ Why should application designers consider adding support for XKMS?
- ☐ In what circumstances is a key recovery system useful?
- ☐ What type of private key does not normally require key recovery?

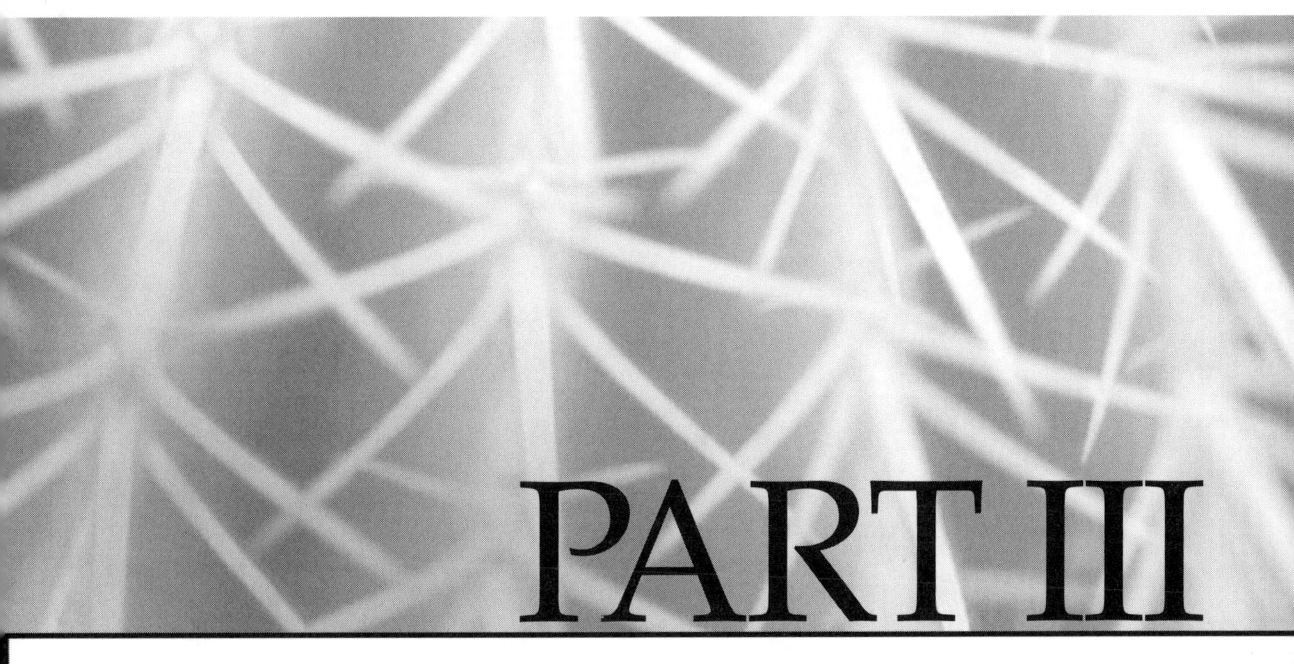

PART III

Security in SOAP: Presenting WS-Security

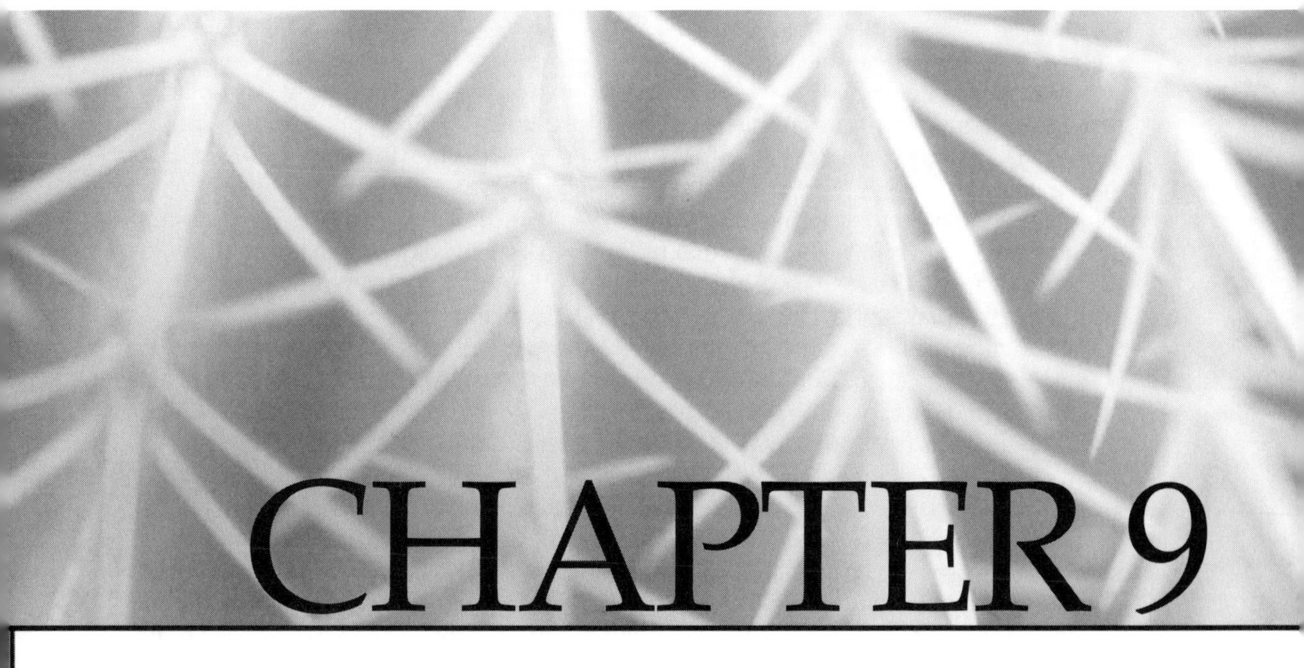

CHAPTER 9

WS-Security

So far, the technologies that we have covered in this book have been either primarily for XML security (for example, XML Signature and XML Encryption) or applicable to the advantages of XML to information security functionality such as key management or access control rules (for example, XKMS, XACML). WS-Security, by contrast, is primarily for securing SOAP messages. It addresses the SOAP security issues discussed in Chapter 3. We've seen that technologies such as XML Signature, XML Encryption, and SAML can be used for purposes other than Web Services security. WS-Security explains how they are used for Web Services security in particular.

WS-Security defines how security tokens are contained in SOAP messages, and how XML Security specifications are used to encrypt and sign these tokens, as well as how to sign and encrypt other parts of a SOAP message. In practice, this means defining the XML elements and attributes that are used to enclose tokens into SOAP messages, and the means to enclose XML Signature and XML Encryption into SOAP.

WS-Security is part of a road map from IBM and Microsoft that includes later specifications such as WS-Trust, WS-Policy, and WS-SecureConversation. It can be used apart from these specifications, but it should be understood in the full context of the "WS-*" specifications.

This chapter uses the Web Services Enhancements 1.0 for Microsoft .NET (WSE) for hands-on familiarity with WS-Security.

INTRODUCTION TO WS-SECURITY

WS-Security has undergone a number of incarnations. It was initially released by Microsoft in October 2001. Then, in April 2002, IBM and Microsoft released their joint "Security in a Web Services World" document. This defined a security framework for Web Services, the first of which to be released (in conjunction with VeriSign) is WS-Security. Later specifications for Web Services security include WS-Trust, WS-Policy, and WS-SecureConversation. June 2002 saw WS-Security submitted to the OASIS standards body, home of SAML and XACML. A Web Services Security group was formed in OASIS in order to develop WS-Security as an OASIS standard.

The definitions of element names for packaging security tokens into SOAP messages are the practical "nuts and bolts" part of WS-Security. Sitting above this is a conceptual model that abstracts different security technologies into "claims" and "tokens." The additional security road map specifications build on these concepts, solidifying them into XML specifications and explaining how to apply for a security token, how tokens are linked to identity, and how security information may be associated with a Web Service.

WS-Security Abstractions

Web Services are designed to allow software from disparate companies to communicate together. They provide a level of abstraction above different platforms and programming languages, allowing different systems to communicate in a loosely coupled fashion. As well as using different platforms and programming languages, communicating companies may well use different security technologies. One company may use Kerberos, while another may consume X.509 certificates. Just as Web Services themselves provide a level of abstraction for companies to link their business logic, the IBM/Microsoft *Security in a Web Services World* road map provides a level of abstraction for companies using different security technologies to communicate securely using SOAP. This level of abstraction means not only that existing security infrastructure can be used for Web Services security, but that new security technologies can also be incorporated.

Tokens and Claims

Claims are statements about a subject either by the subject or by a relying party that associates the subject with a property, such as identity or entitlements. Read the preceding sentence again, because this can seem like a roundabout definition. A claim says something about a subject (end user or entity) that may be used for an access control decision. A token is an XML representation of security information, including claims. A token may either be signed or unsigned. An example of an unsigned token would be a password or symmetric encryption keys used as shared secrets. Examples of signed security tokens are X.509 digital certificates (which are signed by a certificate authority) or a Kerberos ticket. If an unsigned token is used, then confidentiality must be assured to ensure that the token is not intercepted by a third party. As we learned in Chapter 2, when sending a security token, proof of possession of the token must be ensured. It isn't as simple as putting an X.509 certificate into a SOAP message, because a third party could take that X.509 certificate and copy and paste it into another message.

The WS-Security model also caters to SOAP endpoints and intermediaries. The model defines scenarios where the integrity and confidentiality of SOAP messages is ensured while the messages traverse intermediaries. In addition, it describes scenarios where the intermediaries themselves perform security functionality—for example, a SOAP "firewall." Additional specifications, including WS-Trust and WS-Policy, will define how security tokens are issued. The request and issuance of security tokens will also make use of Web Services. Let's look at these additional specifications first, before diving into WS-Security itself. It is important to frame WS-Security in the context of the IBM/Microsoft Web Services Security Roadmap.

IBM/Microsoft Web Services Security Road Map

WS-Security is just the first of the Web Services security specifications to be released as part of the IBM and Microsoft Web Services security road map. These specifications are shown in Figure 9-1.

Looking at Figure 9-1, you can see that the specifications are being produced from the bottom up. SOAP is at the base of the diagram. There is nothing under SOAP, of course, because SOAP is transport-independent. WS-Security sits above SOAP in the diagram because it provides a means of encrypting and signing portions of a SOAP message, using XML Signature and XML Encryption, and for enclosing security tokens in a SOAP message to represent claims.

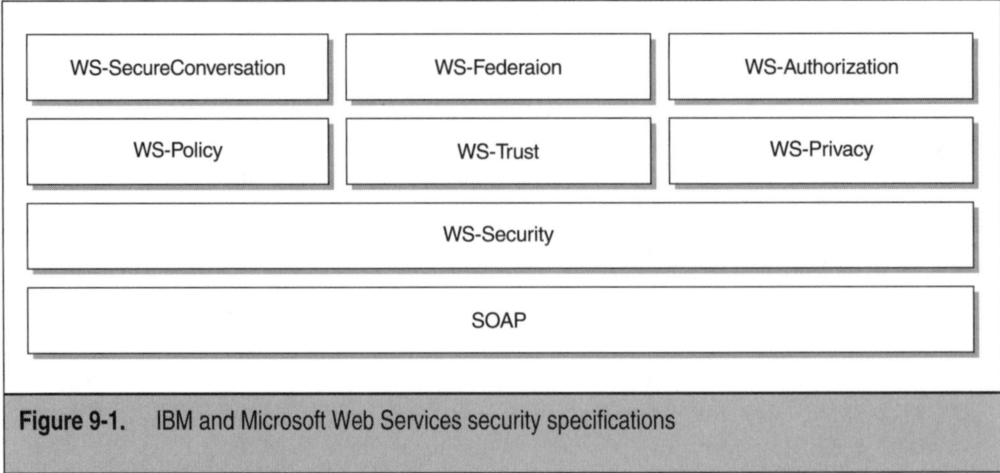

Figure 9-1. IBM and Microsoft Web Services security specifications

Walking through this stack of Web Services security specifications from bottom to top, we can see that each specification depends on its predecessors, mutually building a complete security context for Web Services.

WS-Policy

WS-Policy allows organizations that are exposing Web Services to specify the security requirements of their Web Services. These security requirements include the supported algorithms for encryption and digital signatures, privacy attributes (such as which parameters must be encrypted), and how this information may be bound to a Web Service. The binding to a Web Service will most likely take the form of a WSDL binding, in order to attach policy information to the definition of Web Service. WS-Policy allows organizations initiating a SOAP exchange to discover what type of security tokens are understood at the target, in the same way that WSDL describes a target Web Service. For example, one organization may only consume Kerberos tickets while another organization may only understand X.509 certificates.

WS-Trust

WS-Trust defines how trust relationships are established. Trust relationships can be either direct or brokered. In the case of brokered trust, a "trust proxy" is used to read the WS-Policy information and request the appropriate security token for enclosure in the SOAP message. A trust proxy requests security tokens from an issuer of security tokens. WS-Security will be used to transfer the required security tokens, making use of XML Signature and XML Encryption to ensure their integrity and confidentiality.

This trust model allows *delegation* and *impersonation*. This means that the trust proxy can insert security tokens into the SOAP message that represent the end user. Remember from Chapter 3 that because SOAP is not sent directly by end users, but on their behalf, the SOAP message must contain security information that maps back to the end user.

WS-Privacy

We saw in Chapter 3 that privacy is implemented using confidentiality and access control, and concerns the context and sensitivity of information that is being communicated. Similarly, WS-Privacy uses a combination of WS-Policy, WS-Security, and WS-Trust to communicate privacy policies. These privacy policies are stated by organizations that are deploying Web Services, and require that incoming SOAP requests contain claims that the sender conforms to these privacy policies. The WS-Security specification is used to encapsulate these claims into security tokens, which can be verified.

WS-Privacy explains how privacy requirements can be included inside WS-Policy descriptions. WS-Trust is used to evaluate the privacy claims encapsulated (using WS-Security) within SOAP messages against user preferences and organizational policy. This "Russian doll" model means that the "WS-*" specifications depend on each other.

WS-SecureConversation

SSL is widely used for point-to-point authentication and confidentiality of Web Services communications. We saw in Chapter 3 that message-level security is required for SOAP traffic that may traverse intermediaries. In addition, Web Services traffic cannot be guaranteed to use HTTP, so replying on SSL for authentication and confidentiality is not appropriate. WS-Security defines the use of security tokens within SOAP messages, when combined with XML Signature and XML Encryption, to provide proof of possession and confidentiality of the claims that these tokens encapsulate. When a SOAP message is received, the security token is evaluated and checked against a security policy. However, this process must be repeated for each incoming SOAP message. This is obviously a performance issue, because there is no concept of a session for a group of SOAP messages.

WS-SecureConversation fills this gap, by allowing a requestor and a Web Service to mutually authenticate using SOAP messages and establish a mutually authenticated security context. This security context uses session keys, derived keys, and per-message keys. Like SSL, WS-SecureConversation builds upon the fact that symmetric encryption is faster than asymmetric encryption. By going through the process of using asymmetric encryption to negotiate a symmetric key *once*, this key can be used for a series of SOAP messages. This means that each SOAP message does not have to go through a lengthy and intensive process of message-level authentication. The choreography of the session key negotiation is likely to be similar to that of SSL, meaning that the description of WS-SecureConversation as "SSL at the SOAP level" is valid.

WS-SecureConversation builds upon WS-Security and WS-Trust to securely exchange context (collections of claims about security attributes and related data) in order to negotiate and issue keys. WS-SecureConversation is designed for the SOAP message layer, where messages may traverse a variety of transports (SMTP, HTTP, and so forth) and intermediaries (not all of whom may the trusted). The use of WS-SecureConversation does not preclude the use of transport-level security across point-to-point links.

WS-Federation

Like WS-SecureConversation, WS-Federation also builds upon the specifications that underpin it. It explains how federated trust scenarios may be constructed using WS-Security, WS-Policy, WS-Trust, and WS-SecureConversation. "Federation" in this case involves brokering between different security specifications—for example, communication between a party who understands Kerberos and another party who understands X.509 digital certificates to allow an end user to authenticate to one party, but then use a Web Service exposed by the other party. WS-Policy and WS-Trust are used to determine which tokens are consumed, and how to apply for tokens from a security token issuance service. WS-Federation acts at a layer above WS-Policy and WS-Trust, indicating how trust relationships are managed.

WS-Authorization

This specification has a number of overlaps with XACML, which we encountered in Chapter 7. WS-Authorization describes how access policies for a Web Service are specified and managed. This specification is flexible and extensible with respect to both authorization format and authorization language. It supports both ACL-based authorization and RBAC-based authorization.

WS-Security Elements and Attributes

The WS-Security specification defines XML elements and attributes to enclose security tokens inside SOAP messages, and describes how XML Signature and XML Encryption can be used for confidentiality and integrity of these tokens (and other content) within the SOAP messages. Information is grouped together within blocks. There is a block for a username-and-password combination, a block for a binary security token (for example, an X.509 certificate), and blocks for encrypted and signed information. Let's walk through these blocks.

Security Block

The Security element in WS-Security is contained within the SOAP header. It is structured within the SOAP message as follows:

```
<S:Envelope>
    <S:Header>
            ...
        <Security S:actor="http://www.vordel.com/appml/" S:mustUnderstand="1">
            ...
        </Security>
            ...
    </S:Header>
    ...
</S:Envelope>
```

In the example, the SOAP mustUnderstand attribute is set to 1 to indicate that the Security header entry is mandatory for the recipient to process. If the recipient cannot process the security information, the processing will fail.

Because a single SOAP message may contain more than one Security header block, targeted at separate receivers, the SOAP actor attribute is used to indicate which security tokens are targeted at which Web Services. This is necessary when a SOAP message is routed through at least one intermediary on the way to its endpoint. The SOAP actor attribute is not mandatory for the Security element. However, if more than one Security header block is present in a SOAP message, then only one Security header block can omit the SOAP actor attribute and no two Security header blocks can have the same SOAP actor value. A single Security block cannot contain security tokens targeted at different recipients. If no SOAP actor attribute is present in the Security element, the Security block can be consumed by any intermediary but may not be removed by any of the intermediaries.

As well as enclosing security tokens, the Security header block presents information about the use of XML Signature and XML Encryption in the SOAP message. An XML Signature or XML Encryption block within the SOAP message may refer to another section of the Security block. This situation occurs, for example, if an XML Signature KeyInfo section, contained within the Security block, references an X.509 certificate that is also contained within the Security block. When a subelement of a Security block refers to another subelement, an ID is used to link the two together. We will see an example of this later in this chapter, in the section entitled "BinarySecurityToken Used with XML Signature."

UsernameToken

The UsernameToken block defines how username-and-password information is enclosed within SOAP. As we saw in Chapter 3, SOAP messages are not sent from end users, so it will not be usual for passwords typed by end users to find their way into SOAP messages. If end users are authenticating using username and password, then it is more appropriate to issue a SAML authentication assertion or Kerberos ticket in order to represent the user's authentication act. However, two companies may agree on the use of a username/password combination as a shared secret, to be used for authentication of SOAP messages.

The following listing shows an example of a UsernameToken block within a SOAP message:

```
<S:Envelope xmlns:S=http://www.w3.org/2001/12/soap-envelope
            xmlns:wsse="http://schemas.xmlsoap.org/ws/2002/07/secext">
    <S:Header>

        <wsse:Security>
<wsse:UsernameToken xmlns:wsu="http://schemas.xmlsoap.org/ws/2002/07/utility">
    <wsse:Username>NNK</wsse:Username>
```

```
      <wsse:Password Type=" wsse:PasswordDigest ">FEdR...</wsse:Password>
      <wsse:Nonce>FKJh...</wsse:Nonce>
      <wsu:Created>2001-10-13T09:00:00Z </wsu:Created>
    </wsse:UsernameToken>
        </wsse:Security>
            ...
    </S:Header>
    ...
</S:Envelope>
```

In this listing, the SOAP envelope is defined first, with the WS-Security block placed in the header of the message. Notice that the namespace is "http://schemas .xmlsoap .org/ws/2002/07/secext." That is because the WS-Security Addendum, issued by Microsoft, VeriSign, and IBM in August 2002 (and not July, as the namespace suggests) is being used. The August 2002 Addendum builds upon the April 2002 WS-Security specification in order to allow for the use of a nonce ("number once"—see Chapter 2) and timestamps within UsernameToken in order to guard against replay attacks. If these were not used, there would be a danger that the message could be intercepted by a third party, re-sent, and re-authenticated. The use of transport and session layer security also provides point-to-point authentication and confidentiality, and WS-SecureConversation allows for the use of a session that traverses SOAP intermediaries. The password, in this case, is a shared secret between the requestor and the Web Service, which must be protected from eavesdroppers or potential replay attackers.

As we learned in Chapter 2, the use of a nonce or timestamp must be accompanied by a digital signature so that an intruder cannot simply change the value of the nonce or timestamp without detection. In the "BinarySecurityToken Used with XML Signature" section, we will see how an XML Signature is enclosed within a WS-Security block.

BinarySecurityToken

A UsernameToken, as we've just seen, encloses XML data. However, not all security data may be as easily enclosed in XML. If a claim is based on a binary token, such as an X.509 digital certificate or a Kerberos ticket, a different encoding is required. Therefore, WS-Security defined a BinarySecurityToken structure to enclose non-XML security tokens. It is formed as follows:

```
<BinarySecurityToken Id=...
                           EncodingType=...
                           ValueType=.../>
```

The Id attribute of the security token is used for referencing from elsewhere in the SOAP message. We will see in the next subsections how it is used in the context of XML Signature, where a signature points to an X.509 certificate that may be used to validate the signature. The ValueType attribute contains a qualified name that defines the value type of the encoded binary data. It may make use of XML namespaces. Examples of ValueType include wsse:X509v3 for an X.509 v3 digital certificate, wsse:Kerberosv5TGT for a Kerberos ticket-granting ticket, and wsse:Kerberosv5ST for a Kerberos ticket.

The EncodingType attribute is used to specify the encoding format of the binary data (for example, wsse:Base64Binary for base64-encoded binary data or wsse:HexBinary for XML Schema hex encoding). An example BinarySecurityToken is shown here:

```
<wsse:BinarySecurityToken
            xmlns:wsse="http://schemas.xmlsoap.org/ws/2002/04/secext"
            Id="myToken"
            ValueType="wsse:X509v3"
            EncodingType="wsse:Base64Binary">
            MIIEZzCCA9CgAwIBAgIQEmtJZc0...
         </wsse:BinarySecurityToken>
```

NOTE XML Signature also provides mechanisms for encoding X.509 certificates, using ds:KeyInfo, and this may provide additional flexibility.

Let's look now at how the BinarySecurityToken is used with XML security within SOAP, beginning with XML Signature.

BinarySecurityToken Used with XML Signature

Binary security tokens include Kerberos tickets and X.509 digital certificates. When combined with proof of possession of the key associated with the security token—for example, using an XML Signature—binary security tokens may be used for authentication.

Let's see an example of a BinarySecurityToken block being referenced by an XML Signature block within a SOAP message:

```
<?xml version="1.0" encoding="utf-8"?>
<S:Envelope xmlns:S="http://www.w3.org/2001/12/soap-envelope"
            xmlns:ds="http://www.w3.org/2000/09/xmldsig#"
            xmlns:wsse="http://schemas.xmlsoap.org/ws/2002/07/secext"
            xmlns:xenc="http://www.w3.org/2001/04/xmlenc#">
   <S:Header>

      <wsse:Security>
         <wsse:BinarySecurityToken
                     ValueType="wsse:X509v3"
                     EncodingType="wsse:Base64Binary"
                     Id="X509Token">
                  MIIEZzCCA9CgAwIBAgIQEmtJZc0rqrKh5i...
         </wsse:BinarySecurityToken>
         <ds:Signature>
            <ds:SignedInfo>
               <ds:CanonicalizationMethod Algorithm=
                     "http://www.w3.org/2001/10/xml-exc-c14n#"/>
               <ds:SignatureMethod Algorithm=
                     "http://www.w3.org/2000/09/xmldsig#rsa-sha1"/>
```

```
                <ds:Reference URI="#bodydata">
                  <ds:Transforms>
                     <ds:Transform Algorithm=
                           "http://www.w3.org/2001/10/xml-exc-c14n#"/>
                  </ds:Transforms>
                  <ds:DigestMethod Algorithm=
                       "http://www.w3.org/2000/09/xmldsig#sha1"/>
                  <ds:DigestValue>EULddytSods:DigestValue>
               </ds:Reference>
            </ds:SignedInfo>
            <ds:SignatureValue>
              BL8jdfToEb1l/vXcMZNNjPOVEWRj3dfj32lsf2weWE
            </ds:SignatureValue>
            <ds:KeyInfo>
                <wsse:SecurityTokenReference>
                    <wsse:Reference URI="#X509Token"/>
                </wsse:SecurityTokenReference>
            </ds:KeyInfo>
        </ds:Signature>
      </wsse:Security>
   </S:Header>
   <S:Body>
      <tru:StockSymbol Id="bodydata" xmlns:tru="http://quotes.com/payload">
        QQQ
      </tru:StockSymbol>
   </S:Body>
```

To understand the preceding listing, work from the bottom up. The "StockSymbol" child of the SOAP Body element contains an Id attribute. The content of this attribute is "bodydata." Look at the XML Signature data that is contained within the Security block inside the SOAP header. The Reference section of the XML Signature points to the "bodydata" Id attribute of the StockSymbol element in the SOAP body. This is what is being signed. By looking at the XML Signature block in the Security block, you can see that it is familiar from Chapter 4. It contains a digest of the signed data, information about which algorithms are used, and, of course, the signature itself.

The KeyInfo section of the XML Signature points to a WS-Security BinarySecurity Token, using the new SecurityTokenReference element. The URI attribute of the Reference subelement of the SecurityTokenReference points to the X.509 certificate contained at the top of the SOAP message. The X.509 certificate carries the Id "X509Token" to link to the XML Signature.

We have seen that it is often the best practice to discard the X.509 certificate within the SOAP message, and instead pull the X.509 certificate from an LDAP directory. In that case, however, the KeyInfo section provides information about which X.509 certificate to retrieve in order to validate the signature.

BinarySecurityToken Used with XML Encryption

A BinarySecurityToken block can also be associated with an XML Encryption block. We saw in Chapter 5 that XML Encryption contains a KeyInfo section, which indicates which public key was used to encrypt the symmetric key that was used to encrypt the data. The following code listing is adapted from the WS-Security specification. Notice that the KeyInfo contains distinguished name information from an X.509 certificate. This indicates to the recipient that the corresponding private key is to be used to decrypt the symmetric key used to decrypt the data. Notice that the XML Encryption data in the Security block points to the encrypted data within the body of the SOAP message using the "enc1" Id.

An XML Signature is also used in this example. A transform called RoutingTransform is intended to isolate the routing information and the body of the SOAP message. This transform isolates the information which is signed.

```
<?xml version="1.0" encoding="utf-8"?>
<S:Envelope xmlns:S="http://www.w3.org/2001/12/soap-envelope"
            xmlns:ds="http://www.w3.org/2000/09/xmldsig#"
            xmlns:wsse="http://schemas.xmlsoap.org/ws/2002/04/secext"
            xmlns:xenc="http://www.w3.org/2001/04/xmlenc#">
   <S:Header>
      <m:path xmlns:m="http://schemas.xmlsoap.org/rp/">
         <m:action>http://quotes.com/getQuote</m:action>
         <m:to>http://quotes.com/stocks</m:to>
         <m:from>mailto:mark@vordel.com</m:from>
         <m:id>uuid:84b9f5d0-33fb-4a81-b02b-5b760641c1d6</m:id>
      </m:path>
      <wsse:Security>
         <wsse:BinarySecurityToken
                     ValueType="wsse:X509v3"
                     Id="X509Token"
                     EncodingType="wsse:Base64Binary">
         MIIEZzCCA9CgAwIBAgIQEmtJZc0rqrKh5i...
         </wsse:BinarySecurityToken>
         <xenc:EncryptedKey>
             <xenc:EncryptionMethod Algorithm=
                        "http://www.w3.org/2001/04/xmlenc#rsa-1_5"/>
             <ds:KeyInfo>
               <ds:KeyName>CN=Mark O'Neill, O=Vordel, C=US</ds:KeyName>
             </ds:KeyInfo>
             <xenc:CipherData>
```

```
                <xenc:CipherValue>d2FpbmdvbGRfE0lm4byV0...
                </xenc:CipherValue>
             </xenc:CipherData>
             <xenc:ReferenceList>
                 <xenc:DataReference URI="#enc1"/>
             </xenc:ReferenceList>
         </xenc:EncryptedKey>
         <ds:Signature>
            <ds:SignedInfo>
               <ds:CanonicalizationMethod
                  Algorithm="http://www.w3.org/2001/10/xml-exc-c14n#"/>
               <ds:SignatureMethod
               Algorithm="http://www.w3.org/2000/09/xmldsig#rsa-sha1"/>
               <ds:Reference>
                  <ds:Transforms>
                     <ds:Transform
                            Algorithm="http://...#RoutingTransform"/>
                     <ds:Transform
                  Algorithm="http://www.w3.org/2001/10/xml-exc-c14n#"/>
                  </ds:Transforms>
                  <ds:DigestMethod
                   Algorithm="http://www.w3.org/2000/09/xmldsig#sha1"/>
                  <ds:DigestValue>LyLsF094hPi4wPU...
                   </ds:DigestValue>
               </ds:Reference>
            </ds:SignedInfo>
            <ds:SignatureValue>
                     Hp1ZkmFZ/2kQLXDJbchm5gK...
            </ds:SignatureValue>
            <ds:KeyInfo>
                <wsse:SecurityTokenReference>
                    <wsse:Reference URI="#X509Token"/>
                </wsse:SecurityTokenReference>
            </ds:KeyInfo>
         </ds:Signature>
      </wsse:Security>
   </S:Header>
   <S:Body>
      <xenc:EncryptedData
                  Type="http://www.w3.org/2001/04/xmlenc#Element"
                  Id="enc1">
         <xenc:EncryptionMethod
              Algorithm="http://www.w3.org/2001/04/xmlenc#3des-cbc"/>
         <xenc:CipherData>
```

```
            <xenc:CipherValue>d2FpbmdvbGRfE0lm4byV0...
            </xenc:CipherValue>
        </xenc:CipherData>
    </xenc:EncryptedData>
  </S:Body>
</S:Envelope>
```

Error Handling in WS-Security

There are a number of errors that can occur when a SOAP message formatted using WS-Security is processed. These include the following scenarios:

- **Security token type unsupported** Note that the use of WS-Policy and WS-Trust will allow organizations to communicate information about which types of security tokens they can understand.
- **Invalid security token** This error occurs, for example, if a security token has been corrupted en route to the recipient. It also occurs if the signature over the security token does not validate, or if an encrypted security token cannot be decrypted.
- **Security token cannot be authenticated** If an X.509 certificate is received in a BinarySecurityToken block and the issuer cannot be determined, or if the certificate does not match those that are contained in a local LDAP directory for authentication, then this is the appropriate error type.
- **Referenced security token unavailable** This would occur, for example, if an XML Signature KeyInfo section references an X.509 digital certificate, but this certificate is not present in the SOAP message.

Notice that some of these errors involve failures of processing, whereas others involve unsupported security tokens. SOAP Faults, as defined in the SOAP 1.1 and SOAP 1.2 specifications, are used by a recipient to indicate to the sender that an error occurred processing a message.

SOAP Fault includes a FaultCode parameter that conveys the type of error that occurred. When an unsupported token is received, the wsse:UnsupportedSecurityToken fault code should be used. If an unsupported cryptographic algorithm is referenced in the SOAP message, the fault code should be wsse:UnsupportedAlgorithm.

TIP If a message cannot be processed due to a failure of signature or decryption, there is a chance that the incoming message may have been a denial of service attack or a cryptographic "clogging" attack designed to cause disruption to a signature validation or decryption application. In that case, it would be unwise to provide reinforcement to the sender, so it may be wiser to simply not return an error message to the sender of the SOAP message.

If a SOAP Fault message is to be returned due to a processing failure, the fault codes to use are as follows:

- **wsse:InvalidSecurity** This fault code may be used if the contents of the Security block in the SOAP header cannot be processed.
- **wsse:InvalidSecurityToken** This fault code is self-explanatory—the security token provided in the SOAP message may be invalid due to a broken signature, or due to corruption of the token itself.
- **wsse:FailedAuthentication** This is used if the security token cannot be authenticated or authorized.
- **wsse:SecurityTokenUnavailable** This is used if the security token referenced in the SOAP message is not available in the SOAP message or from another location, such as an LDAP directory or an XKMS service.

SAML AND WS-SECURITY

During the early part of 2002, when SAML and WS-Security were receiving a lot of press attention, it was commonplace for journalists to write articles with a "WS-Security vs. SAML" theme. This was misleading because WS-Security and SAML solve different problems: SAML explains how security assertions may be expressed in XML format, whereas WS-Security explains how security information is contained in SOAP messages.

The WS-Security Profile for XML-based Tokens, published in August 2002, explains how SAML information is enclosed inside SOAP messages. A "SOAP binding" for SAML was lacking in the SAML 1.0 specification, so this is now provided by WS-Security.

The following code listing explains how a SAML v1.0 assertion is contained within a SOAP message:

```
<?xml version="1.0" encoding="utf-8"?>
<S:Envelope xmlns:S="http://www.w3.org/2001/12/soap-envelope"
            xmlns:ds="http://www.w3.org/2000/09/xmldsig#"
            xmlns:wsse="http://schemas.xmlsoap.org/ws/2002/04/secext">
    <S:Header>
        <wsse:Security>
            <saml:Assertion
                      MajorVersion="1"
                      MinorVersion="0"
                      AssertionID="SecurityToken-ef375268"
                      Issuer="CompanyX"
                      IssueInstant="2002-07-23T11:32:05.6228146-07:00"
                    xmlns:saml="urn:oasis:names:tc:SAML:1.0:assertion">
                ...
            </saml:Assertion>
            ...
```

```
        </wsse:Security>
    </S:Header>
    <S:Body>
    </S:Body>
</S:Envelope>
```

The SAML assertion is contained within a Security block, which is contained inside the SOAP header. A SAML assertion may be digitally signed or encrypted, in a similar manner to how other security tokens may be signed and encrypted using WS-Security. The processing of a SAML assertion, contained in a WS-Security formatted SOAP message, should not be different from the processing of any other type of security token expressed using WS-Security.

Code Example: Using the Microsoft WSE

The Microsoft WSE is a downloadable tool that allows Visual Studio .NET developers to build Web Services applications that make use of technologies such as WS-Security. It is available at the following URL: http://msdn.microsoft.com/webservices/building/wse.

The code examples provided with the Microsoft WSE make use of C# as their programming language. The .NET Common Language Framework (CLR) is used. Let's look at a code example for the creation of a SOAP message containing a digital signature and an X.509 digital certificate.

First, the security and XML processing functionality from the .NET platform is required for this program, so the following code pulls in the required packages:

```
using System;
using System.Collections;
using System.ComponentModel;
using System.Windows.Forms;
using System.Security.Cryptography;
using System.Text;

using Microsoft.Web.Services;
using Microsoft.Web.Services.Security;
using Microsoft.Web.Services.Security.X509;

using Microsoft.Web.Services.QuickStart.X509;
```

Let's look at code that calls a Web Service that adds two numbers, similar to the Web Service we encountered in Chapter 3. This code is based on an example provided with the WSE in the \Samples\QuickStart\Clients\X509Signing\ folder.

```
// Instantiate an instance of the web service proxy
AddNumbers serviceProxy = new AddNumbers();
SoapContext requestContext = serviceProxy.RequestSoapContext;
// Configure the proxy
```

```
ConfigureProxy(serviceProxy);
// Get our security token
X509SecurityToken token = GetSecurityToken();
if (token == null)
 throw new ApplicationException("No key provided for signature.");
// Add the signature element to a security section on the request
// to sign the request
requestContext.Security.Tokens.Add(token);
requestContext.Security.Elements.Add(new Signature(token));
// Call the service
Console.WriteLine("Calling {0}", serviceProxy.Url);
int sum = serviceProxy.AddInt(a, b);
```

You can see that the WS-Security model is reflected in the preceding code listing. An X.509 security token is requested and then a digital signature is added to the SOAP message, referencing this X.509 token. The code to request the X.509 certificate is shown here:

```
public X509SecurityToken GetSecurityToken()
{
  X509SecurityToken securityToken;
  // open the current user's certificate store
  // X509CertificateStore store =
     X509CertificateStore.CurrentUserStore(X509CertificateStore.MyStore);
  bool open = store.OpenRead();
  try
  {
    // Open a dialog to allow user to select the certificate to use
    //
    StoreDialog dialog = new StoreDialog(store);
    Microsoft.Web.Services.Security.X509.X509Certificate cert = null;
    cert = dialog.SelectCertificate(IntPtr.Zero, "Select
    Certificate", "Choose a Certificate below for signing.");
    if (cert == null)
    {
      throw new ApplicationException("You chose not to select an X509
      certificate for signing your messages.");
    }
    else if (!cert.SupportsDigitalSignature || !cert.key == null)
    {
      throw new ApplicationException("The certificate must support digital
      signatures and have a private key available.");
    }
    else
    {
      securityToken = new X509SecurityToken(cert);
    }
    }
```

```
      finally
      {
        if (store != null) { store.Close(); }
      }
      return securityToken;
    }
  }
}
```

A dialog box is used to ask the user to choose which certificate they will employ from their local certificate store. The StoreDialog object is used for this purpose. An X509Certificate object is used to load the certificate, and it is checked to ensure that it supports the use of a digital signature, and that the corresponding private key is available. As we know from Chapter 2, it is the private key that is used to produce a digital signature, and the corresponding public key may be enclosed with the signature in the message. Providing the private key is available, the X.509 certificate is loaded into an X509SecurityToken object and returned.

As you can see from the code listings, the use of WS-Security does not presuppose any knowledge of the structure of the SOAP messages that are created. However, it is important to understand the model and abstractions of WS-Security—the use of tokens and the signing and encryption of these tokens, as well as other data in the SOAP message. The .NET platform allows the developer to take advantage of the power of these abstractions without the requirement to delve into the XML itself.

CHECKLIST

- ☐ Read the "Security in a Web Services World" road map document at http://www-106.ibm.com/developerworks/webservices/library/ws-secmap. The WS-Security specification is just the first of the specifications in this road map. However, the concepts, including tokens and claims, will carry through into later specifications, such as WS-Policy and WS-Trust.
- ☐ Ensure that any Web Services security product your company uses supports WS-Security. WS-Security is arguably the most important Web Services security specification, because it explains how XML security relates to SOAP, and will underpin many later specifications.

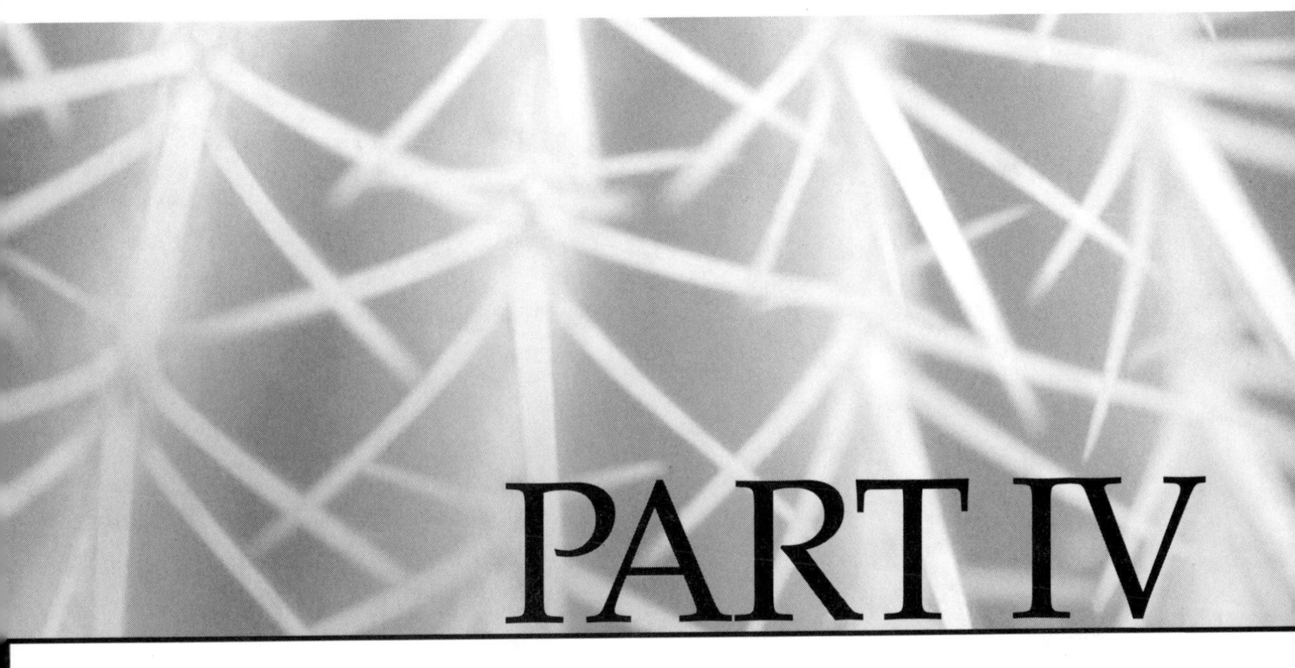

PART IV

Security in Web Services Frameworks

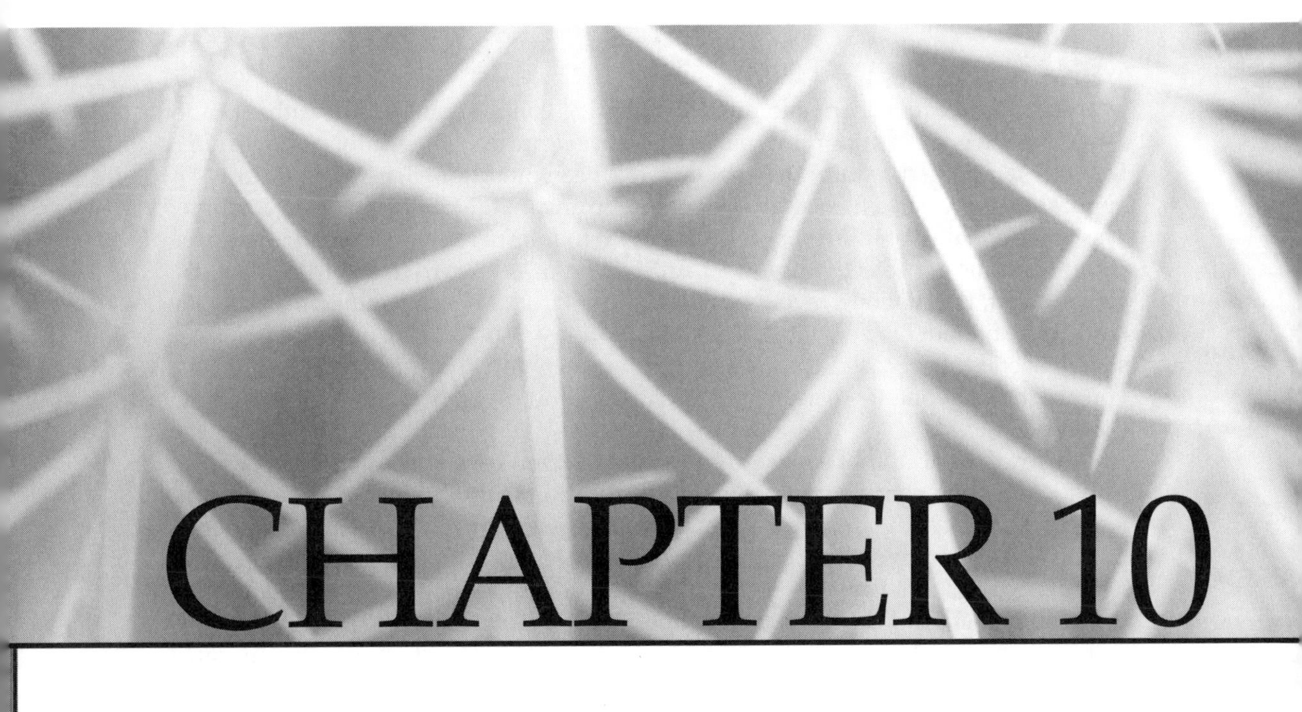

CHAPTER 10

.NET and Passport

Secure applications strive to provide integrity, confidentiality, and authentication. Data integrity is important to users because it protects their information from being modified or indicates that data has been modified. For example, an application can track a file's digital signature to ensure that it has not been corrupted. The confidentiality of information is important to Internet users. After all, there are several reasons to protect your e-mail address, home address, password, and credit card number. Encryption prevents malicious users from eavesdropping on connections. Authentication identifies that you are who you say you are. It usually involves a shared secret (often based on a password) between you and the server. As long as you are the only one who knows the password, you can be uniquely identified by the server.

Microsoft has brought several technologies to the Web Services arena in order to provide integrity, confidentiality, and authentication to the Internet experience. First, we'll take a look at the Kerberos protocol. Kerberos is a distributed authentication protocol designed to protect users' credentials from interception. Next, we'll take a look at Microsoft's Passport technology. Passport functions as a single sign-on technology, very much like Kerberos, but does not currently have the benefit of being a standard. As a result, Passport's application infrastructure is being migrated to Kerberos 5. Finally, we'll peruse the .NET framework and see the contributions Microsoft is making to Web Services security.

Throughout this chapter, we'll focus on Security, capital S. Just because there is a .NET function to encrypt a data stream with Triple-DES, doesn't mean the application is secure. Malicious users can attack the Web server itself through buffer overflows or exploits downloaded from well-known Internet sites. They can also attack the application's session management, cookies, database connectivity, and code. Obviously, it's important to know what features of Passport and .NET provide security, what their limitations are, and what types of attacks will always exist.

TICKET, PLEASE: A KERBEROS OVERVIEW

Kerberos is an authentication system designed to work in an environment where the client is not fully trusted. In short, a Kerberos distribution center (KDC) accepts a password from the user and gives that user a ticket that contains a session key. However, the content of the ticket is encrypted by a secret key known only to the server. In this way, a client must have a valid password and ticket in order to access services protected by Kerberos, but the client cannot view or modify the ticket. The user presents this ticket to application servers, which check the validity of the ticket and permit access based on the result.

The client first requests and receives a ticket granting ticket (TGT) that is used for authentication to the KDC. Then, the client requests and receives a ticket granting service (TGS) that is used for authentication to an application server. The goal of Kerberos is to protect credentials using encryption, prevent replay attacks, and serve as a centralized authentication system (single sign-on). Figure 10-1 illustrates a simplified version of the ticket granting steps. This is merely an introduction to the concept of tickets. We've ignored several steps such as key exchange, but these are handled by the protocol.

A Kerberos ticket contains a realm (similar in concept to a Windows domain), the server name, the session key, the client realm, the client name, and two time values for validity start and end. The session key and validity times are the most important part of the ticket for authentication purposes. The session key is used to identify the user and the validity times are used to protect against replay attacks.

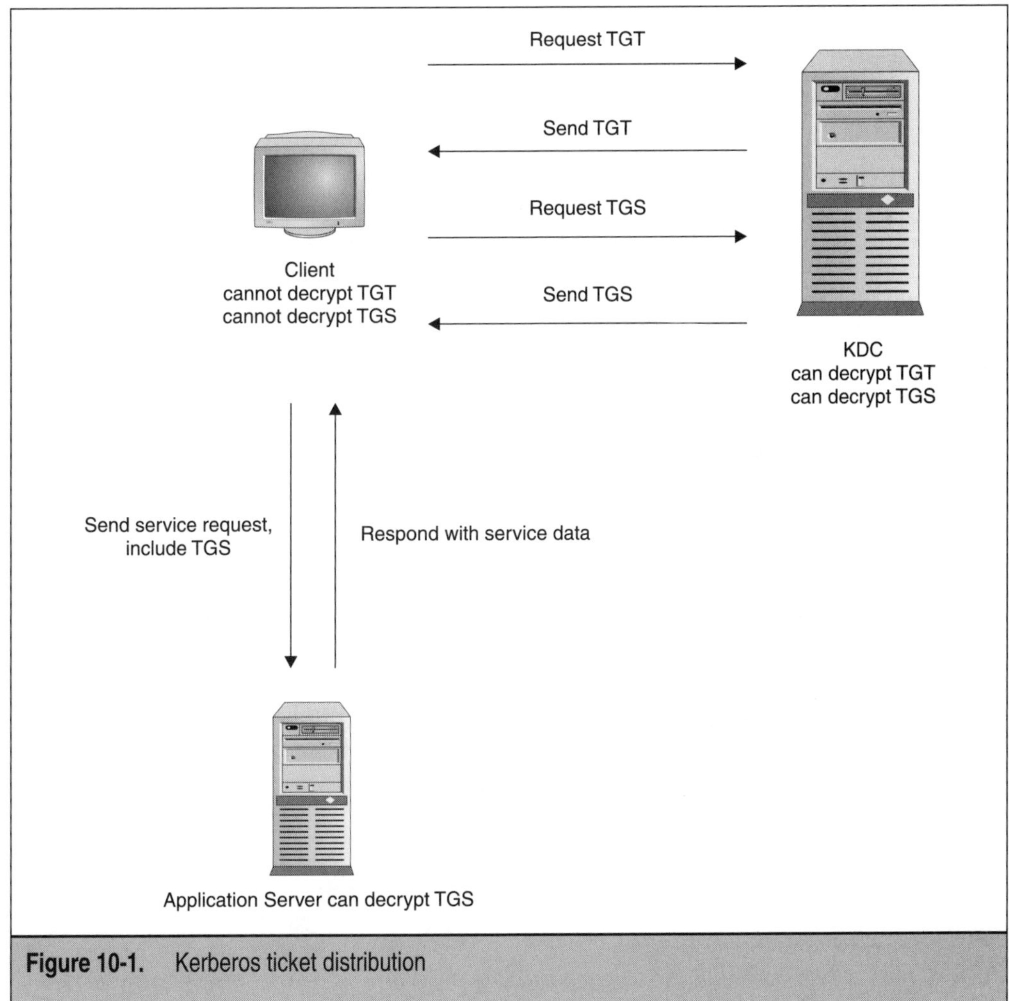

Figure 10-1. Kerberos ticket distribution

PASSPORT

Microsoft's Passport technology is a single sign-on implementation that eases user interaction among authentication-based applications. Theories of world domination aside, the goal of Passport is to provide a uniform, distributed network that performs a few simple functions. One of the most important of these functions is authentication. A user can carry a single Passport credential among several Web applications that support the Passport scheme. In this manner, the user need only manage a single login name and password in order to access disparate applications. In other words, a user authenticates to Passport, Passport provides a cookie, and the user presents this cookie to the Web application. Thus, it functions much like Kerberos tickets.

Prelude to the Login Process

For a third-party application to use Passport, it is imperative that the application server and the Passport server exchange a secret key. This key is used to encrypt sensitive data that must be transmitted between the two servers. For example, a user authenticates to a Passport server and receives a cookie that contains her login name and home mailing address. This cookie is encrypted with a specific secret key. Figure 10-2 shows a high-level description of the key exchange process between the Passport server and the partner application server. Next, the application server must be able to decrypt this cookie value in order to be able to access the user's login name and home mailing address. If the application server and the Passport server did not share a secret key, the application server would not be able to validate the Passport MSPAuth cookie.

On the other hand, if the secret key were based on information supplied by the user, then the Passport server, the application server, and the user would be able to decrypt the MSPAuth cookie. Generally, users (that is, people) are a poor source of random data necessary for strong secret keys. Thus, the user could cause a poor secret key to be generated. This would expose the cookie to a successful dictionary attack, permitting malicious users to obtain confidential personal information. Even so, if the user knows the secret key, she can easily decrypt the cookie and modify values—values that could circumvent security of the application server.

The secret-key exchange between the Passport server and application server happens out of band via a secure e-mail attachment using public-key encryption. Obviously, the secret key must remain "secret," so care is taken to protect the keys from interception. This can be physical exchange, or any trusted exchange ranging from RFC 1149 to couriers with notarized files.

SECURITY ALERT There is no established key management program for Passport. Secret keys do not have a built-in expiry. However, simple key management for negating expired or compromised keys is accomplished by the kv, key value, parameter in Passport. If a compromised secret key belongs to key value 2 (kv=2), both Passport and the application server will "retire" that key and no longer accept it as valid.

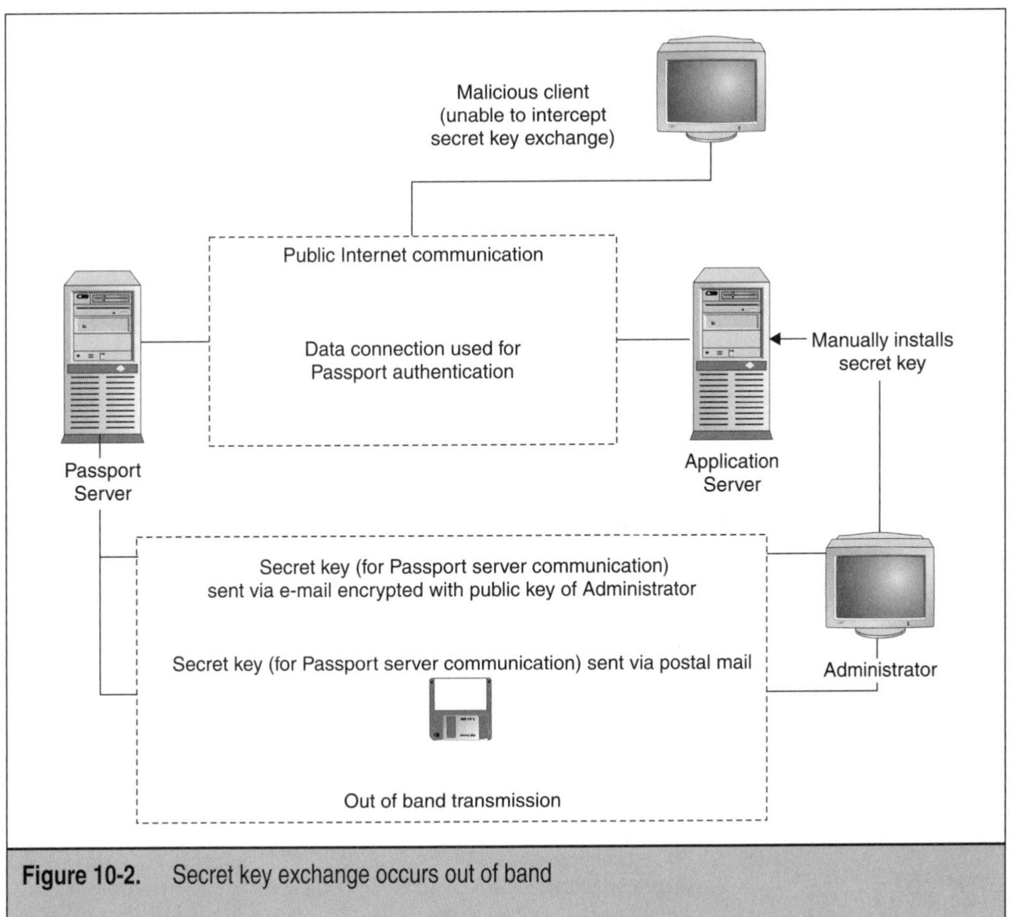

Figure 10-2. Secret key exchange occurs out of band

The Login Process

When a user first visits an application server that supports Passport authentication, that user does not have any tokens to identify her account. The application server requires valid credentials, so it redirects the user to a Passport server for authentication. One parameter of the HTTP redirect includes a Return URL (ru) value that contains a URL to which the user will return once authentication succeeds. At the Passport server, the user provides a correct e-mail address (the login name) and password. Next, the Passport server takes the ru value and redirects the user back to the original application along with two or three new parameters in the URL. These new parameters are the Passport cookies that will be decrypted by the application server, inspected for validity, and set as session cookies in the user's browser. Table 10-1 describes each cookie.

Cookie	What It Contains
MSPAuth Ticket, encrypted	PUID, the user's 64-bit unique identifier Two timestamps: last refresh, last manual sign-in. These timestamps are present to reduce the chances of a successful replay attack and to optionally force users to reauthenticate after a designated period. Saved-password flag, key version verification, and any flags set by network servers. Key version (kv) value, used to select the appropriate decryption key. Note: The user's e-mail address and password are not in this key and are not shared with the partner application.
MSPProf Profile, encrypted	
MSPSec Ticket Granting cookie (TGT), encrypted	Sent over HTTPS only. Used for silent authentication to partner applications, or to correlate the validity of the MSPAuth cookie.

Table 10-1. Passport Cookie Description

Programmatically, an application uses the IsAuthenticated method on the Passport.Manager object to verify a user's MSPAuth cookie. This method returns a True or False value, depending on the validity of the cookie. Additionally, the application can enforce a strict policy to control the level of confidence for a user's cookie. The IsAuthenticated method accepts TimeWindow, ForceLogin, and SecureLevel parameters. Regardless of the values for ForceLogin or SecureLevel, the TimeWindow value is always checked.

- **TimeWindow** A number between 100 and 1000000 that represents the number of seconds (over a minute to about 11 days) after which a user must reauthenticate. The method of reauthentication is controlled by the ForceLogin parameter.
- **ForceLogin** A Boolean value (True/False). A value of True requires users to have entered their password within the TimeWindow. A value of False permits users to continue as authenticated as long as they have received a ticket within the TimeWindow. Set this to True if you wish to set hard time limits on user access to an application. For example, an online banking application might require users to reenter their password every 30 minutes (TimeWindow = 1800, ForceLogin = True) regardless of activity. On the other hand, an e-commerce application might wish to permit users to browse its catalog for an entire day without interrupting the experience to request the password (TimeWindow = 86400, ForceLogin = False).

- **SecureLevel** A number that can be either 0, 10, or 100. This qualifies how the sign-in process must have occurred. An unspecified number or 0 indicates normal authentication; a user supplies an e-mail address and password. Specifying 10 requires that authentication take place over a secure channel; a user must access Passport over HTTPS and have a Return URL that uses HTTPS. Specifying 100 requires that authentication take place over a secure channel and that the user supply a 4-digit PIN. This is a form of two-factor authentication.

SECURITY ALERT Short TimeWindow values reduce the chances of replay attacks by limiting the amount of time during which a cookie is valid. There is also a HasTicket property for the Passport Manager object, but it only checks for the presence of a ticket, not the ticket's TimeWindow.

Notice that the user's Web browser serves as an intermediary for all communication. The application server requires authentication, but sets the Return URL and instructs the user (via an HTTP redirect) to go to a Passport server. The Passport authenticates the user, provides the Passport cookies, then sends the user back to the application server via the Return URL. The application server and Passport server do not communicate directly. Figure 10-3 illustrates this process.

The cookies used in this authentication process are similar to the tickets granted by the Kerberos DC. One of the most important pieces of the Passport cookie is the Passport User ID (PUID). The PUID is a 64-bit number that is unique to every user.

Often, the cookies are sent over HTTP. An astute question would be, Why is a cookie secure even if it is transmitted over HTTP? After all, anyone could intercept the HTTP request and view the cookie. The answer is that the Passport cookie, like a Kerberos ticket, cannot be decrypted by the client because the client does not know and has not supplied the encryption key. Each Passport cookie value (ticket) is encrypted with the 168-bit Triple DES algorithm based on a secret key shared by the Passport authentication server and the Web application server. This is the secret key exchanged out of band when the partner application server is first deployed.

Attacks Against Passport

When an application uses Passport to authenticate users, it does not need to provide methods for managing passwords. In fact, the login name (e-mail address) and password are not supplied by Passport to the partner application. This has a security byproduct beneficial to users. For example, consider two applications: Violet and Rose. If the Violet application server were compromised, only the data stored by Violet would be exposed. The user's Passport credentials are still safe. A malicious user would not be able to use information from Violet to log in to the unrelated Rose application.

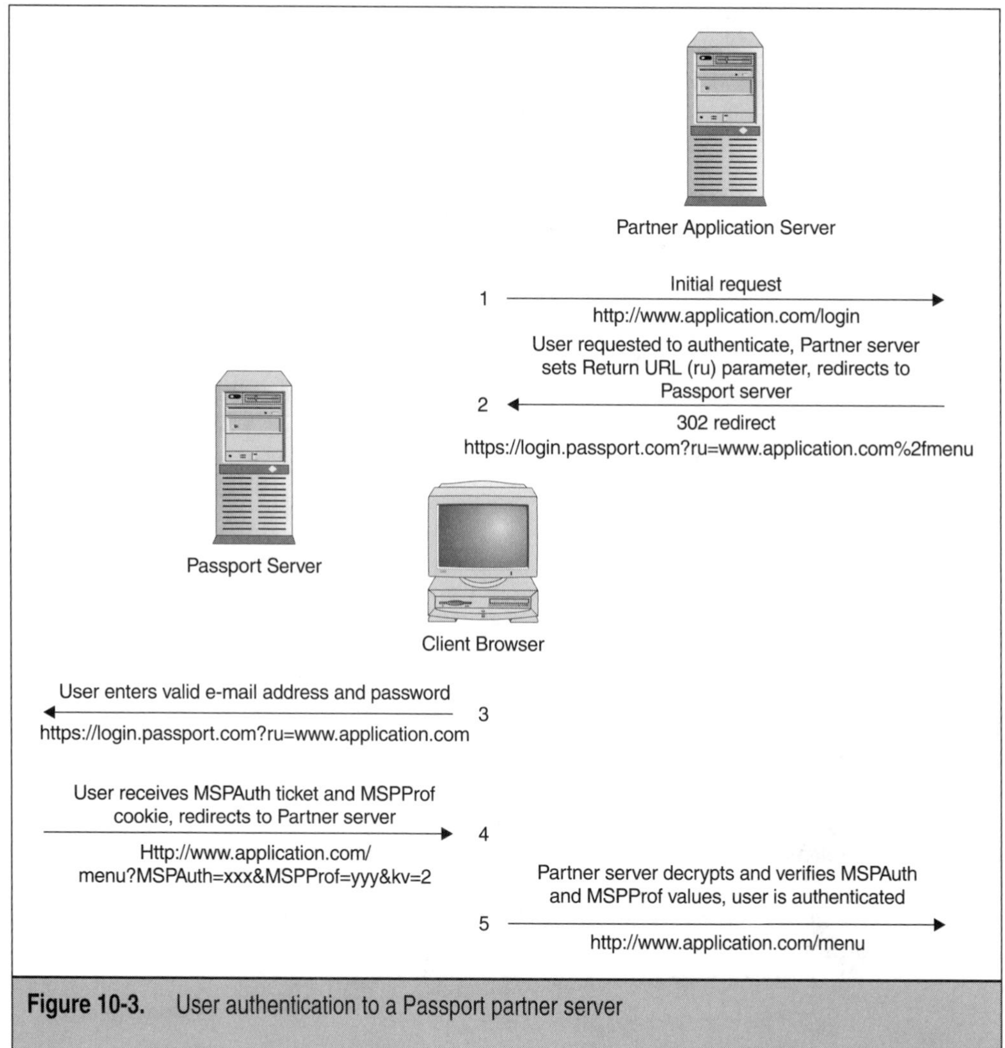

Figure 10-3. User authentication to a Passport partner server

Of course, if a user's login name and password are stolen, that account is compromised. In order to compromise these two pieces of data, a malicious user would have to accomplish a feat similar to one of these scenarios:

- Steal the username and password from the victim's own computer.
- Sniff the username and password as they are submitted to the Passport server. Currently, all Passport authentication must be done over SSL, which mitigates the likelihood of success for this attack.
- Steal the username and password from the Passport server. Any authentication system faces this risk.

Because a cookie may be transmitted over HTTP, it is possible that it could be sniffed by a malicious user. This exposes the cookie to a replay attack. Fortunately, Passport provides the TimeWindow mechanism to reduce the potential success of such an attack.

Malicious Partner Applications

Theoretically, a malicious party could set up a rogue partner application that uses Passport for authentication. This would be an attack against users' Passport credentials. Even though the malicious partner application would be able to decrypt the Passport ticket (MSPAuth) and Profile (MSPProf), it would not be able to harvest Passport accounts. In this scenario, only the user's optionally supplied information and PUID would be exposed. Remember, the user's password is never supplied to the partner application, only the user's ticket upon successful authentication. Even so, if a user's profile contains home mailing address, birth date, and gender, the malicious application would be able to gather that personal information. Passport can collect the following information:

- First name
- Last name
- Country/region
- State
- ZIP code
- Time zone
- Gender
- Birth date
- Occupation
- Accessibility

Even though all of this information can personally identify a user, Passport only requires two fields: a username (e-mail address) and password. There are further restrictions on how information is collected and used when the account is tied to a minor. So, users under 18 years of age (based on the birth date provided by the user) have additional privacy protections.

Privacy

In addition to the security risks of Passport, or any single sign-on system, users are concerned about the privacy of their information. Strong application security gives users a sense of comfort about their information, from credit card numbers to home mailing addresses. An application can use encryption to hide data from malicious eavesdroppers. Digital signatures can be used to validate the end user and the application to each other. The types of data collected, how those data are tracked, and to whom their access is granted lies more in the realm of policy than technical security measures; but it illustrates how important it is for the application developers to consider all of the users' concerns.

Passport also requires that peer applications implement Platform for Privacy Preferences (P3P) for their users. The user's browser must support P3P, which is the case for the most common browsers. Basically, P3P enables a user to specify the types of personal information a Web application may collect. This is to make it easier for users to understand the privacy stance of a Web application and have some ability to control how their personal information is disseminated.

WEB SERVICES AND .NET

Whereas Passport does not currently have a SOAP interface, Microsoft's .NET services already provide methods for implementing SOAP. It supports a variety of platforms and programming languages.

Framework

The .NET framework applies a sandboxing technique for application code that is reminiscent of Java. Application code falls into one of two groups: managed or unmanaged. The terms "managed" or "unmanaged" are in relation to the Common Language Runtime (CLR). Managed code, as defined within .NET, is controlled by a CLR host. The host is typically an ASP.NET ISAPI filter for IIS (for servers) or Internet Explorer (for clients). The host controls several aspects of code execution:

- **How it is placed into memory** Memory management leads to more efficient use of resources and protection of data during exceptions.
- **Exception handling** Buffer overflows and other user-generated errors can be handled to a greater degree. The ability to catch more errors or to "break securely" by default limits the attack vectors for a malicious user. Managed code should be able to catch more errors.
- **Assemblies** A programmer-friendly feature that describes a specific set of files and their version numbers for an application. One byproduct of this is that programmers can be assured of compatibility and functionality because code libraries (DLLs) correspond to specific applications. Thus, upgrading a DLL for one service application will not break functionality for a service application that requires a different DLL version.

Managed code is found in class libraries, such as cryptographic algorithms. Class libraries provide fundamental interfaces for data objects and access methods. An application built from the ground up to rely on class libraries will have more inherent security than a legacy application run from a .NET server.

SECURITY ALERT A CLR host can conceivably run on any operating system or in embedded devices. Consequently, functions that access files ultimately fall into the security controls of the underlying operating system, not the CLR. Managed code with a poorly written input validation function could expose files outside of the Web document root.

The unmanaged code category would include most applications written for IIS today. There is only minimal separation of processes, memory, and security contexts. All of these can lead to buffer overflows and privilege escalation.

Security in .NET applications comes from three sources:

- **Code Access Security** This enforces security within the application in order to control file access, component access, and memory access. For example, it could be used to limit access to the G:\data directory so that a ViewProfile service may access the directory, but an UpdateEmail service cannot. In Visual Basic and C#, the PrincipalPermissionAttribute controls code access based on Name (the user's account on a Windows 2000 domain, for example), Role (the group a user belongs to), Action (Deny, PermitOnly, RequestMinimum, RequestRefuse, and other security actions that explicitly allow or deny a command), or whether the user is authenticated or the object allows access.
- **Evidence-Based Security** Perhaps the most well-known aspect is Authenticode, which is related to assemblies. This enforces security based on certification of the code in question. This level enforces security based on environment, such as code origin (whether the origin is a URL or a, specific, Internet Explorer Security Zone).
- **Role-Based Security** This enforces security based on authentication and authorization of the user. On Windows platforms, the user is tracked by a security identifier (SID) that is checked each time a resource is requested or role is assumed.

On a system level, you can use the mscorcfg.msc Management Console to view the current settings for .NET assemblies, for remoting services (how remote services interact with your system), for code access security policy, and to configure managed applications. Figure 10-4 shows the basic MMC snap-in for the .NET framework.

Significant security options are available for Enterprise, Machine, or User permission sets. A permission set can be configured to permit or deny everything from accessing SQL databases with blank passwords, to defining which hosts can be trusted with Web access, to read/write/append access to individual files, to assembly

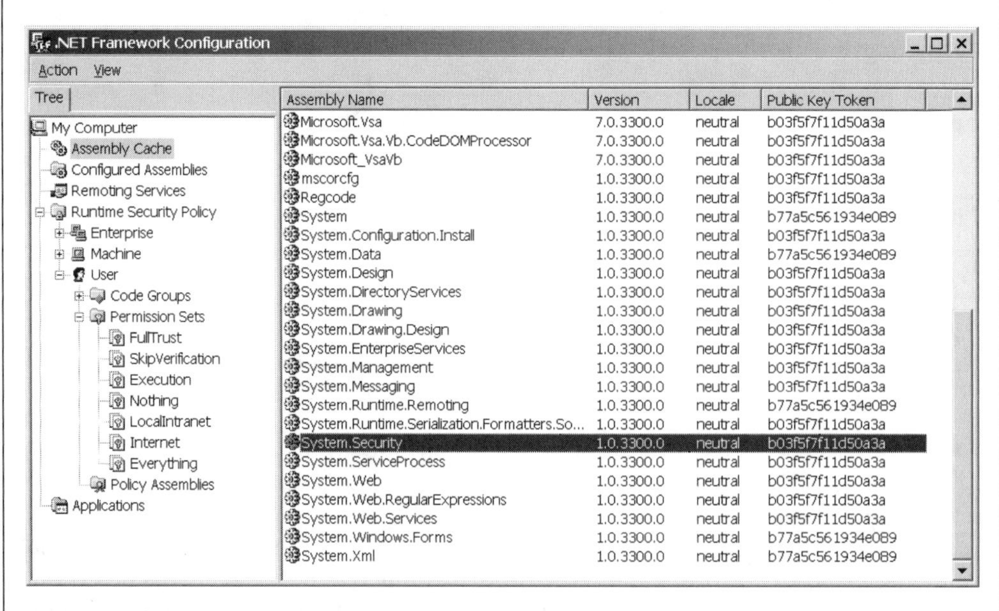

Figure 10-4. Viewing assemblies with the .NET Framework Configuration console

permissions. Figure 10-5 shows the MMC menu for creating a new permission set. Figure 10-6 shows the specific options you can set for an assembly.

Threats Against .NET Services

Like any Web Services application, a .NET application can be written insecurely. The majority of attacks against a .NET site are probably invalid input attacks. These attacks manipulate data to something that the server does not expect.

Input Validation

Input validation attacks take advantage of weak parsing functions and programmers who place too much trust in the client application. One of the most efficient, yet insecure, methods of input validation is to use client-side JavaScript in the Web browser. The JavaScript routines might be smart enough to strip out invalid characters, but it is trivial to bypass such methods. Input validation attacks can lead to user impersonation, privilege escalation, and arbitrary file access.

SQL Injection

SQL injection is a specific subset of input validation that can enable malicious users to extract arbitrary data from a database. A good method of mitigating such attacks is

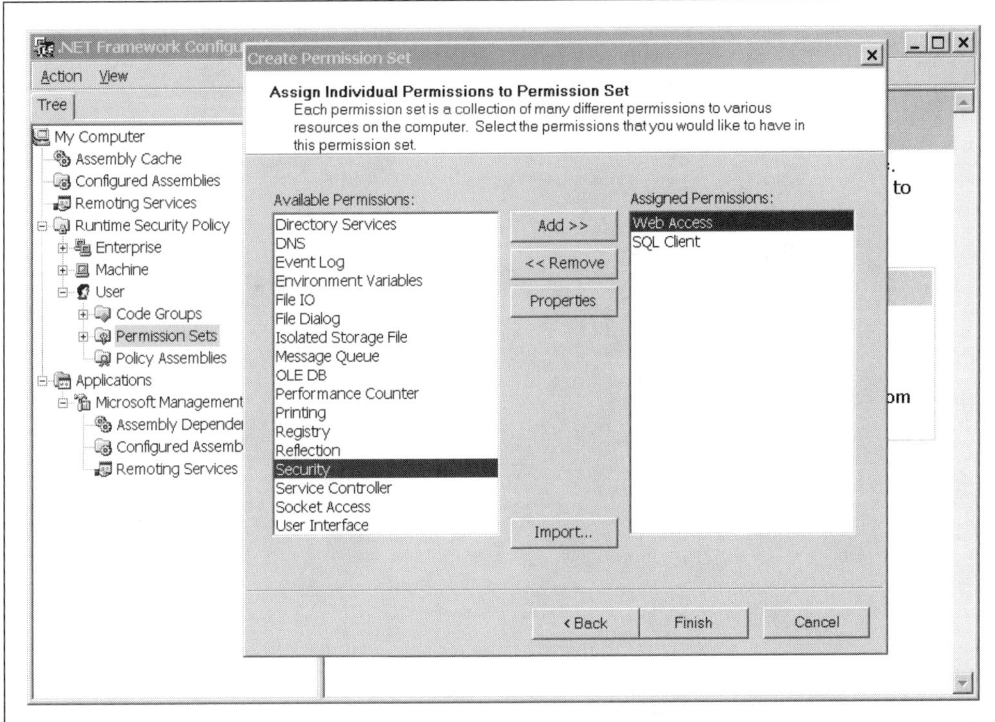

Figure 10-5. Creating a new permission set with the .NET MMC

to rely on stored procedures. For example, if your application relies on the SqlCommandMethod to execute SQL statements, you should use the CommandType .StoreProcedure as opposed to the CommandType.Text method. A stored procedure receives a parameter list and generates an error if the list varies from the predetermined number of parameters or parameter types. On the other hand, it is easier to insert malicious characters into a SQL query constructed from a string.

Consider this function, written in C# pseudocode:

```
[ SqlCommandMethod(CommandType.Text, "SELECT * FROM Users
  WHERE Password = @Passwd AND ExpireDate > GetDate()") ]
public static DataSet GetAnnouncements(SqlConnection connection, int
moduleId)
{
...functions
}
```

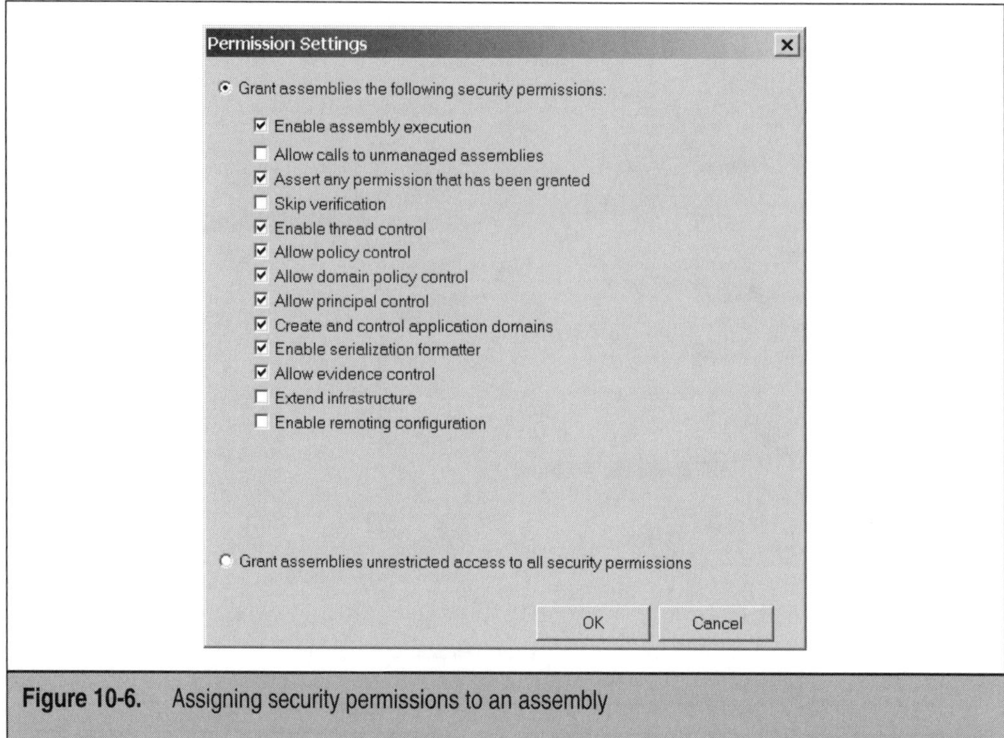

Figure 10-6. Assigning security permissions to an assembly

If the Web application does not perform proper input validation for the @Passwd variables, a malicious user could attempt a SQL injection attack. For example, @Passwd might be manipulated to contain SQL formatting such as "a OR 1=1'--." The final SQL query would end up as "SELECT * FROM Users WHERE Password = a OR 1=1." Thus, the SQL query is reduced to selecting all data (SELECT *) from the table containing user information. Depending on the error handling within the application, a few actions might occur. The application will return an error because it received more fields than it expected. This field information (such as passwords) could be returned in the error string. On the other hand, the application may simply take the first series returned. In that case, the user would log in with the credentials of the first user defined in the Users table.

SECURITY ALERT The .NET version of Microsoft Visual Basic introduces Java's error-handling concept of the try, catch, finally statements. Any time the application must parse user-generated data, place the parsing function within a try statement. The catch statement should handle known possible errors, such as letters entered as a U.S. ZIP code, as well as a default handler for unknown errors, such as receiving null input. Even if the catch statement does not consider every attack, the finally statement should perform a graceful exit of the function and display a polite error message to the user. Remember, this error message should not contain any references to application constants, variables, line numbers, or filenames.

Threats Against .NET Servers

System administrators can easily lose sleep when their .NET applications run on Microsoft's IIS Web server. A vulnerable Web server is often the point of entry into any Web-based application. A buffer overflow or an incorrect parsing algorithm could provide a malicious user access to encryption keys, user data, and application source code. IIS has had a history of such vulnerabilities. For example, Microsoft has issued the following security advisories for IIS:

- **IIS Directory Traversal and Superfluous Decode (MS00-086, MS01-026)** These enabled malicious users to access arbitrary files and run arbitrary commands on the Web server. Placing the Web document root on a drive volume separate from the SYSTEMROOT greatly reduces the impact of this attack.
- **IIS ISAPI DLL buffer overflow (MS01-023, MS01-033)** Buffer overflows in the .printer and .ida ISAPI filters granted malicious users command-line access to vulnerable servers. Removing unused filters from the IIS install would have protected servers.
- **IIS FrontPage Server Extensions (MS01-035)** Another buffer overflow that granted command-line access. Again, removing unnecessary components from the IIS install would have protected many servers.

Attacking Protocols

Servers are always susceptible to denial of service (DoS) attacks. These attacks usually consist of excessive amounts of traffic being sent to the victim Web servers. For example, if the Passport authentication servers were taken down due to a flood attack or a backhoe slicing fiber lines, any partner site that requires Passport authentication would be out of commission as well. A successful DoS attack would be difficult to accomplish against networks specifically designed to handle high bandwidth.

Still, there are some measures you should take to protect your own servers:

- **Apply rate limiting to border routers** Cisco IOS supports committed access rate (CAR) controls with the *access-list* and *rate-limit* configuration options. Using CAR can aid your network against DoS attacks, but requires careful configuration to make sure they work appropriately for your network's average bandwidth, peak utilization, and traffic composition. Here is an example designed to protect against SYN floods. It permits traffic to TCP port 80, but limits SYN packets (new connection requests) while permitting all established connections to continue normally. You would change the numbers 64000 8000 8000 in order to set the average allowable bandwidth and maximum burst numbers:

```
access-list 101 permit tcp any any eq www
  access-list 102 permit tcp any any eq www established
  access-list 103 permit tcp any any syn
  interface <interface> <interface #>
```

```
      rate-limit input access-group 103 64000 8000 8000
conform-action transmit exceed-action drop
```

- **Design redundancy into the network and remove or limit single points of failure** Network equipment such as routers, load balancers, and firewalls should be deployed such that they have failover components. If a single load balancer serves a farm of 20 Web servers, a failure in the load balancer would prevent access to all of the Web servers.
- **Deploy a geographically diverse network** This can be difficult to accomplish for applications that rely heavily on database transactions. However, networks that are distributed geographically are more resistant to power failures, bandwidth flooding attacks, or equipment failure. It is similar to redundancy.
- **Ensure servers are maintained at a current security patch level** If application servers lack security patches, malicious users could more easily create a denial of service or compromise a system. After all, it's easier to bring down a server with only a few dozen packets against a known vulnerability as opposed to flooding the server with millions.

Protecting Your Servers

The IIS ISAPI filters caused a great deal of headaches for administrators. The default installation for IIS is notoriously insecure and includes several items that can be removed in order to make it more secure while not hampering its performance. Here's a quick checklist of recommended settings for IIS:

- Remove all unused ISAPI filters. This is a simple measure that buys a lot of security. Figure 10-7 shows the Properties window from the MMC tool for configuring IIS.
- Place the Web document root on a drive volume that does not contain the system root (WINNT directory). Preferably, this will be a volume that holds no other data but the Web application's code.
- Network access lists should only permit inbound Internet access to ports 80 and 443.
- Network access lists should not allow Web servers to establish outbound Internet connections. This means that the Web server can still answer incoming connections, but the server cannot be used to access an FTP server, a TFTP server, or any other service on the Internet. This makes it more difficult for a malicious user or a worm to use the server as a platform for further attacks.
- Database servers should only use integrated authentication. Regardless, the "sa" user password should not be blank!

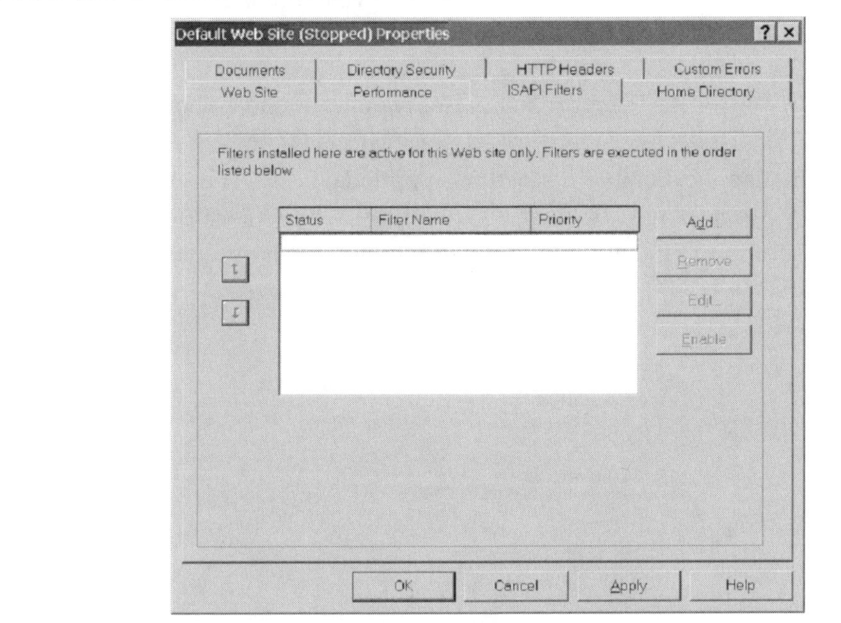

Figure 10-7. Remove *every* unused ISAPI filter.

CHECKLIST

- ☐ Each Web server has been deployed in a secure manner as recommended for its operating system. This includes applying the latest security patches, separating system partitions from Web document roots, and removing unnecessary files from the Web document root.
- ☐ The .NET application uses managed code. Any unmanaged code has been reviewed for input validation and does not perform important functions such as database connections.
- ☐ Strong passwords have been set for all applications, including databases, and remote management methods.
- ☐ The application uses strong exception handling, combined with disabling .NET server's debug output on production systems.

- ☐ Applications perform strong server-side input validation. Content is checked for value (numeric boundaries), type (integer, string, ZIP code, phone number, name), and length.
- ☐ The secret key for the Passport and partner application to exchange data has been installed and a copy of the secret key is stored on a secured host.
- ☐ The partner application has defined what optional Passport user information it will use. Passport only requires an e-mail address and password.
- ☐ Privacy settings (P3P) have been defined for the partner application.

CHAPTER 11

The Liberty Alliance Project

This chapter offers a technical introduction to the Liberty Alliance Project (also referred to as "Liberty" for short). The Liberty Alliance Project is an effort, initiated by Sun Microsystems and now involving more than 120 companies, with the goal of facilitating authentication on the Web for both human users and automated mechanisms (both types referred to as "Principals" in the Liberty technical documentation). Though enhanced authentication technologies for automated mechanisms will become as equally critical as for human users (particularly for Web Services), the examples of this chapter will focus on human Principals since we, as humans, are personally familiar with the challenges of handling multiple local identities. The technical details presented are based on Liberty Alliance Project specifications that were released in July of 2002 (available from the Liberty Web site at http://www.projectliberty.org).

Readers are encouraged to first visit the Liberty Web site to view the multimedia general introduction to Liberty before delving into the technical details presented in this chapter.

WHAT DOES THE LIBERTY ALLIANCE PROJECT HAVE TO DO WITH WEB SERVICES?

What does the Liberty Alliance Project have to do with Web Services? The goal of Web Services is to make it easy for varied organizations to link their systems. The goal of Liberty is to allow different Web sites to cooperate on behalf of their clients to facilitate more seamless and intuitive experiences. In some cases, this cooperation will entail Web Services communication among multiple Web sites on behalf of those Principals.

When Web Services are being performed on behalf of a human Principal, what happens when that individual has identities registered with some of those organizations? For example, suppose a Principal's preferences at one organization ought to determine the response of a Web Service request from another organization with which the Principal is also affiliated. Will those organizations' Principals have to log in at each organization that participates in the overall Web Service? For an efficient, cost-effective, and profitable Web Service, the elimination of unnecessary human interaction is paramount.

So, for Web Services to reach their full potential, a means of federating existing Web identities and enabling single sign-on is necessary—and that is the purpose of the Liberty Alliance Project.

But in addition to the value of cross-domain authentication of humans, there is a need for cross-domain authentication of automated mechanisms, namely applications calling Web Services. These applications, too, will often need to be authenticated, as they interact with other Web Service–enabled applications over the Web. For example, digital media content providers may only allow their content to be accessed through Web Services by media players known to have certain digital rights management (DRM) capabilities. A media player requesting content from one or more content providers would first need to be authenticated, perhaps by proxy, through an identity provider that specializes in registering DRM-certified media players.

Terms to Remember

Before we go any further, some common Liberty terms and namespaces need to be highlighted.

Identity Provider

A provider of Principals' identities that asserts the authenticity of a Principal to other identity providers and service providers (defined next).

Service Provider

This is a provider of services that the Principal may wish to use, but that does not assert the authenticity of a Principal to other providers.

Provider

This can be either an identity provider or a service provider.

Circle of Trust

A circle of trust is a community of service providers and identity providers with business relationships that have joined together to enable new secure experiences for the Principals whose identities they hold.

Principal

Principals are the entities who have, or will have, one or more identities on the Web. Principals will often be human users, but as Web Services make it easier for various software and devices to interact over the Web, it must be remembered that they, too, may be seen as Principals. The Liberty Alliance Project documentation intentionally uses the word "Principal" rather than "user" to emphasize this reality.

Local Identity

This is the identity a Principal has with a specific provider.

Federated Network Identity

This is a set of local identities that recognize each other's existence and can work with each other through Liberty protocols.

Namespace Prefixes Used

The following namespace prefixes are used in this chapter:

- **ds** XML Signature (http://www.w3.org/2000/09/xmldsig#)
- **saml** SAML assertion namespace (urn:oasis:names:tc:SAML:1.0:assertion)
- **samlp** SAML protocol namespace (urn:oasis:names:tc:SAML:1.0:protocol)

Example Players

The examples in this chapter will be based on a scenario involving the following characters:

- **Joan** A Web user who wishes she didn't have to keep track of so many local identities.
- **IDP1** An identity provider through which Joan has her primary identity information. Joan will leverage her identity at IDP1 in order to simplify the burden of tracking local identities.
- **BigWebRetailer** An online retailer at which Joan has a local identity and which is part of IDP1's circle of trust.
- **Delivery** A worldwide parcel delivery company at which Joan has a local identity and which is part of IDP1's circle of trust.

The following sections illustrate the Liberty-defined communications that will occur among the three Web sites above in order to enable more seamless browsing and purchasing experiences for Joan.

Creating Circles of Trust Among Identity Providers and Service Providers

In order to protect users' privacy and organizations' reputations, exchanging identity information only makes sense among organizations that have established trust relationships and the legal agreements to back up those trust relationships. (Liberty does not attempt to standardize what these legal agreements among providers would contain.)

Once a legal framework has been established between an identity provider and a service provider, the first technical step required is the exchange of metadata. Provider metadata primarily consists of the URLs of those endpoints that a provider hosts and that other providers must be aware of; its communication is accomplished through the exchange of provider descriptors. Specifically, the identity provider publishes an identity provider descriptor, and the service provider publishes a service provider descriptor.

Both types of descriptors contain the following information.

ProviderID

This is a provider's identifier (a URI).

ProviderSuccinctID

This is a succinct provider identifier.

KeyInfo (from the XML Signature Namespace)

This is the provider's public key (see Chapter 8 for information on public key management).

SoapEndpoint

This is the provider's SOAP endpoint.

SingleLogoutServiceURL

This is the URL to which logout notification messages are to be sent.

SingleLogoutServiceReturnURL

Once single logout has been achieved, this is the URL to which further incoming logout notification messages will be redirected.

FederationTerminationServiceURL

This is the URL to which federation termination notices are to be sent.

FederationTerminationServiceReturnURL

Once a federation has been terminated, this is the URL to which further federation termination notices will be sent.

An identity provider descriptor also includes a `SingleSignOnServiceURL` element to identify where authentication requests are to be received.

A service provider descriptor includes the following additional information.

AssertionConsumerServiceURL

This is the URL for receiving assertions from identity providers.

FederationTerminationNotificationProtocolProfile

This is the profile of the Federation Termination Notification Protocol that the identity provider should use.

SingleLogoutProtocolProfile

This is the profile of the Single Logout Protocol that the identity provider should use.

AuthnRequestsSigned

If "true", this indicates that the service provider always signs its authentication requests.

Example: IDP1 and BigWebRetailer Create a Circle of Trust IDP1 and BigWebRetailer want to enable their users' identities to be federated; IDP1 is always on the lookout for means of better serving its users, and BigWebRetailer wants to make it easy for IDP1's users to find, purchase, and deliver products.

Here is the IDP1's identity provider descriptor:

```
<IDPDescriptor>
  <ProviderID>http://www.idp1.xom</ProviderID>
  <ProviderSuccinctID>K2H6H9</ProviderSuccinctID>
  <ds:KeyInfo>...</ds:KeyInfo>
  <SoapEndpoint>http://www.idp1.xom/soap</SoapEndpoint>
  <SingleLogoutServiceURL>
      http://www.idp1.xom/liberty/slo
  </SingleLogoutServiceURL>
  <SingleLogoutServiceReturnURL>
      http://www.idp1.xom/liberty/slo_return
  </SingleLogoutServiceReturnURL>
  <FederationTerminationServiceURL>
      http://www.idp1.xom/liberty/term
  </FederationTerminationServiceURL>
  <FederationTerminationServiceReturnURL>
      http://www.idp1.xom/liberty/term_return
  </FederationTerminationServiceReturnURL>
  <SingleSignOnServiceURL>
      http://www.idp1.xom/liberty/sso
  </SingleSignOnServiceURL>
</IDPDescriptor>
```

Here is BigWebRetailer's service provider descriptor:

```
<SPDescriptor>
  <ProviderID>http://www.bigwebretailer.xom</ProviderID>
  <ProviderSuccinctID>084NYY</ProviderSuccinctID>
  <ds:KeyInfo>...</ds:KeyInfo>
  <SoapEndpoint>
      http://www.bigwebretailer.xom/soap
  </SoapEndpoint>
  <SingleLogoutServiceURL>
      http://www.bigwebretailer.xom/liberty/slo
  </SingleLogoutServiceURL>
  <SingleLogoutServiceReturnURL>
      http://www.bigwebretailer.xom/liberty/slo_return
  </SingleLogoutServiceReturnURL>
  <FederationTerminationServiceURL>
      http://www.bigwebretailer.xom/liberty/term
  </FederationTerminationServiceURL>
  <FederationTerminationServiceReturnURL>
      http://www.bigwebretailer.xom/liberty/term_return
```

```
  </FederationTerminationServiceReturnURL>
  <AssertionConsumerServiceURL>
      http://www.bigwebretailer.xom/liberty/assertion_consumer
  </AssertionConsumerServiceURL>
  <FederationTerminationNotificationProtocolProfile>
      http://projectliberty.org/profiles/fedterm_soap
  </FederationTerminationNotificationProtocolProfile>
    <SingleLogoutProtocolProfile>
      http://projectliberty.org/profiles/slo_soap
  </SingleLogoutProtocolProfile>
  <AuthnRequestsSigned>1</AuthnRequestsSigned>
</SPDescriptor>
```

Once IDP1 and BigWebRetailer have exchanged their descriptors, they will know to which URLs the different messages that comprise the Liberty protocols should be sent.

Single Sign-On

Single sign-on means enabling a user to sign on once, and then, without having to sign on again, access different domains that would normally be outside the scope of the primary sign-on domain. Right now, on the Web, a typical user needs to have separate local identities for almost every service she or he wants to use and then must sign on to each one individually. While it is possible for large Internet content providers to let their registered users access a variety of services (for example, e-mail, newsgroups, stock tracking) with one local identity, such integration does not normally extend outside the domain of the content provider. Hence most Internet users maintain separate identities for each banking, billing, travel, interest group, e-mail, and so forth service that they want to use. Undoubtedly, the annoyance of having to keep track of so many different identities with their varying identification (for example, username, system-defined name, e-mail address) and authentication requirements (for example, password rules) dampens the enthusiasm to use the Web and limits what the Web can do for the user.

Recognizing that the lack of a practical single sign-on architecture is no longer just a nuisance but a major obstacle to advancing the Web, Liberty takes advantage of SAML authentication assertions to accomplish single sign-on among members of a circle of trust. Figure 11-1 illustrates how Joan can be presented with her personalized BigWebRetailer page, yet be authenticated behind the scenes by IDP1.

1. Joan goes to the BigWebRetailer Web site.
2. BigWebRetailer redirects Joan to the IDP1 Web site so that it can authenticate her.
3. Once authenticated, Joan is returned to the BigWebRetailer Web site.

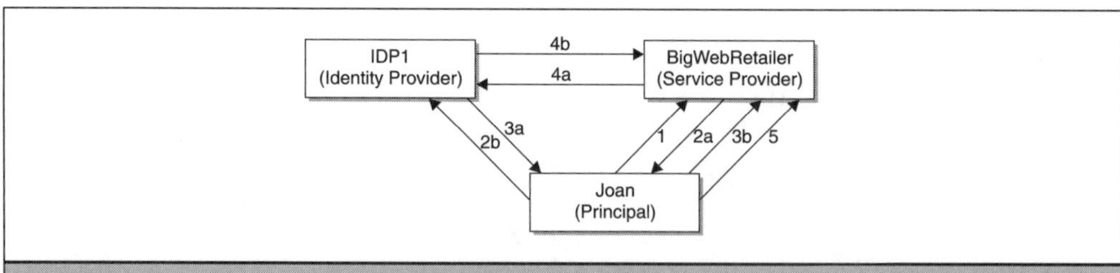

Figure 11-1. Joan (the Principal) is authenticated by IDP1 (her identity provider) when she browses to her personalized BigWebRetailer (her service provider) Web page.

4. The SAML artifact created when Joan was redirected is accessed by BigWebRetailer, then sent by BigWebRetailer to IDP1. IDP1 returns a SAML authentication assertion to BigWebRetailer.
5. If the SAML authentication assertion's digital signature is valid, BigWebRetailer presents Joan's personalized page to her.

Though at first sight being able to sign on once for every potential service may seem ideal, this need not be the most appropriate view of single sign-on. Most of us would certainly like to limit the number of identities we need to maintain, but not necessarily limit them to just one. Indeed, it may make sense to have a separate home identity, work identity, family identity, and so on. The ultimate goal is not one single identity, but to make it possible for a Principal to have just the number of identities she or he wants to have, no more and no less, and to let the Principal control what information is passed among federated identities. (Because "single sign-on" may in fact not be the most appropriate description of what Liberty enables, sometimes the phrase "simplified sign-on" is used instead.)

Identity Federation

Before IDP1 and BigWebRetailer can offer the convenience of single sign-on to Joan, they must first establish a shared identifier for Joan, After all, if IDP1 is to issue an assertion as to the authentication status of Joan and have BigWebRetailer be able to use it, IDP1 and BigWebRetailer have to be able to agree that it is indeed Joan for whom the assertion was created. Both IDP1 and BigWebRetailer must share some common identifier for Joan so that they can use it in their communications on her behalf. The process by which IDP1 and BigWebRetailer establish this shared identifier is called identity federation.

Both identity federation and the subsequently enabled single sign-on are realized through Liberty's authentication protocol in which a provider sends an `AuthnRequest` (authentication request) message to an identity provider and receives an `AuthnResponse` (authentication response) message in return. An `AuthnRequest` message extends SAML's request type and specifies the following.

Provider ID

This is the requestor.

IsPassive

This indicates whether the identity provider may actively query the Principal or not.

ForceAuthn

If set to "true", the identity provider must authenticate, or reauthenticate, the Principal before responding. Note: `IsPassive` must be set to "false" if ForceAuthn is set to "true."

Federate

This indicates whether the corresponding identities are to be federated or not.

Protocol Profile

This is the protocol profile that the service provider wishes to use for the response. If the element is not specified, the default protocol profile is

```
http://projectliberty.org/profiles/brws-art
```

AuthnContext

This is information regarding the preferences of the service provider with respect to how the Principal should be authenticated.

RelayState

This is state information that will be relayed back in the response.

The returned `AuthnResponse` message contains a SAML authentication assertion with these Liberty-defined extensions:

IDPProvidedNameIdentifier This is the name identifier that the identity provider will use for the Principal and that the requesting provider will also use unless it wishes to specify another one through a `RegisterNameIdentifierRequest` message (described later in "Name Registration").

AuthnContext This is the authentication context that was used by the identity provider when it authenticated the Principal. The requestor may check this information to see if it is equivalent to the requested authentication context and/or is acceptable. Authentication context refers to the processes, technologies, and mechanisms used by the identity provider in order to authenticate Principals.

ReauthenticateOnOrAfter

This is a time when the requestor should request a reauthentication from the identity provider.

SessionIndex

This indicates to which session between the requestor and identity provider the `AuthnResponse` pertains. This value, if specified, is used when coordinating the single logout of the Principal.

Example: Joan Chooses to Federate Her *BigWebRetailer* Local Identity with Her *IDP1* Local Identity

In this example, we follow the process that IDP1 and BigWebRetailer follow and the messages they exchange in order to enable single sign-on for Joan. Because it is the concept of identity federation that Liberty defined (as opposed to the subsequent SSO that SAML enables), we concentrate on the identity federation process here.

Before looking at what happens when Joan federates her identities, it will be helpful to consider what the situation looks like beforehand. At this point, both IDP1 and BigWebRetailer have directories listing Principals, their authentication, and other local identity information. IDP1's directory entry for Joan might look like this:

```
<IDP1_Users xmlns="http://www.idp1.xom/namespaces/users">
...
<User UID="Joan_IDP1">
  <AuthenticationInfo>...</AuthenticationInfo>
  <Info>
    <EMail>
      <Address>Joan_IDP1@idp1.xom</Address>
   <Boxes>...</Boxes>
  </EMail>
  <Contacts>
    <Contact>
      <Name>...</Name>
      <Address>...</Address>
    </Contact>
    ...
  </Contacts>
  ...
  </Info>
</User>
...
</IDP1_Users>
```

BigWebRetailer's directory entry for Joan might look like this:

```
<BigWebRetailer_Customers
    xmlns="http://www.bigwebretailer.xom/namespaces/customers">
...
<Customer CID="Joan_BWR">
 <AuthenticationInfo>…</AuthenticationInfo>
 <Address>29 Quandary Road</Address>
 <Preferences>
  <Preference>Kayaking</Preference>
 </Preferences>
</Customer>
...
</BigWebRetailer_Customers>
```

Note that in the above directory examples, none of the XML is predefined by Liberty: Liberty does not define how providers are to store their cross-authentication information, only how they transfer that information. The preceding XML examples are only intended to illustrate how exchanged Liberty information might be handled by two independent organizations.

One fine day, Joan decides to buy a gift for her nephew through BigWebRetailer. This time when Joan logs into BigWebRetailer, she is offered the opportunity to federate her BigWebRetailer identity with her IDP1 identity, and she accepts. Consequently, BigWebRetailer sends an `AuthnRequest` message to IDP1 indicating:

- Joan's BigWebRetailer and IDP1 local identities are to be federated
- IDP1 must authenticate Joan upon receiving the request

The AuthnRequest message sent by BigWebRetailer to IDP1 would appear as follows:

```
<AuthnRequest
    RequestID="9kdk-48vj-k93e"
    MajorVersion="1" MinorVersion="0"
    IssueInstant="2002-10-20T19:31:17-05:00">
  <ds:Signature> ... </ds:Signature>
  <ProviderID>http://www.bigwebretailer.xom</ProviderID>
  <ForceAuthn>1</ForceAuthn>
  <IsPassive>0</IsPassive>
  <Federate>1</Federate>
  <ProtocolProfile>
    http://projectliberty.org/profiles/brws-post
```

```
  </ProtocolProfile>
  <AuthnContext>
    <AuthnContextClassRef>
      http://projectliberty.org/schemas/authctx/2002/05/Password
    </AuthnContextClassRef>
  </AuthnContext>
  <RelayState>EWRJKLCVZXIUODFSAKJL</RelayState>
</AuthnRequest>
```

Upon receiving the previous request, IDP1 authenticates Joan and returns an `AuthnResponse` to BigWebRetailer:

```
<AuthnResponse
    ResponseID="39di-o20x-apci"
    InResponseTo="9kdk-48vj-k93e"
    MajorVersion="1" MinorVersion="0"
    IssueInstant="2002-10-20T19:31:27-05:00">
  <samlp:Status>
    <samlp:StatusCode Value="saml:Success"/>
  </samlp:Status>
  <saml:Assertion MajorVersion="1" MinorVersion="0"
   AssertionID="2349-7543-8320"
   Issuer="http://www.idp1.com
   IssueInstant="2002-10-20T19:31:22-05:00"
   InResponseTo="9kdk-48vj-k93e"
   xsi:type="AssertionType">
  <saml:Conditions NotBefore="2002-10-20T19:31:22-05:00"
    NotOnOrAfter="2002-10-20T21:31:22-05:00">
   <saml:AudienceRestrictionCondition>
    <saml:Audience>http://www.bigwebretailer.com</saml:Audience>
   </saml:AudienceRestrictionCondition>
  </saml:Conditions>
  <saml:AuthenticationStatement
    AuthenticationInstant="2002-10-20T19:31:22-05:00"
    SessionIndex="3"
    ReauthenticateOnOrAfter="2002-10-20T21:31:22-05:00"
    xsi:type="AuthenticationStatementType">
   <saml:Subject xsi:type="SubjectType">
    <saml:NameIdentifier>
      qwert
    </saml:NameIdentifier>
    <IDPProvidedNameIdentifier>
```

```
      qwert
    </IDPProvidedNameIdentifier>
   </saml:Subject>
  </saml:AuthenticationStatement>
  <ds:Signature>...</ds:Signature>
 </saml:Assertion>
 <RelayState>EWRJKLCVZXIUODFSAKJL</RelayState>
</AuthnResponse>
```

The AuthnResponse includes an IDPProvidedNameIdentifier that BigWebRetailer, unless it chooses to replace it, will use as an alias for Joan. At this point, the information in IDP1's directory entry for Joan now looks like this:

```
<IDP1_Users xmlns="http://www.idp1.xom/namespaces/users">
...
<User UID="Joan_IDP1">
 <AuthenticationInfo>...</AuthenticationInfo>
 <Liberty xmlns="www.idp1.xom/namespaces/liberty/circleoftrust">
  <FederatedIdentities>
   <FederatedIdentity
     Domain="www.bigwebretailer.xom"
     NameIdentifierIn="qwert"
     NameIdentifierOut="qwert"/>
  </FederatedIdentities>
 </Liberty>
 <Info>
  <EMail>
   <Address>Joan_IDP1@idp1.xom</Address>
   <Boxes>...</Boxes>
  </EMail>
  <Contacts>
    <Contact>
      <Name>...</Name>
      <Address>...</Address>
    </Contact>
    ...
  </Contacts>
  ...
 </Info>
</User>
...
</IDP1_Users>
```

while in BigWebRetailer's directory, the entry for Joan looks like this:

```
<BigWebRetailer_Customers>
...
<Customer CID="Joan_BWR"
xmlns="http://www.bigwebretailer.xom/namespaces/customers">
 <AuthenticationInfo>...</AuthenticationInfo>
 <Liberty xmlns="www.idp1.xom/namespaces/liberty/circleoftrust">
  <FederatedIdentities>
   <FederatedIdentity
     Domain="www.idp1.xom"
     NameIdentifierIn="qwert"
     NameIdentifierOut="qwert"/>
  </FederatedIdentities>
 </Liberty>
 <Address>...</Address>
 <Preferences>
  <Preference>Kayaking</Preference>
 </Preferences>
</Customer>
...
</BigWebRetailer_Customers>
```

NOTE In each of the previous two examples, a new element named "Liberty" has been introduced to carry the identity federation information. This is introduced only for clarity—Liberty did not define or stipulate how identity and service providers should store this information. For simplicity of this chapter's examples, we will assume members of the IDP1 circle of trust have agreed to use a common format for storing Liberty information, though in reality this need not be the case.

Taking a closer look, we see the IDP1 directory entry for Joan now has

```
<FederatedIdentity
  Domain="www.bigwebretailer.xom"
  NameIdentifierIn="qwert"
  NameIdentifierOut="qwert"/>
```

which means that when IDP1 is communicating with BigWebRetailer and wants to reference Joan, it will use the opaque name identifier of "qwert." Also, when IDP1 receives a message from BigWebRetailer regarding Joan, BigWebRetailer will use the opaque name identifier of "qwert" until it selects another name identifier (as the next section will explain). Similarly, the `FederatedIdentity` entry in BigWebRetailer's directory entry for Joan indicates the same information.

Name Registration

As illustrated by the previous example, at the conclusion of the Liberty authentication protocol, the identity provider and service provider are both using the same name identifier for the Principal. This may be fine for the identity provider who got to specify the name identifier, but may not be acceptable to the service provider who needs to at least ensure the name identifiers it manages are unique, and who, furthermore, may want to use a name identifier that fits in with the way it allocates name identifiers.

Consequently, Liberty provides a means by which a service provider can specify the name identifier it will use for the Principal. This is accomplished by having the service provider send a `RegisterNameIdentifierRequest` message to the identity provider that specifies the following.

ProviderID

This is the identity of the provider issuing the request.

IDPProvidedNameIdentifier

This is the name identifier set by the identity provider (and which the identity provider will continue to use to refer to the Principal).

SPProvidedNameIdentifier

This is the name identifier that the service provider will use to refer to the Principal.

When the identity provider receives the `RegisterNameIdentifierRequest`, it updates its alias information accordingly and returns a `RegisterNameIdentifier Response` to the requesting provider indicating that the provider-provided name identifier is now effective.

Example: BigWebRetailer Requests the Use of a Different Name Identifier for Joan To request a different name identifier for IDP1 to use for Joan when communicating with BigWebRetailer, BigWebRetailer sends this `RegisterNameIdentifierRequest` to IDP1:

```
<RegisterNameIdentifierRequest
  RequestID="DKDI-EIEW-UWIQ"
  MajorVersion="1" MinorVersion="0"
  IssueInstant="2002-10-20T09:32:02-05:00">
 <ds:Signature>...</ds:Signature>
 <ProviderID>http://www.big.webretailer.xom</ProviderID>
 <IDPProvidedNameIdentifier>
   qwert
 </IDPProvidedNameIdentifier>
 <SPProvidedNameIdentifier>
   yuiop
 </SPProvidedNameIdentifier>
</RegisterNameIdentifierRequest>
```

Example: IDP1 Responds to BigWebRetailer's Name Identification Request Upon receiving BigWebRetailer's request to use a particular name identifier, IDP1 uses the name identified by the `IDPProvidedNameIdentifier` element to determine which Principal is the subject of the request, which happens to be Joan, and updates the name identifier it will use when referring to Joan in messages to BigWebRetailer. IDP1 then indicates its acceptance of the proposed name identifier with a `RegisterNameIdentifierResponse` message:

```
<RegisterNameIdentifierResponse
  ResponseID="CMDE-SKQP-ZIWU"
  InResponseTo="DKDI-EIEW-UWIQ"
  MajorVersion="1" MinorVersion="0"
  IssueInstant="2002-10-20T19:32:12-05:00"
  Recipient="http://www.bigwebretailer.xom">
 <ds:Signature>...</ds:Signature>
 <samlp:Status>
  <samlp:StatusCode Value="saml:Success"/>
 </samlp:Status>
</RegisterNameIdentifierResponse>
```

With new name identifier in place, the information in Joan's IDP1 directory entry looks like this:

```
<IDP1_Users xmlns="http://www.idp1.xom/namespaces/users">
...
<User UID="Joan_IDP1">
 <AuthenticationInfo>...</AuthenticationInfo>
 <Liberty xmlns="www.idp1.xom/namespaces/liberty/circleoftrust">
  <FederatedIdentities>
   <FederatedIdentity
     Domain="www.bigwebretailer.xom"
     NameIdentifierIn="yuiop"
     NameIdentifierOut="qwert"/>
  </FederatedIdentities>
 </Liberty>
 <Info>
  <EMail>
   <Address>Joan_IDP1@idp1.xom</Address>
   <Boxes>...</Boxes>
  </EMail>
  <Contacts>
    <Contact>
      <Name>...</Name>
      <Address>...</Address>
```

```
    </Contact>
    ...
  </Contacts>
  ...
 </Info>
</User>
...
</IDP1_Users>
```

The information in Joan's *BigWebRetailer* directory entry looks like this:

```
<BigWebRetailer_Customers xmlns="http://www.bigwebretailer.xom/namespaces/customers">
...
<Customer CID="Joan_BWR">
 <AuthenticationInfo>...</AuthenticationInfo>
 <Liberty xmlns="www.idp1.xom/namespaces/liberty/circleoftrust">
  <FederatedIdentities>
   <FederatedIdentity
     Domain="www.idp1.xom"
     NameIdentifierIn="qwert"
     NameIdentifierOut="yuiop"/>
  </FederatedIdentities>
 </Liberty>
 <Address>...</Address>
 <Preferences>
  <Preference>Kayaking</Preference>
 </Preferences>
</Customer>
...
</BigWebRetailer_Customers>
```

Now, suppose Joan also chooses to federate her Delivery identity within IDP1's circle of trust and in the process of doing so, IDP1 selects the name identifier of "asdfg" to refer to Joan when communicating with Delivery, and Delivery selects the name identifier of "hjkln" to refer to Joan when communicating with IDP1. Here's what IDP1's and Delivery's directory entries for Joan would look like (for simplicity, we assume Delivery's directory architecture happens to be identical to IDP1's and BigWebRetailer's):

```
<IDP1_Users xmlns="http://www.idp1.xom/namespaces/users">
...
<User UID="Joan_IDP1">
 <AuthenticationInfo>...</AuthenticationInfo>
 <Liberty xmlns="www.idp1.xom/namespaces/liberty/circleoftrust">
  <FederatedIdentities>
   <FederatedIdentity
     Domain="www.bigwebretailer.xom"
```

```
      NameIdentifierIn="yuiop"
      NameIdentifierOut="qwert"/>
    <FederatedIdentity
      Domain="www.delivery.xom"
      NameIdentifierIn="hjkln"
      NameIdentifierOut="asdfg"/>
   </FederatedIdentities>
  </Liberty>
  <Info>
   <EMail>
    <Address>Joan_IDP1@idp1.xom</Address>
    <Boxes>...</Boxes>
   </EMail>
   <Calendar>...</Calendar>
   <Groups></Groups>
   <Contacts>
     <Contact>
       <Name>...</Name>
       <Address>...</Address>
     </Contact>
     ...
   </Contacts>
   ...
  </Info>
 </User>
 ...
 </IDP1_Users>
```

The information in Joan's *Delivery* directory entry looks like this:

```
<Delivery_Customers xmlns="http://www.delivery.xom/namespaces/customers">
...
<Customer CID="Joan_D">
 <AuthenticationInfo>...</AuthenticationInfo>
 <Liberty xmlns="www.idp1.xom/namespaces/liberty/circleoftrust">
  <FederatedIdentities>
   <FederatedIdentity
     Domain="www.idp1.xom"
     NameIdentifierIn="asdfg"
     NameIdentifierOut="hjkln"/>
  </FederatedIdentities>
 </Liberty>
 <Address>...</Address>
 <Preferences>
  <Preference>Next day</Preference>
 </Preferences>
```

```
</Customer>
...
</Delivery_Customers>
```

A key privacy-enabling feature of the Liberty specifications is the requirement placed on the identity provider to ensure that the name identifiers it uses for a Principal must be unique across the multiple service providers that a particular Principal may federate to. Returning to the example, while IDP1 uses the string "qwert" to identify Joan in transactions with BigWebRetailer, it uses the string "asdfg" to identify Joan to Delivery. Consequently, BigWebRetailer and Delivery are not given any hook on which they could inappropriately (without Joan's consent) share information about Joan.

Liberty Leading Web Services

This chapter has so far concentrated on how Liberty enables single sign-on for Principals. We have seen that the only information that an identity provider and service provider need exchange about a Principal is a meaningless identifier that can act as an alias to that Principal. But, if we consider the directory entries that IDP1, BigWebRetailer, and Delivery all maintain for Joan, we can imagine another class of information that could be shared.

Looking at the stylized directory entries, we notice there are some attributes that are likely to be duplicated across all the different providers; Joan's e-mail and shipping address are two such examples. The implication of this duplication is, of course, that the burden of maintaining this information and keeping it up-to-date and synchronized falls squarely on Joan. If the information changes (when she moves, changes her e-mail, and so forth), it will not be easy for Joan to update all the different copies.

If such information were to be stored at a single Web site, it would be much simpler for Joan to keep it up-to-date. When other Web sites required this information, they would issue a request to the storing site for the particular piece. The storing site would release the information to the requestor only if the request was in conformance with the Principal's privacy preferences for their personal information. The advantage to the requesting site is clear as well—they are no longer responsible for storing this information or providing interfaces for its maintenance, and have a greater chance of it being up-to-date.

Liberty will use Web Services to enable this sharing of Principal attribute information. The following examples discuss how the different providers at which Joan has federated her identities can use Web Service messages in order to go beyond single sign-on for Principals.

Example: Joan Buys a Gift Through BigWebRetailer and Ships It Using Delivery Now that Joan has federated her IDP1, BigWebRetailer, and Delivery local identities, it becomes much easier for her (and the Web Services acting on her behalf) to use the Web to accomplish multidomain tasks.

Joan wants to buy a gift for her nephew through BigWebRetailer and ship it using Delivery. Thanks to Liberty, Joan's federated network identities, and her prior selection of personal and privacy preferences, IDP1, BigWebRetailer, and Delivery can work seamlessly together sharing the minimal amount of information about Joan needed to get the job done. Let's look at the highlights of the process using psuedocode to illustrate RPC Web Service calls.

Once Joan has bought the gift for her nephew, BigWebRetailer immediately displays a list of Joan's preferred shippers. How does BigWebRetailer know who Joan's preferred shippers are? By asking IDP1 with which shippers Joan has federated her identities in IDP1's affinity group.

```
// BigWebRetailer's source code

// Use IDP1's AffinityGroup.Query() web service to find out which shippers are
// Joan's federated network identity.  The first parameter is BigWebRetailer's
// alias it uses for Joan when communicating with IDP1.
 List shippers = IDP1.AffinityGroup.Query("yuiop", "shippers");

// Display list of shippers to Joan through GUI and note which one she selected
 Shipper shipper = GUI.Display("Select a shipper", shippers);
```

Joan has selected Delivery as her shipper. BigWebRetailer now needs to inform Delivery that Joan wants to ship her item through them. Because BigWebRetailer is not permitted to know the alias Joan uses with her selected shipper, and the selected shipper is not permitted to know which alias Joan uses for BigWebRetailer, BigWebRetailer asks IDP1 (through a Web Service) for the shipper's alias for Joan—which it will return encrypted with the shipper's encryption public key:

```
EncryptedAlias encryptedAlias
    = IDP1.AffinityGroup.QueryAliasByProvider("yuiop", shipper);
```

In the above call, the first parameter is BigWebRetailer's alias for Joan and the second is the shipper's identity. IDP1 determines which user is being queried by matching the specified alias with the caller (BigWebRetailer) to determine the user is Joan. Then IDP1 finds out the alias for Joan used by the specified provider (Delivery), encrypts that alias so only Delivery can decrypt it, and returns it to BigWebRetailer.

With the encrypted alias, BigWebRetailer can now call Delivery's Web Service for delivering an item for a user. The shipper in the following Web Service call would, of course, represent Delivery.

```
shipper.Deliver(item, encryptedAlias, uriForGUI);
```

Once BigWebRetailer's application has called Delivery's `deliver()` Web Service, Delivery looks to IDP1 to obtain Joan's list of contacts so Delivery can automatically present a list of possible destination addresses to Joan. Doing so saves Joan the labor of reentering her nephew's address (and possibly making an error doing so). Delivery's source code looks like this:

```
// Delivery's source code
WebService method Deliver( Item item, EncryptedData encryptedAlias,
                                                          URI uriForGUI) {

  // Get decrypted form of alias
  Alias alias = decrypt(encryptedAlias);

  // Get contacts from IDP1's GetContacts() web service for the alias
  Contacts contacts = IDP1.Principal.GetContacts(alias);

  // Ask Principal to select an address; the list of addresses is generated from
  // the Principal's list of contacts.
  Address addressRecipient = GUI.Display("Select the recipient's address",
                                                      contacts, uriForGUI);


 // Ship item to recipient's address
 ship(item, addressRecipient);
}
```

Now, what would have happened without Liberty? BigWebRetailer would have had no way of knowing which shipping companies Jane deals with other than by having Jane specify one. Once transferred to Delivery's Web site, Jane would have to log in again, and Delivery would have required Jane to enter all the details about the recipient's address.

Just because a Principal has chosen to federate her or his local identities does not mean any local identity should necessarily have access to *all* information within another local identity. In fact, Liberty allows federations to be unidirectional, so, for example, IDP1 may have no access to information under Joan's BigWebRetailer identity. But, thanks largely to XML, access can be more than an all or nothing proposition; for example, Joan may prefer that BigWebRetailer not have access to her *IDP1* list of contacts and that certain contacts remain inaccessible to her non-IDP1 local identities. Providers may wish to consider an XACML-enabled approach to define which local identity information is accessible to other providers.

Defederating a Local Identity

Principals must be able to defederate their identities. In other words, a Principal who has previously federated an identity must be able to remove that identity from the federation of identities she or he has established.

There are myriad reasons why defederation might happen. For human users, it may simply be that a user decides she or he prefers maintaining separate identities or perhaps wants to federate an existing service provider identity with another identity provider. For B2E scenarios, an employee's identity would need to be defederated when that employee left the company. For automated Principals, it may often be that federation is only required for a specific activity period, and therefore it makes sense to simply federate at the beginning of that activity period and defederate at the end of it.

To defederate an identity, a `FederationTerminationNotification` is sent from the service provider (to which the identity is registered) to the identity provider. The `FederationTerminationNotification` message specifies the following.

ProviderID

This is the identifier of the provider in which the local identity specified by the name identifier is registered.

saml:NameIdentifier

The name identifier referencing the local identity is to be defederated.

Example: Joan Defederates One of Her Local Identities Joan decides to defederate her Delivery identity. The following message would then be sent to IDP1 on her behalf:

```
<FederationTerminationNotification
  RequestID="8052-4827-9288"
  MajorVersion="1" MinorVersion="0"
  IssueInstant="2002-10-20T19:39:15-05:00">
 <ds:Signature>...</ds:Signature>
 <ProviderID>http://www.delivery.xom</ProviderID>
 <saml:NameIdentifier>hjkln</saml:NameIdentifier>
</FederationTerminationNotification>
```

Single Logout

Single logout, is of course, essential to the security of a single sign-on system. In Liberty, a `LogoutNotification` is sent to all providers other than the one in which the Principal has directly logged out. A Principal may initiate a single logout from either an identity provider or service provider. If initiating a single logout from an identity provider, that identity provider alerts all other affiliated providers that the Principal is logging out, and those providers then log out the Principal. If a Principal initiates a single logout from a service provider, that service provider alerts the identity provider which then alerts the other service providers.

The `LogoutNotification` message specifies the following.

ProviderID

This is the provider issuing the notification.

saml:NameIdentifier

This is the name identifier of the Principal that logged out.

SessionIndex

This is the same session index that was specified in the authentication assertion during sign-on. If no session index was specified at sign-on, no session index is required at logout.

Example: Joan Logs Out from BigWebRetailer

```
<LogoutNotification
  RequestID="OWKC-IWZZ-DCEI"
  MajorVersion="1" MinorVersion="0"
  IssueInstant="2002-10-20T19:41:18-05:00">
 <ds:Signature>...</ds:Signature>
 <ProviderID>http://www.bigwebretailer.xom</ProviderID>
 <saml:NameIdentifier>
   yuiop
 </saml:NameIdentifier>
 <SessionIndex>3</SessionIndex>
</LogoutNotification>
```

Security in Liberty

Because this chapter's primary purpose is a basic introduction to Liberty, it has focused on the fundamental mechanisms for managing network identities without going too deeply into the security protections that are an essential part of realizing Liberty.

Due to the paramount importance of authentication in Web Services security, the Liberty protocol itself and its implementations must be absolutely secure if they are to be of any use at all. Consequently, Liberty makes use of XML Signature and encryption to protect the authenticity, integrity, and confidentiality of its messages. We have also seen that Liberty makes use of SAML assertions and that XACML would be valuable for fine-tuning what information about a Principal may be accessed and how. Liberty, then, provides an excellent example of how many of the security technologies discussed in this book complement each other.

Liberty also minimizes the risk of attack by being designed to work without exchanging information that would unnecessarily expose user information. For example, opaque name identifiers (for example, "nhyujmkil") are used to refer to users rather than a user's local domain identifier (for example, "JoeSmith").

Liberty Today, Liberty Tomorrow

Liberty's current focus is on enabling more seamless interactions between Principals and the multiple Web sites with which they maintain identities. The primary identities are the Principals, and Web businesses authenticate each other in order to provide new experiences to these Principals—using Web Services to accomplish this. Consequently, Liberty can be thought of as a consumer of Web Services technology. It is also possible to imagine the opposite relation —Web Services (unrelated to a Principal's browsing experiences) using some of the same concepts, technologies, and infrastructure established by Liberty—for instance, the concept of SAML authentication assertions being used to enable third-party mediated trust could be applied to Web Services; a SOAP client first authenticating to a SAML authentication authority (through a SOAP interface) in order to receive a SAML assertion that could be presented to the desired Web Service as an identity token.

Give Me Liberty or Give Me Passport

As well as the Sun-initiated Liberty Alliance Project, Microsoft has put forth the .NET Passport initiative as a means to achieve a cohesive authentication experience for Internet Principals. Passport's current model (that of Passport.com being the single authentication authority) is very different than Liberty's distributed model. But the Passport roadmap includes support for Kerberos and it is likely that Passport could support something more akin to Liberty through Kerberos's support for cross-realm authentication. At the time of writing, it should be noted that while much good work has gone into both Liberty and Passport, historically we are only at the beginning of tackling the challenges of network identity management. New Web technologies (including many of those detailed in this book) have been most successful and profitable when competitors cooperate to produce the best solution. Fortunately, it appears at present that, while technical challenges remain, it may very well be that Liberty and Passport will work together.

Indeed, there are scenarios currently possible in which Passport and a Liberty circle of trust could meaningfully coexist. For instance, if a Liberty identity provider were to also join the Passport community (as a member Web site), it would be possible for a Principal to authenticate to Passport in order to access their account at the identity provider—which could subsequently issue a SAML authentication assertion such that the Principal could access their identities at Liberty-federated service providers. The Liberty identity provider would play the role of a bridge between the two communities and map the different protocols.

The recent submission of WS-Security (of which Microsoft was an initial author) to OASIS, and its modification to support SAML as a peer of Kerberos tickets and X.509 certificates, is an encouraging sign for more meaningful interoperability between Passport and Liberty. Microsoft has indicated that Passport and its TrustBridge product will build on WS-Security and Kerberos, and has given some indication that it will use SAML to some extent. Additionally, many of the same companies working on Liberty are also active in SAML and will contribute to WS-Security.

CHAPTER 12

UDDI and Security

Two words not often found in the same sentence are "UDDI" and "Security." UDDI is a complex specification and, until the recent version 3, avoided any mention of security. However, security must be applied to UDDI when it is used "in the wild." This chapter outlines how this might be achieved, using the technologies that the reader has learned about in the book so far.

UDDI OVERVIEW

UDDI is the Universal Description, Discovery, and Integration protocol. It is designed to allow Web Services to be easily located and subsequently invoked. UDDI allows companies to make public their contact and organizational details, the Web Services that they offer, and the set of interfaces available for public or private access. The latter is important because UDDI registries can be operated as public or private services, depending on organizational requirements and security concerns.

There are six types of data permitted to reside in a UDDI registry:

- businessEntity
- businessService
- bindingTemplate
- tModel
- publisherAssertion
- operationalInfo

UDDI repositories store both business information and service information. Business information is stored in the white pages and the yellow pages, and uses the businessEntity dataType. The white pages contain data concerning the identity of an organization and appropriate contact information. The yellow pages store information about services provided by a particular organization, and use the businessService data type. The organization of data in traditional telephone directories is also based on white and yellow pages: the former allows organizations to be located through an alphabetical search process. The latter allows for category-based lookups to be performed, utilizing semantic relationships between particular types of goods and services and the providers of those goods and services.

Service information is stored in the green pages. The green pages introduce a new type of service information that's obviously not part of a traditional phone book: a bindingTemplate data type, and a tModel data type. A bindingTemplate specifies the locations of services provided by an organization and information about the interfaces provided to the service, while the tModel is concerned with defining the precise definition of each service by using a taxonomy. Figure 12-1 shows the structure of the business

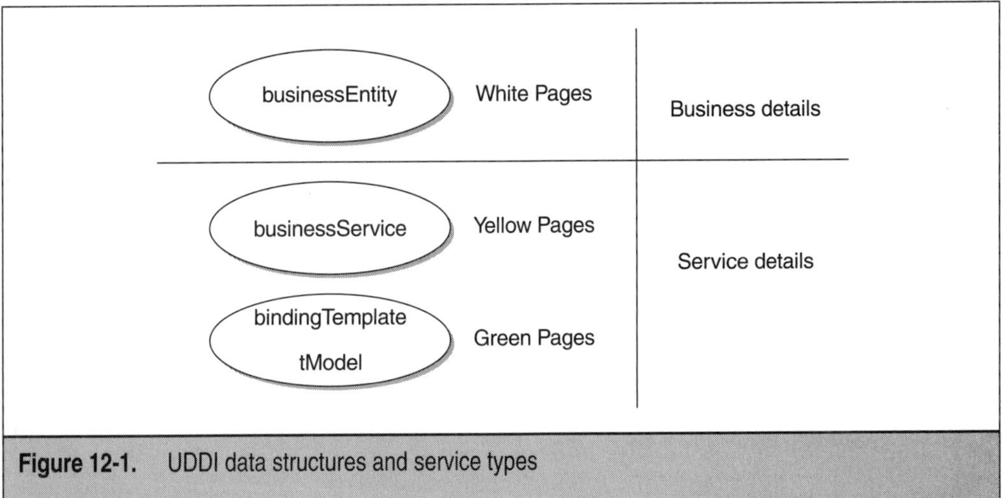

Figure 12-1. UDDI data structures and service types

and service information within a UDDI registry, and the relationships between each page type (white, yellow, and green) and the relevant data models.

The final data type is publisherAssertion, which is a claim to a relationship between two parties asserted by at least one of the parties involved. In a security context, publisherAssertions are obviously important.

A businessEntity element, in the white pages, has three attributes and eight elements. The three attributes are

- **businessKey** Uniquely identified by a universally unique identifier (UUID), and thus uniquely identifies each businessEntity
- **authorizedName** A string containing the person that created the businessData entry
- **operator** A string containing the name of the site that controls the definitive record for the businessEntity

The eight elements are

- **discoveryURLs** Defines file-based discovery procedures
- **name** Name of the businessEntity
- **description** Describes the nature of the organization's business
- **contacts** Lists any contact persons for the businessEntity
- **businessServices** Describes any services at a high level
- **identifierBag** Contains industry data that uniquely identifies the businessIdentity

- **categoryBag** Contains industry data, using the North American Industry Classification System (NAICS), and product data, using the Universal Standard Products and Services Classification System (UNSPSC)
- **dsig:SignatureElement** Optional digital signature

More information about NAICS can be obtained from http://www.census.gov/epcd/www/naics.html, while UNSPSC definitions are listed at http://www.unspsc.org/.

A businessService element in the yellow pages has two attributes and four elements. The two attributes are

- **businessKey** Uniquely identified by a UUID, and thus individually distinguishes each businessEntity
- **serviceKey** Uniquely identified by a UUID, and thus individually distinguishes each service

The six elements are

- **name** Name of the businessEntity
- **description** Describes the nature of the organization's business
- **bindingTemplates** Contains a technical description of the services provided
- **categoryBag** Contains industry and product data using NAICS and UNSPSC
- **dsig:SignatureElement** Optional digital signature
- **A businessService** Can be associated with multiple bindingTemplates

To work with UDDI, you will need access to a set of libraries and APIs that map between your particular platform and the XML schema that specifies the data types and operations that can be performed against a registry. For J2EE, this means that you will need a customized third-party API that maps Java methods to the appropriate SOAP calls. IBM has released an API called UDDI4J, which is what we will use for the examples in this chapter.

Let's examine how UDDI works in practice by performing a search on a UDDI test registry using IBM's UDDI4J API, which allows J2EE to utilize Web Services. The following code shows a test client that connects to the test registry, and returns details of businesses whose names start with "IBM Software" and "IBM Financial":

```
import org.uddi4j.*;
import org.uddi4j.client.*;
import org.uddi4j.datatype.*;
import org.uddi4j.request.*;
import org.uddi4j.response.*;
import org.uddi4j.util.*;
import org.uddi4j.transport.TransportFactory;
import java.util.Vector;
```

```
public class SearchRegistry
{

   public static void main (String args[])
   {
      System.setProperty(TransportFactory.PROPERTY_NAME,
      "org.uddi4j.transport.ApacheAxisTransport");
      System.setProperty("org.uddi4j.logEnabled","true");
      UDDIProxy px = new UDDIProxy();
      try
      {
         px.setInquiryURL(
         "http://www-3.ibm.com/services/uddi/v2beta/inquiryapi");
         Vector tokens = new Vector();
         tokens.add(new Name("IBM Software"));
         tokens.add(new Name("IBM Financial"));
         FindQualifiers fq = new FindQualifiers();
         Vector q = new Vector();
         q.add(new FindQualifier("sortByNameAsc"));
         fq.setFindQualifierVector(q);
         BusinessList bl = px.find_business(tokens, null, null,
         null,null,fq,50);
         Vector v  = bl.getBusinessInfos().getBusinessInfoVector();
         for (int i = 0; i < v.size(); i++)
         {
            BusinessInfo bi = (BusinessInfo)v.elementAt(i);
            System.out.println(bi.getBusinessKey()+" : "+
            bi.getNameString()+" : "+bi.getDefaultDescriptionString());
         }
      }
      catch (Exception e)
      {
         e.printStackTrace();
      }
   }
}
```

The program performs the following actions in sequence:

1. Sets the transport type to be SOAP, provided by Apache Axis.
2. Enables verbose logging to standard output.
3. Constructs a new UDDIProxy object, which is used to invoke operations on a remote UDDI server.
4. Sets the UDDI registry target to be the IBM UDDI v2 test registry.

5. Creates a vector of search tokens for "IBM Software" and "IBM Financial."
6. Sets the result of the search to sort by ascending alphabetical order from the business entity names.
7. A BusinessList object is returned from a call against the UDDIProxy object, passing the tokens and search qualifiers, such as the maximum number of entries to search for.
8. A vector *v* is created, containing the business information details for all business that matches the search tokens.
9. The business key, business name, and description are then printed to standard output in a colon-delimited format.

A sample output is shown here:

```
CF23AA90-C706-11D5-A432-0004AC49CC1E : IBM Financial Transaction
  Services : IBM Financial Transaction Services
0764DF70-FBA3-11D5-8C49-0004AC49CC1E : IBM Software Enterprise
  Integration : We make complex tasks easy.
DE10B100-DA6B-11D6-835F-000629DC0A7B : IBM Software Group
Canberra :null
AB4483A0-F623-11D5-9094-0004AC49CC1E : IBM Software Region North
:Test business
```

The search process implemented in this code demonstrates the Inquirer role of UDDI, and it is described by the underlying UDDI Inquiry API. The complementary role is that of Publisher, where entries are recorded by a service provider using the UDDI Publication API. All of the discussion that follows concerning UDDI security concerns the roles of Inquirer and Publisher.

SECURING TRANSACTIONS WITH THE UDDI SERVICES

UDDI has been widely touted by vendors and commentators as a method of automating business processes on a grand scale by enabling the automatic discovery of new business partners and the subsequent invocation of the appropriate remote services. While it's true that UDDI does have the potential to automate business processes, trust relationships are typically developed over many years between businesses rather than by a simple search process. For example, by using the white and yellow pages, your local "agent" software may identify ten different suppliers of a set of widgets, and the green pages may identify the interfaces and data models required for the invocation process. However, if you don't have a trust relationship with any of the vendors, how can you be assured that they will be able to deliver? While this issue is not unique to UDDI, because all new business partners need to be vetted as per normal business practices, the level of automation in identifying potential partners means that some kind of certification authority or business brokerage may need to act as an intermediary before public UDDI registries are used to the full extent.

Underlying these concerns about trust are some key security issues that need to be addressed by developers. These concerns revolve around the roles of Publishers and Inquirers, authentication of Publishers and methods for authorizing their ability to publish, and authentication of Inquirers and their ability to access published services that they know about—or services that they discover. By focusing on understanding the implicit and explicit issues surrounding authentication and authorization of UDDI users, the potential of UDDI may become more of a reality than the current hype.

Explaining the UDDI Roles

Like a telephone book, a UDDI registry defines two types of access to the data contained within the registry: an Inquirer, which can search for information but cannot update or insert records, and a Publisher, which can update or insert records. Clearly, allowing an Inquirer to update or insert records in the registry would be disastrous: competitors would be able to undermine each other's entries to prevent potential customers (Inquirers) from reliably retrieving details of Publishers. In turn, Publishers should only be able to insert new records when authorized to do so, and should only be able to update their own records.

Publishers

UDDI Publishers are allowed to insert new records into the registry, and are allowed to update existing records that they own. In order to perform insertions or updates, Publishers must be authenticated. This requires registration at the registry site to be performed before publishing can occur. Authentication is through a simple username/password token combination. When invoking a Publisher API call, these credentials are passed to the server, requiring Secure HTTP (HTTPS) transport to ensure that the plaintext form of authentication credentials cannot be sniffed. For the IBM test registry, the Publisher API can be accessed through https://www-3.ibm.com/services/uddi/testregistry/protect/publishapi. Alternatively, authentication can be performed by some other means such as SAML or Kerberos. As we will see in the "Authenticating and Authorizing Publishers" section of this chapter, a key issue is authorizing what activities authenticated Publishers can engage in.

Inquirers

UDDI Inquirers are allowed to access the UDDI registry in a read-only form. Inquirers can search for business organization details, services offered by individual businesses, and the invocation format of those services. By default, UDDI Inquirers are not authenticated, since they are not allowed to publish data in the registry. However, this is problematic because there may be service types and registry entries that should only be available to registered users, rather than the general public. Access to the registry is usually provided by vanilla HTTP, because there is no exchange of authentication credentials. For the IBM test registry, the Inquiry API can be accessed through http://www-3.ibm.com/services/uddi/v2beta/inquiryapi.

Subscribers

Subscribers play a special inquiry role, where they are notified about specific types of insertions and updates made to a registry, including the businessEntity, businessService, bindingTemplate, tModel, and publisherAssertion entries. Subscription is based on a set of preferences that determine the extent of the subscription. Support for subscription is not a requirement for supporting UDDI v3, so you may need to check with your vendor and/or service provider that subscription is supported. Unlike a normal Inquirer, a Subscriber is generally a piece of software.

One of the key differences between a Subscriber and an Inquirer is that Subscribers must be authenticated by a registry node before their requests can be honored: the authInfo token may be used with the subscription API to transmit authentication tokens.

Subscription allows the following operations on the registry:

- Subscribers can be alerted to new businesses that are entered into the registry. This may be useful for the formation of dynamic virtual enterprises, where runtime binding of services is supported by discovery of new partners and the services they offer.
- Changes to existing services and service definitions can be monitored by service owners, and by service users. This allows service owners to be alerted to any unauthorized changes that are made to their services, and allows service users to be notified of any modifications required to continue to successfully interface with the service.
- Integration of public and private registry data is possible, because private registries can subscribe to receive updates on changes to public data, while not compromising their own security by allowing public access to their data and interfaces.
- Subsets of public registries can be maintained and updated on a subscription basis, without data having to be reloaded manually.
- Integration of data from multiple registries can be automated to a large extent, allowing specific industries and portals to reduce duplication and detect inconsistencies more quickly.

Authenticating and Authorizing Publishers

Authentication services are available to Publishers by using the get_authToken interface. Authentication is typically performed by using a simple username and password combination. To prevent the possible interception of cleartext usernames and passwords, HTTPS is always used to publish data to the registry. This provides security at the transport layer. The SOAP request looks like this:

```
<get_authToken cred="XYZ123" generic="2.0" userID="wattersp" xmlns="urn:uddi-org
:api_v2"/>
```

In this example, the username is "wattersp" and the password is "XYZ123." The SOAP response looks like this:

```
<authToken xmlns="urn:uddi-org:api_v2" generic="2.0" operator="
 www.ibm.com/services/uddi">
    <authInfo>
...
    </authInfo>
</authToken>
```

The <authInfo> token that is returned can then be used for subsequent operations that require authentication on the server. The following messages require the Publisher to be authenticated according to the Publisher API:

- **add_publisherAssertions** Adds an assertion about two businesses, defined by a publisherAssertion document, to a Publisher's set of stored assertions.
- **delete_binding** Removes a bindingTemplate from the registry based on the company's UUID.
- **delete_business** Removes a businessEntity from the registry based on a UUID. Associated businessServices, publisherAssertions, and bindingTemplates will also be deleted.
- **delete_publisherAssertions** Removes publisherAssertions from the registry based on the UUID of a specific publisherAssertion.
- **delete_service** Deletes a specific businessService from the UDDI registry given a UUID.
- **delete_tModel** Prevents tModels identified by a UUID from being used, while not actually deleting them.

- **discard_authToken** Ends an authenticated session for the current client.
- **get_assertionStatusReport** Returns a report on all publisherAssertions owned by a specific businessEntity identified by a UUID.
- **get_authToken** Retrieves an authentication token based on a username and password.
- **get_publisherAssertions** Retrieves a list of publisherAssertions for a specific businessEntity.
- **get_registeredInfo** Retrieves the business registration and tModel data for a specific businessEntity.
- **save_binding** Inserts a new bindingTemplate into the registry.
- **save_business** Inserts a new businessEntity into the registry.
- **save_service** Inserts a new businessService into the registry.
- **save_tModel** Inserts a new tModel into the registry.
- **set_publisherAssertions** Inserts a new publisherAssertion into the registry.

Authenticating the Publishers

The following code sample demonstrates how Publishers are authenticated to perform restricted operations within the UDDI registry:

```
 public static void main (String args[])
{
    System.setProperty(TransportFactory.PROPERTY_NAME,
    "org.uddi4j.transport.ApacheAxisTransport");
      System.setProperty("org.uddi4j.logEnabled","true");
      UDDIProxy px = new UDDIProxy();
        try
      {
            px.setPublishURL(config.getProperty(
"https://www-3.ibm.com/services/uddi/v2beta/protect/publishapi"));
            AuthToken t = proxy.get_authToken("wattersp",
            "XYZ123");
            String a=t.getAuthInfoString());
            System.out.println("get_authToken: "+a);
      }
       catch (Exception e)
```

```
        {
                e.printStackTrace();
        }
}
```

The program performs the following actions in sequence:

1. Sets the transport type to be SOAP, provided by Apache Axis.
2. Enables verbose logging to standard output.
3. Constructs a new UDDIProxy object, which is used to invoke operations on a remote UDDI server.
4. Sets the UDDI registry target to be the IBM UDDI v2 test publishing registry over HTTPS.
5. Creates a new AuthToken object by the response from a get_authToken message.
6. Assigns the AuthInfo data to a string variable and prints it to standard output.

Every publishing operation—whether inserting records for new businesses, services, tModels, or assertions—must use this authentication method.

Determining if the Publisher Is Authorized to Publish a Web Service

Using the XML-Signature Syntax and Processing specification, UDDI allows the elements businessEntity, businessService, bindingTemplate, tModel, and publisherAssertion to be digitally signed in UDDI v3. This is in contrast to the fairly open identification model of prior versions of UDDI, where almost anyone could register a businessEntity or other element with no identification requirements. By digitally signing these elements, Subscribers and Inquirers can place a higher level of trust in material received from the registry that purports to be published by a specific company or organization.

In terms of authority to publish information in the registry, a list of business organizations that are responsible for creating all of the businessEntity and tModel objects is maintained. Thus, when a Publisher is authenticated, they have direct access to the entries that they have created in the registry. Figure 12-2 shows the interface for the IBM test registry. Here, a new businessEntity is being defined by an authenticated Publisher. When the Publisher has completed the definition, it will be published, but only that Publisher will be able to modify or delete the businessEntity and its associated objects.

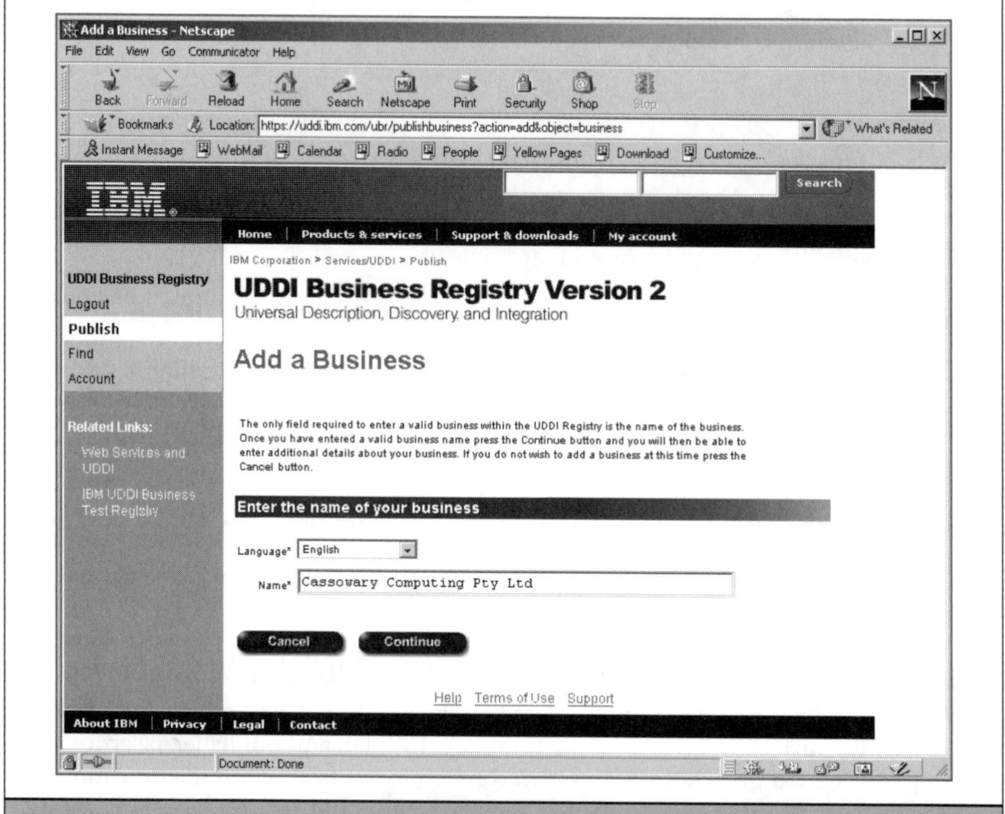

Figure 12-2. Inserting a new businessEntity record into the IBM test registry

A similar interface is provided for defining tModels by authorized Publishers, as shown in Figure 12-3. Here, an authenticated Publisher can define the tModel name, description, overview URL, and a UNSPSC description of the associated industry. Once again, only the authenticated Publisher can modify this data once it has been saved to the registry.

Every site that runs a UDDI registry (whether private or public) must decide on policies for authenticating Publishers and authorizing their activities. Typically, these controls will be implemented through native services—Active Directory, for example, implements many of the security elements associated with the Microsoft UDDI implementation. The methods for authenticating Publishers require standards wherever an assertion is made about the identity of a Publisher from registry to registry. This is where the Secure Assertions Markup Language (SAML) can play a key role in

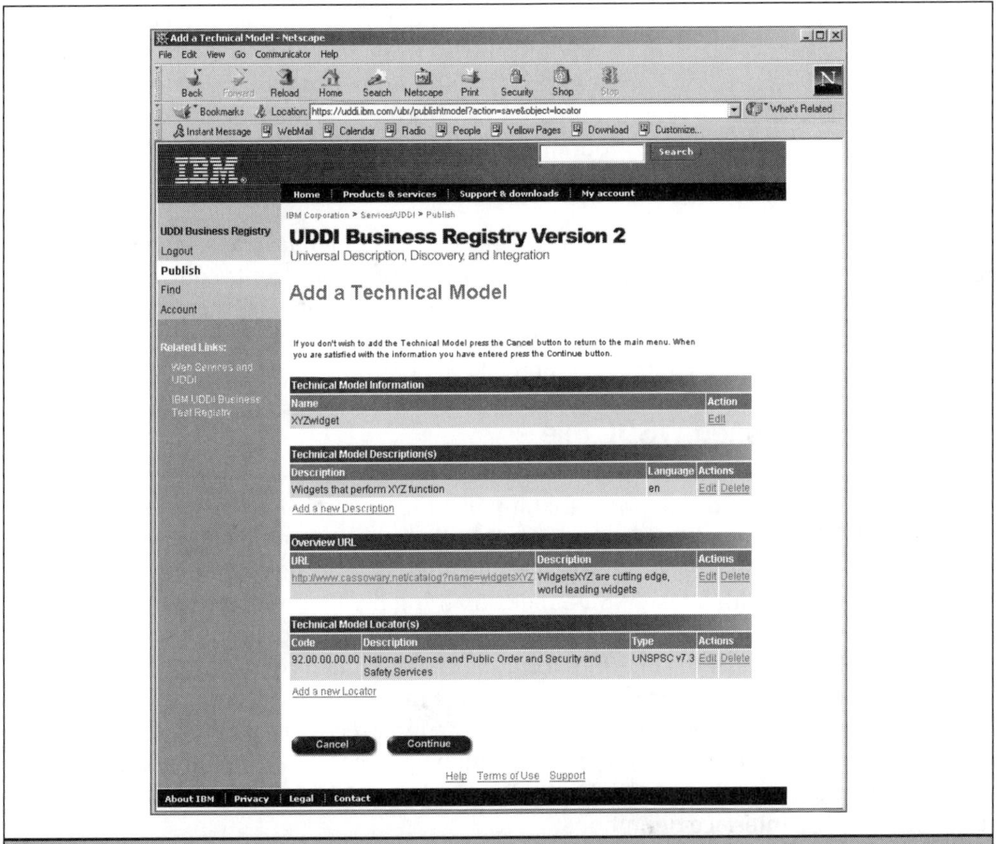

Figure 12-3. Inserting a new tModel record into the IBM test registry

providing "single sign-on" authentication services. SAML is described in more detail in the section "The Role of SAML in UDDI."

One of the benefits of placing strict controls on the authentication and authorization of entries being published in the directory is the increased authenticity that can be established for both Subscribers and Inquirers. For example, if a Subscriber can trust the fact that an authenticated company has digitally signed content in the directory, then a manual check of credentials by the Subscriber is no longer required (as may have been necessary in UDDI v2). In addition, Inquirers can specify that only signed entries be returned as a result of directory queries. This reduces the time required to process requests, since only verified data is returned. The increased confidence associated with digital signing may convince more organizations to participate in the public directory scheme.

Because only authentic Publishers can sign content by using their own private key, a UDDI registry cannot claim to be holding entries from a company unless they have illegally obtained access to the private key. This scenario is unlikely because private keys are not released in the public domain. In addition, when data is moved between registries as a result of entity promotion, any tampering can be automatically detected by Subscribers and Inquirers, and the results of a search containing invalid data can be ignored.

Nonrepudiation of transactions is also critical for commercial transactions, because different parties can sign data to ensure that a record of all electronic contracts, for example, can be stored with integrity. Being able to prove that an agreement was accepted through digital signing of UDDI data is critical to the development of dynamic virtual enterprises in the commercial arena.

Signing the Published WSDL File

Digital signing is a key issue to ensure the integrity of data in a registry. However, what about the integrity of interfaces that involve the dynamic lookup of services through WSDL? As with all networked services, there is a potential for spoofing to occur—that is, for a wily cracker to replace a genuine WSDL file containing valid interface definitions with a fake WSDL file containing invalid interface definitions. For example, a money market service might process electronic cash transactions between member banks. If the interface for transferring millions of dollars electronically was slightly tampered with to point to a spoof site that provided technically correct interfaces for the transaction, the money would be incorrectly transferred without the knowledge of the sender. How can this problem be overcome? Again, digital signing provides a solution by allowing WSDL files to be signed as a means of establishing the authenticity of the interface definitions.

XML digital signatures have a specific syntax associated with a set of processing rules. While this is fairly complicated, most applications only require a subset of all possible elements to be implemented. The basic procedure for signing an object—such as any of the main UDDI registry objects—is that a message digest is computed from the data and then added to a new element from which a new digest is then computed. It is this second digest that is then signed. The <Signature> element is used to represent the output of this process. Elements that can be encapsulated by a <Signature> element include the following:

- **<SignedInfo>** Contains the signed data.
- **<CanonicalizationMethod>** Defines the algorithm that is used to canonicalize the data to be signed.
- **<SignatureMethod>** Specifies the algorithm used to sign the data, including implementations of the DSA and RSA methods.
- **<DigestMethod>** Algorithm used to compute the message digest, such as SHA-1 or MD5.

- **<SignatureValue>** The actual signature data.
- **<DSAKeyValue>** Contains a key that can be used to confirm the signature.

The Role of XML Encryption in UDDI: Screening Services

The XML encryption syntax and processing specification (http://www.w3.org/TR/xmlenc-core/) defines some standard methods for encrypting data that is embodied in XML. The output of the encryption process is yet another XML element that contains a secure version of the original element. Encryption, in the context of UDDI, can be a useful way of protecting data against accidental interception by an unauthorized party, or against deliberate attempts at seizure. In order to use XML encryption, the following steps must be implemented by an application:

1. An encryption algorithm must be selected.
2. A key must be acquired or generated.
3. The data must be encrypted.
4. The output must be encoded as part of an EncryptedType structure.
5. The EncryptedData element is then created.

Let's look at an example where two strings need to be entered into a UDDI registry, or any other SOAP application. Now, imagine that two parameters were to be transmitted to the registry: the first, to be encrypted, contains the string "Security reports - top secret" (param1), while the second contains the string "Security reports - public access" (param2). The request looks like this:

```
<SOAP-ENV:Body Id="Body">
<mns:someMethod xmlns:mns="http://www.cassowary.net/xml/SOAPTest.xsd" SOAP-
ENV:encodingStyle="http://schemas.xmlsoap.org/soap/encoding/">
<EncryptedData xmlns:xenc="http://www.w3.org/2001/04/xmlenc#"
Type="http://www.w3.org/2001/04/xmlenc#Element">
<EncryptionMethod Algorithm="http://www.w3.org/2001/04/xmlenc#tripledes-cbc" />
<ds:KeyInfo xmlns:ds="http://www.w3.org/2000/09/xmldsig#">
<ds:KeyName>cassowary.net</ds:KeyName>
<ds:KeyValue>AQIAAANmAAAApAAA5K/BnmTnOlaIklEQGEfk4oN/D/l2QeU7LQzGgT8CiC+u7CZm
2S6gGcLhvtU6SJyoLoFPIFcD5X8E2ego/qzAhX3XEGMOJJb48RbVuFZpr0Utl2Py
K+i9c0giA4htBx/M2/0qsYZIPigN+x6DdbjVfsF3dvkFRw1nUdurU1XZxZw=</ds:KeyValue>
</ds:KeyInfo>
<CipherData>
<CipherValue>V5lJ64cqW46ETzSYuzWVqjPEbJm+DRDP0PpbsqoT6QCYlONEwr4wO2py3NFQHvdm
jkH9S13wmkmT1UfvMFShwMwx6WNH7KKZly/qQAhfw+c=</CipherValue>
</CipherData>
</EncryptedData>
<param2 xsi:type="xsd1:string">Security reports - public access</param2>
</mns:someMethod>
</SOAP-ENV:Body>
```

This request uses 3DES to encrypt the contents of param1 and supplies the appropriate <KeyValue> and <CipherData>, as well as passing the contents of param2 in the clear. The response is as follows:

```
<SOAP-ENV:Body>
<tns:someMethodResponse SOAP-
    ENV:encodingStyle="http://schemas.xmlsoap.org/soap/encoding/">
<EncryptedData xmlns:xenc="http://www.w3.org/2001/04/xmlenc#"
    Type="http://www.w3.org/2001/04/xmlenc#Element">
<EncryptionMethod Algorithm="http://www.w3.org/2001/04/xmlenc#
    tripledes-cbc" />
<ds:KeyInfo xmlns:ds="http://www.w3.org/2000/09/xmldsig#">
<ds:KeyName>paulwatters.com</ds:KeyName>
</ds:KeyInfo>
<CipherData>
<CipherValue>LKnCWXepHRS8ararQo8WiuqnUfcO+PKZyt5ok8fRlTnAiNqgAdwW
qv/kX4YhAoFcxepWMslqnkRvkbTU+LztN9477URhVY2xWZ1AKgKlJI7w4MjeDtMx
pKiSuqaf/S4ET8Yi5lfN9mrBiW44DvKqMB6ZDsgZipY4Ec7Un5kM1pjkjKmr9KjlY
eqygBk8Nlu8</CipherValue>
</CipherData>
</EncryptedData>
</tns:someMethodResponse>
</SOAP-ENV:Body>
```

In this example, the data returned from the method call is also encrypted.

Authenticating and Authorizing Subscribers

As described earlier, the Subscriber role differs from the Inquirer role because the former must be authenticated, while the latter does not have to be. While the UDDI v3 specification provides for optional access control on the basis of X.509 certificates, there may be some differences in the way that authentication and access control are handled internally by different products. It is likely that some form of inquiry-driven authentication and authorization would be required by some businesses before access to any registry could be granted. A further level of authenticity for Publishers that may be useful to Subscribers is the XML-Signature Syntax and Processing specification (http://www.w3.org/TR/xmlsig-core?), which allows Publishers to digitally sign their own content stored in a registry, providing a level of authenticity beyond that which is available in current public test registries.

Authenticating the Subscriber

In order to create a subscription, a service needs to be developed to process notifications from the registry as they are received, using only one bindingTemplate. Generally, these notifications will be received from the registry using SOAP. A set of criteria defined by a subscriptionFilter must be developed, to ensure that the notifications only contain data relevant to the application. An authInfo token is required for authenticating the client in all cases. The following shows one example of how a subscription can be implemented securely:

```
<save_binding xmlns="urn:uddi-org:api_v3">
         <authInfo>...</authInfo>
         <bindingTemplate bindingKey=""serviceKey="uddi:myServiceKey">
            <description>secure subscription service</description>
            <accessPoint URLType="https">
                 https://cassowary.net/notify_subscriptionListener
            </accessPoint>
        <tModelInstanceDetails>
         <tModelInstanceInfo tModelKey=
           "uddi:uddi.org:v3_subscriptionListener" />
           </tModelInstanceDetails>
      </bindingTemplate>
</save_binding>
```

In this example, a secure subscription service is made available on https://cassowary.net/notify_subscriptionListener along with the appropriate authInfo token.

Determining if the Subscriber Is Authorized to "Discover" a Web Service

Subscribers do not have free and open access to changes that occur within a registry. They must be authenticated, and their access may be still further restricted. Different registries may or may not support subscription at all. Rules may also be defined that determine the level of access given to Subscribers, and in the future billing services for access subscriptions may also be imposed. (The latter certainly opens up opportunities for creating new businesses using UDDI.)

There are two forms of subscription that are supported: asynchronous and synchronous. Asynchronous subscriptions use the notify_subscriptionListener API to automatically alert Subscribers when a notifiable activity occurs. Alternatively, synchronous subscription uses the get_subscriptionResults API and allows regular polling of the directory to receive notification of all changes made to the registry since the previous access. Subscriptions can be identified by the subscriptionKey element.

Subscribers can be authorized for specific time periods, from seconds to years. This prevents default access to Subscribers who have not actively resubscribed and who may need to be authenticated again.

The Role of SAML in UDDI

Access control in UDDI registries is controlled by a set of optional authorization policies. The element authInfo is used to provide information that can be used for authorization decisions for a specific type of user, whether Subscriber, Publisher, or Inquirer. The SAML markup language can be used to assert authorizations in the form of X.509 attribute certificates.

One important aspect of UDDI is the fact that multiple registries can be used concurrently. For example, in a financial application, one registry might contain customer records while another registry might contain supplier records. While it's possible that an Inquirer could be authenticated separately by each registry, it would be much easier if a single sign-on process could be implemented. More importantly, some registries might only allow access to their data if you have been authenticated by a separate registry. Authentication procedures for secure group communications currently require new keys to be issued to group members if a change is made to the group's membership. While techniques for dynamically modifying group membership without having to issue new keys is an area of active research[1], centralizing authentication reduces the proliferation of keys and authentication tokens (which change over time). This approach reduces administrative costs because a single authentication server can be utilized by a number of different registries, and ensures consistency of access granted across multiple services.

The Security Assertion Markup Language (SAML) uses XML to pass authentication tokens and authorization data between different Web Services, including UDDI. A SAML assertion can be made about users or systems, and typically concerns the identity of the user or system. Assertions can also be made about the types of access that a correctly identified user should be able to access. SAML supports quite complex types of assertions about users, systems, and their attributes, and uses SOAP over HTTP to service authentication requests. SAML requires that individual authorities take responsibility for authentication and authorization.

One of the interesting applications of SAML to UDDI is the ability for a user to be authenticated locally, and for that authentication to be asserted later to a business partner's application. Because the user, once authenticated, can have their access controls enforced by the remote system, the business partner's systems are protected from incorrectly identified external users. In addition, the usage of the external user can be strictly controlled. The authentication can be time-based, so that the identity of an external user may only be validated for a certain time period. Most importantly, because the user has been authenticated by a trusted business partner, their identity and actions cannot be repudiated.

---

1 I have to confess that I am currently working on secure group communications.

```
<samlp:Request MajorVersion="1" MinorVersion="0"
  RequestID="6fbhGHH7g76628+/sdas2nfDDSSW=">
  <samlp:RespondWith>AuthenticationStatement</samlp:RespondWith>
    <samlp:AuthenticationQuery>
      <saml:Subject>
        <saml:NameIdentifier Name="SecureDatabase"/>
        <saml:SubjectConfirmation>
          <saml:ConfirmationMethod>
            http://www.oasis-open.org/committies/security/
                   docs/draft-sstc-core-25/password
          </saml:ConfirmationMethod>
          <saml:SubjectConfirmationData>
            AbcDEf43a445A=
          </saml:SubjectConfirmationData>
        </saml:SubjectConfirmation>
      </saml:Subject>
    </samlp:AuthenticationQuery>
</samlp:Request>
```

The different elements in this request can be described as follows:

- **AuthenticationQuery** An authentication query
- **AuthenticationStatement** A statement of authentication
- **RequestID** A unique token that identifies the authentication query, and that matches the InResponseTo field in the response
- **Subject** Describes the system or user to be authenticated

The response for this request is shown here:

```
<samlp:Response InResponseTo="6fbhGHH7g76628+/sdas2nfDDSSW="
  MajorVersion="1" MinorVersion="0"
  ResponseID="7ghH77Hsgjjy++98hfhBB7fgdg=">
  <samlp:Status>
    <samlp:StatusCode Value="samlp:Success"/>
  </samlp:Status>
  <saml:Assertion AssertionID="+8gjJJJHG7shgHHgy88Uh9iiU4e="
    IssueInstant="2002-11-01T12:00:00.001" Issuer="cassowary.net"
    MajorVersion="1" MinorVersion="0">
    <saml:Conditions NotBefore="2002-11-01T12:00:00.001"
      NotOnOrAfter="2002-03-03T15:03:58.466"/>
```

```
      <saml:AuthenticationStatement
        AuthenticationInstant="2002-03-03T14:33:55.201"
        AuthenticationMethod="http://www.oasis-open.org/committies/security/
docs/draft-sstc-core-25/password">
          <saml:Subject>
            <saml:NameIdentifier Name="SecureDatabase"
             SecurityDomain="card:SQLDatabase"/>
            <saml:SubjectConfirmation>
              <saml:ConfirmationMethod>
                http://www.oasis-open.org/committies/security/docs/draft-sstc-
                core-25/password
              </saml:ConfirmationMethod>
            </saml:SubjectConfirmation>
          </saml:Subject>
        </saml:AuthenticationStatement>
  </saml:Assertion>
</samlp:Response>
```

Here, the Subject element is authenticated, with a set of time restrictions and a unique AssertionID, which is an identifier for the assertion being made.

CHECKLIST

- ☐ What are the six types of data permitted in a UDDI registry?
- ☐ What are the attributes of a businessEntity element?
- ☐ What are the attributes and elements of a businessService element?
- ☐ What are UDDI Publishers allowed to do?
- ☐ How are Subscribers authenticated?

PART V

Conclusion

CHAPTER 13

ebXML

Although not a Web Services technology, ebXML is covered in this book because it also makes use of XML and SOAP to enable electronic business. We will concentrate on those aspects of ebXML that impinge particularly on security.

EBXML

ebXML (or electronic business XML) is a series of standards jointly developed by OASIS and UN/CEFACT, whose stated objective is to provide an open XML-based infrastructure enabling the global use of electronic business information in an interoperable, secure, and consistent manner by all parties.

Historically, it can be regarded as an evolution of Electronic Data Interchange (EDI). Some businesses have been deploying EDI to exchange documents like purchase orders, quotations, and invoices for two decades, but its use thus far has been mainly confined to larger corporations. Some 95 percent of the Fortune 500 companies use EDI, for example, whereas only as few as 20 percent of small or medium enterprises do. The slow take-up of EDI among smaller companies is largely dictated by cost and complexity. EDI systems have proven expensive and burdensome to deploy, and while the expense and trouble can be justified for large organizations, this is not the case for smaller companies where the transaction volume is obviously lower. Another significant barrier to EDI take-up internationally (especially) has been the bifurcation of standards—EDI within North America has adopted the ANSI X12 standards, while the rest of the world generally uses UN/CEFACT standards.

ebXML is intended specifically to address the EDI-related issues discussed above, and enable businesses of any size, anywhere on the planet, to do business electronically. We will explain how ebXML aims to achieve this by very briefly summarizing the major components of the ebXML standards. These components can be divided into the areas discussed in the following sections.

Business Processes

The business process module of the ebXML standards attempts to formalize and standardize business interactions into a series of fundamental models and transactions that can be implemented directly by software.

Collaboration Protocol Profile and Agreement

An ebXML collaboration protocol profile is essentially the mechanism whereby an ebXML-enabled entity announces its capabilities and services to the outside world. A collaboration profile agreement is generated when two potential trading partners investigate each other's profiles and discover a common set of messages and processes they can usefully deploy to enable e-business between the two parties.

Message Services

This module describes the communications model for ebXML messages. Essentially, this can be summarized as a MIME/multipart message structured as per the SOAP messages with attachment specification, transmitted using HTTP, HTTPS, or SMTP.

Registry Information and Services

The registry is a key concept in ebXML. The registry is a directory, or database, that stores business processes, messages, and company profiles.

Two obvious points present themselves when reviewing the previous list and comparing it to the Web Services standards discussed in the rest of this book. First, there is a significant overlap between the ebXML registry concept and UDDI. Some would argue that UDDI may well end up delivering this functionality for ebXML. Second, the ebXML concept of standard business processes implies that ebXML is almost taking the reverse approach to Web Services, since ebXML is specifying electronic business interaction from a very high-level approach, whereas Web Services just specify a lower-level framework for generic communications.

Having presented a very brief summary of the major components of ebXML, we will now move on to discussing the security implications and risks of ebXML deployment.

EBXML SECURITY OVERVIEW

The good news from a security aspect is that ebXML was conceived and designed from the ground up with security in mind, in contrast to other protocols or standards where security was never considered at all at the design stage. The bad news is that the requirements and details in the specifications have to be implemented correctly, methodically, and with the most rigorous attention to detail if ebXML is indeed to meet its security requirements.

Of the four major areas of ebXML previously discussed, it is reasonable to conclude that the major risks are going to occur in two of them: message and registry services. Business processes and collaboration agreements are largely inert from a security point of view, in that although these areas do carry risks, such risks are eliminated by correctly protected message and registry services.

Another important point to make, especially to those coming to ebXML from an EDI background, is that ebXML is intended to be run on a public network—not on the private, leased-line arrangement typically found in EDI. This exposes ebXML deployments to a new form of attack: the "mountaineer" hacker, who will attempt to sabotage, or at least investigate, any publicly exposed service simply because it's there. It's important to bear in mind that because information is going over a public network, we must assume that it can be read and altered in transit unless specific measures have been taken to prevent this.

EBXML REGISTRY SECURITY

We will now discuss the security considerations and factors inherent in using the ebXML Registry.

Overview

The importance of ensuring the authenticity, validity, and integrity of information stored in an ebXML registry is obvious. Remember, the registry contains collaboration protocol profiles, message formats, and business processes. If a malicious attacker were to infiltrate spurious instances of these entities into an ebXML registry, the results could at best be described as chaotic.

Standards Requirements

It would be helpful at this stage to review what the ebXML standards say about security.

Standards Overview

The ebXML standards document for registry services has a full and comprehensive set of security requirements. A number of general points are worth making about these requirements before we proceed to a more detailed examination of them.

The XML Signature standard is used to sign various entities. ebXML allows, but does not require, the embedding of certificates within these signatures. If a party decides not to embed the certificate, ebXML is agnostic as to how to validate the signature.

The confidentiality of messages in transit is suggested, but not required or specified. If HTTP is the deployed transport mechanism, then HTTPS is an obvious mechanism to add an encryption layer. Note, however, that an encryption layer would require prior agreement between the parties, because it's not part of the standard—and in any event would only ensure confidentiality of the communications layer.

In the current version of the specification (ebXML Registry Services Specification v2.0, available online at http://www.ebxml.org/specs/), if you publish information in a registry, it's public and the world can read it. There is no facility to restrict read access to registry contents. Organizations therefore need to be vigilant in considering both the overt and implied information content of what they're publishing to ebXML registries. The overt information, for example, could simply be that a company is now registering as a trading partner in a new sector. The information could connote that a company is trying to establish itself in a market sector currently occupied by a major customer. The decision to publish this is obviously sensitive.

We will now discuss in detail the specific requirements and security mechanisms in the ebXML registry services specification.

Access Control

ebXML registries are required to implement an access control policy that recognizes the following three classes of users:

- **ContentOwner** The entity that submitted the content originally. It has read-write access to its own content.
- **RegistryAdministrator** Has read-write access to all objects in the registry.
- **RegistryGuest** Has read-only access to the registry. The specification notes that a RegistryGuest need not present an authenticating certificate.

Registry Content Security

These parts of the specification describe the mechanisms and techniques used to determine that the information contained in a registry is trustworthy.

The first step in achieving this is to require that all content submitted to the registry must be digitally signed with an XML Signature signature (see Chapter 4). The registry standard, at least in this revision, is lax about identifying who can submit content. Any "known entity" is allowed to submit data, with the identity of known entities presumably being verified by some out-of-band means, such as the manual exchange of certificates.

The originating entity is required to sign the message payload, specifically, as against the message headers. This signature is stored with the content and will be distributed to clients who request this information, so that the content and authenticity of the information can be verified.

ebXML also requires that when a registry distributes information to clients, the registry itself signs the message headers, with this signature including the digests of the payloads. The purpose of this is to ensure the integrity of data in transit. When ebXML Messaging Service is used, this imposes no further requirements because this inherently specifies XML Signature signatures in the SOAP header. When only SOAP With Attachments is in use, however, the requirements for a message header signature must be implemented explicitly.

Registry Security Conclusions

It must be acknowledged that the ebXML registry security requirements are at a fairly early stage of evolution, and operate at a very broad-brush level. They leave much detail to individual implementers. The decision not to require that certificates be embedded in XML Signature signatures, for example, leaves a broad panoply of trust and authentication issues squarely in the hands of those developing and deploying ebXML systems.

EBXML MESSAGE SECURITY

We will now proceed to describe the security requirements for the ebXML message service.

Overview

The ebXML message service specification describes and defines the message enveloping and header document schema that will be used to communicate using ebXML messages. It is intended to be neutral vis-à-vis lower-level protocols, but the current standard provides a binding to HTTP/HTTPS and SMTP. It is intended that other protocols can, and will be, used.

An ebXML message consists of a MIME multipart message, organized in accordance with the SOAP messages with attachment specification. The first MIME attachment in an ebXML message is referred to as the header container, and contains one SOAP 1.1–compliant message. Thereafter, an ebXML message consists of 0 or more additional MIME parts, referred to as payload containers, which hold application-level data. Essentially, this first MIME attachment is where ebXML specifies the location, nature, and format of control, routing, and (of special interest to us) security information.

STANDARDS OVERVIEW

The ebXML messaging specification recognizes that the following security requirements are inherent in any messaging service. These security requirements are described in detail in Chapter 2. Refer to that chapter if you need a reminder.

Authorization and Authentication

Is the person sending this message entitled to send it? Are we sure that the person sending it is actually the person whose identity/authorization is used?

Data Integrity and/or Confidentiality Attacks

Is the message we're processing the message that was actually sent, or has it been altered in transit? Has it been examined in transit by individuals who shouldn't have had access to it?

Denial of Service and/or Spoofing

Can hostile attackers prevent access to a service or facility by legitimate users by sending spurious or multiple messages? Can they lock legitimate users out by pretending to be them?

EBXML STANDARDS OVERVIEW

The standard suggests a variety of measures to ameliorate these risks, and we will now discuss these measures in detail. Before proceeding to these measures, a summary of the specification's requirements and suggestions for generating an XML Signature signature would be helpful.

The first thing to note is that the suggested, but not required, signature algorithm for generating signatures is DSA-SHA1. ebXML implementations must be able to verify signatures using this algorithm.

The signature is required to cover at least the SOAP envelope, but payload signing is at the discretion of the implementation. The SignedInfo element is required to have a Canonicalization element, a SignatureMethod element, and at least one Reference element.

A KeyInfo element is suggested, but not required. The completed namespace-qualified Signature element must be placed in the SOAP envelope element it signs.

It is required that the XML Signature Reference element for the SOAP envelope have a URI attribute value of "", denoting that the signature is intended to apply to the document that contains the signature element. The SOAP envelope reference element is also required to have a Transforms element, whose children must conform to the following requirements.

The first transform must have an algorithm attribute denoting the XML Signature enveloped signature algorithm. The effect of this is to exclude the parent signature element and its descendents.

The second transform must have a child XPath element consisting of the following:

```
<XPath> not (ancestor-or-self::node()[@SOAP:actor="urn:oasis:names:tc:ebxml-msg:actor:nextMSH"]
ancestor-or-self::node()[@SOAP:actor="http://schemas.xmlsoap.org/soap/actor/next"]
)
</XPath>
```

The purpose of this XPath transform is to exclude from the signature material any elements with SOAP actor attributes targeted for the next ebXML message service handler and their descendents, and also to exclude any elements with actor attributes that target the element at the next node (which may change en route).

It is suggested, but not required, that the last transform specify the XML Signature C14N transform, which will canonicalize the SOAP envelope without comments.

Note the required and suggested transforms apply only to the SOAP envelope and its contents. Suitable transforms for message payload nodes are at the discretion of the application.

We will now proceed to examine how ebXML suggests the various risks and dangers previously outlined can be guarded against.

Persistent Digital Signature

The standard requires that the only mechanism used to sign ebXML messages will be the XML Signature standard. This is considered persistent because the validity of the signature can be maintained under this standard even if new element content is added to the message, assuming suitable transforms are specified.

Persistent Signed Receipt

Any ebXML message that has itself been digitally signed may be acknowledged with an XML Signature signed message. The signed receipt must contain an XML Signature Reference element consistent with the message it's acknowledging.

Nonpersistent Authentication/Integrity

The underlying communications protocol could be used to provide a layer of assurance of physical data integrity, and also to provide a level of mutual authentication. TLS, for example, can be used to ensure that messages have not been tampered with in transit, and to confirm that the two parties to an exchange have mutually satisfactory and trustworthy X.509 certificates.

Confidentiality

The standards envisage that the XML Encryption standard, when available, will be used to provide encryption services. Again, this would have the advantage that element content could be added to the document without breaking the encryption. In the absence of XML Encryption, implementations may choose to deploy an encrypting network protocol such as TLS to protect the confidentiality of messages while they're in transit.

Authorization

Authorization services will ultimately be provided for ebXML using SAML. Until SAML is widely deployed and available, authentication can be provided by the underlying communication protocol. For example, mutually authenticated SSL could be deployed to establish the identity of sender and receiver to a reasonable degree of assurance. Once identities have been satisfactorily established, the implementation then could ensure that the entity involved is indeed entitled to access the resource in question, whatever it may be.

Trusted Time Stamps

The standard notes that various efforts are under development to develop standards for services offering trusted time-stamping services, and that ebXML will consider using these as they reach fruition.

MESSAGE SECURITY CONCLUSIONS

It can be seen that the ebXML message specification, as it stands, largely devolves security to three standards, XML Signature, XML Encryption, and SAML. Pending the widespread uptake of these standards, in particular XML Encryption and SAML, security for ebXML messaging is going to rest largely on some combinations of old friends such as IPSEC, TLS, and SSL.

CHAPTER 14

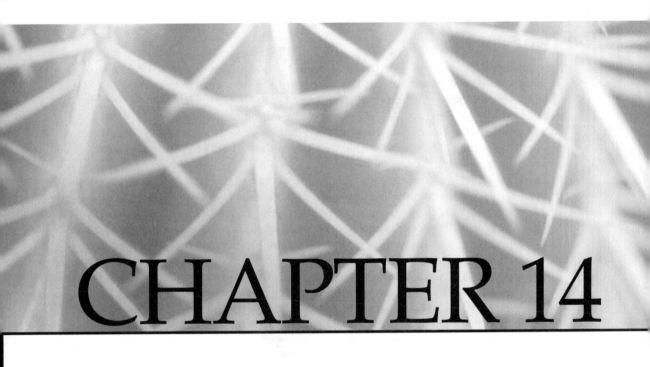

Legal Considerations

In his inspirational book, *The Future of Law* (Oxford University Press, 1996), Richard E. Susskind noted that, as far as law is concerned, one security fence at the top of a cliff is better than any number of ambulances at the bottom of that cliff. In theory, most IT security experts would agree with that seeming truism. In practice, most of them operate to the contrary maxim; namely, that an expensive and messy reactive legal cure is better than a proactive legal risks avoidance policy. There are several reasons for this strategic myopia.

The first of these is cultural. Lawyers tend to operate at one remove from the genesis of most technical and commercial projects. Lawyers view law as a parallel discipline that occasionally may proceed in lockstep with business, but does not need to form an integral part of it. The second reason is a related one. Lawyers and commercial people tend, respectively, to concentrate on the rarefied and on the newsworthy aspects of law. Certainly, any of the modish legal areas mentioned in passing under the heading "Legal Security Is Holistic" (in the concluding part of this chapter) can have a periodic operational relevance to online contracting—or to product/system design.

However, this chapter is concerned with distinguishing between law that may have an occasional relevance to online contracting and law that is fundamental to it, and will focus on the latter. In IT circles, the upshot of a misplaced attention to abstruse legislative moot points is a corresponding indifference towards workaday legal fundamentals—the settled common law basics of contract law and of evidence—that should inform the architectural specification of any secure online system from the outset.

This chapter outlines those common law basics and places them in a security context before applying them to some particular security technologies.

THE ROLE OF CONTRACT LAW AND EVIDENCE IN ONLINE SECURITY

As noted in Chapter 2, security, even from a purely technical standpoint, has negative and positive aspects: it is both a barrier to entry and a portal for privileged access. This chapter builds on the positive aspect of security by describing how it can also, literally, "secure the law."

While there is a general appreciation of this symbiosis between law and security, it is evident that too much security is still applied unthinkingly. Few would dispute the truism that "security is a process, not a product." Despite that, "security" is too often viewed as a fit-and-forget panacea. It isn't. All security is *applied* security.

By itself, the term "security" does not support a precise definition. Security is a mere shopping list of technical products and technical and human processes and procedures. Panic or comfort buying of security products may have a counterproductive effect. More security can result in worse security. If you know that your PC/system is unsecured, you may at least exercise some caution when using it.

Conversely, greater business misfortunes are likely to befall someone who acts in ignorance of technical vulnerabilities. Such complacency is often exacerbated by a blinkered reliance on a security product that may provide strong but incomplete security. Ironically, the greatest commercial calamities are likely to befall those users who, despite being technically aware, remain ignorant of the negative legal implications of such technical vulnerabilities. We need to be able to justify our security spending by reference to defined security and legal benefits. We need to ask ourselves: "If security is the answer, then exactly what is the question?"

The following part of this chapter suggests what that "clarifying question" should be, and then attempts to demystify both law and security by isolating the main components of each, and by considering where and why they relate to each other.

If Security Is the Answer, Then Exactly What Is the Question?

The question is unequivocal: *What security do you need to contract online?* In generic terms, which security items do you need from that list? Why do you need them?

Culturally, we have been conditioned to think narrowly of online security as a tangible, often technical response to a range of equally tangible and mostly technical issues. However, the value of technology does not stop there. Most societies depend on a stable and impartial system of justice to rein back, and provide a bulwark against, abuses of commercial and political power. For instance, it is a truism that businesses cannot function in a society where courts are corrupt and where, as a consequence, contracts may be flouted with impunity.

Up to now, societies have looked to the checks and balances of their constitutions as the guarantors of those bedrock systems of justice. In the 21st century, when so many relationships with and between businesses and with government departments are already being conducted online, it is clear that traditional checks and balances are struggling to cope with the vulnerabilities of online contracting. This is where technical security measures can also play a wider legal role—by *positively securing the legal components of a contract*. Citizens and businesses alike depend on a shared framework of fundamental legal conceptual components.

Until we remind ourselves of what those fundamental legal components are, we cannot begin the technical process of securing them in a systematic manner.

Legal Components: A Primer

Two definitions of "contract" are extant in common law. The classical common law definition holds that a contract is ". . .a promise or set of promises which the law will enforce."[1] A hybrid, civil law–influenced definition holds that a contract is ". . .an agreement giving rise to obligations which are enforced or recognized by law."[2] The second limb of each definition—enforceability by law—inhabits a shared conceptual

1 *Chitty on Contracts* (26th ed.) Volume

2 Treitel, *The Law of Contract* (9th ed., 1995)

space. That aspect is directly relevant to the issues considered in this chapter. Generally, in common law jurisdictions, a validly formed contract comprises four components:

- **Offer** The terms of the offer must be clear and unambiguous.
- **Acceptance** The acceptance must be final and unequivocal.
- **Consideration** In other words, "money or money's worth." It goes without saying that a recipient of goods or services must pay for them (apart from the limited instances where a promise is contained in a deed, under seal). Incidentally, note that "payment" does not have to be monetary; and, in the absence of fraud or mistake (and apart from various consumer protection laws), the law generally has little interest in investigating the commercial adequacy of any consideration.
- **Intention to create legal relations** The parties must have intended to form and be bound by a contract. Historically, this stipulation has been imported into the common law from civil law jurisdictions where no doctrine of consideration exists. Practically, courts assume that (for instance) business-to-business contracts are attended by the requisite legal intent.

In other (perhaps more intuitive) words, online contracting depends on an ability to prove

- *What* was agreed?
- *When* was it agreed?
- *Who* agreed to it?

Since much of the remainder of this chapter assumes a working knowledge of digital signatures and of public key encryption, the next section is a brief reminder of information set out in greater detail in Chapter 2.

NOTE The rash of e-commerce and digital signature laws enacted in most jurisdictions the world over neither significantly add to nor detract from those component principles. They do not prescribe any technical standards. Generally (there are some residual exceptions that are outside the scope of this chapter), they confine themselves to bland confirmatory statements. The following extract from the Electronic Signatures in Global and National Commerce Act is typical of similar provisions in European Union ("EU") directives and in domestic EU enactments: "...a signature, contract, or other record relating to such transaction may not be denied legal effect, validity, or enforceability solely because it is in electronic form..."

Digital Signing

Public key cryptography is a mathematical transformation based on key pairs. The sender and the recipient at either end of a communication channel will each have a key pair containing a public key and a corresponding private key. Public key signatures and encryption ensure

- **Authenticity and integrity** Data encrypted by the sender's private key can only be decrypted by the sender's public key. Both the data and the validating public key must be correct if validation is to be positive. "Correct data" means that the data's integrity has been protected; "correct public key" means that the sender has been authenticated (details below).
- **Confidentiality** Data encrypted with the recipient's public key can only be decrypted with the recipient's private key. Hence, only the recipient can decrypt the data.

This key-pair system is an essential component of a legally binding virtual infrastructure. By contrast, symmetric key cryptography (where sender and recipient rely on one so-called "shared secret" key) is susceptible to a "man in the middle attack." A "shared secret" is a contradiction in terms; and, if one party decides subsequently to renege on a contract and deny that he or she ever sent a particular communication, they need only claim that the key has been intercepted and used by a third party—or even by the other party.

NOTE Benjamin Franklin once observed: "…three may keep a secret, provided two of them are dead…"

The key-pair system means that it is computationally infeasible to derive the private key from knowledge of the public key.

This is what happens during a digital signing:

1. The sender prepares a string of data; for example, a purchase order expressed in XML.
2. To save processing power and time, the sender prepares a "hash" (essentially a short, unique, mathematically derived summary) of this document.
3. The sender encrypts the hashed document with the sender's private key. This encrypted hash is the actual digital signature.
4. The sender sends the digital signature and, if required, the original data (if confidential, this original data can be further encrypted) to the recipient.
5. The recipient verifies the sender's digital signature with the sender's public key. The signature will either contain the public key or point to the relevant directory. This authenticates the sender's identity.
6. The recipient then repeats step 2 to create a duplicate hash of the original data, using the same hash algorithm as the sender.
7. The recipient compares the two hashes. If they are identical, the recipient is assured thereby that the data has not been altered after signing by the sender.

8. Finally, the recipient obtains a digital certificate from a certificate authority (or from the sender) and validates it. Validation confirms the authenticity of the sender. This will confirm the sender's public key, name, and other specified information. The digital certificate will have been itself signed by the certificate authority.

At this point, it is useful to look at how the law deals with electronic and ink signatures, and to address some of the more prevalent misconceptions.

Dispelling the Myths

A digital signature is simply a particular kind of electronic signature; the terms are not synonymous. As yet, there has been no narrowly exclusive statutory or judicial definition of "electronic signature." That term could include methods as diverse as facsimile signatures, a typed name at the bottom of a plain e-mail message, an e-mail origination header, a digital signature, a biometric method, a personal identification number ("PIN"), a smartcard, and so forth.

CAUTION Digital signatures are sometimes also confused with *digitized* electronic signatures. These are graphical representations of a handwritten signature, such as those that UPS and Federal Express use. These are not bound to signed data. Their stand-alone evidential value is slight. They must not be confused with digital signatures proper.

Section 2 (8) of the Uniform Electronic Transactions Act provides a typical legislative definition of an electronic signature:

> "[a digital signature is]…an electronic sound, symbol, or process attached to or logically associated with a record and executed or adopted by a person with the intent to sign the record."

Similarly, Article 2 of the EU's Digital Signatures Directive provides a typical legislative definition of a digital signature:

> "…[an] electronic signature [is one] which…is uniquely linked to the signatory…is capable of identifying the signatory…is created using means that the signatory can maintain under his sole control; and…is linked to the data to which it relates in such a manner that any subsequent change of the data is detectable…"

Such legal definitions are open-ended. They try to balance forward-looking technical agnosticism with legal stipulations deriving directly from the four legal elements of a contract set out previously. Such stipulations do little more than reflect the common law evidential fundamentals that an ink signature must also satisfy.

Apart from some classes of contracts falling under residual aspects of the Statute of Frauds, neither statute law nor common law seeks to stipulate or define the mechanics of the contractual signing process. The reason for this is obvious: the legal fundamentals of a contract (set out previously) are self-contained. There is no legal need for lawyers also to concern themselves with mandating signing or with the mechanics of signing. Any misguided common law or statutory incursions into this area would do little but add confusion and inflexibility into clear and settled common law rules governing the creation of a contract.

NOTE In early Bavaria, certain commercial deals were only concluded once the youngest male present had had his ears boxed. Similarly, illiterate signatories still mark an "X" in lieu of signing their name. Equally, in the Irish Supreme Court decision in *Casey v. Irish Intercontinental Bank* [1979] I.R. 325 (S.C.), a lawyer instructed a secretary to type out the material terms of an agreement on headed notepaper. The lawyer did not sign the typed letter. Despite this, the Irish Supreme Court held that the lawyer had adopted the heading as his signature, with legally binding effect.

In strict legal theory then, a contract doesn't depend on any signature; it depends on the will of the contracting parties. Practically, it also depends on there being an incontrovertible means of proving that contracting will. While a traditional ink signature is a useful evidential tool, it is important not to become confused between the contract itself, and the means of signifying consent to it. Technical purists often point out, with justification, that a digital signature is not directly analogous to an ink signature. In one sense, this is a technical truism: a digital signature involves a necessary separation of initial creation and subsequent usage.

This separation does not exist in the paper world. This is an obvious point, but it bears stressing. While an ink-on-paper signature can be forged, it is almost impossible to re-create or to reuse. A forger could not cut out an existing paper signature with a pair of scissors and affix it to a subsequent contract! However adept the forger, minute differences are inevitable, and a handwriting expert (doubtless aided by a handwriting analysis software product) will be able to detect these. By stark contrast, an unsecured private key on a PC might, in theory, have been used by anyone.

However, this carping, while based on factual technical distinctions, is in danger of missing the legal point. It is not legally material that the technical mechanisms involved in a digital signing are not sequentially congruent with the technically trite process of putting pen to paper. What matters is that either process is understood to be, and is capable of being, a reliable means of signifying the signer's consent to the contents of an e-mail or a document.

From a legal standpoint then, it is arguable that the loose use of the word "signature" to describe the process whereby one signifies consent to a contract by electronic means is legally efficient. Everyone understands the legal effect of signing a document—you are signifying that you both understand the terms of a contract and that you agree to be bound by these terms. The widespread use of the traditional word "signature" to describe the (admittedly technically distinct) process of denoting understanding and consent online will obviate any arguments that might otherwise have arisen. If a less familiar term than "digital signature" had been adopted, it is likely that individuals, out of cynicism or genuine error, might have claimed that they "failed to realize" that they had in fact given their consent to a contract.

See also the discussions under the headings "Digital Signatures: Legally Neutral Until Secured" and "Digital Signatures: An Emerging Legal Hierarchy," later in this chapter.

Mapping Legal Components to Technical Security Components

Each of the conceptual legal components previously outlined (together with the practical proof component) maps directly to a number of technical security approaches/components. This is summarized in Table 14-1.

What Was Agreed?

All commercial systems, be they paper or virtual, depend on the absolute inviolability of agreed contractual data. If you buy *x* amount of shares in Solid PLC from your access point to an online system, you do not expect to find that, by the time it arrives on the recipient's machine, your agreement has been altered to now record that a third party has purchased *x*-times-10 shares in Shaky PLC. Effectively, data security *is* Internet security. It would be a quixotic endeavor to attempt to secure the multiplicity of routes and systems that make up the open Internet. In any event, much modern commercial data needs to be transported in a manner that permits a variety of access permissions.

As we saw in Chapter 3, the security of XML traffic over the Internet requires *security in the message* (that is, in the SOAP message). Transport security protects data while it is in transit. Message-level security acts on the data itself. This point is best illustrated by a physical-world analogy. Assume you have sent a postcard from San Francisco to London. While it is in transit, it is protected from being modified or read because it is locked in a container on a freight train, or locked in the back of a mail truck. However, when the postcard is stored overnight at a mail depot, it can be read. The *message itself* is not secured. The stages in the journey (the "hops" in Figure 14-1) are secured, but the message itself is not secured.

Now assume, by contrast, that instead of sending an open postcard, you have sent the same message in an envelope with a wax seal, or in a locked metal dispatch box.

Legal Component	Maps To	Security Components Needed
What was agreed?	⇨	Data security Internet security
When was it agreed?	⇨	Time stamping
Who agreed to it?	⇨	Certificate security Private key security
Proof: trustworthy audit trails	⇨	System security LAN internal security LAN perimeter security

Table 14-1. Linking Law to Security

The message itself is now secured. The hops continue to be secured (the locked container on the freight train, the locked mail truck), but the message itself has now been secured as well.

That analogy works for electronic mails. A single e-mail message may pass through many e-mail servers before it reaches its destination. The message will be secured during those "hops" between e-mail servers. However, while the message is sitting on a particular e-mail server, the administrator of that server or a third-party hacker can read the message. This is why simply securing the transportation between each e-mail server is insufficient. We must also secure the e-mail message itself (see Figure 14-1).

NOTE In many cases, we need to think in terms of securing against disclosure as much as we already do in terms of securing against attack. For instance, mere disclosure of trade secrets or the contents of patent applications will destroy their commercial value.

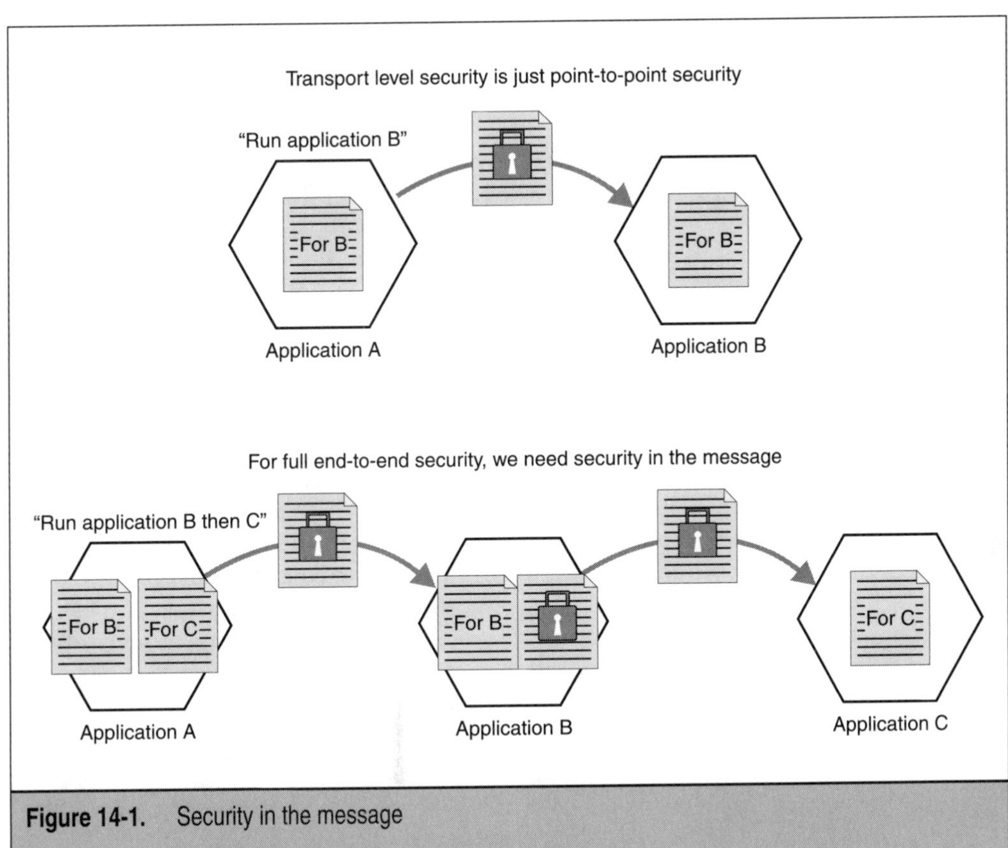

Figure 14-1. Security in the message

When Was It Agreed?

At common law, any agreement without an express or obvious effective date will normally be void for uncertainty. However, merely stipulating an effective date is not in itself proof against a "replay attack," even in a paper environment. Assume that you have faxed signed instructions to your bank to transfer money to a previously nominated third party. If an agent of the third party intercepts and resends the fax, the bank may well transfer a further amount.

Messages that have been sent electronically, and that have been digitally signed, are just as vulnerable to such replay attacks. The potential for fraudulent repeat contracting is obvious—a hacker intercepts your message and sends it again. However, the corollary of such replay attacks can have equally damaging legal consequences. Where a system receives two identical (but genuine) messages from another system (for example, at 11:00 p.m. "Sell 100,000" and at 11:01 p.m. "Sell 100,000"), then it may ignore the second message on the assumption that it is a replay attack.

However, since the second message may have been sent before the first message, but received secondly because of network delays, there is in fact no way to ascertain which of the messages might be a replay attack. Legally, no safe assumptions can be made about either message; and both will need to be discarded. However, once you are aware of such legal issues, you can look to a variety of technical solutions.

TIPS You can secure your digital signature solution against replay attacks by making sure that the signature data includes a timestamp; or you can include a "nonce" in your messages. A nonce, standing for "number once," is a value that changes with each transmitted message, thereby ensuring that no two valid messages can be identical.

Who Agreed to It?

Legally, the "key to online contracting is in the key." How and where private keys are respectively distributed and stored has important legal consequences. Clearly, if a key issuer makes only a cursory effort to verify that I am who I say I am before allocating a private key to me, then it follows that I could, if I wished, readily obtain a false online identity. However, even a rigorous system of identity checking will be undone if I am then permitted (or even required) to store my private key in an insecure place.

In the latter scenario, while the key may originally have corresponded to the real me, this initial identity matching will be negated as soon as an impostor uses my key to impersonate me. In the XML Signature specification, the W3C organization readily admits that this point of legal vulnerability is partly a policy issue that technology by itself cannot fully guard against:

> ". . .signer authentication is an application decision (e.g., does the signing key actually correspond to a specific identity) that is supported by, but out of scope, of this specification."[3]

This is a restatement of the "security is a process, not a product" truism mentioned earlier. It follows that private keys must be stored securely. Ideally, they should be stored on a hardware token that may itself have additional PIN and/or biometrics security. The evidential implications of a range of private key storage methods are developed in the section "An Emerging Legal Hierarchy," later in this chapter.

Built-in Safeguards

Much of the legal debate about digital signatures focuses on a key security aspect. We tend to overlook the fact that digital signatures provide two additional, built-in legal safeguards that traditional ink signatures cannot match:

1. A digital signature is bound to the data that is signed. If the data changes, the signature becomes invalid. This is not the case for a handwritten signature. If I sign the last page of a 300-page legal agreement, and then page 77 is replaced with a new and slightly—but materially—changed page 77, there is no way of detecting this change purely by examining my ink signature.

2. Chapter 2 explains how, if used properly, digital signatures can guarantee data integrity. This is distinct from their role in linking a signer's identity to signed data. In the case of a handwritten signature, there is no guarantee of such integrity. There is only a link to the signer's identity.

Trustworthy Audit Trails

We have already noted that all commercial systems, be they paper or virtual, depend on the absolute inviolability of agreed contractual data. Inviolability in this context carries the additional sense of being inviolable from attack or destruction for a period sufficient to ensure that, if need be, the courts can refer back to a contracting party's

---

3 XML-Signature Syntax and Processing-W3C Recommendation, February 12, 2002

obligations so as to enforce that party's compliance with them. This is the stuff of conventional, defensive online security: Internet usage policies for employees, continually updated antivirus software, firewalls, and daily backups stored off-site.

NOTE EU and U.S. data protection laws provide additional justifications for storing data securely. Increasingly, they are also starting to prescribe adherence to best technical practice and approaches.

Broadly speaking, all of the preceding working legal principles have been settled law in all key commercial jurisdictions for generations. They have a strategic importance to online security that eludes the merely operational significances of more narrowly focused laws (for instance, those laws dealing with data protection, or with spam). Once we start to prioritize law into the essential and the merely important, it is then a relatively simple matter to look at any technological product or context and ask oneself the anchor question: "legally, does this work?"

Let's put that question to a number of important security technologies.

APPLYING THE LAW TO PARTICULAR TECHNOLOGIES

Clearly, law mainly has relevance to those technologies that claim to secure the conceptual legal components listed in Table 14-1. Technologies such as digital signatures, SAML, SSL, and biometrics variously concern themselves with technical issues such as user authentication and data integrity. Effectively, such technical issues are indistinguishable from legal issues. Before considering those individual technologies, it is helpful briefly to consider the amalgam of technologies and technical approaches that make up Web Services.

Web Services: An Overview of Legally Relevant Technical Trends

It may be helpful to view Web Services as being an important milestone in the development of the Internet as a tool for business, as opposed to being some sort of overnight technological paradigm shift. Previously, communication between software applications across networks used complex protocols such as CORBA and DCOM. Increasingly, however, standards vendors are using Web technologies (such as HTTP and XML) for automated communications processes.

Despite the fact that there are several standards vendors still jostling for market position, it is clear that there is a shared trend towards application integration at increasingly specific (and therefore increasingly useful) levels, and that this drive towards greater integration is accelerating. This growing convergence, despite its unruly nature, is now sufficiently significant that it has been dignified with its own name—hence Web Services. It may be a new departure, but it still contains many of the broad characteristics of a PKI structure.

However, the underlying technology has been simplified. For instance, previously, a certificate request was sent to a certificate authority as a PKCS#10 message; that is, not using the Web. By contrast, in Web Services architecture, XKMS is used to send a semantically equivalent key validation message, formatted as XML, over the Web. The advantages of this new approach are simplicity (many programmers and applications already know XML and may not have been familiar with complex and specialized cryptographic formats such as PKCS#10) and interoperability (many firewalls block all ports apart from Web and e-mail ports).

One can also receive information about the status of a key in an XML format. This is also part of the XKMS specification. Apart from the fact that XML is being used, and that the information flow uses the Web, the underlying processes are the same. The user applies for a secured public key (now using X-KRSS instead of PKCS#10) and then the recipient of a signed document checks the status of the public key in question through an online key validation service (now an XKMS "trust utility" with an XML/SOAP interface).

In addition, XML Signature is a means of representing a digital signature as XML, and also has special provision for the case where the signed information is itself written in XML. While an XML signature is almost semantically equivalent to the older PKCS signature format, the advantage of an XML signature is that it can be understood by a wide variety of applications.

From a legal perspective, there are two noteworthy aspects to the foregoing:

- The Web is being used increasingly as a communications channel for embedded communications processes.
- In keeping with this greater use of the Web, private keys are more likely to be stored in a key store that is directly accessible by a Web browser.

Legally, is either of those technical trends material?

Evidential Credibility of a Web Services Architecture

Web Services' drive towards greater integration convenience carries within it a commercial pressure not to use awkward security methods that may be viewed as disproportionate to the vulnerabilities of the medium.

SECURITY ALERT As far back as 1885, Justice Stephen remarked that "Laws ought to be adjusted to the habits of society, and not aim at re-moulding them...custom, and what is called common sense, regulate the great mass of human transactions. If...the law deviates from these guiding principles, it becomes a nuisance. If you require people to take precautions which they feel to be practically unnecessary, and which are alien to their habits of life, the only practical result is that they will prefer the risk of the penalties of neglect to the nuisance of taking the precaution."

Quoted in Section 17 of the Statute of Frauds, 1 LQR 1, 6 (1885)

The next two sections examine the varying legal implications of the three main types of private key storage that may ensue. From a purely evidential perspective, such differing storage methods create at least three types of digital signature. Obviously, digital signatures are not peculiar to Web Services; the following observations about digital signatures have a general applicability to digital signatures in any online context.

We should be aware of any legal implications of a typical Web Services architecture platform. Where security vulnerabilities are manifestly inherent in the design of a network systems architecture, there is a greater likelihood that people who wish to repudiate their contractual liabilities will point to the statistical probability of an attack on that network to strengthen their arguments for such repudiation. From a legal standpoint, the perceived statistical likelihood of an attack could be more damaging than an actual attack.

The convenience of using Web Services must be weighed against the precautions that must be taken to ensure the legality of Web Services transactions. However, provided that, for instance, the SAML assertions used in Web Services are kept secure (discussed later), the attacks that should concern us are those that may be capable of compromising private key security.

Digital Signatures: Legally Neutral Until Secured

The legal validity of any online trading model that relies on stand-alone digital certificates (see next section) depends largely on the likelihood of *key theft* (effectively, identity theft) being statistically unimportant enough that a court could reasonably discount it.

Law is a pragmatic discipline. It operates to certain working assumptions. For instance, it assumes that you are innocent. In fact, you may not be. However, the prosecution is obliged, in criminal matters, to prove otherwise. In contractual matters, courts assume that your ink signature at the end of a paper contract is in fact yours. It does not automatically assume that your ink signature must be someone else's and thereby require you to prove otherwise in each disputed case.

The obvious fact that paper documents and signatures are at least as susceptible to fraudulent manipulation as their online equivalents has never been a bar to their providing a legally binding mechanism and context for paper-based contracting. Theoretically, paper documents and signatures can easily be falsified and forged. This is understood and accepted as the trade-off for having a generally efficient system. No one has ever suggested that pen and paper should be scrapped, despite the reality of these vulnerabilities. Instead, the pragmatic emphasis in the paper world is on understanding the vulnerabilities of the paper contracting process so that business and legal communities can best accommodate and manage them.

Similar working assumptions (confirmed by statutes) hold for electronic (including digital) signatures. The positive assumption of legitimate private key usage could only be displaced if, as noted, digital signatures were to become widely discredited in fact. This is unlikely. Digital signatures are expected to match, not surpass, the legal effects of ink signatures.

It is important to keep this aspect in perspective by looking critically at ink signatures. A written signature on paper is nothing more than a convenient method by which contracting parties signify that they are willing to accept rights and obligations set out in the wording of a contract, and that the terms of the contact have been agreed upon and are fully understood by all parties. However, once someone can demonstrate fraud, the influence of drugs/alcohol, forgery, insanity, duress, or mistake, then that contract, despite its being in paper-and-ink format, will be null and void.

Digital signatures are no different. E-commerce laws the world over tend only to give negative clearance to digital signatures by stating simply that they shall not be denied legal effectiveness and admissibility as evidence solely on the grounds that they are in electronic form. No one can guarantee that every single digital signature will always be capable of being verified. By itself, this will be of limited legal significance. Online attacks can only undermine the legal credibility of digital signatures generally if the volume and seriousness of such online attacks are such that digital signatures become widely discredited. Given the intrinsic qualities of public key cryptography, and that related security continues to mature, it is unlikely that this will happen.

Digital Signatures: An Emerging Legal Hierarchy

Not all digital signatures are of equal standing. Some digital signatures may be linked to "self-signed" certificates. Legally, the status of these do-it-yourself (DIY) signatures is more akin to train tickets than that of (say) national passports, in that they are only notionally linked to the user. However, the legal limitations of such so-called digital signatures are widely understood; and, if they are to be used in a critical online environment, they will invariably be augmented with other identity checks (such as personal questions carried out over the telephone or by e-mail) in real time.

This means that there is an emerging hierarchy of digital signatures. For convenience, these may be described as being linked to

- **Stand-alone digital certificates** Given out after an exhaustive series of identity checks, including face-to-face identity checks; and where the private key is thereafter stored as securely as possible, perhaps on a hardware token that may itself have additional PIN or biometrics security, such as RSA Security's SecurID product. Their intrinsic evidential value is likely to be prima facie conclusive.
- **Corroborative digital certificates** Given out after a rigorous series of identity checks (which may rely mainly on an exchange of paper correspondence concerning individual specific matters such as banking or share-ownership details), and where the private key may thereafter be either stored on a hardware token (or smart card) or on a Web repository. Legally, their intrinsic evidential value is high. In addition, where they are used in conjunction with additional real-time identity checking (such as using personal question checks conducted by telephone or over e-mail), their evidential value is likely to be prima facie conclusive.

- **Disposable digital certificates** Self-signed, without being linked to any third-party identity provider. Legally, their intrinsic evidential value is slight, though they may assist in corroborating paper-based or affidavit evidence.

The Web-centric nature of a Web Services environment means that stand-alone digital signatures may not always feature in it. Corroborative digital signatures may on occasion be used. This means that any assessment of the legally binding nature of a particular Web Service will need to be a holistic assessment of the entire service. One needs to assess not only how the certificates are managed and how the private keys are stored, but also how the wider implementation aspects (such as corroborative identity checks) will be carried out.

Incidentally, it is worth noting that this approach differs little in principle from the kind of legal scrutiny that would have been directed towards policy details in a classical PKI environment. All that is different about the approach to legal scrutiny required by the Web Services model is that the scrutiny is directed towards a de facto entire-service implementation policy, as opposed to a formalistic written set of PKI policies that typically concentrated more narrowly on key issuance and storage.

SAML: The Legality of "Distributed Trust"

Security Assertion Markup Language, or SAML, is a means of reporting and vouching for a prior act of user authentication or authorization, or a user's attribute (for example, credit status). However, any such "SAML assertion" (discussed later in the chapter) is not in itself an act of user authentication. This seemingly trite distinction has important legal liability and legal security implications.

This section discusses those legal implications and makes some practical suggestions. That discussion is prefaced by, respectively, a short lay guide to SAML assertions and a summary of the differing legal effects of the two main kinds of prior authenticating acts.

What Are SAML Assertions?

SAML uses XML to encode messages relating to user authentication and user authorization. A SAML assertion is an automated assertion describing (or related to) a prior act of online authentication by an individual person, or to an act of authorization relating to that person. *Assertions* and *profiles* are important components of the SAML specification. SAML profiles are sets of rules describing how to put SAML assertions into particular use-case protocols as such protocols evolve to meet particular commercial/ user requirements.

Currently, there are SAML profiles for single sign-on to Web sites; and the OASIS Security Services Technical Committee is developing a profile for SAML assertions to be contained in SOAP messages. Typical SAML assertions include

- **Authentication assertions** Asserting that the user has proved her or his identity. Note that SAML does not mandate a particular type of prior authenticating act.

- **Attribute assertions** Asserting that, for example, the user has certain spending limits.
- **Authorization assertions** Asserting that, for example, the user is authorized to access a particular database or is authorized to purchase a particular item.

Browser/Artifact Profile: A Typical SAML Deployment The simple browser/artifact profile depicted in Figure 14-2 (below) involves a user logging onto, and being authenticated at, one particular site. SAML assertions allow that user to access related sites without having to reauthenticate herself or himself.

What Is an Authenticating Act?

Legally, an authenticating act is any action by you that establishes your individual identity. This rarely needs to be an absolute identification, it need only be proportionate to the value of the situation requiring the identification. Online, the two main types of authenticating act are

- **Usernames + passwords** These are "something you know." Incidentally, companies such as RSA Security develop credit-card-sized hardware password-generating devices—"something you have." These provide stronger authentication security than usernames + passwords.
- **Digital signatures** These authenticating acts have overlapping legal effects (see Table 14-2 on the next page).

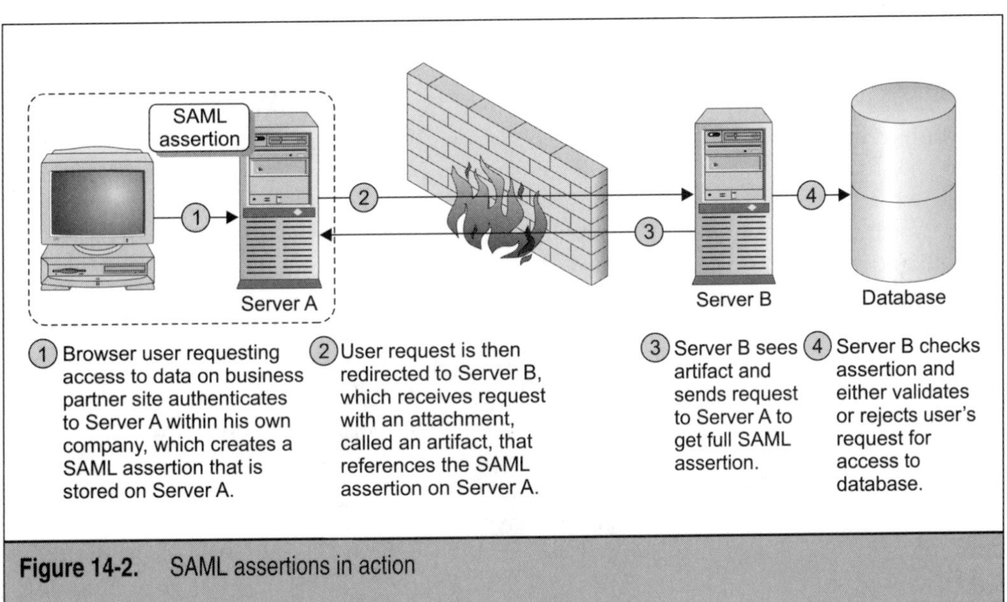

SAML assertion
Server A
1
2
3
4
Server B
Database
1 Browser user requesting access to data on business partner site authenticates to Server A within his own company, which creates a SAML assertion that is stored on Server A.
2 User request is then redirected to Server B, which receives request with an attachment, called an artifact, that references the SAML assertion on Server A.
3 Server B sees artifact and sends request to Server A to get full SAML assertion.
4 Server B checks assertion and either validates or rejects user's request for access to database.

Figure 14-2. SAML assertions in action

Authenticating Act	Legal Effect
Username + password	Weak authentication No guarantee of (contractual) data integrity Very weak (contractual) nonrepudiation
Digital signature	Strong authentication* Guaranteed (contractual) data integrity Strong (contractual) nonrepudiation* * Provided that, as noted earlier, the digital certificate has only been issued after an exhaustive series of identity checks, including (ideally) face-to-face identity checks, and provided that the private key is thereafter stored as securely as possible, perhaps on a hardware token that may itself have additional PIN or biometrics security.

Table 14-2. Legal Effects of Authenticating Acts

SAML Assertions: Legal Implications

Paradoxically, even though SAML is itself a security technology, it must itself be securely deployed—and it must be deployed in a network that has already been separately secured.

SAML Is Not a Guarantor A SAML assertion is a mere messenger. It is not a guarantor. While it should be abundantly clear that the reliability of a SAML assertion is wholly dependent on the reliability of the original authenticating act, this obvious point must be highlighted. Otherwise, there is a human tendency to become seduced by the plausibility of the intervening SAML technology; and to overlook the fact that, in legal reality, little, of any, stand-alone legal merit may have been asserted to.

For instance, technical papers on SAML tend to describe a SAML authentication assertion as an assertion that the user has "proved" his or her identity. This overstates the legal effect of, for instance, a mere username + password combination. In that case, it would be more accurate to state that the user has *attested* to his or her identity. This caveat applies especially to SAML assertions derived from prior digital signature authentication, such as are required by the Browser/Post SAML Profile. No amount of subsequent SAML assertions can transform an insecurely obtained digital certificate into a legally binding digital certificate.

Currently, SAML assertions are primarily designed to assert to acts of authentication and authorization, and issues directly relating thereto. SAML assertions are not *in themselves* about issues of contractual data integrity or contractual nonrepudiation. SAML assertions typically occur in a user-access context. That context typically occurs prior to any transmission of additional contractual data (as opposed to authentication data) by the user. Accordingly, SAML assertions have little direct relevance to contractual data-integrity issues. Further, a SAML assertion only goes to prove that a designated user accessed system x at y hours. Beyond that, a SAML assertion is not an activity log.

Of itself, a SAML assertion is of little relevance in refuting attempts by a user to deny that she or he had entered into a particular contract.

Securing SAML Assertions Throughout, this chapter stresses the importance of online security in helping to create a legally binding architecture. The same principles apply to SAML assertions. When SAML assertions communicate between different networks, the initiating server (server A in Figure 14-2) creates and stores the SAML data locally. Potentially, the SAML data exchange and the underlying data storage both are points of technical and legal vulnerability. It is essential that commercial and legal planners should be aware of such vulnerabilities, and of the obvious remedies.

To prevent replay attacks, the latest Web Services Security Addendum document[4] recommends the following:

> "In order to trust Ids and timestamps, they SHOULD be signed using the mechanisms outlined in WS-Security. This allows readers of the IDs and timestamps information to be certain that the IDs and timestamps haven't been forged or altered in any way. It is strongly RECOMMENDED that Ids and timestamp elements be signed. Note that since the Timestamp header is mutable, signatures need to be associated with individual elements. Timestamps can also be used to mitigate replay attacks. Signed timestamps MAY be used to keep track of messages (possibly by caching the most recent timestamp from a specific service) and detect replays of previous messages. It is RECOMMENDED that timestamps and nonces be cached for a minimum of five minutes to detect replays, and that timestamps older than five minutes be rejected in interactive scenarios."

Ideally, such data exchanges should also be encrypted separately, instead of needing to rely on any surrounding channel encryption. In Figure 14-2, server A's SAML assertions must only be capable of being accessed or interrogated by server B, not by an unauthorized third-party server.

In this context, commercial and legal planners should keep abreast of evolving SAML security standards. SAML 1.1 looks set to resolve many of the legal issues. In particular, there is a growing recognition that SAML 1.1 needs to provide more complete information about the authentication context of differing authentication methods. This should resolve the legal error, already noted, of appearing to confer parity of legal status on a disparate range of weak and strong authentication methods.

Liability In a typical scenario, a SAML assertion generated by company A's server will be instrumental in securing access to company B's confidential database system for user X. Effectively, B is relying on A's assertion about X's credentials. If A's SAML deployment is insecure, untold commercial damage to B may ensue at the hands of X.

---

4 Published at www.-106.ibm.com/developerworks/webservices/library/ws-secureadd.html?dwzone=webservices. Copyright © International Business Machines Corporation, Microsoft Corporation, VeriSign, Inc. 2002

Prima facie, B could sue A. Contractually, such liability trapdoors can easily be avoided by A's prior insistence on some prudent apportionment and limitation of liability/hold harmless clauses. Otherwise, it is not difficult to see the scope for fractious and technically involved lawsuits.

The Value of SAML

Commercially, SAML is a timely mechanism; both for solving the repeat authentication logjam for users and for simplifying automated back-office machine-to-machine trading. Provided that commonsense security and liability issues are addressed in the manner outlined, SAML assertions can be relied upon as being authoritative distributors of trust between disparate companies and sites.

SSL: Legally, How Secure Is It?

The contractual effect of Secure Sockets Layer (SSL) differs dramatically, depending on its use context. SSL uses encryption and digital certificates as normal, but usually does so to authenticate the server only. SSL allows a confidential "secure pipe" to be established for the duration of a communications session. This suffices to allow the confidential communication of the user's input to the Web site. In this way, SSL can operate without the complexities of a full PKI infrastructure.

Effectively, SSL is one half of a normal PKI structure. It is indicated in a business-to-consumer model whereby consumers order goods over the Internet. While consumers have an obvious requirement to verify the identity of the retailer company at the server side, any legal requirement that this verification be mutual is mostly negated by the deployment advantages of concentrating the technology and the legality at the server. Accordingly, one-way SSL has obvious legal limitations in a mutual, "at-arms-length" business-to-business context.

Biometrics: Is Seeing Believing?

Biometrics is the generic term for a variety of scientific methods for measuring and statistically analyzing biological data. In information technology, "biometrics" usually refers to technologies for measuring and analyzing human body characteristics such as fingerprints, eye retinas and irises, voice patterns, facial patterns, hand measurements, keystroke patterns, and DNA profiling. For instance, biometric fingerprint devices are security systems that claim to offer a secure means of access to online systems (or buildings) by identifying you from your fingerprint.

Fingerprint and other biometric devices consist of a reader or scanning device, software that converts the scanned information into digital form, and a database where the biometric data is stored for comparison with the biometric data entered when a user tries to gain access. In converting the biometric input, the software identifies specific points of data as match points. Using an algorithm, the match points are processed to a value that can be compared with biometric data scanned when a user tries to gain access.

For decades, popular science fiction films have familiarized us to such biometric devices. This factor, together with their dramatic and tangible user effects, means that biometric devices enjoy a popular security credibility that, for instance, digital signatures struggle to match.

However, in this instance, popular intuition errs on the generous side. Biometric devices have a role as secondary security/authentication methods, but their value as frontline, or sole, legal authentication methods is questionable. The theoretical vulnerability in any biometric device lies in the fact that the user's unique details will be checked against a database on each occasion that the device is used. Theoretically, it is possible to hack into a database holding a set of individual biometric records and to map them to a false identity.

Fooling Security

During 2002, a Mr. Tsutomu Matsumoto, a cryptographer at Yokohama National University in Japan, was able to bypass biometric authentication security by using basic DIY skills and $10 worth of household supplies. Using the free-molding plastic you can buy at DIY stores, Matsumoto made a plastic mold of his finger. He then poured in some liquid gelatin (you can buy it in grocery stores) and let it solidify. This crudely made fake finger fooled 80 percent of fingerprint detectors tested by Mr. Matsumoto. Perhaps more alarmingly, using a digital camera and some basic etching techniques, he was also able easily to re-create effective fake fingers from stray fingerprints. Such fake fingers could (literally) be pressed into action as perfect accessories to a physical security attack. Simply mold the transparent gelatin finger over your own. Watching security guards will not suspect anything as you press your own finger onto the sensor. After it lets you in under an assumed identity, simply eat the evidence!

CONCLUSIONS

This chapter demonstrates that, in both law and security, there can be no unthought absolutes:

- Legal security is holistic.
- Security also depends on cultural mores. (Consider the security anomaly that is off-site electronic voting.)
- The best security is designed to fail.

Legal Security Is Holistic

In line with the "padlock on a paper bag" axiom, there is little point in applying all or any of the preceding security measures to a systems architecture that is itself legally vulnerable in other ways. For instance, you may wish to configure your system automatically to send copies of signed data to an Oracle database to ensure efficient storage and subsequent data interrogation.

Further, for litigation planning, you may also wish to generate digitally signed audit trails. Many applications keep logs of their activities; for example, "signed document on 12/12/2002 at 12:10 p.m.; sent document on 12/12/2002 at 12:11 p.m." Such log files should also be digitally signed, ideally using a tamperproof hardware device.

CAUTION In the broadest sense, legal security eludes even the above. While the following are outside the scope of this chapter, you should also check that your Web site design complies with GUI disability laws; that your autoresponder is not inadvertently binding you into unwanted contracts by responding in legally binding terms to every casual query; that you have highlighted any of your onerous click-through trading terms with a specific "accept" button; that your harvesting of potential customer information is not contravening data protection laws; that your bulk mailings do not contravene any anti-spam laws; and that your site is compliant with distance selling legislation.

Effective Security Depends on Shared Cultural Assumptions

Most prison security systems depend heavily on the cultural assumption that prison wardens are not motivated to release prisoners. Since the majority of wardens obviously are not so motivated, the prison security system works. ATM machine security depends heavily on a common-sense materialistic assumption that it is not in our interests to reveal our ATM card PINs. That assumption is overwhelmingly correct; and, again, the system works. Digital signature security, like credit card security, depends on an equally common-sense assumption that it is not in our best interests to allow our private key to fall into third-party hands, thereby running the risk of incurring fraudulently attributed contractual liabilities to unknown parties.

Such assumptions disintegrate in the case of electronic voting in political elections, where such voting is carried out away from a polling booth. From a straightforward technical security perspective, electronic voting is problematic in any event. Contracting parties use digital signatures to bind contractual obligations to named individuals. By contrast, online voters are at pains to remain anonymous. Further, contracts usually exist in a wider context. That context can be a telling source of corroborative evidence to settle a contractual dispute. However, online voting is a once-off event—it is deliberately designed so that there should not be any corroborative evidence of a voter's intentions.

Arguably however, off-site online political voting's greatest security threat is a cultural one: voter apathy. In the West, a significant minority of potential voters is alienated from party politics. They do not vote. They have no incentive to maintain the security of their online votes. In fact, they have every incentive, particularly in marginal constituencies, illegally to sell their votes to unscrupulous party activists.

Strong security and effective policies can guard against *identity theft* to a court's satisfaction. However, where a politically indifferent and mercenary voter is voting unsupervised, there is little that even the best security can do to prevent fraudulent *identity selling*. Once such voter fraud is credibly alleged, a court may have to draw the usual obvious and damning conclusions about motive and opportunity. It is difficult to see how any binding democratic process could be founded on such uncertainty.

The foregoing is certainly not to decry security generally, nor to seek in any way to diminish its usually positive legal effects. It simply serves to illustrate that law and technology both exist in a cultural context. This theme—that legal security is a managed, holistic process—runs through this entire chapter. The fact that off-site electronic political voting can be fatally compromised by something as un-technical as a countervailing popular culture simply serves to highlight the importance of maintaining an aggregate approach to legal security.

The Best Security Is Designed to Fail Successfully

Chapter 2 used the sealed bunker analogy to demonstrate that a hermetically sealed security system is, paradoxically, an unusable security system. Equally, law must always be arguable to some extent if it is to avoid degenerating into fascism. Instead of casting about for a nonexistent technical silver security bullet, the real-world issue for both law and security is a pragmatic matter of deciding *to what extent* a security infrastructure can and needs to be resistant to technical attack, or to subsequent legal challenge.

This legal pragmatism is already at work in online security. We have seen, for instance, that the legal effectiveness of a digital signature is mutable—its legal force is in part dictated by the effectiveness of a people-dependent security policy that determines how the private key should be allocated and stored. Proportionality and context can also be critical factors. We have also seen how, in a consumer-to-business context, one-way SSL security is technically and legally adequate, but that it would fail to meet reasonable legal expectations about authentication and proof in a business-to-business context.

Security risks, and their attendant legal risks, are no different from any other risks. They can be managed, but short of ceasing all online activity, they cannot be eradicated. Perhaps the best analogy is vehicle safety. Certain automobile manufacturers concentrate on "passive safety" such as airbags and crumple zones. Other more thoughtful manufacturers lay equal stress on "active safety" such as agile and secure handling, efficient interior ergonomics to reduce driver fatigue, and powerful engines to allow for safer overtaking maneuvers.

The danger with passive safety is that it engenders complacency. The driver retreats into a cocoon and expects/hopes that the barrier security devices will be proof against all external attacks from other road users. This is a "wait and hope" policy. In other words, it's no policy. By contrast, a driver who has learned to rely on active safety is fully alive to the constant possibility of danger and is, as a result, better prepared to take early and effective preemptive action.

Similarly, the best security professionals will never claim to have eradicated risks. A keen awareness of the possibility of failure guards against complacency and ensures that any security failure will be a *managed failure*. We can best control the security and legal consequences of an anticipated and managed failure. We are relatively helpless in the face of an unexpected failure.

Accordingly, the challenge for security professionals is to implement security measures that take equal account of technical, people-dependent, legal, and cultural contingencies—and that apply these thoughtfully to particular situations. The law does not expect that we can create failproof systems. No court would even give any credence to such a wild claim. However, the law does expect that security professionals will implement security measures that

- Demonstrate a clear understanding of the core legalities that must be secured
- Are capable of keeping security attacks to a *de minimis* level

These are not the stuff of absolutist or extravagant "snake oil" ambitions. They are realistic and achievable goals. We have already noted how, from a legal standpoint, the perceived statistical likelihood of an attack could be as damaging as an actual attack. However, provided we can achieve such goals, our security will have secured the legal components of a contract in the first place; and by keeping *successful* physical attacks to a *de minimis* level, our security will also have negated even the possibility of any retrospective legal challenge that would seek to attack a particular contract by discrediting an entire architecture.

In legal security, the possibility of failure is, paradoxically, our most effective security ally.

CHECKLIST

- ☐ Demand practical answers to primary questions: "Why, exactly, do I need any security before I can contract online? Which security items do I need?"
- ☐ Ask whether the security items you select will enable your system to tell you
    - ☐ *What* was agreed?
    - ☐ *When* was it agreed?
    - ☐ *Who* agreed to it?
- ☐ Put security into your data. It's not enough to secure the transport-channel.
- ☐ Secure your private key.

- ☐ Be legally critical of digital certificates. Legally, a "stand-alone" digital certificate is not the same as a "corroborative" digital certificate. Legally, neither is the same as a "disposable" digital certificate.
- ☐ Deploy SAML critically. SAML is useful, but it is legally neutral. Do not commit the cardinal legal error of believing that SAML can intervene to confer parity of legal status on a disparate range of weak and strong prior authentication methods.
- ☐ Ignore anyone who either enthuses about or dismisses law or legal security in categorical or alarmist terms.

APPENDIX

Case Studies

This section of the book explains the technologies, products, and standards discussed in the rest of this book using several case studies of projects. This book started with a theoretical look at security, at Web Services, and at how security and Web Services relate together. This relationship works both ways: long-standing security problems may now be solved using Web Services, while the use of Web Services demands new security technologies. In this section, we look at how the technologies we've learned about can be put into practice. We will see various deployment models for Web Services security, including the use of authentication portals that talk to Web Services to present information to end users, and the use of XML gateway/XML firewall products to manage and control access to Web Services.

LOCAL GOVERNMENT SERVICE PORTAL

This first case study takes an old problem (deploying a Web site to a large user group whose members are authenticating using various methods) and applies a new solution (Web Services).

Project Overview

This project involved a local government authority that wishes to make available a range of services on its Web site portal to a variety of users, with varying levels of authentication and access granted depending on the identity of the user in question.

Web Services is attractive for government integration projects, because governments typically have very diverse and mutually incompatible systems, but also have a requirement for these systems to share information. Integration via a service-oriented architecture means that the various government systems do not need to be tightly integrated, which in turn means that technologies and solutions can be enhanced or swapped out without the change propagating to other systems and causing disruption.

The use of Web Services in government started with the use of Web Services within government systems, before the use of outward-facing Web Services. End users will continue to mainly use portals—not Web Services—for the foreseeable future to communicate with governments. Businesses, however, will migrate to the use of Web Services for government communication—for example, the filing of tax returns. The first step, underpinning these later steps, is for services-oriented architecture to be adopted for systems integration between government systems. Combined with Web Services security, this allows users authenticated through the portal to access services without the requirement to reauthenticate.

Security Factors Identified

The main security risk is the authentication issue. Although back-office systems are not being exposed directly using publicly available Web Services, an end user who has authenticated to the portal may request information that is fetched on their behalf using SOAP. In this case, it is important that information about the end user's authentication travels with the SOAP message.

The use of a Web portal introduces Web site security challenges. It is important that the solution is not vulnerable to attacks mounted against the Web server itself, such as denial of service attacks and buffer-overflow attacks, or that it be vulnerable to attacks on other applications that are present on the same Web server.

Security Measures Deployed

It was decided that for the first release there would be two methods of user authentication available. One would be via a standard Web browser interface, using usernames and passwords over SSL. More trusted clients would be issued with client SSL certificates. Both these clients would communicate solely with the service portal. This would in turn communicate with the back-end systems using SOAP. The fact that there was no access to the back-end systems other than by authenticated users mitigated the concerns about these systems being compromised, but required that authentication cannot be bypassed. Web Services used in this project required the presence of a SAML authentication assertion issued by the government portal. This ensured that any attempt to bypass the authentication system and send a SOAP message directly to the Web Service would not be successful, because this SOAP message would not contain a valid SAML authentication assertion. As well as the use of SAML assertions within the SOAP messages, firewalls and routers are used to ensure that the internal Web Services use a private subnet, accepting no internal connections from the outside world.

WS-Security is used to package the user authentication information into the SOAP message. The SAML assertion conveys both the strength of the authentication and the identity of the user, thereby allowing the destination systems the autonomy to make their own decisions about which privileges should be granted.

FOREIGN EXCHANGE TRANSACTIONS

Our next case involves a fairly typical example of automating a high-value transaction process for a financial institution, in this case one involving foreign exchange.

Project Overview

This real-life case study involved a merchant bank in one of the larger European Union countries. The bank was involved in a thriving and substantial foreign exchange business with larger commercial organizations.

Typically, such organizations would have requirements for non-Euro currencies in the 1 to 10-million range, and would have between one and six weeks notice of such requirements. They would fax the bank a purchase order when the requirement became apparent, noting the date by which the amount was required. The bank was then trusted to secure the required amount at the optimum exchange rate, subject to the time requirements. When the bank judged the moment to be ripe, it would execute the transaction and notify the customer by fax, noting the interest rate achieved. (Yes, we did use the word fax in those sentences!). The bank took a small percentage commission of each transaction.

The manual, fax-based system worked largely because the service was targeted at very high-value transactions, and was at the time offered to less than a hundred customers. The bank had realized that if it could extend the service to more customers, it would benefit in two ways: first because the service was inherently profitable, and second due to its purchasing power in the foreign exchange markets being enhanced.

Clearly, a system based on a manual exchange of faxes would have to be replaced, because it was already producing a significant error rate under current loads. Consultants were engaged to suggest an electronic replacement.

The solution deployed was based on a client-side Web browser interface accepting and directing input to a corporate intranet application server, which in turn communicated using SOAP to the bank's systems.

Security Factors Identified

The bank was compelled by its regulatory authority to maintain records for ten of all foreign exchange transactions over 10,000 Euro in value. Under the manual system, this was achieved by simply photocopying the faxes and storing both the copy and the original faxes in separate, secure storage facilities. The bank's management had significant concerns, largely justified, about the durability and persistence of electronic records. This is mentioned not so much as a security issue, but more an example of the pragmatic, nitty-gritty snags that are frequently encountered when developing high-security systems that handle high-value transactions. Financial institutions care, deeply, about six and seven figure sums of money, and have deeply ingrained traditions and practices when dealing with such sums.

Authentication of client requests was quickly identified as a significant issue, although not perhaps as crucial as would initially be suspected. The accounts to which the foreign funds were eventually transferred, even in the manual system, were communicated to the bank "out of band," when the organization in question was first established as a customer, and could only be modified by written intervention of the company's finance director—again, transferred out of band (by motorcycle courier). It was decided at an early stage to maintain this practice, because it eliminated the risk of a compromised client transferring monies to the compromiser's designated bank account. This meant the most a compromiser could achieve was mischief, rather than actual gain.

Internal threat was identified as a significant risk. The bank's staff was well paid, but this project, perhaps more than most, raised the possibility of a single, successful fraudulent transaction being a "Rio retirement fund," where a successful perpetrator could enjoy financial security for life. The staff, of course, potentially had the ability to change the predefined destination account numbers previously discussed.

Mischief at the client's site, involving attacks from their staff, was also a consideration. While we could envisage no direct possibility of gain from such mischief, there was always the risk of a disgruntled employee entering spurious transactions for some reason.

Direct denial of service attacks were not a major consideration, because the project's Web Services were never intended to be made public, and those to whom it would be made known would always be known to the bank in advance.

Confidentiality of transactions in transit was also considered desirable, because a company's foreign exchange transactions are obviously commercially sensitive information.

Security Measures Deployed

No definitive solution presented itself to the archival problem, although agreement was ultimately reached with the regulatory authority that a piecemeal solution of storing electronic records on a variety of media (tape, CD-ROM, high-density floppies) would be acceptable.

Regarding the internal threat, it was concluded that the key risk factor was the point at which customer account details were being modified. It was decided that protection against alteration to such systems was to be provided by smartcard access, with the smartcards being held by some 30 different officers of the bank. When a customer update was required, the system would be notified and would then nominate, at random, four of the smartcard holders, who would need to present their cards before the update could go ahead. Thus, a fraudulent update of customer details would require collusion between four random members of the bank's staff. This was considered acceptable both by the bank's management and by its insurers, who were prepared to underwrite fraudulent usage coverage for the bank under this system.

The client authentication issue was resolved by the use of SAML. The client would authenticate as usual to his or her corporate application server. Then, a SAML authentication assertion would be obtained for the user in question and packaged into a SOAP message. This message would then be dispatched to the bank's systems, using

HTTP over mutually authenticated SSL. The bank's frontline systems would then extract the identity of the purported client from the authentication assertion and examine it to determine who issued the assertion. The assertion was digitally signed using XML Signature, and therefore the issuer was verified by first validating the XML Signature (to ensure that the assertion hadn't been tampered with) and then ensuring that the signer was trusted. Applications that provide this SAML verification functionality, using XML Signature validation, include Vordel's VordelSecure product. Following successful processing of the SAML authentication assertion, a SAML authorization decision request is sent to the internal authorization systems. At this point, either an authorization decision assertion is issued and the transaction proceeds or the user authentication presented is inadequate and the transaction is disallowed.

Note that there are two security contexts here: one in which the application server of the bank's client authenticates itself to the bank via the authenticated SSL, and another in which individual users authenticate themselves via an interplay of the client access control system and the bank's access control system.

XML GATEWAY ROLLOUT

This final case study examines the use of an XML security product in order to provide security for an organization's XML-based communications with its partners. This case study includes the concept of an XML firewall. It also walks through the configuration of a product for the security of Web Services.

Project Overview

A large financial services company required the ability to secure and monitor all XML traffic entering and leaving their private network. This large organization had multiple entry points and multiple exit points, which required security. XML data would be received from a wide variety of partners, though not from the general public. The organization required the establishment of an XML gateway prior to the actual deployment of Web Services.

Security Factors Identified

Because this XML gateway must receive XML data from the outside world, it must not be susceptible to direct attack itself. This would include vulnerabilities to a denial of service attack or to a buffer-overflow attack. It was important, therefore, that a security gateway should not itself be a point of vulnerability. A policy was devised for the use of locked-down operating systems and Web servers. This involved the application of security patches as they were issued and the blocking of all unused TCP/IP ports. A firewall was configured to ensure that low-level attacks were blocked, and it was mandated that SSL would always be used for encryption and mutual authentication of all HTTP traffic received by the XML gateway.

The next security factor that was identified was the existence of multiple entry points to the organizations, all of which may receive XML traffic. If XML security was only deployed at a single gateway, then it would be like deploying border guards at only a single border crossing and asking smugglers to "helpfully" only use that border crossing. A distributed solution, enforcing security across all XML entry points, was required instead. However, a further security issue was triggered by the use of a distributed architecture. If policies must be replicated across different gateways, there were dangers that version control would become out of sync.

A further security factor was that a variety of protocols and XML filtering functionality was required. When XML data was received, it first had to be checked to ensure that it was targeted at a Web Service intended to be available to partners. Once the target of the XML data was discovered, a policy had to be enforced for that Web Service. This meant that XML security policies had to be configurable *per service*, because some services may require more security than others. Requests to Web Services that were not supposed to be publicly available had to be blocked. The organization also required that the XML sent to each Web Service was appropriate, requiring it to be validated against an XML Schema at the gateway.

Incoming messages were to be authenticated using digital certificates contained within SOAP messages. It was important that the signature would convey proof of possession of the corresponding private key. This was achieved by including a timestamp within the signed data. In the future, it is planned to use WS-SecureConversation in order to negotiate a session key for the communication.

Finally, the organization wished to be alerted when XML messages were blocked by their XML gateway. They did not require this information for each individuate blocked XML message, but wanted to be able to raise an alert if the number of blocked messages for any given security rule exceeded a certain level.

Security Measures Deployed

Part of this project involved XML firewalling functionality. XML firewalling was defined as filtering XML traffic based on the content of the traffic, as opposed to identity-based access control that involves filtering XML traffic based on the sender of the traffic. An XML firewall performs similar functionality to a traditional firewall, except at the SOAP application layer.

An XML firewall is similar in concept to an application-level gateway firewall. Application-level gateways filter packets at the application layer. They are aware of what traffic meant for specific applications should look like. For example, an application layer gateway knows the difference between Web traffic and telnet traffic, even though both use TCP/IP. Application-specific commands and user activity can be logged. These firewalls are relatively processor-intensive. An application-level gateway will know that if it is protecting an e-mail POP server, the command "USER" is allowed and takes one parameter (that is, the username). Anything else is not allowed. For example, traffic that looks like telnet traffic directed to the POP server will be blocked.

Many firewalls have been configured to only allow Web (HTTP, SSL) and e-mail (POP, SMTP) traffic to pass. Other TCP/IP ports, and other protocols, are routinely blocked. SOAP is often "tunneled" through the Web ports (80 for HTTP, 443 for SSL), effectively disguised as normal Web traffic. This is generally not done for malicious reasons, but rather for pragmatic reasons because all other ports are blocked. In particular, SOAP is very frequently bound to HTTP. When a traditional firewall examines a SOAP request received over HTTP, it might conclude that this is valid HTTP traffic and let it pass. Firewalls tend to be all or nothing when it comes to SOAP. A SOAP-level firewall should be capable of the following:

- Identifying if the incoming SOAP request is targeted at a Web Service that is meant to be available.
- Identifying if the content of the SOAP message is valid. This is analogous to what happens at the network layer, where IP packet contents are examined. However, at the application layer it requires data that the Web Service expects.

Note that an XML firewall only provides part of the functionality that is required in this case study. This is because, as well as requiring only the appropriate data to enter the organization, only the appropriate *senders* of the data should be allowed. Firewalls do not typically provide security based on identity. However, firewalls are often combined with VPNs, which provide this functionality. The firewall/VPN combination is comparable to an XML gateway that combines XML Firewalling with identity-based access control using WS-Security and SAML.

For this case study, the organization used the VordelSecure product, which combines XML firewalling functionality with access control using WS-Security and SAML. Let's walk through the configuration of this product in order to re-create the settings used in this case study.

VordelSecure uses a tool called a Security Management Wizard to set security policies for XML traffic. Policies are set up *per service*, with the Web Service identified using a combination of SOAP endpoint, method name, method URI, and SOAP action. Look at Figure A-1 and you will notice that a Web Service called Calc has already been set up.

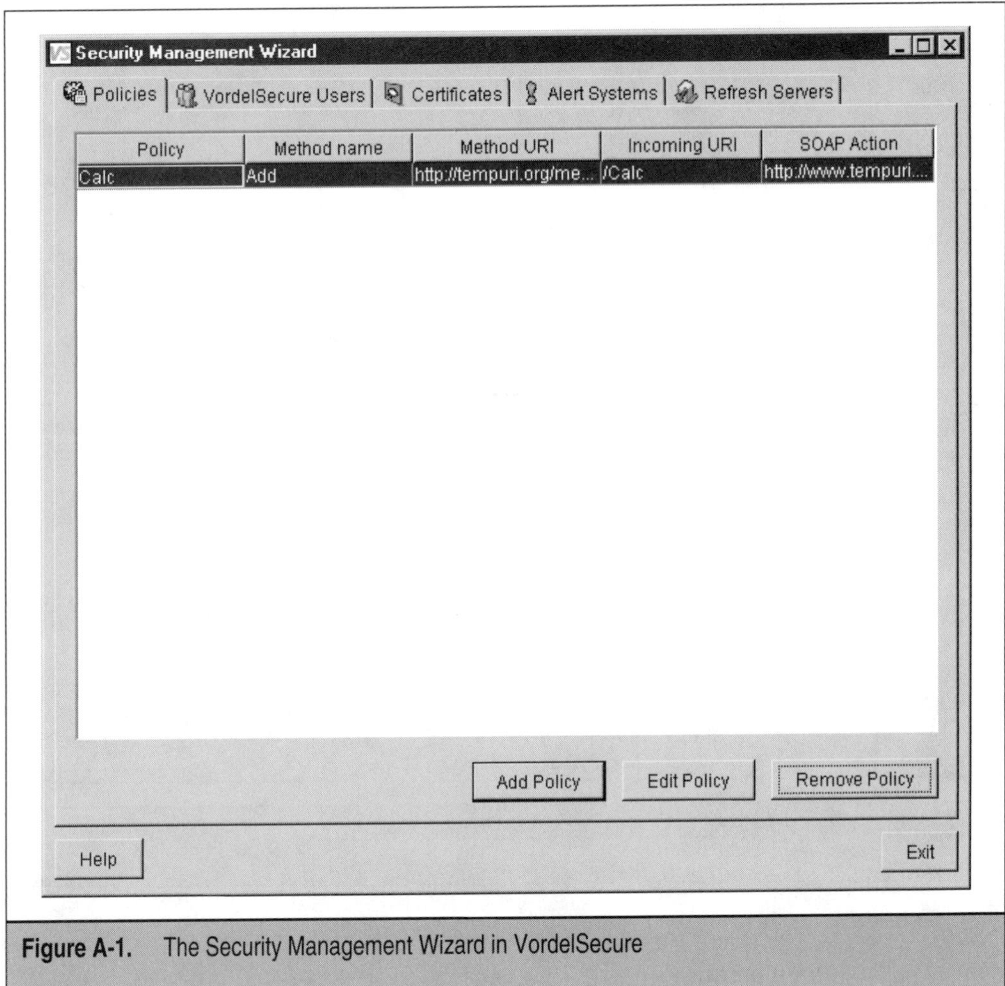

Figure A-1. The Security Management Wizard in VordelSecure

Click Add Policy in order to set a policy for an XML gateway. The enforcement of this policy can be distributed across multiple XML gateways, using VordelSecure's distributed architecture. Notice that there is an option to load a policy from a WSDL file, rather than configuring it manually (see Figure A-2).

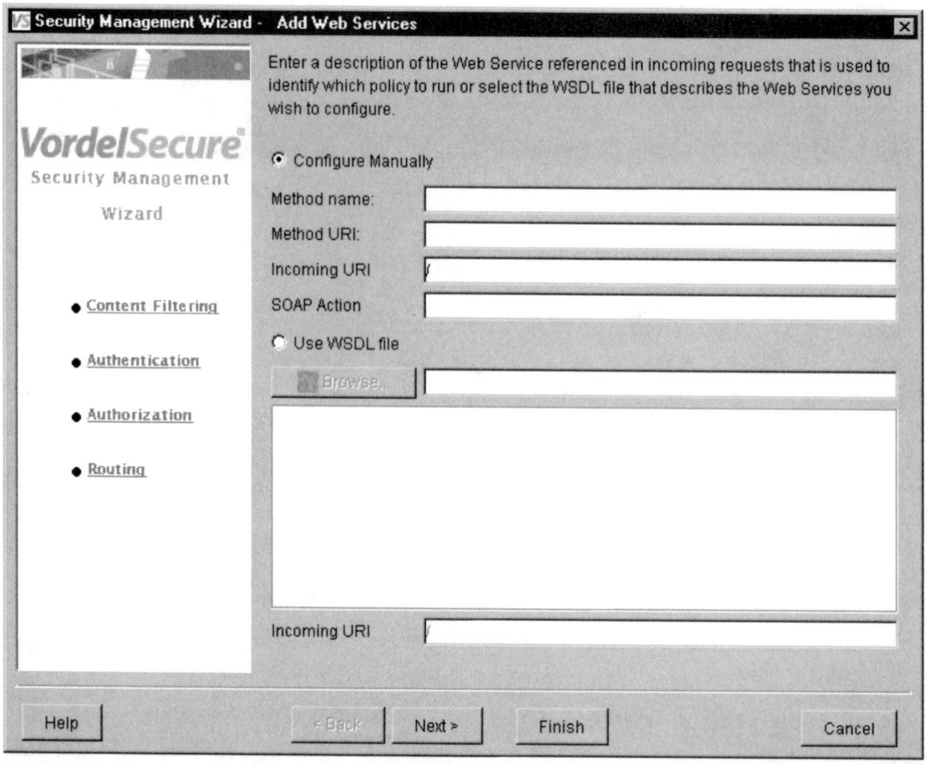

Figure A-2. Loading a Web Service description in VordelSecure

Because policies are enforced on a per-service basis, it is important that the service is defined accurately so that VordelSecure can identify the target of traffic it receives. If the target cannot be identified, the XML communication in question is dropped by VordelSecure.

The configuration screen shown in Figure A-3 gives the option to use a preexisting security policy to configure the traffic to this Web Service.

Notice in Figure A-3 that the security options for the Web Service are listed on the right of the screen. These range from XML firewall functionality (that is, "content filtering") through to identity-based functionality (that is, authentication and authorization).

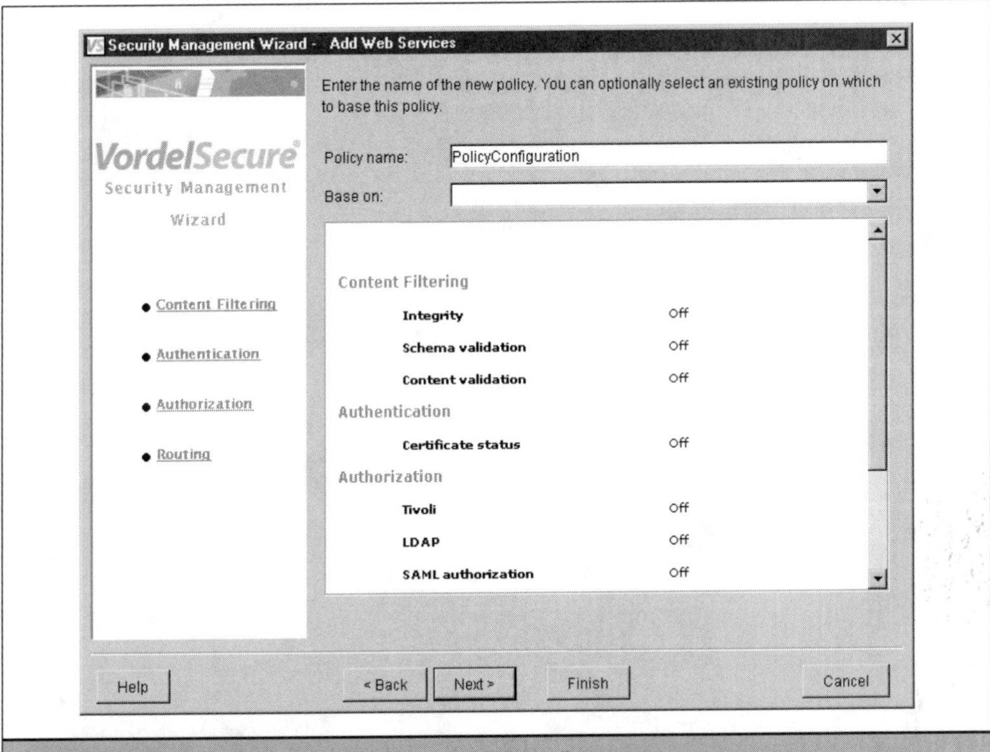

Figure A-3. Basing a security policy on a preexisting policy

Press Next to move to the next screen in order to configure XML Signature validation over the incoming SOAP message. This screen is shown in Figure A-4.

Figure A-4 shows an XML Signature filter being configured in such a way that it will be enforced over the entire SOAP body. The SOAP body is identified using the XPath expressing "//soap:Envelope/soap:Body/*." This is the minimum content of the SOAP message, which must be digitally signed. Note that the SOAP namespace is configured using the Edit button below the XPath selection box. If the WS-Security option is chosen, the administrator can choose which SOAP actor for which XML Signatures will be enforced, or the administrator may choose to enforce XML Signatures for all SOAP actors referenced within the SOAP message.

The next option is to configure an XML Schema to be enforced over the incoming data. This is shown in Figure A-5. Again, an XPath expression is used to narrow down the portion of the SOAP message that must be validated against the XML Schema.

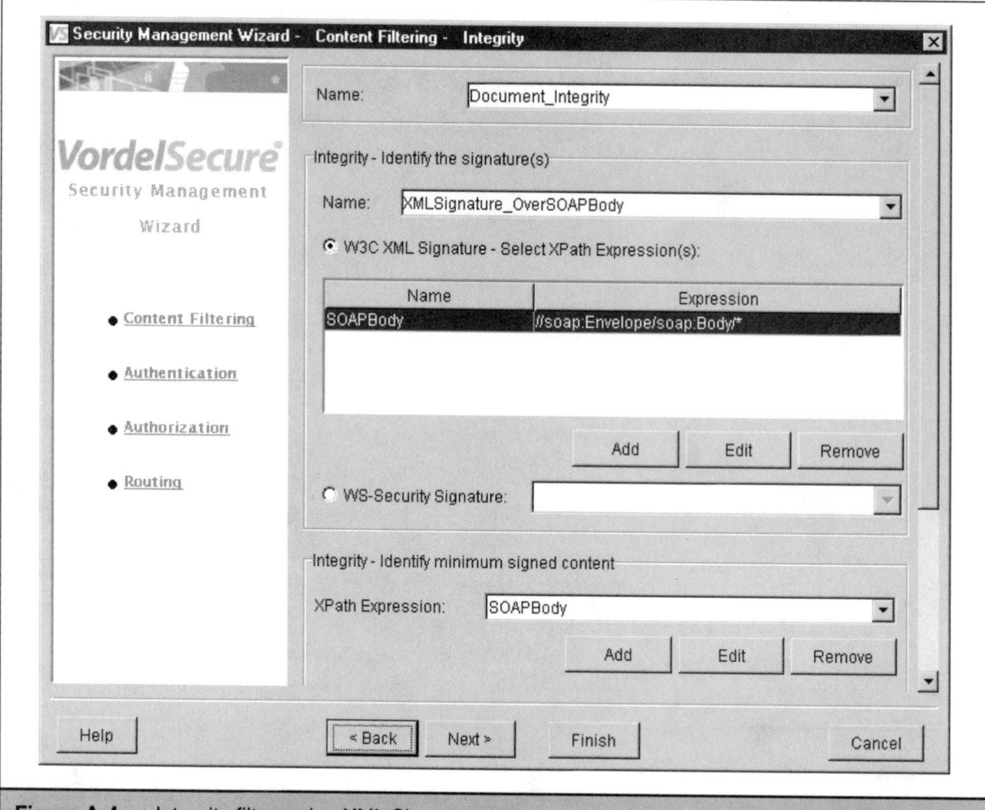

Figure A-4. Integrity filter, using XML Signature

TIP The use of Schema validation is processor-intensive, and is only recommended if the machine on which it is implemented is suitable for high-volume XML processing.

We have already seen XML firewalling based on the integrity of the SOAP body (using XML Signature to validate the integrity) and XML Schema to validate the structure of the SOAP body. It may be required to go a level deeper and look at the content of individual XML elements and attributes. This was not required for this case

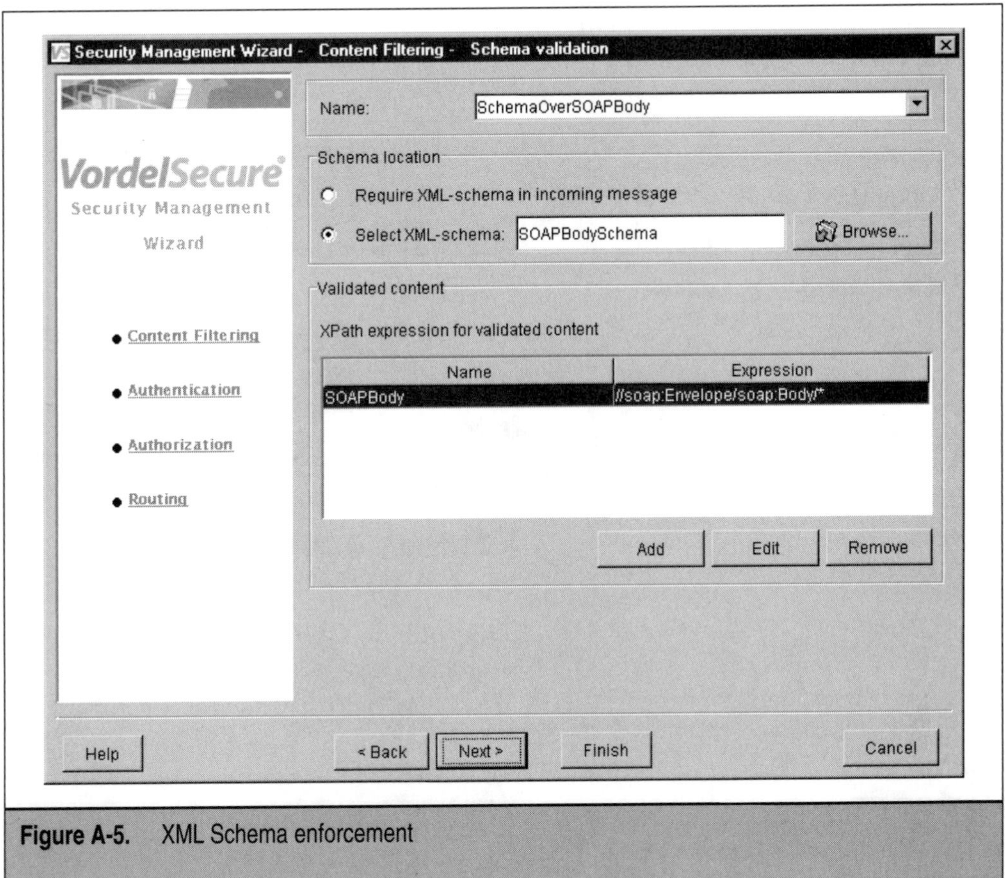

Figure A-5. XML Schema enforcement

study, which only required the integrity and schema validation aspects of XML firewalling.

Next we move on to identity-based security. Figure A-6 shows message authentication using X.509 certificate validation being configured. Recall from Chapter 2 that message authentication using an X.509 certificate requires proof of possession of the associated private key; otherwise, an intruder could simply copy and paste the certificate into a different SOAP message.

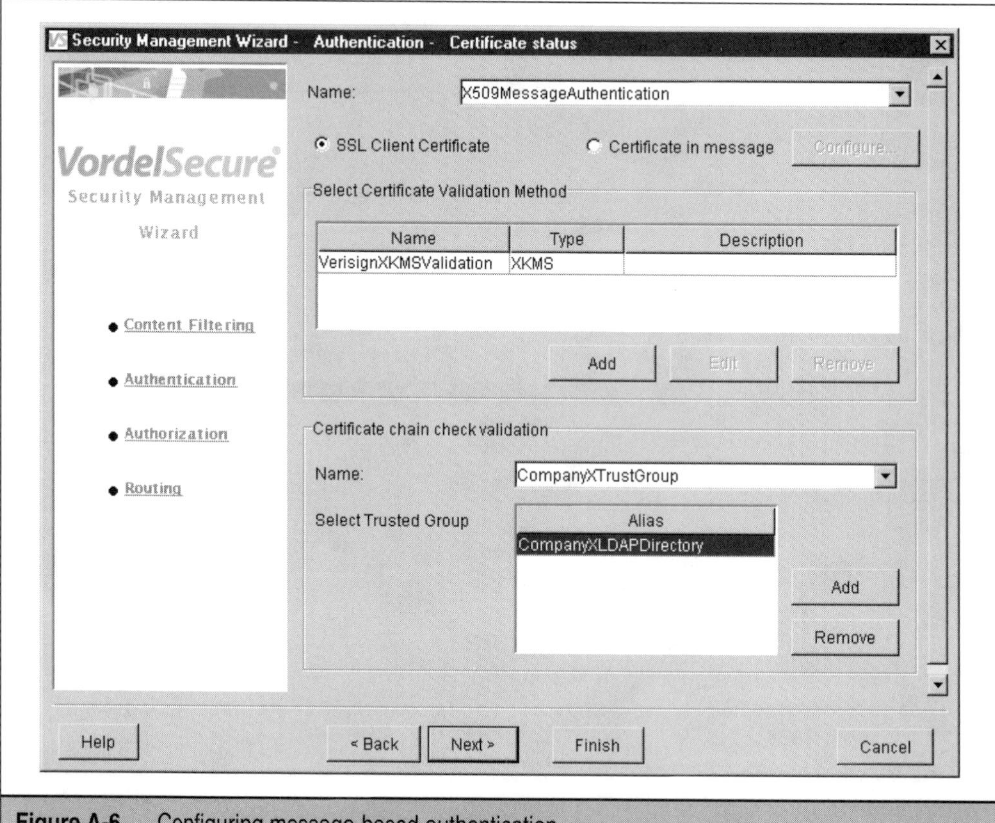

Figure A-6. Configuring message-based authentication

By pressing the Configure button shown in Figure A-6, the administrator can determine which certificate is to be used for authentication, because a single SOAP message may contain multiple XML Signatures, each associated with a different X.509 certificate. The steps for X.509 certificate authentication used in this case study were as follows:

1. Validate the XML Signature associated with the X.509 certificate. Ensure that the appropriate data has been signed. The signed data included a timestamp. This ensured that attempts at replay attacks would be detectable.
2. Ensure that the certificate is still valid. This is done using a SOAP message sent to an XKMS trust service.
3. Ensure that the certificate has been issued by a trusted certificate authority.

Once these steps have been performed, VordelSecure can be configured to send successfully authenticated messages to the target Web Service.

Figure A-7 shows routing being configured for an internal Web Service, so that messages that successfully pass the XML gateway can reach the Web Services that sit inside the organization. In this case study, it was decided not to use SAML because the partners using the Web Service did not have the capability to issue SAML assertions to insert into SOAP messages. In addition, the overhead of issuing SAML assertions to insert into messages sent from the gateway to an internal Web Service was seen as unnecessary.

Recall that the organization in this case study wished to raise an alert if the number of blocked XML messages exceeded a certain amount. Figure A-8 shows this functionality being configured in VordelSecure.

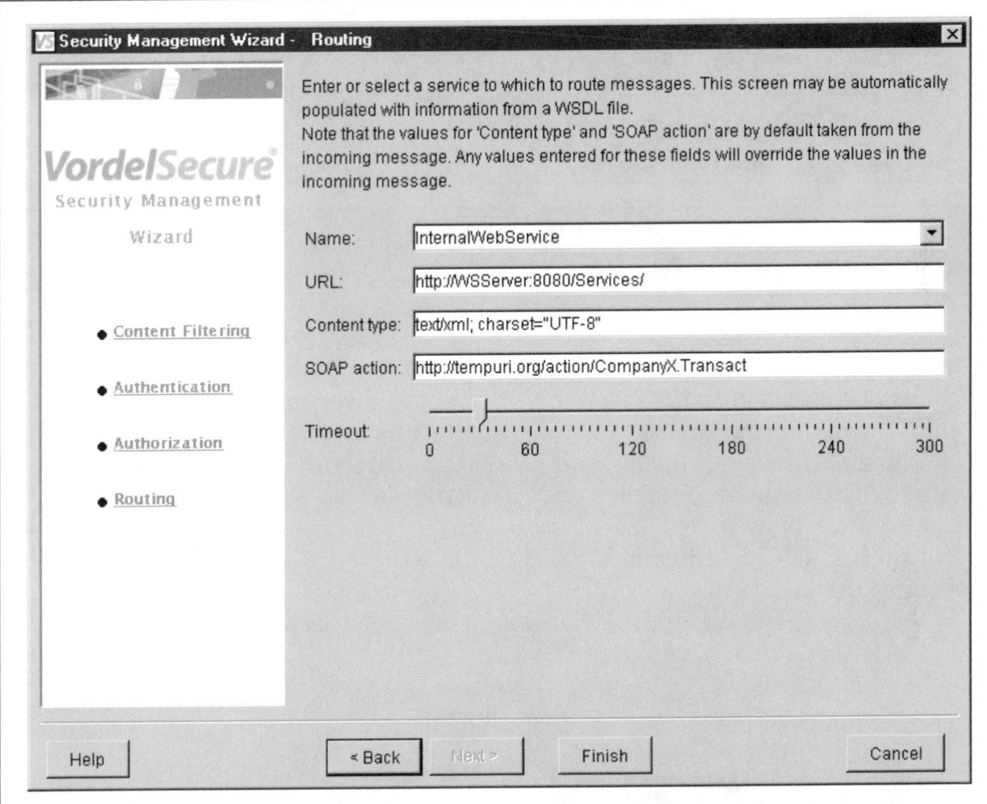

Figure A-7. Routing successful messages from the XML gateway to an internal Web Service

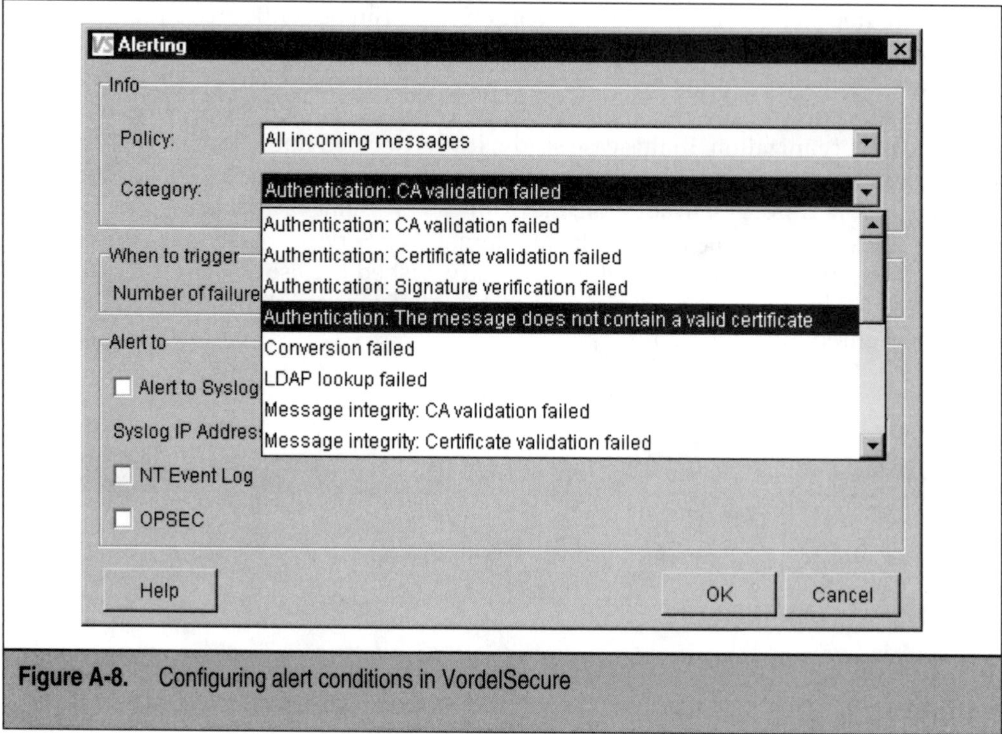

Figure A-8. Configuring alert conditions in VordelSecure

In conclusion, this case study shows an XML security product being used to secure a Web Service, based on XML firewalling—that is, characteristics of the data, and based on which service is being targeted—and based on access control information from within the incoming XML message (in this case, an X.509 digital certificate). In Chapter 9, we saw how a SOAP request containing an X.509 certificate as a security token can be created using C#. Now we have seen how a security policy can be configured to enforce a server-side security policy based on the existence of security tokens within incoming SOAP messages.

Index

A

❖ B

❖ C

❖ D

E

F

G

H

❖ I

 J

❖ K

❖ L

M

N

O

P

R

S

❖ T

U

 V

 W

 X

❖ Z

INTERNATIONAL CONTACT INFORMATION

AUSTRALIA
McGraw-Hill Book Company Australia Pty. Ltd.
TEL +61-2-9900-1800
FAX +61-2-9878-8881
http://www.mcgraw-hill.com.au
books-it_sydney@mcgraw-hill.com

CANADA
McGraw-Hill Ryerson Ltd.
TEL +905-430-5000
FAX +905-430-5020
http://www.mcgraw-hill.ca

GREECE, MIDDLE EAST, & AFRICA (Excluding South Africa)
McGraw-Hill Hellas
TEL +30-210-6560-990
TEL +30-210-6560-993
TEL +30-210-6560-994
FAX +30-210-6545-525

MEXICO (Also serving Latin America)
McGraw-Hill Interamericana Editores S.A. de C.V.
TEL +525-117-1583
FAX +525-117-1589
http://www.mcgraw-hill.com.mx
fernando_castellanos@mcgraw-hill.com

SINGAPORE (Serving Asia)
McGraw-Hill Book Company
TEL +65-863-1580
FAX +65-862-3354
http://www.mcgraw-hill.com.sg
mghasia@mcgraw-hill.com

SOUTH AFRICA
McGraw-Hill South Africa
TEL +27-11-622-7512
FAX +27-11-622-9045
robyn_swanepoel@mcgraw-hill.com

SPAIN
McGraw-Hill/Interamericana de España, S.A.U.
TEL +34-91-180-3000
FAX +34-91-372-8513
http://www.mcgraw-hill.es
professional@mcgraw-hill.es

UNITED KINGDOM, NORTHERN, EASTERN, & CENTRAL EUROPE
McGraw-Hill Education Europe
TEL +44-1-628-502500
FAX +44-1-628-770224
http://www.mcgraw-hill.co.uk
computing_neurope@mcgraw-hill.com

ALL OTHER INQUIRIES Contact:
Osborne/McGraw-Hill
TEL +1-510-549-6600
FAX +1-510-883-7600
http://www.osborne.com
omg_international@mcgraw-hill.com